# Hegel and Christian Theology

# Hegel and Christian Theology

## A Reading of the
## *Lectures on the Philosophy of Religion*

PETER C. HODGSON

OXFORD
UNIVERSITY PRESS

# OXFORD
## UNIVERSITY PRESS

Great Clarendon Street. Oxford OX2 6DP

Oxford University Press is a department of the University of Oxford.
It furthers the University's objective of excellence in research, scholarship,
and education by publishing worldwide in

Oxford New York

Auckland Cape Town Dar es Salaam Hong Kong Karachi Kuala Lumpur
Madrid Melbourne Mexico City Nairobi New Delhi Shanghai Taipei Toronto

With offices in

Argentina Austria Brazil Chile Czech Republic France Greece
Guatemala Hungary Italy Japan South Korea Poland Portugal
Singapore Switzerland Thailand Turkey Ukraine Vietnam

Published in the United States
by Oxford University Press Inc. New York

British Library Cataloguing in Publication Data

Data available

Library of Congress Cataloging in Publication Data

Data applied for
ISBN 0 19 927361-8
EAN 9780199273614

1 3 5 7 9 10 8 6 4 2

Typeset by Kolam Information Services Pvt. Ltd, Pondicherry, India
Printed in Great Britain by
Biddles Ltd, King's Lynn

# PREFACE

In the 1980s a new edition of Georg Wilhelm Friedrich Hegel's *Lectures on the Philosophy of Religion* appeared in German, English, and Spanish. I assisted the principal editor, Walter Jaeschke, in preparing the German text, and I coordinated the English translation by Robert F. Brown, J. Michael Stewart, and myself. This is a critical edition that distinguishes Hegel's four series of lectures (1821, 1824, 1827, 1831), which differ from each other quite significantly, and establishes a critical text for the first three series. The previous editions conflated the lectures into an editorially constructed text that often obscures Hegel's distinctive arguments and emphases. Now it is possible to study Hegel's philosophy of religion on a level of accuracy and insight hitherto unattainable.

After my decade-long engagement with the translation, I needed a break from Hegel and for the next several years pursued other projects. I did, however, edit an anthology of his writings on religion entitled *G. W. F. Hegel: Theologian of the Spirit*. During the past fifteen years several valuable studies have appeared that make use of the new edition, but they do not centrally engage the speculative reconstruction of Christian theology that is accomplished by Hegel's lectures, nor do they provide a close reading of the text as a whole. Thus an opening exists for a book such as the present one.

My view is that Hegel's *Philosophy of Religion* is one of the two or three most important resources from the nineteenth century for theology as it faces the challenges of modernity and postmodernity. The others are Friedrich Schleiermacher's *Christian Faith* and Søren Kierkegaard's *Fragments* and *Postscript*. Hegel, Schleiermacher, and Kierkegaard offer quite different routes beyond the theological impasse posed by the representative thinker of the Enlightenment, Immanuel Kant, and these routes continue to be productive today. The purpose of the present monograph is to make the case as far as Hegel is concerned.

The first two chapters incorporate editorial material I prepared for the anthology. They argue that Hegel's philosophy of religion is a philosophical theology focused on the concept of spirit (*Geist*), and they provide an overview of his writings on religion prior to the philosophy of religion. Chapter 3, based on the *Introduction* to the lectures, analyses Hegel's conception of the object and purpose of philosophy of religion and his critique of the theology of his own time. Chapter 4 examines his approach to Christianity within the framework of the concept of religion, while Chapter 5 focuses on the concept, knowledge, and worship of God; these two chapters draw on materials from the first main part of the lectures, *The Concept of Religion*. The next four chapters, Chapters 6–9, engage central themes of Christian theology as they are presented in the third part of the lectures, *The Consummate Religion*: the triune God as absolute spirit; creation, humanity, and evil; Christ and reconciliation; Spirit and community. Chapter 10 evaluates Hegel's conception of the place of Christianity among the religions of the world as they are presented in the second main part of the lectures, *Determinate Religion*. The concluding chapter draws these materials together into a case for the contemporary theological significance of Hegel. Here I identify six sets of distinctions or currently contested sites and their Hegelian resolution. The resultant categories—spirit, wholeness, narrative, Christ, community, pluralism—are viewed as contributing valuable resources to theological reflection today. I also identify points at which Hegel's thinking about religion and theology needs correction in light of ongoing experience and further reflection.

Oxford University Press is assuming the publication of the *Lectures on the Philosophy of Religion* and of other newly edited and translated lectures by Hegel. I am pleased that this monograph will accompany the reissuing of the text some twenty years after it first appeared. Rupert Cousens, Hilary O'Shea, and Lucy Qureshi helped to make this happen. To them and to the readers for the Press I am grateful.

PETER C. HODGSON

# CONTENTS

# NOTES ON THE TEXT

*Lectures on the Philosophy of Religion*, edited by Peter C. Hodgson, translated by R. F. Brown, P. C. Hodgson, and J. M. Stewart with the assistance of H. S. Harris, 3 vols. (Berkeley and Los Angeles: University of California Press, 1984, 1985, 1987; Oxford: Oxford University Press, 2006).

References to this work are cited in-text by volume and page number. The lecture series from which the citations derive can be determined from the following table.

|  | 1821 | 1824 | 1827 | 1831 |
|---|---|---|---|---|
| Volume 1 |  |  |  |  |
| *Introduction* | 83–112 | 113–147 | 149–184 | 461–464 |
| *The Concept* | 185–256 | 257–364 | 365–449 | 451–460 |
| *of Religion* |  |  |  | 464–474 |
| Volume 2 |  |  |  |  |
| *Determinate* |  |  |  |  |
| *Religion* | 93–231 | 233–512 | 513–699 | 703–760 |
| Volume 3 |  |  |  |  |
| *The* |  |  |  |  |
| *Consummate* |  |  |  |  |
| *Religion* | 61–162 | 163–247 | 249–347 | 351–374 |

A one-volume edition containing the text of the lectures of 1827 is also available (University of California Press, 1988; Oxford University Press, 2005). Corresponding pages of this edition can be found by referring to the German pagination that is printed in the margins of both editions.

This book follows the convention of the English edition regarding the use of lower case for Hegel's philosophical terminology. Thus 'spirit' is written in lower case (including the philosophical name of God, 'absolute spirit'), except when the reference is to the Holy Spirit of the Trinity.

# PART ONE

# Introduction

# I

# Hegel as a Theologian of the Spirit

## HEGEL'S LIFE AND CAREER IN BRIEF[1]

The year 1770 was auspicious for art and thought. The spring of
that year brought the birth of Friedrich Hölderlin and William
Wordsworth, and the winter, Ludwig van Beethoven. Between the
two poets and the composer there was born, on 27 August, one who
achieved in philosophy a greatness comparable to theirs in poetry
and music, Georg Wilhelm Friedrich Hegel. Among the birth-year
mates there was a mystical linkage. Perhaps it is not too fanciful to
suggest that Hegel became the Beethoven of philosophy, and
Beethoven the Hegel of music; for they both sought pattern, harmony, and redemption in and through a world of conflict, dis-
harmony, and suffering. The music of Beethoven, like the
philosophy of Hegel, manifests the awesome tragic wholeness of
life in strikingly beautiful formulations. Hegel shared something
of Wordsworth's nature mysticism, although philosophically he
was closer to the greater genius of Wordsworth's companion and
rival, Samuel Taylor Coleridge, born just two years later. As for
Hegel and Hölderlin, there is sad irony in the fact that the latter's
youthful genius came to a tragic end in madness the same year that
the former's greatest work of genius was published, 1807.

---

[1] This chapter and the next draw upon the editorial introduction and textual
annotations written by the author for *G. W. F. Hegel: Theologian of the Spirit*, ed.
Peter C. Hodgson (Minneapolis: Fortress Press; Edinburgh: T&T Clark, 1997).
Used by permission of Augsburg Fortress Publishers. The definitive biography is
by Terry Pinkard, *Hegel: A Biography* (Cambridge: Cambridge University Press,
2000). For this first section, see also Franz Wiedmann, *Hegel: An Illustrated
Biography*, trans. Joachim Neugroschel (New York: Pegasus, 1968); Jacques
d'Hondt, *Hegel in His Time*, trans. John Burbidge (Peterborough, Ont.: Broadview
Press, 1988); Stephen Houlgate, *Freedom, Truth and History: An Introduction to
Hegel's Philosophy* (London and New York: Routledge, 1991); and Richard Kroner,
'Hegel's Philosophical Development', introduction to *Early Theological Writings*,
trans. T. M. Knox (Chicago: University of Chicago Press, 1948).

4 Hegel as a Theologian of the Spirit

The son of a Württemberg civil servant, the young Hegel attended the Stuttgart *Gymnasium* from 1777 to 1788, where he proved to be an exemplary student and read the classical authors along with Shakespeare, Rousseau, Lessing, Goethe, and Schiller. He seemed headed for a career in ministry, so he entered the theological seminary of Tübingen in 1788, where he formed a close friendship with Friedrich Hölderlin and Friedrich Schelling. Schelling was five years younger than Hegel and Hölderlin but entered the seminary as an exceptionally precocious student only two years after them. These three, finding the theological orthodoxy of their professors stultifying, educated themselves in the political, literary, and philosophical literature of the Enlightenment, and they embraced the ideals of the French revolution with enthusiasm. They also imbibed deeply of the German and Swabian mystics. During this period Hegel began writing fragmentary essays for his own edification, in which among other things he explored the possibility of creating a new folk religion that would integrate all aspects of life.[2]

Hegel completed his studies in 1793, but he did not take up a career in ministry. Instead he accepted a position as house tutor for a wealthy family in Bern, Switzerland, where he had considerable free time and access to a rich library. Here he broadened his knowledge of modern philosophy and studied Immanuel Kant seriously for the first time. He produced more exploratory essays in which he was severely critical of the 'positivity' of Christianity while extolling a Kantian religion of morality. In the fall of 1796, with the assistance of Hölderlin, he obtained a similar tutorial position in Frankfurt, which brought him into closer proximity with his friends. Here he began to explore the possibility of combining the beauty of Greek folk religion with the moral law of Kantianism in the shape of spiritual beauty or love, which he now saw to constitute the heart of Christianity as a religion of spirit. Spirit unifies opposites in a pantheism of love. Several of the fragments written during this period were given the title 'The Spirit of Christianity and Its Fate' when they were published, along with Hegel's other early writings, in 1907 by Herman Nohl.

Upon his father's death in 1799, Hegel received a modest inheritance that allowed him to accept a position as an unsalaried

---

[2] This and other writings on religion prior to the *Lectures on the Philosophy of Religion* are discussed in Chap. 2.

lecturer (*Privatdozent*) at the University of Jena, where he joined Schelling in 1801. Students paid small fees to attend his lectures on logic and metaphysics, the philosophies of nature and spirit, ethics and natural right, and the history of philosophy. These lectures not only provided additional income but also gave Hegel the opportunity to experiment with various elements that gradually evolved into his philosophical system. It was a period of remarkable intellectual fertility for him. His first publications were two book-length essays, *The Difference between Fichte's and Schelling's System of Philosophy*, and a comparative study of Immanuel Kant, Friedrich Heinrich Jacobi, and Johann Gottlieb Fichte entitled *Faith and Knowledge*. In 1806, as Napoleon defeated the Prussian troops at the Battle of Jena, Hegel finished under considerable duress his most famous work, the *Phenomenology of Spirit*, a few hundred copies of which were printed early in 1807.

For financial and personal reasons, Hegel found it necessary to leave Jena. He moved to Bamberg to become editor of a newspaper, but a year later, in 1808, he was fortunate to be offered a position as rector of a *Gymnasium* in Nuremberg, where among other things he taught religion and speculative logic to his pupils. In 1811, Hegel married, began a family, and during the next four years (1812–16) published his *Science of Logic*. The latter work sufficiently established his reputation that in 1816 he was offered university professorships in Heidelberg, Erlangen, and Berlin. The Erlangen and Berlin offers were couched in qualifications, so he accepted the offer from Heidelberg. His lectures there, covering a full range of philosophical topics with the exception of religion, proved to be a great success, and he published in 1817 the *Encyclopedia of the Philosophical Sciences*, a compendium of the entire system of philosophy intended as a textbook to accompany his lectures.

In the next year, 1818, Hegel was recruited by the Prussian Minister of Education, Karl von Altenstein, to become professor of philosophy at the University of Berlin, filling a chair left vacant by Fichte's death in 1814, and there he remained until his death. Through the impact of his books and lectures, Hegel's fame spread throughout Europe, and Hegelianism began to form as a philosophical school. In 1820 he completed a textbook on political philosophy, *Elements of the Philosophy of Right*; it was to be the last book he published (except for revised editions of the *Encyclopedia*). The *Philosophy of Right* generated considerable

controversy because in it as well as in his public activity Hegel
attempted to steer a middle course between revolutionary and
restoration politics. There was considerable political turmoil in
Prussia at the time, and Hegel found himself in the delicate situation of being supported in his office by the aristocratic establishment while sympathizing with liberal reform movements.
Consequently he had numerous enemies on the right and the left,
and his position in Berlin was never completely secure.

In the summer of 1821 Hegel lectured for the first time on
philosophy of religion, which was the final major element of his
system to be elaborated in detail. When these lectures were
repeated in subsequent years—1824, 1827, and 1831—they varied
greatly in structure and content, indicating the fluidity and openness with which Hegel approached this and other topics. He was
constantly appropriating new material and responding to specific
issues and challenges.

In a strict sense the Hegelian system came into existence as a
fixed entity only after Hegel's death, which occurred suddenly on
14 November 1831, during an epidemic of cholera. In little over a
month following his death, his wife, students, and friends had
arranged to publish his collected works, including lecture manuscripts and auditors' transcriptions (*Nachschriften*) on the major
topics covered in Berlin—history of philosophy, logic and metaphysics, and the philosophies of history, art, right, and religion.
With Hegel's voice silenced, his former students and disciples
within a few years fell into warring factions; and the controversy
over Hegel's thought continues to this day.

### SPECULATIVE PHILOSOPHY AND
### THE LOGICAL DEEP STRUCTURE

What Hegel came to call 'speculative philosophy' was indebted to
yet distinct from the 'reflective philosophy of subjectivity'—the
phrase he used to describe, in his early work, *Faith and Knowledge*,
the philosophies of Kant, Fichte, and Jacobi.[3] Speculative

---

[3] The full title of the work is *Faith and Knowledge, or the Reflective Philosophy of
Subjectivity in the Complete Range of Its Forms as Kantian, Jacobian, and Fichtean
Philosophy*. See *Faith and Knowledge*, trans. Walter Cerf and H. S. Harris (Albany:
State University of New York Press, 1977), 53.

philosophy did not avoid the Kantian critical philosophy but attempted to move through and beyond it. Hints toward this end were provided by Fichte and especially Schelling, but Hegel eventually moved in his own direction through an act of high philosophical creativity.

Kant's philosophy starts with empirical, sense experience, received in the form of intuition (*Anschauung*). By application of a priori categories (time, space, causality, substance, etc.), mind constructs these intuitions into a picture of reality. We can never, Kant insisted, get beyond these constructions to know reality or the world as it is in and for itself. The constructed object simply reflects mind back to itself. Nor, obviously, can we have theoretical knowledge of any transcendent, metaphysical ground of reality. The price of (vainly) seeking such knowledge is what Kant called 'transcendental illusion'.[4]

For Hegel there is a 'getting beyond' in the form of a turn, a reversal, such that what is constructed also shows or manifests itself, gives itself on its own terms, which partly correspond to but also enrich and correct consciousness. Something new is known beyond self-knowledge; there is a spiralling ahead, and consciousness proves to be participatory and receptive as well as critical and constructive. Reality is, to be sure, a mirror of consciousness; but *consciousness is also a mirror of reality*. 'Speculation' (from the Latin *speculum*, 'mirror') involves a relationship of double mirroring in which there occurs a reversal in the flow of meaning—from object to subject as well as from subject to object.[5] Where Kant's philosophy ends by imposing strict limits on reason, Hegel's moves on to a science of logic, a philosophy of the categories of thought. Thought is the medium in which the mirroring occurs.

The condition of possibility for this reversal is that subject and object, self and world, the same and the other, participate in, are moments of, an encompassing whole, which Hegel calls variously 'truth', 'actuality' (*Wirklichkeit*), 'the universal', 'the absolute', 'spirit' (*Geist*)—or 'God'. In addition to a first and a second, there is a third, which overreaches the first and the second and is the relationship between them. This relationship or whole is not

---

[4] Immanuel Kant, *Critique of Pure Reason*, trans. Norman Kemp Smith (London: Macmillan, 1929), 300–3 (B 355–9, A 298–302).

[5] On speculative philosophy and theology, see below, Chaps. 3–4.

separable from the component elements but becomes actual, manifests itself, only in their double mirroring. It gives itself in the reversal of relationship between consciousness and object. It is 'transcendental' in the sense of presenting conditions of possibility of their relating; it is not 'transcendent' in the sense of being a supersensible entity or ground apart from them. The whole presents itself in the form of intellectual intuition, which Hegel thought of as analogous to, yet distinct from, Kant's sensible intuition—thus drawing out the implications of Kant's own allusion to intellectual intuition in the *Critique of Judgement*.[6] We intuit the fundamentally rational structure of the whole as we engage in the critical construction of the contents of sense experience into an intelligible world. Intellectual intuition both follows and precedes sensible intuition. Sense experience is not the absolute starting-point of knowledge; something always precedes it.

So the picture we get from Hegel is that of a spiralling movement, a dialectic of mediations in which cognitive novelty occurs, rather than that of a circle of repetition constantly reflecting back on itself or a linear thinking that moves from one disconnected unit to the next. The question for Hegel is whether the spiral remains open-ended such that the three constitutive moments remain irresolved, or whether the spiral converges on a point of indifference— absolute knowledge, the sheer identity of consciousness and object, thought and reality. The latter is the direction taken by Fichte and Schelling—'the night in which all cows are black' (one of Hegel's famous jibes against Schelling's philosophy[7]). If Hegel resisted this direction, then the focal point of the interplay between self, world, and the truth of the whole (God) cannot be the human self or subject as it was for Kant and Friedrich Schleiermacher; nor can it be God as a transcendent entity or supreme being; rather it is the interplay itself, the spiral of mediations among these three elements, which can be represented geometrically as moving in wave-like rhythms (like the helix of the genetic code).

Hegel does make some critical assumptions about this spiral of mediations. The fundamental assumption is that it is essentially rational. This is *his* basic intellectual intuition, shared with

   [6] Immanuel Kant, *The Critique of Judgement*, trans. James Creed Meredith (Oxford: Clarendon Press, 1952), 2. 66.
   [7] *Phenomenology of Spirit*, trans. A. V. Miller (Oxford: Clarendon Press, 1977), 9.

Aristotle:[8] the intuition that thought knows itself (*noēsis tēs noēseōs*) in knowing objects of thought. The condition of possibility of the co-constitutiveness of consciousness and object is the rationality of the whole.

Reason or thought is not something static: it moves and thinks, and it does so in the form of assertions, statements, judgements, arguments, syllogisms. The syllogism (or reasoning to a conclusion) is the basic movement of thought and of life itself.[9] Thought moves between three moments or elements and brings them into relation with one another: the *universal substance or principle* of a statement (U); the *particular quality* or determinate modification of the universal in the case at hand (P); and the *individual subject* about which the statement makes a predication (I). Consider this example of a syllogism about Socrates, which has the logical form: All U is P; I is U; therefore I is P.

> All human beings (U) are mortal (P);
> Socrates (I) is human (U);
> Therefore, Socrates (I) is mortal (P).

According to Hegel, all valid syllogisms can be varied so that each of the three elements assumes in turn the middle or mediating position between the other two. Hence there are three forms or figures for every syllogism: U-P-I (the order of Hegel's system), U-I-P, and P-U-I (the example given above). The effect is to prevent any one of the elements from becoming foundational and the others derivative; rather they are co-constitutive.

Life-processes involve an analogous set of elements: immediacy or identity (corresponding to the universal), differentiation (corresponding to the particular), and synthesis at a higher level of complexity (corresponding to the individual or subjective). Life is rational, and rationality is alive. Hegel must have thought he had 'cracked a code' with this essentially mystical grasp of the dialectic of life and thought. Is it deep insight into truth or totalizing illusion? Deconstruction argues that there is no such code, or at least no single code but an irreducible multiplicity of codes. For

[8] See Hegel's reference to the key passage in Aristotle's *Metaphysics*, 12.7, 1072[b] 18–30, in the *Encyclopedia of the Philosophical Sciences*, § 577 (*Hegel's Philosophy of Mind*, trans. William Wallace and A. V. Miller (Oxford: Clarendon Press, 1971), 314–15; this passage is translated in *Hegel: Theologian of the Spirit*, 53–4 (see 277 n. 21)).
[9] *Encyclopedia*, §§ 183–9 (*The Encyclopedia Logic*, trans. T. F. Geraets, W. A. Suchting, and H. S. Harris (Indianapolis: Hackett, 1991), 259–64).

Hegel the one code manifests itself in an astonishing multiplicity of forms through which it undergoes determinate modification; and thus the articulation of it is as diverse as the topics of philosophy. The three constitutive elements of the syllogism are linked by Hegel with the three main branches of philosophy: science of logic, philosophy of nature, and philosophy of spirit.[10] *Logic* is concerned with the structures and relations of thought itself, for which Hegel uses the term 'the logical' or the 'logical idea' (as distinct from the idea as embodied or realized in the world and consciousness), and it plays the role of universal principle in relation to the whole of philosophy; by itself it is a principle of abstract identity. *Nature* is identified with the particular qualities or determinate modifications of the universal; it plays the role of differentiation and otherness in the philosophical system. *Spirit* (finite human consciousness) is identified with the individuality or uniqueness that emerges from the union of the universal and the particular; it plays the role of reconciliation or return to a more richly constituted whole as mediated through difference: a movement toward the concrete universal or *absolute spirit*.

These linkages seem to be a critical assumption for which Hegel offers no direct justification: there is no prior proof of the truth of a philosophical system. But we can appreciate the alternatives that propelled him to this position. If nature were to become the universal principle, then spirit would be mediated with its particular (now merely logical) qualities by means of nature, and the resulting system would be *naturalism*: Hume, Feuerbach, Marx. If finite spirit were to become the universal principle, then nature would be mediated with its particular (logical) qualities by means of spirit, which would be an instance of *subjective idealism*: Kant, Fichte. Both naturalism and subjective idealism are monisms that tend to reduce everything to one principle: matter or mind. The alternative requires the transcendence of the logical idea as the universal principle rather than its identification with either nature or finite spirit. This transcendence of the idea yields Hegel's *speculative or absolute idealism*. If nature and spirit are to be mediated in such a way that neither is to be reduced to the principle of the other—and Hegel contends that only this mediation conforms to lived experience—then they must be mediated by a middle term

---

[10] *Encyclopedia*, § 187 addition (*The Encyclopedia Logic*, p. 263); §§ 575–7 (*Hegel's Philosophy of Mind*, 314). See further below, Chap. 11, pp. 267–8.

that is the universal principle of both, the logical idea.  Nature, in turn, when it assumes the middle position in the triple mediation of philosophy (as it does in Hegel's own system), prevents finite spirit from collapsing into undialectical identity with pure rationality by disclosing spirit's embodied character and demonstrating that it is not its own principle.  Spirit in middle position raises nature to its essence in the sense that it recognizes nature to be the appearance of the idea in the mode of particularity and externality; in nature, spirit slumbers.  The natural and spiritual mediations also have the effect of bringing the logical idea into relation with that which is other than itself—of preventing it from absorbing all of reality into itself in a pure metaphysical idealism (such as that of Berkeley).

Hegel insists that 'idealism' is not to be understood as the antithesis of 'realism'.  Rather it overreaches and embraces realism.  The idea is the absolute unity of concept and objectivity, of the rational and the real.  Ideality is not something that is given outside of and apart from reality.  Rather, ideality is the *truth* of the finite, of reality.  'This ideality of the finite is the most important proposition of philosophy, and for that reason every genuine philosophy is *idealism*.'[11] 'Consequently, the opposition of idealistic and realistic philosophy has no significance.  A philosophy which ascribed veritable, ultimate, absolute being to finite existence as such, would not deserve the name of philosophy.'[12] As these quotations suggest, by 'idealism' Hegel means *absolute idealism*.  The following comment makes very clear the distinction between subjective and absolute idealism as he understands it:

According to the Kantian philosophy, the things that we know about are only appearances for *us*, and what they are *in themselves* remains for us an inaccessible beyond.  The naive consciousness has rightly taken exception to this subjective idealism, according to which the content of our consciousness is something that is *only* ours, something posited only through *us*.  In fact, the true situation is that the things of which we have immediate knowledge are mere appearances, not only *for us*, but also *in-themselves*, and that the proper determination of these things, which are in this sense 'finite', consists in having the ground of their being not within themselves but in the universal divine idea.  This interpretation must also be called

[11] *Encyclopedia*, § 95 remark, § 96 addition, § 213 (*The Encyclopedia Logic*, 152–3, 286).
[12] *Science of Logic*, trans. A. V. Miller (London: George Allen & Unwin, 1969), 155.

idealism, but, as distinct from the subjective idealism of the critical philosophy, it is *absolute idealism*.[13]

'Absolute' here connotes that which encompasses all relations within itself, including relations with the finite or non-absolute. God as the absolute idea releases or 'absolves' the other to be other, but not totally other. With the classical tradition, Hegel affirms that God has only internal relations; nothing can be 'outside' of God. But within the divine milieu, external relations occur, including between God and world, for the world shares in nature's externality.

Hegel's interpretations of the various domains of experience, while generated out of the logical deep structure, are by no means simply read off from that structure. Rather, experience as it actually presents itself in the realms of history, art, religion, ethics, society, politics, anthropology, and psychology is determinative of the way in which the deep structure concretely appears—and it appears in a rich variety of forms, shapes, variations. The logic functions as a hermeneutical key or paradigm for reading and interpreting experience, but it is a key that must be used experimentally, in the manner of a heuristic device. As we shall discover, of no subject is this truer than Hegel's lectures on the philosophy of religion.

## PHILOSOPHY OF RELIGION AS THEOLOGY

Hegel's intention in addressing religious themes was not clearly understood in his time, and many suspected that he set out to convert the subject matter of theology into a purely immanent, human phenomenon. Or, if that was not the case, then the way in which he reinterpreted Christian doctrines in a strange philosophical conceptuality effectively undercut traditional theism. Hegel, it was believed, was either an atheist or a pantheist.

By contrast with these misrepresentations, Hegel insisted that the proper topic of philosophy of religion is precisely the nature and reality of God. Philosophy of religion cannot properly limit its concern to the phenomenon of religion; rather it must recognize that religion itself encompasses the relationship of human beings to God. Religion intends an actuality that lies beyond it—but this

---

[13] *Encyclopedia*, § 45 addition (*The Encyclopedia Logic*, 88–9).

transcendent referent had been rendered problematic by Enlightenment philosophy, history, psychology, and natural science. Traditionally, the question of the reality-status of God had been addressed within philosophy by metaphysics or natural theology. But the claims of these disciplines were severely questioned by Kant's critique of pure reason. Moreover, the authority of scripture and the historical basis for Christianity had been challenged by critics such as Lessing, and the alternative of a purely rational or natural religion favoured by the Enlightenment was undercut by Hume.

Philosophy of religion came on the scene as an alternative to the discredited metaphysics of natural theology, and according to Walter Jaeschke[14] it faced two options. It could, on the one hand, develop a new philosophical theology within itself, or perhaps borrow one from another source, in order to have a foundation for cognitive knowledge of God and thus provide an adequate account of how religion conceives itself. Or, on the other hand, it could conclude that no such foundation is available and thus 'confine itself to regarding religion as a specifically human expression of life. It has then no right to take what appears as divine to be anything other than human.' The latter option is the one that has prevailed since Feuerbach: the divine is nothing other than the essence of the human projected on a screen of transcendence. Anthropological, sociological, psychological, and historical interpretations of religion have come to the fore, and for them the problematic character of God-talk could be regarded as a matter of scientific indifference.

Hegel, however, took the first option, and he regarded the intimations of the latter course that were already discernible in his time to spell disaster not only for religious faith but also for human culture. Since neither classical metaphysics, nor the Enlightenment rational theologies, nor the Kantian doctrine of moral postulates, nor Schleiermacher's orientation of theology to religious feeling were in his judgement satisfactory accounts of faith in God, Hegel set out to recover the conceptual foundations of religion by creating a postcritical speculative theology of his own. That was the true agenda of his lectures on the philosophy of religion.

---

[14] Walter Jaeschke, *Reason in Religion: The Foundations of Hegel's Philosophy of Religion*, trans. J. Michael Stewart and Peter C. Hodgson (Berkeley and Los Angeles: University of California Press, 1990), 1–9.

Jaeschke points out that Hegel became aware of this agenda only gradually and through sustained reflection.[15] By the end of the Frankfurt period he was clear about the need for a metaphysical renewal of the doctrine of God and religion, but not about how to accomplish it. God could not be the extraworldly, omnipotent superperson of classical theism, or the abstract supreme being of the Enlightenment, or the preceptor and executor of the Kantian moral law. In Frankfurt Hegel began to develop a theory of the divine as the unification of nature and freedom, finite and infinite, but he had not yet arrived at the decisive category of *Geist* (spirit) to describe it. However, basic conceptual decisions were made during Hegel's tenure in Jena and completed by the time of writing the *Phenomenology of Spirit*. On the one hand, philosophy of religion is placed in the context of a reconstructed system of thought. On the other hand, it does not dissolve into logic or purely philosophical knowledge, nor is it a patchwork of ethical and aesthetic considerations. Rather philosophy of religion is a distinctive sort of philosophical or speculative theology, which claims that a postmetaphysical way of thinking about God is possible and that religion is a unique shape of consciousness alongside psychological, ethical, and aesthetic experience. The place of philosophy of religion in relation to the other human sciences was established in the *Phenomenology*, but not its internal form and content. That was achieved only with the *Lectures on the Philosophy of Religion*.

At the very beginning of these lectures, Hegel told his hearers:

God is the beginning of all things and the end of all things; [everything] starts from God and returns to God. God is the one and only object of philosophy. [Its concern is] to occupy itself with God, to apprehend everything in God, to lead everything back to God, as well as to derive everything particular from God and to justify everything only in so far as it stems from God, is sustained through its relationship with God, lives by God's radiance and has [within itself] the mind of God. Thus philosophy *is* theology, and [one's] occupation with philosophy—or rather *in* philosophy—is of itself the service of God [*Gottesdienst*, 'worship']. (1:84)[16]

Such a linkage between theology and philosophy was once found in the Middle Ages, and the time had come to re-establish it, Hegel

[15] See Jaeschke, *Reason in Religion*, 121–8.

[16] In-text references are to *Lectures on the Philosophy of Religion*, 3 vols., ed. and trans. Peter C. Hodgson *et al.* (Berkeley and Los Angeles: University of California Press, 1984–7; Oxford: Oxford University Press, 2006). See Chap. 2, n. 46.

argued, since modern theologians have abandoned their vocation
of knowing *God*, as opposed to knowing only human subjectivity or
investigating only what was *once* believed. Indeed, it is now philosophy rather than theology that preserves and interprets the
central Christian doctrines (1:121–2, 154–8, 168).
Hegel returned to this theme at the end of the lectures. 'The goal
of philosophy is the cognition of the truth—the cognition of God
because God is the absolute truth. . . . Philosophy knows God
essentially as concrete, as the spiritual, realized universality that
is not jealous but communicates itself.' The Enlightenment is not
pleased when philosophy defends the rationality of the Christian
religion or shows that the truth is deposited in religion. The task of
philosophy—or of 'the [branch of] philosophy that is theology'—is
'to show forth the rational content of religion [*die Vernunft der
Religion*]'.[17] Or, expressed slightly differently: 'Philosophy is to
this extent theology', that it presents the reconciliation of God with
the world, this reconciliation being the peace that does not 'surpass
all reason' but is itself precisely reason (3:347).
  Theology, then, is a branch of philosophy that concerns itself
with the knowledge of God and exhibits the rational content of
religion. It does this by raising the symbolic, metaphorical, representational language of religion into a conceptual, scientific terminology—and precisely this is the agenda of Hegel's lectures on
the philosophy of religion. Theology, in brief, is a 'science of
religion' and 'the intellectual science of God' (2:252).
  In the controversies following his death, Hegel would have
aligned himself with the theologians of the Hegelian middle who
sought to carry forward the agenda of a scientific theology (Karl
Daub, Philipp Marheineke, Karl Rosenkranz, Ferdinand Christian Baur),[18] as opposed to the radicals of the Hegelian left
who rejected all religion as mythological and illusory (Bruno
Bauer, David Friedrich Strauss, Ludwig Feuerbach, among
others), and the conservatives of the Hegelian right who sought
to restore orthodoxy or establish a speculative theism or a 'positive'

---

[17] 3:246–7. The variant referring to the '[branch of] philosophy that is theology'
derives most likely from Hegel's marked copy of Griesheim's transcript of the 1824
lectures. In this Hegel is drawing on a tradition that goes back to Aristotle, who
conceived his 'first philosophy' as theology.
[18] Hegel praised Daub and Marheineke specifically in this connection at the
conclusion of his Foreword to Hinrichs's *Religion* (see Chap. 2, n. 41, and *Hegel:
Theologian of the Spirit*, 171).

philosophy of mythology (such as I. H. Fichte, C. H. Weisse, and Friedrich Schelling in his later writings).[19] In the subsequent history of philosophy and theology, however, right down to our own time, the deconstructive critics of the left and the neoconservatives of the right have prevailed against the Hegelian middle. The speculative theology of the latter has been derided as 'ontotheology' by the left and as 'heterodoxy' by the right.

## THEOLOGIAN OF THE SPIRIT

We can with some justification, then, speak of Hegel as a 'theologian'—but why a 'theologian of the spirit'? The answer is that 'spirit'[20] identifies for Hegel the distinctive ontological quality of God. The charge of 'ontotheology' levelled against Hegelianism is correct so long as the term is defined in accord with Hegel's innovative, indeed 'heterodox' approach: these terms of derision can be turned to good effect. According to Cyril O'Regan, Hegelian ontotheology contends that the shared content of theology and philosophy is truth or God, and that this content can be known, but also that the dominant form of knowledge encapsulated in the Christian metanarrative is seriously deficient. Thus Hegel undertook a speculative redescription of the narrative, oriented to the trinitarian self-manifestation of God in 'moments' or 'epochs' that can also be grasped in logical or conceptual form as the foundational structure of reality itself. The being of God (the *ontos* of *theos*) discloses itself to be not pure immediacy or abstract substance or 'supreme being' (*höchstes Wesen*) but rather 'spirit' (*Geist*) in the sense of energy, movement, life, revelation, differentiation, and reconciliation.[21] Spirit designates a God who is intrinsically self-revelatory, self-manifesting; God is not locked up

---

[19] For a thorough discussion, see Jaeschke, *Reason in Religion*, chap. 4.

[20] I follow the 'down' style of the English edition for Hegel's philosophical terminology. Thus 'spirit' is written in lower case (including the philosophical name of God, 'absolute spirit') except when preceded by a definite article ('the Spirit'), which signifies a reference to the (Holy) Spirit of the Trinity.

[21] Cyril O'Regan, *The Heterodox Hegel* (Albany: State University of New York Press, 1994), 3. O'Regan argues that Hegel's postcritical reconstruction of ontotheology draws upon resources in a heterodox tradition that goes back to Gnosticism, Neoplatonism, and medieval and early modern mysticism (Meister Eckhart, Joachim of Fiore, and Jacob Boehme)—a tradition of which O'Regan himself is critical. Another study, which explores the influence on Hegel's

within godself but is knowable and related to the world. Spirit is not an aspect or person of the divine Trinity but the Trinity as such and as a whole, considered as an encompassing act or process of creating, communicating, consummating—an act by which God's own being is engendered and accomplished as well as that of the world.[22] Such a position represents a sharp break with traditional metaphysical theology, the Kantian critique of which Hegel shares, but he insists that God is the most actual of subjects—absolute intersubjectivity—rather than being merely a human projection or an ethical postulate. Any theology worthy of the name is in this sense an ontotheology.

Hegel's decisive breakthrough to this insight came in the *Phenomenology of Spirit*, which assumed the dramatic pattern of a *Bildungsroman*, a novel of formation and development. When the parentheses are removed from the *Phenomenology*, it is clear, says O'Regan, that the ultimate subject of becoming is neither the human individual nor society but God, the transcendental signified—or, in Hegelian terms, neither subjective spirit nor objective spirit but absolute spirit. Thus Hegel gives an ontotheological as opposed to a merely anthropological reading of the metanarrative. The emergent subjectivity of both individual human beings and the human community are elements in the becoming of the divine (inter)subjectivity. This whole process is what Hegel means by *Geist*.[23]

The evolution of Hegel's theology of spirit can be traced in writings that precede the *Lectures on the Philosophy of Religion*. In one of the essays comprising 'The Spirit of Christianity and Its Fate' (1799), hints occur that spirit is the condition of possibility for a nonextrinsic relationship between the divine and the human, which is a relationship of spirit to spirit, a unity that embraces difference. 'The hill and the eye which sees it are object and subject, but between humanity and God, between spirit and spirit, there is no such cleft of objectivity and subjectivity; one is to the other an other only in that one recognizes the other.' In reflecting

---

pneumatology of Luther and Lutheran pietism, is Alan M. Olson, *Hegel and the Spirit: Philosophy as Pneumatology* (Princeton: Princeton University Press, 1992), esp. chap. 3. A considerable portion of Olson's study (chaps. 4–6) is devoted to the relationship between Hegel and Hölderlin, and especially to the impact of the latter's madness on Hegel's interpretation of spirit.

[22] See O'Regan, *The Heterodox Hegel*, 20–1, 29–30, 45–9.
[23] Ibid., 52–4, 56–7.

on John 4:24 ('God is spirit, and they that worship him must worship him in spirit and in truth'), Hegel writes: 'How could anything but a spirit know a spirit? . . . Faith in the divine is only possible if in believers themselves there is a divine element which rediscovers itself.' Believers are not illumined by an exterior light; 'on the contrary, their own inflammability takes fire and burns with a flame that is their own'.[24] Hegel is employing here characteristically mystical language and spiritual images. The christology contained in this essay is also pneumatological: Jesus is one who is filled by the Spirit, who proclaims the inbreaking kingdom of God as a communion of the Spirit (consisting in harmonious love and renewing life), and who must depart so that the Spirit may come and dwell within the community.[25]

In *Faith and Knowledge* (1802), the concept of absolute spirit is present—it is the true infinite that includes finitude within itself and overcomes it—but the category 'spirit' itself is lacking. At the beginning of the Jena lecture fragment, 'The Resumption of the Whole into One' (1802–3), Hegel remarks that 'in religion the ideal shape of spirit is real, while its real side is ideal'. This means that the ideality of the divine takes on an empirical reality that reflects spirit back to itself. The goal of religion is 'to let spirit appear in spiritual shape', as opposed to the sensuous shapes of nature and art.[26]

Spirit is the highest of the stages of consciousness whose odyssey is traced in the *Phenomenology of Spirit* (1807); it appears when reason, which mediates the difference between consciousness and self-consciousness, assumes the shapes of ethical life, art, religion, and philosophy. In the preface to this work a definition of spirit begins to be fashioned. 'That substance is essentially subject is expressed in the notion that represents the absolute as *spirit*—the most sublime concept, one appertaining to the modern age and its religion.'[27] The spiritual on the one hand is what is essential, substantial, or has being *in itself* (consciousness); on the other hand, it relates itself to itself, it knows itself as subject in relation to an object recognized to be other than itself, it has being *for itself*

[24]  *Early Theological Writings*, 265–6 (see chap. 2, n. 5).
[25]  Ibid., 271–3.
[26]  *System of Ethical Life and First Philosophy of Spirit*, p. 179 (see Chap. 2, n. 15).
[27]  *Phenomenology of Spirit*, 10–18. Page references are to the Miller translation, but passages quoted in the following paragraphs are from the translation found in *Hegel: Theologian of the Spirit*. See Chap. 2, n. 18.

(self-consciousness). Yet in its being outside itself it remains within itself, that is, it has being *in and for itself*, and as such it is reason or *spiritual substance*. *Absolute* spirit is that spiritual substance whose recognitive relationships are all internal to itself: it is the whole that embraces all otherness, everything finite and determinate, indeed exteriority as such, within itself. *Finite* spirit, by contrast, recognizes otherness to subsist outside it, and it finds itself involved in relationships that limit and restrict it; just this is the meaning of its finitude. Common to absolute spirit and finite spirit is that both entail relationships of consciousness. Spirit is free, pure, rational relationality, which presupposes sense as the soil of objectification and difference but is itself metasensual.

The etymological and biblical association of spirit with fluid natural forces (wind, breath, light, fire, water) is present but remains below the surface for Hegel. Spirit *is* the vitality or energy that gives and sustains life, but for human life it is the energy and relationality of consciousness that is distinctive. Consciousness is of necessity embodied, just as God is embodied by the world; without the world God is absolute idea but not yet absolute *spirit*. Thus spirit presupposes the sensuous but transfigures it, raises it to pure thought, which is the most concentrated form of energy. The German term *Geist* has at its root the idea of being moved powerfully, as in fear or amazement, a movement associated with the sudden drawing in or expelling of breath. In this way it is linked to the Hebrew, Greek, and Latin words for 'spirit', all of which carry the base meaning of 'breath' or 'wind'. *Geist* also means, in a more restrictive sense, 'mind', and thus it supports the cognitive twist Hegel applies to the concept of spirit. Strictly speaking, one should say 'recognitive', since it is relationships of *recognition* that constitute spirit.[28]

The interpretation of spirit in the *Phenomenology* is further specified when the Christian or revelatory religion is examined.[29] Here absolute spirit is known to be 'knowledge of itself in its divestment: spirit is the being that is the process of retaining identity with itself in its otherness.... Consequently in this

---

[28] For the etymology of *Geist*, see Steven G. Smith, *The Concept of the Spiritual: An Essay in First Philosophy* (Philadelphia: Temple University Press, 1988), 9–11. On the connection between spirit and recognition, see Robert R. Williams, *Recognition: Fichte and Hegel on the Other* (Albany: State University of New York Press, 1992). My reading of Hegel has been influenced in a number of ways by Williams.

[29] *Phenomenology of Spirit*, 453–78.

religion the divine being is revealed. Its revelatoriness consists manifestly in this, that what it is, is known.' It is known as *spirit*, 'as essence that is essentially self-consciousness'.[30] Something is hidden from consciousness if its object is only an alien other and if consciousness does not know its object as itself. The true shape of spirit is to be revelatory self-consciousness; and God is manifest as the universal self or self-knowing subject, which encompasses within itself all finite subjects.

Another striking formulation is found when Hegel turns in the *Phenomenology* to the third of the trinitarian figures.[31] The truth is neither identity (sameness) nor difference but the movement between them, the process by which they turn into each other. With respect to God and the natural world, we can say that the divine is natural and human to the extent that God is *not*, or does not *remain*, merely essential being (*Wesen*); while nature and humanity are divine precisely *in* their essential being, as distinct from their determinate and finite being (*Dasein*). But in *spirit* 'the two abstract sides are posited as they are in truth, namely as sublated', both annulled and preserved (*aufgehoben*). Thus spirit designates the relationship of the divine to the human and the human to the divine, and in this way it acquires a religious as well as an epistemological and ontological connotation. With respect to the divine Trinity, the 'Holy Spirit' is the third moment or element, in which the first two elements, the abstract being of the 'Father' and the concrete, crucified being of the 'Son', are annulled and preserved. Reconciliation occurs in the third moment as spiritual unity in which distinctions are present as sublated moments; reconciliation is the substance of spiritual community, the community constituted by the indwelling of the Spirit.

Hegel's later writings do not advance beyond the *Phenomenology* as far as a theoretical conception of spirit is concerned, but the language in which this conception is formulated is often simpler and clearer. At the beginning of the treatment of 'Absolute Spirit' in the *Encyclopedia of the Philosophical Sciences* (§ 554), there occurs the following concise statement: 'Absolute spirit, while an identity that is eternally self-contained, is likewise an identity that is returning and has returned into itself [from difference].' It is this return that evokes religion, which 'is to be seen as proceeding from and located in the subject no less than as proceeding from absolute

---

[30] *Phenomenology of Spirit*, 459.        [31] Ibid., 471–8.

spirit'. The religious relationship is not merely a human product but the doing of absolute spirit itself, 'which is present as spirit in its community'.[32]

Spirit is obviously a central theme of the *Lectures on the Philosophy of Religion* and of the reading of these lectures in the chapters that follow, especially Chapters 6 and 9. For the moment it is worth noting a passage in the 1824 lectures that seems to gather up much that Hegel strives to say about spirit, and says it with striking imagery: 'Spirit is an eternal process of self-cognition in self-consciousness, streaming out to the finite focus of finite consciousness, and then returning to what spirit actually is, a return in which divine self-consciousness breaks forth' (3:233). The image of 'streaming out' captures the fluid quality that spirit quintessentially is. A variant to this passage from Hegel's miscellaneous papers (3:233 n. 191) contains even more vivid imagery:

Spirit is an eternal process of self-cognition, dividing itself into the finite flashes of light of individual consciousness, and then re-collecting and gathering itself up out of this finitude—inasmuch as it is in the finite consciousness that the process of knowing spirit's essence takes place and that the divine self-consciousness thus arises. Out of the foaming ferment of finitude, spirit rises up fragrantly.

These passages are notable both for the clarity with which eternal spirit is understood to be the energy suffusing the whole process while remaining dependent upon the process for its self-actualization, and for the use of sensuous mystical images—'streaming out', 'finite flashes of light', 'the foaming ferment of finitude', the 'fragrance' of spirit—that are indebted to Meister Eckhart and Jacob Boehme.

Whether reliance on such sources represents a dangerous heterodox swerve away from the mainstream of Christian theology on Hegel's part, or whether it opens up the possibility of fresh insight into central Christian themes, is a matter to be considered in the chapters that follow.

[32] For references to the *Encyclopedia*, see Chap. 2, n. 37.

# 2

# Hegel's Writings on Religion

Hegel did not address the topic of religion only for the first time in his Berlin lectures of 1821. The opportunity to develop a full series of lectures on the philosophy of religion did not come until after his arrival in Berlin. But there was no topic in which he had a deeper and more abiding interest, as evidenced from his days as a theological student in Tübingen through the years in Jena and Nuremberg. The present chapter provides a survey of Hegel's writings on religion from the 1790s to the early 1820s.[1]

## EARLY THEOLOGICAL WRITINGS

In his earliest essays Hegel was concerned with how religion might become a vital, integrative, ethically transformative force in not only the personal life of individuals but also the cultural, social, and political life of a people (*Volk*), a concern that remained within him until his last days. The youthful Hegel was convinced that Christianity, in either dogmatic-supernaturalist or enlightened-rationalist dress, was no longer such a force, and for this reason he was attracted to the ancient Greek public or folk religion (*Volksreligion*). But he knew already in 1793–4 that the Greek ethos could not be restored in the modern world, and this was just the dilemma that at the time seemed irresolvable. Gradually he became aware that one must come to terms with actuality as it presents itself to one's own time and place, and that the rational is always already present in it—'the rose in the cross of the present'

---

[1] The writings discussed in this chapter are anthologized in *G. W. F. Hegel: Theologian of the Spirit*, ed. Peter C. Hodgson (Minneapolis: Fortress Press; Edinburgh: T&T Clark, 1997), and the analysis draws from the editor's introduction and annotations to that volume. Quotations are from the translations prepared for this volume, which in some cases differ substantially from previously published translations.

demanding of us 'hard labour', as he expressed it in the Preface to the *Philosophy of Right*.[2] The later Hegel's hard labour was in part that of releasing the transformative power of Christianity from its dogmatic and rationalist encrustations.

## Religion is One of Our Greatest Concerns in Life

One of these early essays, written as he completed his theological studies at the University of Tübingen in 1793, addresses religion as 'one of our greatest concerns in life'.[3] It has more the character of a series of musings about loosely connected themes than of a focused essay. First, Hegel is interested to explore the interplay of sensuality, subjectivity (heart, feelings), and reason (notably practical reason) in religion. Religion is a matter of heart, not of dogma or teaching, yet some form of positive religion and religious instruction is necessary. In this connection, a distinction is necessary between authentic reason or wisdom (*Vernunft*), and Enlightenment understanding or intellect (*Verstand*)—a distinction that remains fundamental for Hegel thereafter.

The author waxes eloquent in his critique of objective, institutional religion, yet at the same time he wants to makes religion a public force, not a merely private piety. His ideal of a public religion is the folk religion (*Volksreligion*) of the ancient Greeks: it imbues the soul with power, enthusiasm, spirit, and it forms a universal community of the spirit free of idolatrous, fetishistic beliefs. At the same time he sees the need for the continuance of private religion, which is concerned with the training of individuals, inducements to virtue, and the provision of comfort and care. Just how the tension between public and private religion might be adjudicated is not further explored.

In the final part of the essay, which is the most connected, Hegel lays out three elements in the constitution of a folk religion: (a) its

[2] G. W. F. Hegel, *Elements of the Philosophy of Right*, ed. Allen W. Wood, trans. H. B. Nisbet (Cambridge: Cambridge University Press, 1991), 22.

[3] *Three Essays, 1793–1795: The Tübingen Essay, Berne Fragments, The Life of Jesus*, trans. Peter Fuss and John Dobbins (Notre Dame: University of Notre Dame Press, 1984), 30–58; excerpted in *Hegel: Theologian of the Spirit*, 39–57. We see already in this early essay the extent to which Hegel was sensitive to the sensuous and cultic aspects of religion, and this helps to explain why later he insisted on the validity of sensible intuition (*Anschauung*) and imaginative representation (*Vorstellung*) as modes of apprehending truth, alongside that of the philosophical concept (*Begriff*).

teachings must be founded on universal reason, which affirms the all-transcending love of God; (b) it must engage both the heart and the imagination, and thus it is made up of concepts (doctrines), essential customs (myths), and ceremonies (sacrifices as expressions of gratitude);[4] (c) all of life's needs are bound up with it, so it is essential that religious doctrines and practices not be cut off from the rest of life. The cultivation or education of a people as a whole requires both folk religion and political institutions. It is evident that the young Hegel and his friends are exploring the possibility of becoming enlightened religious educators, of creating a new folk religion that might accomplish in their own time what the Greeks accomplished in theirs. But Hegel also recognizes this to be nothing but a wistful dream, appropriately embodied in a mythological figure ('the genie of nations'), and the essay ends with the sober remark that this 'fair youth . . . has fled from the earth'.

## The Spirit of Christianity and Its Fate

In his early writings, Hegel explored and tested several religious options. During the Tübingen years (1788–93), it was primarily the ideal of a folk religion, as we have just seen. While he was in Bern (1793–6), Immanuel Kant's religion of morality had a major impact and served as the basis of Hegel's critique of the 'positivity' (the historical, institutional, and dogmatic forms) of the Christian religion. After moving to Frankfurt in 1796, however, Hegel sought a 'spiritual' enrichment of both folk religion and the Enlightenment. Richard Kroner suggests that if the soul of Greek religion was beauty, and if the reason of Kantian philosophy was morality, then Hegel concluded that the ultimate truth was moral or spiritual beauty, and this truth he discovered in the Christian Gospel in the form of love—a love that assumed concrete shape in the figure of Jesus. This is the thesis of the essays collected by Herman Nohl under the title 'The Spirit of Christianity and Its Fate' (written over a period of several months in 1798–9).[5]

---

[4] This is the beginning of Hegel's later analytic distinction, applied to each of the determinate religions in the philosophy of religion lectures, between abstract concept, concrete representation, and community or cultus.

[5] Herman Nohl (ed.), *Hegels theologische Jugendschriften* (Tübingen: J. C. B. Mohr, 1907). A portion of this work was translated by T. M. Knox as *Early Theological Writings*, with an introduction and fragments translated by Richard Kroner (Chicago: University of Chicago Press, 1948; r.p. University of Pennsylvania Press,

One of these essays[6] is the earliest version, and one of the clearest, of Hegel's speculative theology of incarnation. From romantic devotee of Greek folk religion and enlightened critic of positive religion, Hegel evolved in a few years into a passionate defender of Christian mystery. The unity of divine and human nature is 'pure life' from which all determinacy and opposition is removed, and thus it cannot be grasped by reflection but only by intuition and inspiration. The activity of the divine is a unification of spirits, and only spirit can grasp and embrace spirit. Hegel thinks that the Jewish culture of the time was unsuited to spiritual comprehension, yet Jesus and the Johannine evangelist, both obviously Jewish, succeeded in expressing deep spiritual insight despite conceptual and linguistic limitations.

Thus Hegel is attracted to the logos doctrine of the Gospel of John, but he also draws attention to the 'son of God' and 'son of humanity' language common to all the gospels and presumed to derive from Jesus himself. The relation of a son to a father 'is a living relation of living beings, a likeness of life'. 'Father and son are simply modifications of the same life, not opposite essences.' Each individual is a part and at the same time the whole, the living relatedness. In a living thing, 'the part of the whole is one and the same as the whole': there is one tree, yet every branch is a tree if planted. Thus 'son of God' expresses a 'modification' of the divine, and likewise 'son of humanity' is a modification of the human, an individual subsumed under the universal, 'humanity'. Now these two sons are conjoined in Jesus of Nazareth. 'The son of God is also son of humanity; the divine in a particular shape [*Gestalt*] appears as a human being.'[7] The particular gestalt in which the divine appears is simply a human shape, the shape of one who lived, taught, and died in a particular way, and in whom is represented the whole of humanity.

This connection is a 'holy mystery' because it is life itself, and thus it can be grasped only mystically or by faith, not by the objectifying categories of the two-natures doctrine. God is the existential counterpart (*Gegenstand*), not the epistemological

---

1971). Kroner's statement cited above is on p. 9. The remainder of Nohl's edition was translated by Fuss and Dobbins as *Three Essays*.

[6] 'The Religious Teaching of Jesus', *Early Theological Writings*, 253–81; excerpted in *Hegel: Theologian of the Spirit*, 58–71.

[7] *Early Theological Writings*, 262; cf. 256–62.

object (*Objekt*), of faith. Faith is a relationship of spirit to spirit, a feeling of harmony, or unification. 'Faith in the divine is only possible if in believers themselves there is a divine element which rediscovers itself . . . in that on which it believes.' Here Hegel imbibes of mystical images (light, fire) and is pointing toward a mystical gnosis, both of which locate him in a heterodox trajectory of Christian tradition. 'Only a modification of the Godhead can know the Godhead.'[8]

Faith is, however, only the beginning of a relationship that culminates in friendship. As long as Jesus remained physically present, his followers remained believers only. Even this objectivity must be removed to enter into a purely spiritual relationship with God, animation by the Holy Spirit. Thus Hegel makes much of the Johannine saying that Jesus must depart in order for the Spirit to come (John 14:16; 16:7). With the transition from Jesus to the Spirit there occurs a transition from faith in a counterpart to an actual living in and with Christ. The divine is now present in the disciples as in Jesus; the purely inward unity of love and friendship is accomplished. The culmination of faith is 'the return to the Godhead whence humanity is born', and this return 'closes the circle of human development'.[9]

Jesus himself articulated this idea with the image of the kingdom of God. The word 'kingdom' is inadequate to express the 'divine unification of humanity' if, as its political usage suggests, it means a union through domination and subjugation as opposed to 'the beauty of the divine life of a pure human fellowship', which is utterly free. Yet properly construed, the kingdom of God 'comprises the whole of religion as Jesus founded it', a communion of life in God—a beautiful idea, to be sure, but one flawed by an 'incompleteness' that would give fate power over it. This incompleteness, Hegel hints, was its attempt to overleap nature, its flight from the division and struggles of real life, and its failure to achieve practical implementation other than on the smallest scale. The 'fate' of Jesus and the church—the fate of the spirit of Christianity—is an unresolved tension between the inner truth of the gospel and the exigencies of the external world.[10]

---

[8] *Early Theological Writings*, 266.  [9] Ibid., 272–3.
[10] Ibid., 277–81.

JENA WRITINGS

*Faith and Knowledge*

In 1801 Hegel moved from Frankfurt to Jena, where he began his university career as a lecturer, and where his relationship with Friedrich Schelling was renewed. Together Hegel and Schelling edited *The Critical Journal of Philosophy*, and in the first issue of the second volume (July 1802) Hegel published a lengthy essay, *Faith and Knowledge*, which followed by less than a year his first acknowledged publication, *The Difference between Fichte's and Schelling's System of Philosophy*. According to its title page, the topic of *Faith and Knowledge* was to be 'the reflective philosophy of subjectivity in the complete range of its forms as Kantian, Jacobian, and Fichtean philosophy'. Whereas in the earlier work J. G. Fichte had been contrasted with Kant, now he was seen as the logical culmination of Kant's critical philosophy. Critical philosophy is 'reflective philosophy' in the sense that what the mind knows is a 'reflection' of its own subjective categories. Against Kant's epistemological scepticism, F. H. Jacobi asserted the immediate certainty of religious knowledge or faith, while Fichte completed the reconciliation of finite reason with religious faith already implicit in Kant. For both Kant and Fichte, in Hegel's view, faith is subjected to the criteria of autonomous reason and loses its grounding in the self-manifestation of the absolute, upon which is based what Schelling and Hegel called 'speculative' intuition, which mirrors the truth of the whole rather than simply its own limited subjectivity. In opposition to the rationalistic reduction of faith, which Hegel regarded as characteristic of Enlightenment culture, true philosophical knowledge depends on the religious consciousness and experience of the absolute—not an alien, transcendent, other-worldly absolute but an immanent absolute that subjects itself to negation in the historical Good Fridays of this world.

The introduction to this work[11] argues that the Enlightenment and its aftermath, which Hegel calls 'the culture of reflection', has succeeded in destroying both faith and knowledge. Reason has

[11] *Faith and Knowledge*, trans. Walter Cerf and H. S. Harris (Albany: State University of New York Press, 1977), 55–66. Cf. *Hegel: Theologian of the Spirit*, 72–82.

dismissed religion as merely positive, and itself has become mere intellect or understanding, knowing nothing except that it knows nothing. The void of knowing is filled with the subjectivity of longing and divining; the latter is called 'faith', but it is not true faith in the sense of having a counterpart or a relationship other than to itself.

The turn to subjectivity, which is the principle of the 'North' or of Protestantism, is in itself an authentic turn, for beauty and truth do present themselves as feelings, persuasions, love, which establish contact with the subjectivity of the believer, and the latter must be constructively engaged in the act of knowing. Objectively speaking, the 'sacred grove' of the ancients has been reduced to 'mere timber' for moderns.[12] There is no gainsaying this, but it is still possible to attain sublimity in the form of feeling, eternal longing, perfect vision, blissful enjoyment.

Religion ought to resist the empirical doctrine of happiness (eudaemonism), which orients values solely to this world, but in fact it succumbs to it. The fixed principle of this culture is that the finite is absolute, the sole reality. Opposed to it is another fixed principle, namely that the absolute is the eternal, the incalculable, the inconceivable, the empty—an incognizable God beyond the boundary of reason. But a God who is utterly opposed to the finite is limited by the finite and in this respect is finite as well. Thus piety readily passes over into self-help: 'the poetry of Protestant grief ... is transformed into the prose of satisfaction'. John Locke and the eudaemonists, argues Hegel, have transformed philosophy into empirical psychology; theirs is a subjectivity whose reason is solely immersed in finitude, renouncing any intuition or cognition of the eternal. The philosophies of Kant, Fichte, and Jacobi, despite their intentions to the contrary, are the 'completion and idealization' of this empirical psychology. By setting up infinity as the antithesis of the finite, they make it finite too; they achieve only an idealism of the finite, of a subjectivity that reflects itself back to itself. So these philosophies are 'nothing but the culture of reflection raised to a system'. Human beings 'are not a glowing spark of eternal beauty, or a spiritual focus of the universe, but an absolute sensibility'. Humans may have faith in a realm beyond the barrier that cannot be crossed, but this merely adds a touch of 'alien supersensuousness' to their underlying sensibility. It is

---

[12] *Faith and Knowledge*, 57.

rather as though a painting were permitted to depict only the melancholy longing of human faces but not the gods themselves. Or, to vary the artistic metaphor, it is ironic to complain, as these philosophers do, of being deprived of one's deprivation when after seeing only the feet of a figure the whole work of art is revealed. The fact is that they want to hold on to their precious finitude, whereas the true infinite 'consumes and consummates' finitude.[13]

In the conclusion, following detailed analyses and critiques of Kant, Jacobi, and Fichte, Hegel sums all of this up in the pithy statement that these modern philosophies have 'recast the dogmatism of being into the dogmatism of thinking, the metaphysic of objectivity into the metaphysic of subjectivity'. Dogmatism remains, taking on 'the hue of inwardness, of the latest cultural fashion'. Hegel cleverly turns the two dogmatisms against each other. By negating false objectivism (the metaphysic of objectivity), reflective philosophy (the metaphysic of subjectivity) plays a necessary though transitional role in the birth of speculative philosophy. It represents the moment of nothingness, the pure night of infinity, of infinite grief, the feeling that 'God godself is dead'. But this 'speculative Good Friday' is recognized by speculative philosophy to be only a moment of the supreme idea, of the absolute, through which it must necessarily pass in order to achieve its resurrection to the serene freedom of its shape, which is the shape of spirit. This is because the true absolute, the true infinite, includes finitude within itself and overcomes it. Only when finitude has come into its own through reflective philosophy—the speculative Good Friday—is the absolute able to rise into its true and infinite subjectivity, to come into its own as absolute *spirit*.[14]

## The Resumption of the Whole into One

In lectures at the University of Jena Hegel began to construct a philosophical system, experimenting with a number of approaches during a period of intense creativity from 1801 to 1806. In the earliest of these system outlines (1802–3), he envisioned a fourfold division rather than the triadic plan (logic, nature, spirit) he

---

[13] Ibid., 58–66.
[14] Ibid., 89–91; *Hegel: Theologian of the Spirit*, 83–4.

arrived at just a year later.[15] Following an introduction consisting of logic or 'the science of the idea as such', there would be a philosophy of nature, concerned with the realization of the idea in nature as its 'body', and a philosophy of ethical life (*Sittlichkeit*) as the 'real spirit' (human beings in their social-political-cultural existence) that the idea generates for itself. For the conclusion to his system,[16] Hegel intended to take up religion as 'the resumption of the whole into one, the return to the primitive simplicity of the idea'. Religion is no longer regarded merely as part of social or ethical life (as it was in Hegel's Tübingen and Bern writings) but as the highest synthesis of theoretical (logical) and practical (ethical) cognition, and hence as the culmination of the whole system, which begins with the theory of the absolute and ends with the experience of the absolute. Here for the first time in Hegel's thought we glimpse the place of religion in relation to the whole of philosophy. Religion rather than purely philosophical know-ledge is the culminating moment, but it is to be a new, philosoph-ical religion of the spirit. In later versions of the system, ethics and religion are incorporated into the philosophy of spirit, and religion is regarded as not the final but the penultimate moment (of which Christianity remains the consummate expression), superseded in form (but not content) by speculative philosophy.

Hegel also hints in this fragment at the internal structure of philosophy of religion. He identifies three forms of religion as it appears in world history, corresponding to the logical moments of identity, difference, and mediation. The problematic running through all the forms is how spirit takes shape in the world, i.e. how the ideality of spirit becomes real and how its real side is ideal:

---

[15] Most of these materials have been lost, and we are dependent on information provided by Karl Rosenkranz in *Georg Wilhelm Friedrich Hegels Leben* (Berlin, 1844; r.p. Darmstadt: Wissenschaftliche Buchgesellschaft, 1969). Rosenkranz pro-vides (133–41) a summary of and quotations from a lecture fragment dating from this period that describes how Hegel moved from ethical life to religion and found in the latter the culmination of his philosophy. This is one of the most important texts of the Jena period, for it contains ideas of germinal importance for Hegel's treat-ment of religion in later writings, and it shows the evolving, fluid character of his thought (including some experimentation with ideas derived from Schelling). Rosenkranz's text has been translated by H. S. Harris as an appendix to the 'System of Ethical Life' in *System of Ethical Life and First Philosophy of Spirit*, ed. and trans. H. S. Harris and T. M. Knox (Albany: State University of New York Press, 1979), 178–86. Selections from this material are found in *Hegel: Theologian of the Spirit*, 85–91.

[16] According to Rosenkranz, *Hegels Leben*, 179.

for religion there is no *Geist* without *Gestalt*, no spirit without sensible or intellectual configuration. The first form of religion, that of identity, typifies nature religion and the religion of art, both of which are seen to be historically embodied by Greek religion; here the shape of spirit is that of nature (the old Greek mythologies) and of the beautiful human figure (the Greek dramatists and philosophers).

The second form, that of difference, seems to encompass a disparate totality made up of Jewish, Roman, and Christian religions. For all of these religions, the gods are dispelled from nature (the womb of identity), but with differing results. Judaism is left with the anguish of infinite separation between the divine and the human; Roman religion substitutes for its dismembered gods an abstract, dead universality; while Christianity re-establishes a oneness with the absolute in a single human being. The Christian idea of reconciliation is elaborated in the form of a Trinity, which re-enacts the moments of the dialectic: absolute thought (the Father), creation (the eternal and incarnate Son), the realized identity of objective world and eternal thought (the Holy Spirit). Hegel adds this notable remark: 'The divinity in which [reconciled] love finds its own felicity must come to be the *Mother of God* herself.'[17] Is this a reference to a fourth person of the Godhead, the holy Mary, forming a divine quaternity? Or is the Mother of God another name for the figure of comfort and regeneration, the Holy Spirit? There is precedent for the latter in certain strands of Gnostic and Syrian Christianity, which subsequently influenced German pietism (Gottfried Arnold, Hermann Francke, Count Zinzendorf). In any event, this is a thought experiment to which Hegel did not return (although in the *Phenomenology of Spirit* he does say that the love of the spiritual community is symbolized by the figure of the mother).

The third form of religion in world history is envisioned to be a philosophical religion of the Spirit. Hegel imagines that through the mediation of philosophy a new form of world religion will emerge out of Christianity. Catholic beauty and holiness have been destroyed by Protestant worldliness and cannot be brought back; yet nature and world have not truly been reconciled in Protestantism, and there remains only a secular form of infinite grief. What is called for is a new religion of a free people, a religion

---

[17] *System of Ethical Life*, 184.

in which reason 'has found once more its reality as an ethical spirit, a spirit which is bold enough to assume its pure shape on its own soil and in its own majesty'. Hegel seems to be playing once again with the ideal of a folk religion, but this too is a thought experiment that is not repeated in later writings. Perhaps its place is taken by the portrayal in the Berlin philosophy of religion lectures of the kingdom of the Spirit; however, the latter represents the fullest realization of the Christian ideal, not the establishment of a post-Christian religion. These various explorations bear testimony to the fertility of Hegel's mind during the years in Jena.

PHENOMENOLOGY OF SPIRIT

Hegel's most famous work was completed rapidly and under duress in the autumn of 1806 and was published early the next year. Not only was he in need of funds from the publisher, but also Napoleon's army was advancing on Jena. Shortly thereafter Hegel decided to leave Jena for financial and personal reasons; he was not to resume a university professorship until 1816 in Heidelberg. *The Phenomenology of Spirit* was intended as an introduction to Hegel's 'System of Science', the first main part of which did not appear until the publication of the *Science of Logic* in 1812–16.[18]

*Preface*

The Preface to the *Phenomenology*[19] was written after the work was completed and is one of the most lucid presentations of Hegel's

[18] A satisfactory translation of the *Phenomenology of Spirit* does not yet exist (a problem that should be rectified when a new translation appears from Cambridge University Press). The discussion and quotations that follow are based on the translation prepared by H. Michael Stewart and Peter C. Hodgson for the selections in *Hegel: Theologian of the Spirit*, 92–136. The German source is *Phänomenologie des Geistes*, ed. Johannes Hoffmeister (Hamburg: Felix Meiner Verlag, 1952), 19–30, 63–75, 473–80, 521–48. The page numbers of A. V. Miller's translation, *Phenomenology of Spirit* (Oxford: Clarendon Press, 1977), are given for reference purposes, although sometimes our translation is closer to that of J. B. Baillie, *Phenomenology of Mind*, rev. 2nd edn. (London: George Allen & Unwin, 1949). For a reading of the *Phenomenology* from a theological perspective, see Stephen Crites, *Dialectic and Gospel in the Development of Hegel's Thinking* (University Park, Pa.: Pennsylvania State University Press, 1998). Crites also provides an extended analysis of Hegel's intellectual formation and of the early writings and the Jena writings prior to the *Phenomenology*.
[19] *Phenomenology of Spirit*, 1–45.

philosophy. He argues that the subject matter of philosophy, 'the true' or 'the absolute', must be grasped as both substance and subject.[20] 'Substance' signifies what underlies all that is, the universal essence of things, whereas 'subject' signifies a self-conscious, knowing agent or agency. Traditionally, these are alternative philosophical conceptions of the absolute, but Hegel claims that they belong together in the claim that the absolute is *spirit*. For it is precisely spirit that unifies substance and subject, identity and difference, the ideal and the real, thought and life, through a process of absolution (release) and resolution (reintegration). The religious name of this absolving spirit is 'God', and God must accordingly be understood to become God only through this process. This means that God is not a simple essence or immediate identity but rather an action that negates, ruptures, and reinstates itself, reflects itself back to itself in otherness. The life of God may indeed be expressed as 'the play of love with itself'; but this is merely an insipid idea 'if the seriousness, the anguish, the patience, and the labour of the negative are lacking in it'.[21] Subjectivity entails negation and its labour; it is a *result*, a process, a becoming, not a given.

The divine substance/subject is the truth that is the whole (*das Ganze*). 'But the whole is nothing other than the essence consummating itself through its development.'[22] The divine whole is absolute in the sense that all relations, internal as well as external, . are contained within it. Negation, rupture, and differentiation occur within it; it is not limited by another essence outside it. It is a cosmotheandric whole, not merely a divine whole; it encompasses and constitutes all that is, *cosmos* and *anthropos* as well as *theos*—and as such it is 'spirit'. Hegel expresses this by saying that the true is actual only as a 'system', a structured and interrelated wholeness. This is what is meant, he says, when one refers to 'the absolute as *spirit*', which is the 'most sublime' of modern concepts.[23] It means that the absolute is relational and processual. Spirit is what is actual in a triple mediation: it is essence or has being *in itself* (abstract, ideal divinity); it relates itself to itself or is being *for itself* in other-being (determinate, real worldliness); and in this being outside itself it remains within itself and is thus *in and for itself* (the interplay of ideality and reality, divinity and world).

---

[20] Ibid., 10.    [21] Ibid., 10.    [22] Ibid., 11.    [23] Ibid., 14.

Spirit that knows itself as spirit is knowledge or science, *Wissenschaft.* Such knowledge is the actuality of spirit; it is the fluid or medium in which spirit spiritualizes, the realm spirit builds for itself, the very element that is the stuff of spirit. This 'ethereal element' is 'pure self-recognition in absolute otherness'.[24] Knowledge presupposes otherness and difference, but recognizes itself in the other. Spirit comes to self-recognition through the long and laborious journey of history; the phenomenology of spirit traces the stages along this path. The subject or agent of this historical action is not merely individual human subjects but absolute spirit itself, the whole, the true, the system. Humans as thinkers and doers play a necessary role in this process, but it encompasses and consumes them.

The Preface includes a meditation on the 'tremendous power of the negative', which is the 'energy of thought', the power that drives the dialectic. The negative appears above all as death, the nonactual that deactualizes—that of which all living things have an instinctive dread. Yet 'the life of spirit is not the life that is afraid of death and keeps itself untouched by devastation, but the life that endures death and maintains itself in it. It attains its truth only when, in utter dismemberment, it finds itself.' Spirit gains its power 'only by looking the negative in the face and lingering over it. This lingering over it is the magic power that converts the negative into being.'[25] *Geist* is what goes on, brings new life out of death; the life thus brought forth is deeper, richer, stronger than the youthful innocence on which death has not yet cast its shadow.

*Introduction*

The 'phenomenology' of spirit, Hegel tells his readers in the Introduction to the work, is the 'science of the experience of consciousness'.[26] Consciousness appears in the three basic forms of consciousness, self-consciousness, and reason (chapters 1–5). Reason takes on the shape of spirit (chapter 6) when it achieves ethical and cultural expression (that is, spirit is intrinsically an intersubjective, social category, although the whole process is

---

[24] *Phenomenology of Spirit*, 14.

[25] Ibid., 19. The image of dismemberment (*Zerrissenheit*) forecasts that of Golgotha, the place of skulls, with which the work ends, 493 ('the Golgotha of absolute spirit', Baillie translation, 808).

[26] Ibid., 46–57, quotation from 56.

also spirit); and the highest shapes of spirit are religion, including art (chapter 7), and philosophy or absolute knowing (chapter 8). The journey of spirit through the various shapes of consciousness constitutes for Hegel a veritable *itinerarium mentis in Deum*: the phenomenology of spirit is a religious quest, a pilgrimage.

The primary task of the Introduction is to establish a strong link, indeed a dialectical identity, between cognition and its content, between concept and object, knowing and being. Cognition is not merely an instrument by which to grasp absolute being; it is the absolute itself. It is a common fallacy to think of the absolute as standing on one side and cognition (or consciousness) on the other. Contra Kant, we must recognize that by investigating knowing we are in fact investigating the thing itself. Thus the science of the experience of consciousness, of the path taken by the soul as it journeys through its successive configurations, is not merely an epistemological and anthropological investigation. It is also an ontological and theological one: it is an account of absolute spirit's return to itself through finite spirit's rise to consciousness of the absolute.

The goal is attained when knowing no longer needs to go beyond itself, when it finds its own self, when concept corresponds to object, and object to concept. Hegel does not regard this as an empirical state of affairs attained once and for all—and certainly not in his own time and his own philosophy. Our historical state is rather one of unending quest through countless determinate negations. There is no shortcut that avoids the wealth and detail of determinacy and difference. Every time consciousness thinks it has finally glimpsed itself as its own object, it is driven on to a new shape. This is the very nature of 'absolute knowledge' itself. It is not a blank whole, not a barren identity, but all the endless and inexhaustible details of life that we are tempted to pass over. It is 'absolving' knowledge, releasing itself into the life-and-death struggle of history. It has the quality of wisdom (*phronēsis*) rather than of information (*technē*), of desire (*erōs*) rather than of permanence (*stasis*).

*Religion*

At the beginning of chapter 7 on religion,[27] Hegel offers a famous recapitulation of the preceding chapters of the *Phenomenology*.

---

[27] Ibid., 410–16.

Religion has appeared in the shapes of consciousness hitherto considered, but only from the point of view of consciousness that is conscious *of* absolute being; absolute being in and for itself, the *self*-consciousness of spirit, has not appeared in those forms. This signals a transition from an anthropological to an ontotheological perspective, and it hints that the self-manifestation or self-revelation of the absolute will be a central theme in the discussion of religion proper.

The shapes of spirit appear in a temporal sequence, a history of religions. The religions constitute the determinately existing actuality of the whole of spirit, which *is* only as the differentiating and self-returning movement of these its aspects. The whole of spirit, the spirit of religion as such, is a movement away from immediacy toward the knowledge of what spirit is in and for itself, toward a shape that is perfectly identical with its essence. Hegel believes that this movement attains its consummation in a particular historical religion, Christianity, which consequently is the absolute or revelatory religion. However, the phenomenological arrangement of this progression differs from the historical sequence in which the religions have appeared. There seems to be no single line of advance since each religiocultural trajectory at some point retrogresses, a 'knot' forms, and spirit moves to another trajectory, so that there are in fact many lines in history, which can be 'bundled' but not amalgamated.

Hegel then outlines his phenomenological arrangement of religions, which identifies three major moments or bundles: (1) Immediate religion, or natural religion, in which the distinction between consciousness and self-consciousness has not yet emerged. Spirit remains in immediate unity with itself, or knows itself as its object in natural or immediate shape alone. (2) The religion of art, or Greek religion, where spirit knows itself in a *sublated* natural shape, which is a product of conscious activity, a work of art. (3) The revelatory or Christian religion, where spirit attains its true shape in a self-consciousness that is both divine and human; but the representational form in which this is expressed must still pass over into absolute knowing. This is Hegel's first sustained effort to establish the internal arrangement of philosophy of religion. While the basic knots remain in place, the bundled contents will vary drastically as the treatment is refined in the Berlin lectures two decades later.

*The Revelatory Religion*

At the beginning of the third part of the chapter, Revelatory Religion (*die offenbare Religion*),[28] Hegel is concerned to show how and why the transition occurred from Greek and Roman to Christian religion. The transitions, 'knots', or breaks in history are of critical importance. Hegel's attention to them shows that he does not subscribe to a naively progressivist view of history; rather his vision is deeply tragic, though encompassed within a tragicomic metanarrative for which both alienation and reconciliation are ongoing realities. What happened, on Hegel's version, was that the ethical spirit and beauty of Greek religion was lost in the Roman world, leaving only the finite self with its abstract legal status and its pretentious claim, 'The self is absolute being.' This 'levity' inevitably somersaulted into an 'unhappy consciousness', the recognition that finitude cannot satisfy the human soul. Such was the tragic fate of the certainty of self that aims to be in and for itself alone and is conscious of the loss of all essentiality; it was the anguish that pronounces God to be dead, that knows Greek religion and art now merely to be 'beautiful fruit plucked from the tree'. The Romans, amazingly, celebrated this death of the gods by collecting them in their pantheon; but in so doing they unwittingly brought on the birth pangs of spirit's new emergence.[29] (Hegel's discussion of Roman religion is only a slightly veiled critique of the religious situation of his own time.)

Turning specifically to the revelatory religion,[30] Hegel articulates its core insight in terms of a speculative theory of incarnation. Such a theory has two sides: the first side is the divine becoming human (substance divests or empties itself of itself and becomes self-consciousness); the second is the human becoming divine (self-consciousness divests itself of itself and makes itself into a universal self). There is a divestment of the divine and an exaltation of the human such that the two become one: here Hegel has adopted the classic Lutheran doctrine of the two states of Christ (humiliation and exaltation), but he probes its meaning with astonishing insight. If we had only the latter side, the self-exaltation of the human, then spirit would only be imagined into existence; this is the visionary dreaming (*Schwärmerei*) that conjures divinity out of itself. No, the first side, the divestment of the divine, must

---

[28] *Phenomenology of Spirit*, 453–78.    [29] Ibid., 453–6.    [30] Ibid., 457–63.

also be there as an objective reality in the shape of an actual human being. That spirit is present for the immediate certainty of faith is not merely imagined; rather 'it is actual in the believer'. Consciousness does not set out from its own inner life and connect the idea of God with it; 'rather it starts from an existence that is immediately present and recognizes God in it'. Hegel's position in brief seems to be this: faith *does* have an objective historical referent and point of departure, but it cannot be proved from history that this point of departure has the *significance* attributed to it by faith; the only proof in this instance is the proof of the Spirit.

By descending from its eternal simplicity, the absolute being (the 'Father') attains for the first time its 'highest being'—which is not the remote and inaccessible deity of rationalism, but a divesting, absolving, relational being that comes down into history and makes itself manifest (the 'Son'). Essential being (*Wesen*) becomes existent, determinate being (*Sein, Dasein*)—and this is to say that it becomes spirit (*Geist*), 'the being that is the process of retaining identity with itself in its otherness'. Spirit in the immediacy of self-consciousness is the particular individual Jesus of Nazareth, as contrasted with the universal self-consciousness of the religious community. But this individual human being, 'as whom absolute being is manifest', is subject to the conditions of time, space, and mortality: his being passes into having been and his sensible presence into spiritual presence. This is the passage from the Son to the Spirit.

These temporal and spatial categories, endemic to the representational form of religion, are not adequate to the truth of absolute spirit. Consequently, Hegel moves on[31] to provide a speculative redescription of the central Christian theologoumenon, the Trinity, which contains the true content but in less than adequate form. The three constitutive moments, conceptually expressed, are pure thought, representation, and self-consciousness. *Pure thought* designates the immanent or intradivine Trinity, which is not an empty essence but already the *implicit* fullness of absolute spirit.[32] *Representation* (*Vorstellung*) designates the second moment, that of creation, fall, incarnation, life and death, symbolically encapsulated in the figure of the Son.[33] Representation is not merely an epistemological category but an ontological one. It designates a divine doing, not merely a human knowing. *God* sets godself forth

---

[31] *Phenomenology of Spirit*, 463–4.          [32] Ibid., 464–5.
[33] Ibid., 465–71.

(*vor-stellen*) in and as world; this is an essential element in the process of God's becoming spirit. The referent of representation is real history, not fanciful myth, although what happens in history is often recounted in mythical form.

The third moment is that of *self-consciousness* or infinite inter-subjectivity, which is associated by Christian faith with the Holy Spirit, resurrection, reconciliation, and the community of faith.[34] Hegel observes that 'absolute being' would be an empty name if in truth there were an absolute other to it or an irreparable fall from it. 'Absolute' must mean then that there is nothing with which God cannot be related. Within the divine whole there is genuine other-ness and recalcitrant difference, but it is only when essential being is reflected back into itself that it is spirit. Hegel launches at this point into a complex discussion of the ontological status of good and evil. Evil seems to take two forms: on the one hand, it is a withdrawal into self, a becoming self-centred, in other words a failure to make the move from the first moment to the second; but on the other hand, it is a matter of getting stuck in the second moment, revelling in separation and estrangement, failing to come back into self. In both cases, it is a stopping short of spirit, a failure in spiritualization.

Hegel's discussion of spiritual community and spiritual resur-rection is incredibly rich and dense.[35] He is describing here a process by which the divine being's individual self-consciousness (as Christ) becomes universal, becomes the religious community. Death is transfigured from the nonbeing of the historical individ-ual Jesus into the universality of the Spirit, which lives, dies, and rises daily in the community. Particularity dies away in universal-ity, representation in concept. What dies in the death of the medi-ator is not only 'the already dead husk stripped of its essential being', but also the abstraction of the divine being. The abstract supreme being must die, along with the historical mediator, in order for the concrete universal, world-encompassing Spirit, to be born. Spirit is the movement in which absolutely opposed things recognize themselves as the same and are reconciled. This reconciliation or atonement is a process intrinsic to the divine life, not a satisfaction attained by paying a penalty. It is a present reality, not something that happened once in the distant past or will come only in the distant future.

---

[34] Ibid., 471–3.      [35] Ibid., 473–8.

The community is filled by eternal love, symbolized by the figure of the mother, but this is a love that is only felt, not yet grasped in consciousness. Reconciliation occurs for the community in the heart, but its consciousness is still ruptured. Reconciliation appears to it to lie in the beyond, while the present world is not yet transfigured, does not yet have a spiritual shape. This inward and incomplete character of reconciliation indicates for Hegel the necessity of making one more transition—from revelatory religion to absolute knowing. But does philosophy accomplish the transfiguration of the world any more successfully than religion does?

## ENCYCLOPEDIA OF THE PHILOSOPHICAL SCIENCES

The *Encyclopedia* is the only complete compendium of Hegel's philosophical system. He prepared it for use in conjunction with his lectures, which became expositions of the thesis paragraphs of the printed text. The first edition was published in 1817, less than a year after Hegel's arrival in Heidelberg. In 1818 he was called to Berlin as the successor to Fichte, and there his lectures on the topics covered by the *Encyclopedia* greatly expanded. A second edition was issued in 1827, nearly twice the length of the first; and a third in 1830, only modestly revised from the second. The three main parts of the *Encyclopedia* are the Science of Logic (a shortened version of the book published in 1812–16 and partly revised shortly before Hegel's death), the Philosophy of Nature (the only published version of this portion of Hegel's system, although he lectured frequently on the topic), and the Philosophy of Spirit.

The third part, the Philosophy of Spirit, is in turn divided into three sections: Subjective Spirit (anthropology, phenomenology of spirit, psychology), Objective Spirit (right, morality, ethical life), and Absolute Spirit (art, revealed religion, philosophy). The first two forms of spirit, which specify human existence in its individual and social manifestations, are transcended and unified in the third, which is the richest and most inclusive of Hegel's categories, encompassing divinity and humanity, the infinite and the finite, the ideal and the real, the spiritual and the natural: it is the whole, the true, the free. In art the absolute is known principally in the shape of sensible intuition (*Anschauung*); in religion, in that of spiritual representation (*Vorstellung*); and in philosophy, in that of the speculative concept (*Begriff*). While the forms of knowledge differ, the content is the same.

The organization of this section of the *Encyclopedia* goes back to the first edition of 1817, although the content was considerably revised in 1827. The organization is a modification of that found in chapters 7 and 8 of the *Phenomenology of Spirit*, where Hegel treats in succession 'natural religion', 'the religion of art', 'the revelatory religion', and 'the absolute knowing' of philosophy. The section on 'art' in the *Encyclopedia* includes as a subtext references not only to 'the religion of art' proper, namely Greek religion, but to several of the so-called natural religions as well (in the lectures on the philosophy of religion, this material was expanded greatly to become the section called 'determinate religion'). The section on 'religion' is highly compressed and formal, and it is limited to only one part of the subject, whose place in the whole of the philosophy of religion remained unclear;[36] but nonetheless it contains some very important passages and offers an interesting variation on the internal arrangement of what is here called 'revealed religion' as opposed to 'revelatory religion'. Hegel did not lecture in Berlin on the paragraphs on 'Objective Spirit' and 'Absolute Spirit' in the *Encyclopedia* as such; rather he gave separate and extensive lecture courses on the philosophy of right, the philosophy of art, the philosophy of religion, and the history of philosophy. The *Encyclopedia* continued to be used as a text for lectures on logic and metaphysics, philosophy of nature, and philosophy of subjective spirit.

The section on Absolute Spirit opens with this definition: 'Absolute spirit, while an identity that is eternally self-contained, is likewise an identity that is returning and has returned into itself' (§ 554).[37] Religion, as one of the shapes constituting this return, 'is to be seen as proceeding from and located in the subject no less

---

[36] On the relation of the *Phenomenology* and the *Encyclopedia* to the *Lectures on the Philosophy of Religion*, see Walter Jaeschke, *Reason in Religion: The Foundations of Hegel's Philosophy of Religion*, trans. J. Michael Stewart and Peter C. Hodgson (Berkeley and Los Angeles: University of California press, 1990), 208–15.

[37] Quotations are from the translation by J. Michael Stewart and Peter C. Hodgson in *Hegel: Theologian of the Spirit*, 137–54, based on the third edition of 1830 as edited by Friedhelm Nicolin and Otto Pöggeler, *Enzyklopädie der philosophischen Wissenschaften im Grundrisse* (Hamburg: Verlag von Felix Meiner, 1959), and compared with the new critical edition of this text edited by Wolfgang Bonsiepen and Hans-Christian Lucas in *Gesammelte Werke*, vol. 20 (Hamburg: Felix

than as proceeding from absolute spirit, which is [present] as spirit in its community'. Thus the science of religion must be both anthropological and theological. The two aspects, subjective consciousness and absolute spirit, come together as an inward process in the form of *faith*, which, in worship, sublates the antithesis 'into a spiritual liberation' (§ 555).

Art, as the first of the shapes of absolute spirit, is 'the concrete intuition and representation of implicitly absolute spirit as the ideal' (§§ 556–63). Art needs not only sensuous material but also the given forms of nature, of which the human is the highest because only in it can 'spirit have its corporeality and thus its intuitable expression' (§ 558). Art is a transfiguration, not an imitation, of nature, but absolute spirit cannot be made truly explicit in its shapes; spirit remains hidden beneath or within the shape of beauty, which can achieve only an 'imbuing' of its forms by spirit. Art is a human work, a product of individual genius; the artist is the master of the god, and no divine *self*-manifestation takes place here.

Art and religion are of course closely associated since art is one of the forms by which religious content is expressed. The advent of fine or beautiful art (*schöne Kunst*) portends the decline of the nature religions, which are still bound to sensuous externality. The religion of fine art (Greek religion) and the religion of symbolic art or sublimity (Jewish religion) must have concrete spirituality as their principle. But even these are 'only a stage in liberation, not the supreme liberation itself' (§ 562). Intuition must pass over into revelation.

Revealed religion (§§ 564–71) is thus the second of the shapes of absolute spirit. Authentic religion is revealed by God, who is not jealous, who does not withhold what God is. As spirit, God is intrinsically revelatory, for 'spirit is only spirit in so far as it is *for* spirit'. If God is to be taken seriously in religion, then it is from *God* that the definition of religion must begin. But to grasp what God is as spirit calls for 'profound speculation'. It embraces the following propositions, which Hegel elaborates from a work by the jurist-theologian Carl Friedrich Göschel (who had become his

Meiner Verlag, 1992). The earlier English translation by William Wallace, *Hegel's Philosophy of Mind* (Oxford: Clarendon Press, 1894, r.p. 1971) has been consulted. References are to paragraph numbers. A new translation will be published by Cambridge University Press.

disciple): 'God is only God to the extent that God knows godself; God's self-knowing is, further, a self-consciousness in humanity and humanity's knowledge *of* God, which proceeds to humanity's self-knowing *in* God' (§ 564). The medium of divine revelation and self-knowing is not a directly given oracle from God or a body of sacred teachings but the very process of human consciousness and knowing.

The form of religious knowledge is representational, which means that the constitutive elements of the divine content are understood as phenomena following one another, a web of happenings in temporal succession and spatial dispersion. These finite reflective categories are sublated in faith and worship but not yet translated into speculative concepts (§ 565).

Combining both conceptual and representational forms, we can say that the spheres or elements in which the absolute content presents itself are as follows: universality (immanent Trinity), particularity (creation and governance of the world, the work of the eternal Son), and individuality (the history of redemption, reconciliation, and restoration, the work of the temporal Son who passes into the Spirit) (§§ 565–9). This arrangement goes back to the first edition of the *Encyclopedia* (1817) and is similar to the 1821 philosophy of religion lecture manuscript. It differs from the *Phenomenology* and the later philosophy of religion lectures (1824, 1827, 1831), for which the second moment encompasses both creation and incarnation and is associated with the figure of Christ, while the third moment is that of the community of faith and the Spirit. Hegel experimented with both arrangements. The *Encyclopedia* arrangement is more christological in the sense that the Son is associated with both the second and third moments, sharing the latter with the Spirit (of course it is the indwelling Spirit that makes Jesus to be the Christ, so that what is involved is really a pneumatological christology); while the *Phenomenology* and later philosophy of religion arrangement is more traditionally trinitarian and at the same time more radically pneumatological in the sense that the third moment is exclusively that of the Spirit and is also the consummation of the first two moments.[38] It was typical of

[38] Cyril O'Regan discusses the significance of these two arrangements in *The Heterodox Hegel* (Albany: State University of New York Press, 1994), 235–7. He points out that the Spirit is the 'first among equals' for Hegel, and that Hegelian heterodoxy 'swerves' away from traditional christology, pneumatology, and ecclesiology through the impact of mysticism.

Hegel to engage in such thought-experiments: each approach contains insight and truth, but only the totality of approaches is *the* truth. Philosophy (§§ 572–7) is the unity of art and religion. Artistic intuition is not merely held together to form a whole as in religion; it is also combined into a simple spiritual intuition and then raised to self-conscious thought. Philosophy grasps the *necessity* of the shared content of art and religion as well as of their distinct forms, and thus it is liberated from the one-sidedness of all forms.

This consideration led Hegel to add a lengthy remark to § 573 in the 1827 and 1830 editions on the relationship of philosophy and religion. Both their difference of forms and their identity of content must be recognized. Religion itself, he points out, criticizes its own forms as it approximates speculative thinking or becomes scientific theology. If it does not do so, it will fall prey to rationalistic critiques of the contradictions in faith, by which rationalism advances its own principle of formal identity and finitization of content. Speculative philosophy/theology is reproached for having too little of God in it for positive religion, too much for rationalism and piety. The charge of atheism, that philosophy has too little of God, has grown rare; more common is the charge of pantheism, that it has too much of God. The latter charge arises from modern piety and theology, which eschew any specific knowledge of God and hold only to a God in general, while occupying themselves with merely historical matters (what was *once* believed). But no serious philosophy, claims Hegel in a lengthy excursus, has ever held to pantheism in the strict sense that everything simply *is* God: this is an absurdity.

What is at issue here is the relationship between God and the world, and Hegel offers one of his most lucid discussions of the matter. Reflective understanding separates God as essence from finite, worldly appearance, and then establishes an external, 'incomprehensible' link between them. Speculative philosophy, by contrast, is concerned not with abstract unity or mere identity, the empty absolute, but with concrete unity, which entails at every stage distinctive determinations of which there are a great number and diversity, the last and deepest of which is absolute spirit itself—the determinacy that encompasses all determinations. The critics who bring the charge of pantheism and barren identity 'lose sight of the chief point of interest, namely the manner in which

unity is determinate'.[39] Instead of recognizing unity in the diverse
ways it is determinate, they grasp only the most external and worst
sort of unity, namely composition, which they falsely attribute to
philosophy. On their own compositional view, God would have to
dwell in the interspace of things, and there would be an infinite
splintering of the divine actuality in materiality.
   *The manner in which unity is determinate*: this is a leitmotif of
Hegel's philosophy. It is present in the following summary of the
*Encyclopedia* (§ 574): 'the concept of philosophy... is the logical
idea [*das Logische*] with the signification that it is universality
attested in concrete content as in its actuality. In this manner
science has returned to its beginning: its result is the logical idea
but as a spiritual principle [*das Geistige*].' The movement is from
abstract to concrete, determinate unity. Spirit is the most intense
and also the most diverse sort of unity. The return to the beginning
but with difference inscribes the figure of a spiral, a figure that is
articulated conceptually by the three figures of the philosophical
syllogism. Each of the terms of the syllogism (the logical idea,
nature, spirit) in turn assumes middle position and couples the
other two. In this way concrete, determinate unity is established.
Hegel concludes with a phrase reminiscent of Aristotle: 'The eternal idea that exists in and for itself is eternally active, engendering
and enjoying itself as absolute spirit' (§ 577).[40]


FOREWORD TO HINRICHS'S RELIGION

Hegel took the occasion of writing a foreword to the work of a
former student and future disciple[41] to return to a topic with which
he had long been concerned, the reconciliation of faith and reason,
and also to address a challenge that newly confronted him in 1822.
It is one of his most accessible writings on religion. The reconciliation is not genuine, he argues, if faith has become devoid of

   [39] § 573 remark (*Hegel: Theologian of the Spirit*, 150–1).
   [40] Hegel concludes the *Encyclopedia* with a quotation from Aristotle's *Metaphysics*, 12.7, 1072$^b$18–30, concerning the relationship between thought, being, and
activity.
   [41] H. F. W. Hinrichs, *Die Religion im inneren Verhältnisse zur Wissenschaft*
(Heidelberg, 1822), pp. i–xxviii. The passages quoted here are from the translation
by J. Michael Stewart for *Hegel: Theologian of the Spirit*, 155–71. It is one of the few
statements on religion published by Hegel himself during the Berlin years, and thus
it is an important supplement to his lectures on the philosophy of religion.

content and reason has renounced the cognition of truth. There is no longer any discord between them because there is no longer any object of dispute.

Faith is properly defined as both the subjective fact of being convinced *and* the church's objective creed, its credo. Education is a process of internalizing the truth, which first impinges externally in words and letters. The church is properly engaged in education in both senses—in mediating the doctrinal tradition and in bringing about inner conviction. Conviction comprises the subjective aspect of faith: a 'taking-as-true' (*Fürwahrhalten*) with reasons,[42] in this case the reasons provided by and for representational thinking.

Reason is properly understood as cognition of truth. The Enlightenment critique of reason was necessary because in the doctrinal and metaphysical tradition finite objects of understanding were confused with and represented as eternal truth. But the Enlightenment left thought with *only* finite material and eschewed any possibility of knowing truth in and for itself. Enlightenment theology was left without any known truth or objective content, and thus without any possibility of a *doctrine* of faith (a *Glaubenslehre*).[43]

The mention of *Glaubenslehre* leads Hegel into a discussion of the work recently published by his theological colleague in Berlin, Friedrich Schleiermacher. One suspects that this is a primary occasion for his writing the foreword, since the second volume of Schleiermacher's *Der christliche Glaube* was not published until 1822, and Hegel had been able to take only brief account of the first volume in his philosophy of religion lectures of the previous summer. Schleiermacher and others are claiming that only in the region of *feeling* can spirit still find a place to encounter the eternal; only here can the impulse to truth take refuge. Hegel has no objection to feeling as such, only to the claim that it is the sole or predominant form of cognition. However, Hegel understands 'feeling' (*Gefühl*) as 'sensibility' (*Empfindung*), thus as an indeterminate, sense-based mode of knowledge that can be filled with any content, whereas Schleiermacher intends something quite different by 'feeling', namely a prereflective awareness of the whence and whither of existence. Hegel never seems to appreciate this distinction, and thus he insists that, while there may be a natural

[42] *Hegel: Theologian of the Spirit*, 158.    [43] Ibid., 161.

feeling of the divine, the divine is properly present only in and for spirit, and that spirit consists not in natural life but in being reborn. Animals live according to natural feeling, and if religion is the feeling of dependence, 'a dog would then be the best Christian'.[44] The heart of religion is not a feeling of dependence but a feeling of freedom. Only free spirit can have religion.

The need of our time, as Hegel sees it, is for a substantial, objective content of truth, and this can be provided only by thinking, not feeling. The conviction of faith needs the testimony of the indwelling spirit of truth. Religion requires a science of religion—a theology, whose proper content is not history but present rational cognition. The cognition of God is what raises humans above animals, makes them happy or blessed. Yet at the pinnacle of modern culture is a reversion to the ancient notion that God is uncommunicative—a turn against the revelatory heart of Christianity and spirit. What is theology without cognition of God? Hegel answers with the words of the Apostle: 'a noisy gong and a clanging cymbal'.[45]

## THE FOUR VERSIONS OF THE LECTURES ON THE PHILOSOPHY OF RELIGION

Hegel sought to provide such a cognitive theology in his lectures on the philosophy of religion. Since his assessment of the context in which he was speaking was refined and nuanced in light of new challenges, and since he was continually assimilating new materials, the four series of lectures (1821, 1824, 1827, 1831) differ from each other considerably. The fundamental point of view and theological-philosophical conclusions do not change, but the structure and details of the argument do, and ideas are often formulated in slightly different ways that disclose new angles of meaning. Hegel rarely ever simply repeated himself verbatim: he was thinking as he spoke. The critical edition edited by Walter Jaeschke, Ricardo Ferrara, and myself reconstructs each of the lecture series as a separate text based on the best available sources.[46] My primary

---

[44] Ibid., 166. See 278 n. 6 on Hegel's famous jibe against Schleiermacher.
[45] Ibid., 170.
[46] The work was published simultaneously in German, Spanish, and English. See the Editorial Introduction to volume 1 of the German and English editions. The German edition is *Vorlesungen über die Philosophie der Religion*, ed. Walter Jaeschke,

agenda in the present book is not that of distinguishing the lectures
and elucidating their distinctive internal arrangements, although
I do often trace the nuancing of specific themes from one lecture to
another. A table enables readers to identify the specific lecture
series for each quoted passage or reference.

The one feature of the lectures that remains constant through
the years from 1821 to 1831 is their division, following an *Intro-
duction*, into three main parts: *The Concept of Religion, Determinate
Religion*, and *The Consummate* or *Revelatory Religion*. The present
study offers a reading and interpretation of the *Introduction* in
Chapter 3, of *The Concept of Religion* in Chapters 4 and 5, of *The
Consummate Religion* (Christianity) in Chapters 6 to 9, and of
*Determinate Religion* in Chapter 10. The focus of my effort is on
Hegel's reconstruction of Christian theology rather than on the
lectures as a whole, which in their second main part offer an
extensive discussion of the history of religions.

The first series of lectures was delivered in the summer semester
of 1821. Although Hegel's decision to lecture on the philosophy of
religion was apparently stimulated by the impending publication
of Schleiermacher's *Glaubenslehre*, only a few allusions to this
work are found in these lectures. Fortunately Hegel's lecture
manuscript survives (in the State Library of Prussian Culture in
Berlin),[47] and it can be supplemented by passages from the *Werke*
editions of 1832 and 1840 that are based on a now-lost transcription of the lectures made by Leopold von Henning.

3 vols. (vols. 3–5 in Hegel's *Vorlesungen: Ausgewählte Nachschriften und Manuskripte* (Hamburg: Felix Meiner Verlag, 1983–5)). The English edition is *Lectures on
the Philosophy of Religion*, ed. Peter C. Hodgson, trans. R. F. Brown, P. C. Hodgson, and J. M. Stewart with the assistance of H. S. Harris, 3 vols. (Berkeley and Los
Angeles: University of California Press, 1984–7; Oxford: Oxford University Press,
2006). A one-volume English edition of the lectures of 1827 was published in 1988
(to be reissued by Oxford, 2005). The original edition of the *Lectures*, published as
vols. 11–12 of Hegel's *Werke* (1st edn., ed. Philipp Marheineke (Berlin, 1832); 2nd
edn., ed. Philipp Marheineke and Bruno Bauer (Berlin, 1840)), combined the
sources from different years into an editorially constructed text. Georg Lasson's
edition (4 vols., Leipzig: Verlag von Felix Meiner, 1925–9) distinguished Hegel's
lecture manuscript but amalgamated the other sources. It was a failed attempt to
produce a critical edition, although it yields (through philological reconstruction)
the best version of the 1827 lectures that is available after the destruction of
manuscripts in the Second World War.

[47] It is the only one of Hegel's lecture manuscripts to survive intact. Only
fragments of manuscripts on other topics still exist, most notably introductions
to the lectures on the history of philosophy and the philosophy of world history.
These are collected in vol. 18 of Hegel's *Gesammelte Werke*, ed. Walter Jaeschke

The second series occurred in the summer semester of 1824. The polemic against rationalism and pietism already present in 1821 now was heightened and took on more specific targets, namely, Schleiermacher, Jacobi, and various post-Kantian theologians. For these lectures an excellent transcription by Karl Gustav von Griesheim is available (also in the Library of Prussian Culture), as well as several other transcripts of lesser quality and various miscellaneous papers in Hegel's own hand.

The third lectures, those of the summer semester 1827, shift their focus to a new challenge, potentially a more bitter rival to speculative philosophy than rationalism and the theology of feeling had been, namely the neopietism of F. A. G. Tholuck and other theologians who had begun to attack Hegel's alleged 'pantheism' and 'atheism' by labelling him a 'Spinozist'. Hegel was now at pains to distinguish his own philosophy from pantheism and to affirm the historical roots of Christian faith whereas in the earlier lectures he had attacked historicism. The best transcripts of the 1827 lectures have been lost, and a reconstruction of these lectures is largely dependent on Georg Lasson's edition of 1925–9 supplemented by passages from the *Werke* that are identifiable as deriving from 1827.

Hegel lectured on the philosophy of religion for the last time in the summer of 1831, shortly before his death on 14 November of that year. They clearly establish his philosophical theology as one that mediates between right-wing and left-wing impulses by combining a speculative theology of the Trinity with a political theology of freedom. They also introduce major revisions into the treatment of the determinate religions. All the transcriptions of these lectures are lost, but David Friedrich Strauss made excerpts from one of them when he arrived in Berlin in the autumn of 1831 to study with Hegel, and these excerpts have recently been

(Hamburg: Felix Meiner Verlag, 1995). Hegel was intending to prepare a manuscript of his lectures on the proofs of the existence of God (delivered in the summer semester of 1829) for publication when he died in the autumn of 1831. The manuscript has been lost, but the text was printed in vol. 12 of the *Werke* edition as an appendix to the lectures on the philosophy of religion. A critical edition of this material is found in vol. 18 of the *Gesammelte Werke*. The philosophy of religion manuscript is published not only in the critical edition of the lectures (see n. 46) but also in vol. 17 of the *Gesammelte Werke*, also edited by Jaeschke (1987). By contrast with the paucity of Hegel's own manuscripts, significant numbers of auditors' transcriptions (*Nachschriften*) of lectures are still available. These are being published in critical editions for the first time (see the Bibliography).

rediscovered. They are not, however, sufficient to reconstruct the lectures.[48]

I suggested in Chapter 1 that Hegel's logic functions as a hermeneutical key for reading and interpreting experience, but that it is a key he used experimentally, in the manner of a heuristic device. The *Werke* edition of the 1830s and 1840s presented his lectures on the various topics of philosophy as part of a completed, consistent, unitary system, but we now know that Hegel lectured with an innovative spirit, unwilling ever simply to repeat what he had said before. On no subject was this truer than that of religion. Far from imposing an abstract, a priori schema on the history of religions, Hegel approached this topic as an experimental field in which a variety of interpretative arrangements must be tried out. His evident willingness to incorporate new data and experiment with new schemas suggests that for him speculative philosophy as a whole involves a conceptual play with the logical deep structure in order to arrive at new insights, to grasp connections, differences, types, trends, directions, to understand more fully the inexhaustible wealth of what presents itself in experience. He is not offering empirical descriptions but rather imaginative constructions intended to evoke disclosures of the *truth* of the world in which humans dwell.

For this purpose the medium of oral lectures is ideally suited. Duncan Forbes claims, in his introduction to the *Lectures on the Philosophy of World History*,[49] that Hegel's philosophy 'is best approached in the spirit of Plato's, as something that is in danger of being destroyed or distorted if it is written down'. Forbes points out that Hegel in fact was extremely reluctant to publish and that if one views the *Encyclopedia of the Philosophical Sciences* and the *Elements of the Philosophy of Right* as Hegel viewed them, namely as compendia for courses of lectures, then he published only two books in the strict sense, the *Phenomenology of Spirit* and the *Science of Logic*. These are of course among the greatest works of philosophical literature, but to give them a definitive priority over Hegel's spoken lectures (with which he was almost exclusively

---

[48] For details on the four series of lectures and their sources see the editorial introductions to vol. 1 of the unabridged edition, esp. 1–33, and to the one-volume edition of the lectures of 1827, 15–26.

[49] *Lectures on the Philosophy of World History: Introduction: Reason in History*, trans. H. B. Nisbet with an introduction by Duncan Forbes (Cambridge: Cambridge University Press, 1975), pp. xiii–xiv.

occupied during the last decade of his life) is to treat his philosophy as a closed book, whereas it was an attempt to 'think life', dialectically yet concretely, holistically yet with shrewd insight into detail. The only way to appreciate this kind of thinking, says Forbes, is to 'watch it at work'. One watches it at work in the lecture hall. Once it ceases to be thinking and becomes thought, once it stops speaking and is reduced to an editorial amalgam (as with the older editions of the lectures), it ceases to be a living process and becomes a system. The primacy of speaking on Hegel's part did not entail a romantic attachment to his own subjectivity or intentionality; rather it permitted the process of *thinking* to remain open, fluid, and continuous.

The risk of an interpretation such as the one that follows, which attempts to order the rich matrix of lecture materials into 'elements of a Hegelian Christian theology', is that it will convert Hegel's thinking into thought and treat the latter as a system. In part this is the fate of any interpretation that comes later and does not belong to the original, and irrepeatable, living process. I will resist the tendency to some degree by allowing differently nuanced renditions of common themes to stand side by side, and by attending to the context of important passages. But I introduce my own interpretative arrangements and am also looking for underlying thematic motifs that tie Hegel's theology of spirit together. These, I believe, are motifs that continue to resonate today and are of significance for the work of constructive Christian theology. My purpose in struggling to understand Hegel is to promote our own thinking on these topics and not to present a fixed system of thought.

# 3

# Hegel and the Theology of His Time

The *Introductions*[1] to each of the lectures on the philosophy of religion address several topics, with some variation in content and sequence of treatment as well as in the particulars of analysis. For our purposes the central topics may be identified as follows: (1) a discussion of the object and purpose of philosophy of religion; (2) an analysis of the characteristics of modernity as they pertain to the task of the philosophy of religion; (3) a critique of previous and concurrent theologies; and (4) a hint of the alternative to be provided by speculative philosophy of religion and theology. By addressing these themes Hegel positions himself in relation to the culture, philosophy, and theology of his time.

## THE OBJECT AND PURPOSE OF THE PHILOSOPHY OF RELIGION

The philosophy of religion has as its object not only *religion* as an inherent and necessary feature of human consciousness but also the object of religion, which is *God* or the knowledge of God. As such, it is a branch of *philosophy as a whole*. Hegel elaborates on these points in his introductory remarks.

### Knowledge of God (by Reason Alone)

The lecture manuscript begins with the claim, repeated in the later lectures, that philosophy of religion has the same purpose as the *theologia naturalis* of the school philosophy of the sixteenth to eighteenth centuries, as represented by G. W. Leibniz, Christian

---

[1] These *Introductions* are quite substantial. In the English edition, the *Introduction* to the 1821 lecture manuscript runs to 30 pages; to the 1824 lectures, 36 pages; and to the 1827 lectures, also 36 pages.

Wolff, and A. G. Baumgarten: knowledge of God 'by reason alone', as distinct from what is known of God on the basis of positive revelation (1:83).[2] Hegel goes on to remark (in eloquent, sweeping, poetic language) that God is the beginning and end of all things, the one and only object of philosophy as well as religion. Since the highest task of philosophy is to occupy itself with God, it is clear that philosophy *is* theology, and that one's occupation with and in philosophy is of itself the service or worship of God (*Gottesdienst*) (1:83–4).

Hegel emphasizes that the object of philosophy is the same as the object of religion, namely 'the supreme or absolute object', which exists strictly for its own sake and is radically free and unconditioned; likewise occupation with it must be free and unconditioned. Contra Schleiermacher's emphasis on the feeling of absolute dependence, religious consciousness is the 'absolutely free consciousness', which enjoys its object in the state of 'blessedness' and manifests the glory of God in such a way that everything transient and finite wafts away into eternal harmony (1:113–14).

In the 1824 lectures Hegel reveals his awareness of the novelty of philosophy of religion as an academic discipline. It established itself as a separate philosophical topic only toward the end of the eighteenth century.[3] While his claim, transmitted only by H. G. Hotho, that he is the first to make not only God but religion the object of philosophical treatment, appears doubtful (1:115 n. 7), it is true that he is the first major modern philosopher to elevate philosophy of religion to a central place in a philosophical programme, in effect letting it take over the task of natural theology that had been abandoned by Protestant theologians in favour of revealed, scripturally based theology. Hegel's ultimate objective, as will become evident, is to reconcile natural and revealed theology.

The 1827 lectures acknowledge that while philosophy and religion both engage God and 'serve' God, they do so differently. They differ in the peculiar character of their concern with God

---

[2] Later in the lectures Hegel qualifies the disjunction between natural and revealed theology by arguing that Christianity as the 'revelatory religion' embraces both reason and revelation. What is revealed is rational, and reason itself is revelatory. See below, Chap. 4.

[3] In works by H. P. C. Henke, K. H. L. Pölitz, and L. H. Jakob (see 1:115–16 n. 7).

(the one focused on reason, the other on revelation), and this has led to hostility and suspicion between them. Hegel does not elaborate this point further here but rather goes on to observe that the linkage between religion and philosophy is nothing new. Some of the church fathers (Tertullian, Clement of Alexandria, Origen) drew upon Neopythagorean, Neoplatonic, and Neoaristotelian philosophy; and the scholastic theologians in particular 'built up theology out of philosophy', as evidenced by Anselm's famous remark about 'faith seeking understanding'. Hegel believes that the time has arrived 'when philosophy can deal with religion more impartially on the one hand, and more fruitfully and auspiciously on the other' (1:153–4). The question as to whether Hegel himself exhibits a certain hostility toward and suspicion of theology, and consequently accords philosophy a position of superiority vis-à-vis theology, is one to which I turn at the end of Chapter 9.

*Knowledge of Religion (as It Exists)*

The object of the philosophy of religion is not just God but also religion, or God and religion together. This point is brought out especially in the 1824 lectures. If the object were simply God, then the concept of God could be restricted 'to the sterile result of an abstract essence of the understanding' (1:116). The target here seems to be the Enlightenment understanding of God as the 'supreme being' or 'highest essence' (*das höchstes Wesen*), a conception shared by Immanuel Kant and Friedrich Schleiermacher. From Hegel's point of view, such a God is a sterile abstraction. God is not yet grasped as a living being, as *spirit (Geist)*. To think of God as *Geist* rather than as *Wesen* is to think of God as God is present in religious belief, that is, in the community of faith. 'It will be evident that God can only be genuinely understood in the mode of his being as *spirit*, by means of which he makes himself into the counterpart of a community and brings about the activity of a community in relation to him; thus it will be evident that the doctrine of God is to be grasped and taught only as the doctrine of *religion*' (1:116–17). 'God' and 'religion' are intrinsically relational concepts: God is God only in relation to the knowledge of and faith in God on the part of human communities; and religion is the relationship between God and consciousness. Thus in treating God, philosophy of religion must also treat religion, and vice versa.

The religion that the philosophy of religion seeks to know and comprehend is the religion that already exists and is everywhere present in human culture. The task of philosophy is not to produce religion. 'That would be like trying to introduce spirit into a dog by letting it see spiritual creations, or eat witty remarks, or chew on printed matter' (1:89). While it is possible that religion may be awakened in the soul through philosophical cognition of it, this is neither necessary nor common. Rather, religion is intrinsic to human beings, indeed is what distinguishes them from the animals (1:90–1). It is possessed inwardly, even though it may be outwardly stimulated. Assuming the existence of religion and the need to interpret, not produce it, the principal concern of the philosophy of religion, the 1821 manuscript tells us (1:91), is the relationship of religion in human beings to *everything else* in their world view, consciousness, cognition, purposes, and interests; and when philosophy of religion investigates this relationship, it will encounter the characteristic 'discord' of modernity—a topic to which we shall attend momentarily.

*Philosophy of Religion and Philosophy as a Whole*

Philosophy of religion, while a subdiscipline of philosophy as a whole, thematizes the very heart of philosophy:

Philosophy in general has God as its object and indeed as its only proper object. Philosophy is no worldly wisdom, as it used to be called; it was called that in contrast with faith. It is not in fact a wisdom of the world but instead a cognitive knowledge of the nonworldly; it is not cognition of external existence, of empirical determinate being and life, or of the formal universe, but rather cognition of all that is eternal—of what God is and of what God's nature is as it manifests and develops itself.   (1:116–17)

This is a classic formulation of Hegel's idealism, which is not antithetical to realism but rather understands ideality to be the *truth* of the finite, that which overreaches and embraces the real. A philosophy that ascribes ultimate truth to finite existence as such or posits a disjunction between the real and the ideal is no genuine philosophy. Schleiermacher among others understands philosophy to be a 'worldly wisdom'[4] from which theology as a divine wisdom based on distinctively religious experience and sources

---

[4] Friedrich Schleiermacher, *The Christian Faith*, §§ 16, 19 (see below, n. 14).

must be protected; Hegel will have nothing of such a distinction and separation.

The proper object of philosophy and religion is the same, although philosophy calls it the 'absolute idea' (its conceptual name) while religion calls it 'God' (its representational name). This difference in naming accounts for a certain historical tension between philosophy and religion. But God is more than the absolute or logical idea: God is also *for* godself and thus is spirit, *absolute spirit*. 'That God is spirit consists in this: that he is not only the essence [*Wesen*] that maintains itself in thought but also the essence that appears, the essence that endows itself with revelation and objectivity' (1:119). The name of God as 'spirit' is both conceptual and representational, both philosophical and religious; and one of the tasks of the philosophy of religion as philosophical theology is to bring about a reconciliation of philosophy and religion by thematizing the spirituality of God.

Philosophy focuses both on the absolute in itself and on its process of production, the path by which it comes to be for itself as spirit, which is also the path by which finite consciousness becomes aware of itself as spirit, the path traced by the phenomenology of spirit. Thus God is both the beginning and the end of philosophy, both presupposition and result. God is the result of the other branches of philosophy as they unfold from the science of logic through the philosophy of nature to the philosophy of spirit. In this sense the whole of philosophy is a proof of God. Philosophy of religion, as the last of the philosophical sciences, makes this result its starting-point and focuses on the appearing of God in specific religions as 'the utterly concrete idea' (1:119–21).


CHARACTERISTICS OF MODERNITY

The 'modern' doctrine that humans can know nothing of God[5] undercuts the philosophy of religion project as thus conceived; indeed, it cuts out the very heart of philosophy itself (to say nothing of theology). Such a doctrine has become in our time a settled prejudice, Hegel remarks in his lecture manuscript. The more that knowledge of finite things has expanded, the more

_____

[5] Hegel is alluding especially to Kant, but also to J. G. Fichte, F. Bouterwek, and F. H. Jacobi (see 1:87 n. 15).

the sphere of the knowledge of God has contracted. It is the distinction of our age 'to know an infinite mass of objects, but only of God to know nothing' (1:86–7). While there was once a time when human hearts were restless until they found their rest in God, while there was once a need to know God above all else, 'our age has renounced this need and the efforts to satisfy it; we are done with it' (1:87). Ours is an essentially secular age to which the religious injunction, 'You shall know God', is accounted mere folly. Christ's 'lofty demand' to be perfect as your Father in heaven is perfect 'is an empty sound to the wisdom of our time, which has made of God an infinite phantom far removed from our consciousness, and which likewise has reduced human cognition to a vain phantom of finitude' (1:87–8). How ironic it is to arrive at the conclusion through cognition itself that cognition grasps everything but the truth! 'I declare', Hegel continues, 'such a point of view and such a result to be directly contrary to the whole nature of the Christian religion' (1:88). This is the pressing issue of modernity to which Christian theology ought to fashion a convincing response. But Christian theology itself has mostly acceded to such a view; and Hegel's lectures are intended to fill the void left by theological agnosticism (1:89).

Another characteristic of modern secularism is the opposition between religious consciousness and 'the rest of consciousness', an opposition marked by the setting off of Sunday from the rest of the days of the week during which 'we are concerned with our particular interests and worldly goals' quite apart from any explicit belief in God. This gulf between a secular world and a religious world is even more pronounced when it comes to modern natural science, which constructs a finite system of the universe in which God is not needed and has no place (1:92–3, 102–3). In true piety, no such isolation of religion from the rest of life is possible (1:93–4). The fact that such an isolation has occurred is 'the discord of our times' (1:107)—a theme to which Hegel returns at the end of the lecture manuscript. In similar vein, he refers to the 'plague of the present age', which is the contention that reason not only cannot know God but cannot in the strict sense know any truth at all (1:135).

The doctrine of double truth (a human truth of reason and a divine truth of faith) is a traditional form[6] of this modern discord

---

[6] It can be traced back to the thirteenth century and somewhat later was expounded especially by William of Ockham; cf. 1:130 n. 41.

and present plague. Such a doctrine is philosophically and religiously impossible, Hegel contends. There cannot be two kinds of reason, a divine and a human, any more than there can be two kinds of spirit. 'Human reason . . . *is* reason generally, is the divine within humanity. Spirit, in so far as it is called divine spirit, is not a spirit beyond the stars or beyond the world; for God is present, is omnipresent, and strictly *as spirit* is God present in spirit. God is a living God who is effective, active, and present in spirit' (1:130). In a statement characteristic of the 1824 lectures, Hegel continues: 'Religion is a begetting of the divine spirit, not an invention of human beings but an effect of the divine at work, of the divine productive process within humanity.' Indeed, 'God rules the world as reason' (1:130).

Hegel notes that the Catholic Church rejected the doctrine of double truth,[7] and that 'this cleavage first occurred in the Protestant Church' (1:131–2). Once the cleavage between faith and reason is accepted it is only a matter of time before truth itself becomes a casualty. Modern agnosticism and atheism have their roots in the divided consciousness of Protestantism, the attempt to carve out a realm of faith immune from the critiques of autonomous reason. Catholicism has avoided the cleavage only by binding reason strictly to the authority of the church.

## CRITIQUE OF PREVIOUS AND CONCURRENT THEOLOGIES

As we have seen, Hegel judges that the theology of his time has for the most part acceded to the discordant presuppositions of modernity and thus lacks the resources to provide a rational articulation and defence of central Christian doctrines. The *Introductions* to the several lecture series each provide assessments of the contemporary theological scene.

### Metaphysical Theology

Hegel's proposed alternative does not entail a return to traditional metaphysical theology, which assumes that objects simply are as they are brought before consciousness, and that thinking can go

---

[7]  At the Fifth Lateran Council (1512–17).

straight to its objects without reflecting on them. God is believed to be such an object, and metaphysical theology makes assertions about the ontological status of God: it conceives God as an other-worldly supreme being (*höchstes Wesen*), an abstract essence of the understanding (*Verstandeswesen*), and it does so in categories that project finite distinctions and attributes into infinity. The predicates it attributes to God are one-sided and mutually exclusive, and thus lead to irresolvable antinomies. This is because metaphysical theology remains bound to the disjunctive categories of the understanding and does not rise to the holistic, dialectical thinking of reason. Hegel accepts Kant's critique of precritical ontotheology, which is seen to assume a more or less naive posture toward objectivity.[8] He applies the critique not to the classical theologians (Clement, Origen, Augustine, Proclus, Anselm, Aquinas), with whom he has considerable affinity despite epistemological differences, but to the dogmatics of Protestant scholasticism and to the natural theologies of Leibniz, Wolff, and Baumgarten (see 1:83, 106, 115–17, 121–2). However, metaphysical theology is not a major target of his criticism in the philosophy of religion lectures.

### Rational Theology

Hegel hones in much more thoroughly on the rational, historical, agnostic, and feeling-based theologies of his time. The first of these, the so-called *Vernunfttheologie*, is really based on the disjunctive categories of the understanding (*Verstand*)—in this it is very much like metaphysical theology—and on the method of petty argumentation (*Rasönnement*), rather than on the holistic conceptual thinking of reason (*Vernunft*). This is the theology of the Enlightenment, which turns against the content of specific dogmas

---

[8] See Hegel's discussion of the first and the second of the 'Positions of Thought with Respect to Objectivity' at the beginning of the Science of Logic in the *Encyclopedia of the Philosophical Sciences*, §§ 26–36, 40–60 (*The Encyclopedia Logic*, trans. T. F. Geraets, W. A. Suchting, and H. S. Harris (Indianapolis: Hackett, 1991), 65–76, 80–108). Hegel accepts Kant's critique of the cosmological and teleological proofs of God, but not of the ontological proof, which in his view is, when properly interpreted, the only genuine proof. He does not accept Kant's turn to the postulates of practical reason as a ground of belief in God, but applauds his discussion (in the *Critique of Judgement* (see Chap. 1, n. 6)) of 'intellectual intuition' as that which grasps the concrete and inwardly determined universal (here alone Kant's philosophy shows itself to be 'speculative').

but leaves the doctrinal system of the church largely in place and defends it by rationalistic arguments (1:121–2). For example, it attempts to prove the existence of God from the external, contingent purposiveness of nature, but in the process it reduces God (or the divine wisdom) to something trivial, contingent, and finite. Thus God in his wisdom provides animals with weapons (teeth, claws, stings, etc.) by which they survive, but these can be defeated by other animals or humans, and divinity becomes involved in the calculus of the greater good—for example of cats versus mice and of humans versus bees (1:98–100). This is the reasoning of *Verstand*, not *Vernunft*; and Kant's critique of the teleological arguments of the so-called physicotheology is presupposed in Hegel's discussion of these matters in the lecture manuscript.

Hegel attends in the 1824 lectures to both the exegesis and dogmatics of theological rationalism, as represented by J. F. Röhr, J. A. L. Wegscheider, and especially H. E. G. Paulus. Rational exegesis professes only to promote an understanding of the Word of God contained in scripture (1:122–3). But Hegel points out that where interpretation goes beyond a mere explanation of words to a discussion of the contents and an elucidation of the sense, it introduces its own thoughts and prejudices and is more than mere exegesis. Thus 'the most sharply opposed views are exegetically demonstrated by theologians on the basis of scripture, and in this way so-called holy scripture has been made into a wax nose', twisted into one shape or another (1:123).[9] Theologians naively believe they are expositing scripture when in fact they are merely displaying their own presuppositions and interests.[10]

One of the presuppositions of rationalism is that reason can have no cognition of God—a presupposition profoundly at variance, Hegel notes, with the presuppositions of the biblical writers. Thus rational theology exhibits a 'generally negative tendency

---

[9] An expression with which Hegel was probably familiar through Lessing, and which is traceable back to the twelfth century (see 1:123 n. 30).

[10] Another naive feature of rational exegesis is that it frequently allows the literal historical sense of scripture to stand by substituting a rational explanation for a supernatural, as in the accounts of miracles. It remains oblivious to the presence of myth, symbol, ritual, and constructive theological imagination in religious writings. This point is made with devastating effect by David Friedrich Strauss, although ironically Strauss himself exhibits a rationalist mentality with his penchant for playing off one supernaturalist interpretation against another. See *The Life of Jesus Critically Examined*, trans. George Eliot, ed. Peter C. Hodgson (Philadelphia: Fortress Press, 1972; London: SCM Press, 1973), pp. xxv–xxxi.

toward any content at all in regard to the nature of God'. Such a theology knows only in general *that* God is, but otherwise its God is an empty and dead supreme being, not a concrete living spirit. The latter is what church theology intends by the doctrine of the Trinity ('the key by which the nature of spirit is explicated'), and thus it is not surprising that theological rationalism has neglected this doctrine or rejected it entirely, its abstract categories proving incapable of grasping dialectical distinctions and relations. In criticizing the representational forms of the traditional doctrine, it loses the tradition's deepest insight into the nature of God (1:126–7). Hegel's criticism seems to be directed principally against Schleiermacher, whose theology exhibits certain rationalizing tendencies, although the neglect of the doctrine of the Trinity and the designation of God as a 'supreme being' is common in the deistic literature of the seventeenth and eighteenth centuries (e.g. Herbert of Cherbury) and in the so-called neologians of the eighteenth century (e.g. W. A. Teller and J. G. Töllner) (1:127 nn. 34, 35).

In one of his more scathing remarks, Hegel compares rational theologians with 'the Englishman who didn't know that he was speaking prose': likewise, because they work exegetically and (so they believe) in a passively receptive way, theologians are unaware that they are actively thinking and in this very thinking capable of comprehending the divine (3:261).[11]

### Historical Theology

Another famous Hegelian quip is aimed against the type of theology that wants to adopt only a historical attitude toward religion. Such theologians are like 'countinghouse clerks, who keep the ledgers and accounts of other people's wealth ... without acquiring assets of their own' (1:128, 166). This is a version of theological rationalism that preoccupies itself with the historical development of doctrines but makes no attempt to articulate a contemporary doctrine of faith. In the 1827 lectures Hegel argues that this preoccupation with the historical is a sign that the central Christian

---

[11] Hegel's allusion here is to a dialogue in Molière's *Le Bourgeois Gentilhomme*, where however it is a Frenchman, not an Englishman, who has to be assured that he is indeed speaking prose. Hegel apparently transferred the object of the quip to Isaac Newton, of whose philosophical acumen he had a low opinion. See 3:261 n. 39.

dogmas have lost much of their present, existential significance. The emphasis is placed on past controversies that no longer engage us, or on the contingencies of doctrinal formulation as opposed to the 'depths of spirit' out of which doctrines arose. Interest shifts to psychologizing interpretations that trivialize the doctrine of Christ, who is reduced to a merely human figure, and the doctrine of the Trinity, which is regarded as mere 'decorative timbering'. Ironically, it is now philosophy that retains more of the teachings of the church (speculatively reconfigured) than the prevailing theology does (1:155–9). Hegel's targets here are on the one hand the rationalist historians of dogma such as J. L. Mosheim, J. S. Semler, and C. W. F. Walch, and on the other hand Neopietist theologians such as F. A. G. Tholuck who track trinitarian doctrine to pagan sources and have charged Hegel with 'pantheism' (1:157 n. 17). In this and in other respects, rationalism and pietism are able to make common cause, sharing a fear and suspicion of speculative theology.

### *Agnostic Theology and the Turn to Ethicotheology*

Another spin-off of rationalism is theological agnosticism—the view most effectively espoused by Kant that God cannot be known cognitively, that theoretical reason is limited to objects of sense experience, and that religion must turn to practical reason. Kant's alternative to ontotheology, cosmotheology, and physicotheology is 'ethicotheology', which in his view provides the only valid proof of God, namely that God, as guarantor of the kingdom of ends, is a necessary postulate of action in accord with moral ends.[12] Already in the 1790s Hegel had become convinced of the failure of the moral interpretation of religion; consequently, moral teleology and its accompanying doctrine of postulates are in his view no more persuasive than the physical teleology criticized by Kant. A theology that merely knows in general, in the form of an ethical postulate, *that* God is, has reduced God to an abstraction—the supreme being, a vacuum, a beyond—and has no means of comprehending God as a living spirit (1:126, 167). This is indeed an 'unphilosophy' of 'nonknowing', as F. H. Jacobi dubs it in his appeal to a higher, suprarational knowledge of faith (1:133 n. 46). As we have seen, Hegel regards such a view to be the 'plague

---

[12] See Immanuel Kant, *Critique of Practical Reason*, trans. Lewis White Beck (New York: Liberal Arts Press, 1956), 128–36. See below, Chap. 5, n. 27.

of the present age'—the contention that reason not only cannot cognize God, but also cannot cognize any truth at all (1:135).

In another connection, in the lecture manuscript, Hegel reveals his suspicion of the argument that religious belief is necessary to ethical action (1:199–202). Religion can never properly be a means to an end other than itself. Religion, the religious relationship, the glorification and service of God, is its own end. Nor can it be demonstrated that religion is necessary to anything else: the versatile human spirit can, if it chooses, make use of other means and get along quite well without religion. Pragmatic and utilitarian reasons can be adduced to justify ethical behaviour in accord with Kantian or other criteria of value. A divine guarantor of the kingdom of ends is not needed. The logical outcome of Kantian agnosticism and ethically based theism, Hegel believes, is thoroughgoing atheism.

Is Hegel justified in his critique of ethicotheology? The question is especially pressing in light of the turn to ethics on the part of Emmanuel Levinas and other critics of Hegelian ontotheology. On the one hand, it does seem correct to insist that religion is corrupted by being reduced to a function of some other human activity or interest. On the other hand, a close connection exists between religion and ethics, as Hegel himself recognizes. A religion that does not issue in a transformation of human behaviour is ultimately empty in its worship of God. And ethical activity motivated by the love of God and neighbour, a love of the other for the sake of the other, will issue in quite a different practice than a utilitarian or self-serving ethic. While religion is not a means to nonreligious ends, and while the truth of religion cannot be demonstrated from a moral teleology, religion nonetheless serves as the substantial foundation of ethical life, and divine redemption is at work in social and political institutions as well as in individual hearts. This is Hegel's considered view of the matter.

Hegel's considered view also includes a recognition of the element of mystery or non-knowing in speculative knowledge of God. His objection is to an agnosticism that excludes the possibility of knowledge of God altogether, not to an agnosticism that is a condition of possibility of knowing God. It is the agnostic element that drives thinking beyond understanding (*Verstand*) to reason (*Vernunft*), and that drives reason beyond all its finite forms to its ground in the infinite. The matter can also be posed in terms of the interplay between apophasis (negative theology) and kataphasis (positive theology), although Hegel does not employ these terms. It is the apophatic moment that prevents kataphatic theology from becoming dogmatic and authoritarian, while the kataphatic moment prevents apophatic theology from dissolving into silence or ethical postulates.

The question to be raised with Hegel is whether in speculative philosophy the apophatic element is preserved or whether it is totally submerged in the cognition of God. It can be argued that the apophatic element is in fact preserved in Hegel's distinctive way of moving through and beyond Kant's critique of theoretical reason. He does so by radicalizing the doctrine of antinomies, which gives rise to the dialectical nature of thinking and the recognition that all concrete unities embrace opposing determinations; and by pointing to the moment of negation that is present in the metaphysical proofs of God.[13]

## Theology of Feeling

Hegel develops his critique of the theology of feeling especially in the lectures of 1824, where his attention is focused on Schleiermacher. In claiming that we can have no cognition of God and that God has no inward determinations, the theology of feeling reduces God to a hollow abstraction, a supreme being (1:127). In this respect it is close to both rational and agnostic theology. 'Because knowledge of God does not fall within the comprehension of reason, there coheres with this standpoint the view that consciousness of God is rather sought only in the form of *feeling*—that religion has feeling as its source, and that the relationship of the human spirit to God is to be confined only to the sphere of feeling and is not to be transposed into thought or into comprehension' (1:136). While Hegel has Schleiermacher's *Christian Faith* in mind, he does not provide a close reading of that work or acknowledge the distinction that Schleiermacher draws between ordinary feeling and religious feeling, which is a feeling of *absolute* or *utter* dependence on God, and which as such is the condition of possibility of feelings of relative dependence and freedom in the world.[14] Evidence for this imprecise reading is Hegel's dismissive

---

[13] See *Encyclopedia*, §§ 48, 50 (*The Encyclopedia Logic*, 91, 98).

[14] Friedrich Schleiermacher, *Der christliche Glaube*, 1st edn. (Berlin, 1821–2) §§ 8–9; 2nd edn. (Berlin, 1830–1), §§ 3–4. The second edition was translated into

remark, repeated from his Hinrichs Foreword,[15] 'If we say that religion rests on this feeling of dependence, then animals would have to have religion too, for they feel this dependence' (1:279). This is to regard feeling as a physical sensation or emotion, whereas it is clear that for Schleiermacher religious feeling entails a relationship of consciousness to reality as a whole of which no animal is capable. It is a form of cognition that is prereflective in character and that grounds the human way of being in the world. As such it is actually akin to what Hegel calls intellectual or speculative intuition.

Hegel is closer to the mark in noting that for Schleiermacher the knowledge afforded by religious feeling does not strictly include knowledge of God, whose infinite being is beyond all finite cognitive categories. Thus it is 'declared that we can know only our relation to God, not what God himself is' (1:163). 'Only our relation' points to religion, and thus religion is made an object of investigation but not God's nature and attributes. But the true insight, according to Hegel, is that God is inseparable from God's relations. This is what it means to conceive God as *spirit*: spirit is always *for spirit* and thus intrinsically relational. The being of God is not separable from the religious relationship to God, and vice versa (1:164). The chief criticism of Schleiermacher's theology of feeling is that it does not attain to the cognition of God as spirit, and as a consequence it also de-emphasizes the doctrine of the Trinity (3:75, 81). Schleiermacher does develop a system of divine attributes, which follow from modifications in the feeling of utter dependence, but in the strict sense these do not describe the divine nature but rather aspects of our relationship to God. We relate to God, but God does not relate to us; and without the latter relationship God cannot be fully spiritual and triune. God may relate to godself, but of that relationship, Schleiermacher insists, we know nothing.

In the 1827 lectures, Hegel's attention turns more to Jacobi, who emphasizes that religion entails 'immediacy', of which feeling is one form. God is revealed immediately in the consciousness of human beings, and this immediate knowing is called 'faith'

English under the editorship of H. R. Mackintosh and J. S. Stewart (Edinburgh: T&T Clark, 1928). It is true that Schleiermacher was clearer about this distinction in the second edition of his work, with which Hegel was not familiar, than in the first, to which Hegel responded in his lectures. See 1:136 n. 52, 279 n. 37.

[15] See above, Chap. 2, pp. 46–7.

(1:159–62). As such faith is qualitatively distinct from other forms of (worldly) knowledge. It entails an immediate certainty *that* God is, but is unable to judge *what* God is. Hegel's strategy is not to deny the validity of religious immediacy but to suggest that it represents only the beginning, not the end, of the knowledge of God. Theology must move through and beyond the immediacy of faith and feeling to a mediated knowledge of God's objective being (see Chapter 5 below).

Both Schleiermacher and Jacobi are pointing to the role of subjectivity in religion, and Hegel acknowledges in another context that it is an 'important advance of our age' to recognize the role of subjectivity. But we must not allow subjective consciousness to become disconnected from its object, which then floats into the distance and is inaccessible to reason. It is precisely in the subject that the inseparability of subjectivity and the object exists. The risk of modernity is that subjectivity will become one-sided, will become pure knowledge of itself, devoid of content. 'What has no objectivity has no content.' In this respect our own age is comparable to that of the Roman Empire, which was trapped in a spiritless subjectivity that could only yearn for a beyond (3:166–9). The linkage of the discord of our time with the Roman age and Roman religion occurs more than once in the lectures.

## Atheism and Pantheism

This linkage is also implicit in Hegel's critique of modern atheism and pantheism, for the Roman religion itself (in Hegel's interpretation of it) was atheistic and its pantheon represented the twilight of the deities.[16] Hegel regards atheism as the logical outcome of the theological tendencies of modernity. Rationalist, historicist, agnostic, ethically oriented, and feeling-based theologies are vulnerable to atheism and/or pantheism in so far as they surrender the convictions that God can be known cognitively, that a relationship with God is possible that is not simply a projection of human needs and emotions, and that God is spiritually present and efficacious in the world but is not identical with world processes.

Hegel rarely alludes specifically to atheism in the lectures. The following passage from the 1824 lectures, which occurs in the context of a critique of the theology of feeling, is a significant exception.

[16] See the discussion of Roman religion in vol. 2 (2:190–231, 498–512, 687–99).

If in regard to God we could appeal only to feeling, then we would have to wonder how any kind of objectivity is still attributed to this content, i.e., to God. The materialistic views[17] have been more consistent in this respect. They have regarded spirit and thought as something merely material, a combination of material forces; they have reduced spirit and thought to feeling and sensation, and accordingly taken God and all representations [of God] as products of feeling, and denied objectivity to God. The result is then atheism. God is thus a product of feeling, of my weakness—a product of pain, hope, fear, joy, cupidity, and so forth. (1:136–7)

Precisely whom Hegel has in mind with the reference to 'materialistic views' is uncertain. However, Ludwig Feuerbach, who heard these lectures, later developed just such a view. He argued that religious and theological ideas are the product of feeling and sensation, which are material forces; thus the idea of God is a projection of human needs, and all ideas are in the strict sense imaginative illusions based on physical and socioeconomic realities.[18] Similar views were espoused by other left-wing Hegelians, such as Bruno Bauer, Max Stirner, and Karl Marx. Hegel seems rather uncannily to have anticipated what might follow from the breakdown of speculative philosophy, and thus he himself insists that God must be understood to be what is 'independent in and for itself', that 'God is not simply rooted in feeling, is not merely *my* God' (1:137). He is not accusing the theologies of feeling of materialism but is suggesting that they are peculiarly vulnerable to the reversal of theology into anthropology, and of idealism into naturalism.

Hegel's references to pantheism are more explicit because speculative philosophy itself had been accused of pantheism by theologians who are 'incapable of cognizing God as spirit' and can think of God only as 'something absolutely unworldly' (1:344 n. 163). This topic is addressed specifically in the 1827 lectures in response to attacks on Hegel's alleged pantheism by Tholuck and others (1:375 n. 20). Hegel notes that charges of pantheism had already been brought against Spinoza during the so-called 'pantheism controversy' at the end of the eighteenth century.[19] However, if pantheism means the view that all things simply *are* God,

---

[17] Hegel's marked copy of Griesheim's transcript of the 1824 lectures adds: 'or, as they may otherwise be designated, the empiricist, historicist, and naturalistic views, at least' (1:136 n. 53).

[18] See Ludwig Feuerbach, *Principles of the Philosophy of the Future*, trans. Manfred Vogel (Indianapolis: Bobbs-Merrill, 1966).

[19] The controversy focused around an exchange of letters between Jacobi and Moses Mendelssohn, triggered by G. E. Lessing's alleged deathbed confession that

then no serious philosophy is pantheistic, neither Spinozism, nor Oriental religions, nor the Eleatic philosophers (1:374–7, 432). Rather what is being espoused by these philosophies is that God is the *essence* within individual things, the *universal* within the particular, the *one* within the many, the *substance* within accidents. 'The usual representation of pantheism derives from the practice of focusing on the abstract unity rather than the spiritual unity, and from entirely forgetting that—in a religious representation in which only the substance or the One has the value of genuine actuality—individual things, in this very contrast with the One, have disappeared and no actuality is ascribed to them' (1:376). In the philosophical sense the world has no independent actuality (*Wirklichkeit*), although empirically of course it exists and is 'real'.[20] This is Spinoza's position, according to Hegel, and it is properly described as 'acosmism', not 'atheism' or 'pantheism' (1:376–7). It is not God who is absorbed into the world, but the world into God. However, speculative philosophy, with its triple mediation of logical idea, nature, and finite spirit, consummated in God as absolute spirit in whom distinctions are preserved, not annihilated, avoids both atheism and acosmism, and it certainly is not crude pantheism. It is more accurately described as 'panentheism'—all things have their being or actuality *in* God— but this is not a label that Hegel himself utilizes. His definition of God as spirit says all that needs to be said. The problem is that neither theists nor atheists have any true comprehension of what spirit means.

## SPECULATIVE PHILOSOPHY OF RELIGION AND THEOLOGY

As an alternative to all of these discredited theologies—discredited because inadequate to the needs of the time and to the deep truths of religious tradition—Hegel offers his own approach. It can best

he was a Spinozist and a pantheist. J. G. Herder and Friedrich Schelling also became involved in the controversy. See 1:370 n. 11, 377 n. 31.

[20] Hegel is trading here on a distinction between *Wirklichkeit* (actuality) and *Realität* (reality). *Wirklichkeit* derives from that which is supremely *wirklich* (actual, active), namely God as absolute idea. It belongs to the activity of the idea to posit that which is other than its ideality, namely reality, and to become spirit in the interplay of ideality and reality. *Wirklichkeit* names the interplay.

be characterized as a 'speculative' philosophy of religion and theology. Chapter 1 gave a preliminary definition of 'speculative' as a relationship of double mirroring between consciousness and object, thought and being, such that neither is reduced to a mere reflection (or projection) of the other. Both have reality, and their reality is co-constitutive. Meaning flows between them in both directions, from subject to object and from object to subject. Thought is the medium of the flow. A further discussion of the speculative concept of religion follows in Chapter 4; and the main elements of Hegel's speculative version of Christian theology are treated in Chapters 5–9. For the moment, in the context of the *Introduction*s to the lectures, and as a response to the theologies of the time, three points seem to be of primary importance: that God is essentially rational, that only a speculative approach can reconcile reason and religion, and that to learn to think theologically one must 'go into the water'.

## God as Essentially Rational

The 1824 lectures offer a concise definition: 'God is essentially rational, is rationality that is alive and, as spirit, is in and for itself' (1:139). Very much like the Neoplatonic understanding of *nous*, reason for Hegel is not an inert instrument but a dynamic life-force, the heart and soul of the universe. God is this rationality in the form of self-relating and other-relating spirit. The categories 'spirit', 'reason', and 'God' are essentially identical. If God is rational, God must also be knowable. When we engage in cognitive acts, we are already implicitly knowing God; when we investigate cognition we are investigating God. The means and the end of knowing are one and the same; reason has rationality as its ultimate object.[21]

This is not to say that what rationality is, and therefore what God is, are immediately evident. Rationality cannot be embraced by any of the finite categories of the understanding, and in this sense it is a mystery. It is the highest mystery, the highest truth, which demands reverent silence as well as the most rigorous philosophical speculation. Hegel points out that the Neoplatonic philosophers, Proclus in particular, connected speculative thought

---

[21] Hegel shares with Aristotle the conviction that thought knows or thinks itself in knowing the objects of thought. See Chap. 1, n. 8.

with the idea of 'mystery' as inherited from Greek religion (1:382 n. 44). 'The speculative idea is opposed not merely to the sensible but also to what is understandable; for both, therefore, it is a secret or mystery.... *Mysterion* is what the rational is; among the Neo-platonists, this expression already means simply speculative philosophy' (3:280). Thus, as we have seen, an apophatic moment is introduced into Hegel's principally kataphatic orientation, just as negation plays a critical role in his dialectical method.

The 1827 lectures offer a similar formulation: the object of philosophy of religion is 'God himself, *absolute reason*'. As absolute reason God is absolute spirit. 'Absolute spirit is knowledge, the determinate rational knowledge of its own self. Therefore when we occupy ourselves with this object it is immediately the case that we are dealing with and investigating rational cognition, and this cognition is itself rational conceptual enquiry and knowledge. So the [Kantian] requirement [to investigate cognition first] proves to be completely empty. Our *scientific cognition is itself the required investigation* of cognitive knowing' (1:170).

Religion entails passing over into the region of the absolute content or absolute truth, for which finite categories of thought are no longer appropriate (1:170–1). Kant showed that the finite categories serve only for the cognition of phenomena and not of the truth. As a consequence, the representational form of the doctrines of faith, which employ such finite categories, must be superseded by conceptual thinking. Both a deconstruction of representational forms and a reconstruction in conceptual language are necessary. The concept grasps the inseparability of distinguished categories and elements, such as 'heaven' and 'earth', which in their very difference imply and require each other. The true (*das Wahre*) is the unity of all distinctions: immediate and mediated knowledge, subject and object, thought and being, representation and concept. By themselves these aspects are one-sided: their truth is in their unification, but this is a unification in which differences are not extinguished but sublated (1:172–3).

### The Reconciliation of Reason and Religion

The antinomy between reason and religion, or knowledge and faith, is false from the start. Neither rational cognition nor the absolute content of religion, the concept of God, should have to give up anything. Christianity goes farthest in this direction of any of the religions, Hegel believes, but for it too cognition remains at the level of representation, and contemporary theology draws back into feeling rather than advancing to the concept, which alone is capable of reconciling thought and its content because it is the form most adequate to the content (1:104–8).

Because it does not abandon the content, speculative philosophy of religion or theology is closer to positive Christian doctrine than the so-called rational theology (1:129, 139–40). Much more of dogmatics is preserved in speculative philosophy than in contemporary dogmatics, for classical dogmatics presupposed the rationality of faith and gave its doctrines intellectual formulation (1:168). Similarly, in part 3 of the lectures Hegel remarks that today philosophy is pre-eminently what is essentially orthodox, maintaining and preserving the basic truths of Christianity (3:262); it is now philosophy that protects the dogmas of church doctrine from the theologians.

## On Going into the Water

The only way to learn to think theologically is to engage in acts of theological cognition.

The initial demand is that we should first investigate reason generally, the cognitive capacity or conceptual thought, before proceeding to cognition. . . . We picture the project of cognition as though it were something that came about by means of an *instrument* with which one wants to grasp the truth. On closer consideration, the demand that we should first cognize this instrument is inappropriate, however plausible it may seem. The critique of the cognitive capacity is a stance taken by Kant's philosophy and by our time. It was believed that a great discovery had been made at this point, but, as so often happens in life, the belief was a mistake. . . . Reason is to be investigated—but how? It must be investigated rationally, it must be cognized. This is possible only through rational thinking, through rational cognition; any other way it is impossible. (1:138; cf. 132–9)

Hegel makes the point with a homely anecdote. The demand that we ought not to begin philosophizing (or theologizing) until we have investigated the preconditions of doing so is like that of a Scholastic[22] 'who does not want to go into the water until he has

---

[22] On the origins of this anecdote, see 1:169 n. 51. In the 1824 lectures, quoted here, the Scholastic becomes a 'Gascon', probably through a transcriptional error on the part of Griesheim.

learned to swim. To learn to swim one must go into the water' (1:139, 169).

Hegel's critique of the theology of his time is principally that it is afraid to go into the water. It preoccupies itself with epistemological prolegomena, turns to anthropological, historical, and psychological considerations, and forever defers the question of God, failing to provide a satisfactory contemporary alternative to classical metaphysical theology. If it were to start thinking, it might surprise itself. Thinking is not simply an instrument by which to grasp the truth; it is the truth itself in all its beauty and mystery.

If we were to translate Hegel's admonition to go into the water into its meaning for theology in *our* time, we might say that it calls for the courage of conviction and the courage of experimentation. The courage of conviction means the determination not to surrender the deep truths of religious faith, but to think through them boldly, yet critically. Religion has nothing to fear from bold thought dedicated to the truth. The courage of experimentation means the recognition that all our thoughts are really thought-experiments, constructions of the human imagination—not, hopefully, as projections of human needs and illusions, but as fragile responses to what gives itself in experience. Gift, not need, is what solicits thinking. Knowing that our thinking is, or has the capacity to become, a construction that reflects an aspect of, indeed a self-manifestation of, the inexhaustible mystery, and that it must negotiate with many other such constructions, is a postmodern version of the speculative insight. It is an insight that liberates us to think.

PART TWO

# Elements of a Hegelian Christian Theology

# 4

# Christianity and the Concept of Religion

## THE THREEFOLD DIVISION
## OF THE PHILOSOPHY OF RELIGION

The one element that remains constant across all the lecture series is their division into three main parts: *The Concept of Religion, Determinate Religion*, and *The Consummate* or *Revelatory Religion.* The *Introductions* to each of the series provide a 'division of the subject' or a 'survey of the treatment of our subject': 1:109–12 (1821), 1:141–7 (1824), 1:174–84 (1827), 1:462–3 (1831).[1] The rationale for this division is set forth in the 1821 manuscript and changes little thereafter: first to be considered is the *concept of religion* as a representational and scientific presupposition; then the *development* of the concept, which means the positing in determinate reality of what is contained in the concept, or as expressed in the terms of Hegel's logic, the elevation and perfection of the concept into the *idea* as the unity of concept and reality;[2] and finally the *consummation* of the determinations of the concept

---

[1] The 1827 lectures repeat this information in the form of a 'survey of previous developments' at the beginning of the third part (3:262–71). These surveys also include summaries of the internal divisions of the three parts, and the latter divisions do vary considerably from one lecture series to the next. In fact, in the case of the 1824 lectures, the summary of *The Concept of Religion* in the *Introduction* differs from the actual presentation of it in the ensuing lectures (see 1:141 n. 64).

[2] See 1:324; 3:264–5. Hegel's logic defines the idea as 'the true in and for itself, the absolute unity of concept and objectivity' (*Encyclopedia of the Philosophical Sciences*, § 213). As such the idea forms a bridge between the science of logic and the philosophy of nature: the idea 'resolves to let the moment of its particularity . . . go forth freely from itself as nature' (§ 244). My translations; cf. *The Encyclopedia Logic*, trans. T. F. Geraets, W. A. Suchting, and H. S. Harris (Indianapolis: Hackett, 1991), 286, 307. The idea makes the transition from logic (the categories of being, essence, and concept) to reality (nature and spirit). This transition corresponds theologically to God's creation of the world.

through the return of the concept into itself, which means that the absolute idea ('God as spirit in the form of truth and revealedness') is now fully an object of consciousness (1:110–11). This consummation occurs in the Christian religion, while the earlier, determinate religions 'constitute the stages of transition for the concept of religion on the way to its consummation' (1:112).

The 1827 lectures expand on the rationale by first establishing an identity between the *method* of a science such as philosophy of religion and its *content*, which is nothing other than 'the self-explicating concept' (1:174). This means that *truth* and *method* are ultimately one,[3] and that scientific procedure follows from the movement of the subject matter itself. Thus the first moment in the philosophical treatment of religion is the concept itself, and the second moment is the determinateness of the concept, the concept in its determinate forms. These forms are already contained implicitly in the concept, which is like a seed from which an entire tree unfolds. The forms are not literally 'preformed' in the concept but are 'enveloped in a spiritual manner' and subsequently emerge into determinate existence. This emergence is not something forced on the concept from outside; 'rather it is the free concept that impels itself to its own determinateness'. Initially, religions in their finite typifications stand over against each other, but the development of the concept continues such that 'it comes forth to itself out of its determinateness, out of its finitude. . . . This *re-established concept* is the infinite, true concept, the *absolute idea* or the *true religion*' (1:175–6).

This return of the concept to itself seems to involve a transcendence of the historical determinacy through which the concept has emerged. If so, then it is difficult to understand how any historically determinate religion such as Christianity could simply *be* the absolute, true, and consummate religion—which nonetheless is understood to be an *existing* religion, something that must come to pass in history (1:141). Indeed, a tension is discernible between the historical forms of Christianity and the speculative redescription of it in the third part of Hegel's lectures. Despite this tension, Hegel clearly privileges the Christian religion as most adequate to

---

[3] This is the central thesis of Hans-Georg Gadamer's philosophical hermeneutics, *Truth and Method*, 2nd rev. edn., trans. Joel Weinsheimer and Donald G. Marshall (New York: Crossroad, 1989). Gadamer comments on Hegel several times in this connection (see esp. 464).

the concept. But why should only one religion provide the launching pad for the completion of the concept of religion in history? Is not Hegel's speculatively reimagined religion of the 'Concrete Spirit' (Paul Tillich's expression, which I shall employ later) more plausible and even more adequate to the concept if it draws upon the resources of all the great religious traditions? After all, the concept is formed in the matrix of history as a whole, and (as Hegel himself knew) the history of religions cannot be ordered into a linear trajectory culminating in Christianity. Even if we affirm that the consummate religion emerges from a diversity of religions, we may have difficulty grasping the idea of a historically existing religion that is no longer determinate and finite. These are questions that Chapter 10 will have to address.

The concept of religion is essentially the concept of God, or of God and humanity together, and this togetherness is what Hegel calls 'spirit'. It is spirit that is active throughout, both in the concept (spirit's abstract, logical, potential form), in the realization of the concept in history, and in the return of the concept to itself.

Spirit, if it is thought immediately, simply, and at rest, is no spirit; for spirit's essential [character] is *to be altogether active*. More exactly, it is the activity of *self-manifesting*. 'Manifesting' signifies 'becoming for an other'. As 'becoming for an other' it enters into antithesis, into distinction in general, and thus it is a *finitizing* of spirit.... Spirit that manifests itself, determines itself, enters into existence, gives itself finitude, is the second moment. But the third is its manifesting of itself according to its concept, taking its former, initial manifestation back into itself, sublating it, coming to its own self, becoming and being *explicitly* the way it is implicitly. This is the rhythm or the pure eternal life of spirit itself.   (1:176–7)

This passage (from the 1827 lectures) makes it clear that the three main parts of the philosophy of religion correspond to the moments in the life of God as absolute spirit. The same pattern repeats itself in diverse ways within each of the parts, for it is absolute spirit in its threefold mediation that is active through the length and breadth of history. Here method (the structure of the philosophy of religion) follows from the movement of the subject matter (absolute spirit).

Our task in this chapter is first to determine what Hegel's distinctive definition of the concept of religion is, and then to examine how Christianity as the consummate religion relates to the concept of religion. In so far as the actual content of the concept of religion comprises the concept of God (the abstract being, knowledge, and worship of God), this aspect of the topic will be addressed in Chapter 5.

## THE CONCEPT OF RELIGION

### The Empirical Approach to Religion

Hegel arrived at an adequate definition of the concept of religion only gradually. The 1821 lectures approach the definition via a circuitous route through a description of religion drawn from empirical experience, a demonstration of the necessity of the religious standpoint in human life, and a delineation of religion vis-à-vis art and philosophy. The essential elements are present, but they are presented confusingly.

The 1824 lectures systematize much of this material and offer an intriguing comparison of 'empirical' and 'speculative' approaches to religion (1:257–9; the comparison does not reappear in 1827. The empirical approach is in vogue today, says Hegel, because it starts with immediate experience or 'feeling', defines religion as a modification of feeling, and then moves on to other forms of religious consciousness (1:261–88). But because it limits itself to finite categories of consciousness, it can never arrive at what in Hegel's view is distinctively religious, namely the actual relationship of finite and infinite spirit. It can never get off the ground, so to speak.

The empirical approach comes to an impasse (1:277–88). It knows that, although God and myself appear to be undividedly one in feeling, in fact religious consciousness 'in more determinate form' is aware of the antithesis between myself as a finite, feeling, particular subject and God as the infinite, independent, universal object. How, then, is a relationship between the finite and infinite possible? From the point of view of empirical observation, only two options seem plausible: either God remains what is totally other and beyond, the negation of finitude, of which I can have no cognitive knowledge; or finitude itself is what is exhaustively real and good, existing solely for itself. Finitude is related either *negatively* to God or *affirmatively* to itself; it cannot be related *affirmatively* to *God*. Finitude attempts to bridge this gulf in the form of 'reflective' knowledge, which appears philosophically as 'understanding' and religiously as 'representation', but from this point of view the infinite remains either an incomprehensible beyond or a mere projection of the finite. The negative relationship to God is expressed in the feeling of utter or absolute dependence, as described by Schleiermacher. The affirmative relationship to the self is the basis of modern atheism, from Kant and Fichte onward. Only from the point of view of reason or thought is it possible to conceive the infinite as that which 'overreaches' the finite, both encompassing and transcending it as an 'affirmative infinitude' (1:288–310). Here the perspective shifts from finite consciousness to the infinite self-mediation of spirit. There is no way of passing over from the finite to the infinite unless the infinite itself constitutes the passage; but this is already the speculative insight.

What Hegel calls 'empirical observation' is a more restricted operation than a phenomenological description of religion. Phenomenology is already implicitly speculative, as we shall discover by examining the role of phenomenology in the speculative concept of religion. But first we must achieve an understanding of speculative philosophy and of the speculative concept of religion.

*Speculative Philosophy*

'The speculative' for Hegel, we have said, involves a relationship of double mirroring between consciousness and object. Reality is a *speculum* or mirror of the consciousness that is engaged in acts of knowing. But consciousness is also a *speculum* of the ultimate reality that manifests itself, makes itself known through our acts of knowing it. A reversal in the flow of meaning occurs—from object to subject as well as from subject to object. As opposed to naive realism, speculative thought knows that there is no direct knowledge of objects, but knowledge mediated through the categories of thought (and the interests of the knower[4]). As opposed to naive idealism, speculative thought knows that mind does not

---

[4] The emphasis on the interests of the knower is a post-Hegelian development (through Marx, Nietzsche, and Freud, etc.), which, according to Jürgen Habermas, represents a critique and radicalization of Hegel's theory of knowledge (itself a critique and radicalization of Kant's epistemology). See Jürgen Habermas, *Knowledge and Human Interests*, trans. Jeremy Shapiro (Boston: Beacon Press, 1971). This is not to say that Hegel himself is unaware of the role of human interests in knowledge. His essay on 'The Varieties of Historical Writing' in the Introduction to the *Lectures on the Philosophy of World History* shows that he is. See the translation

simply create reality or project fantasies, but rather is the medium through which reality manifests itself. Objective knowledge is possible, but reflectedly, not directly. Speculative philosophy is a postcritical way of maintaining the connection between subject and object such that neither is reduced to a shadow of the other. They are connected because they share in the actuality of the rational and the rationality of the actual.[5]

The connection between subject and object, or thought and being, the ideal and the real, is not one of identity. Thus Hegel is at pains to insist that speculative philosophy is not a crude pantheism for which everything is simply identical (1:374). Rather it is a study of unity *in its concrete determinations*. 'Likewise', he continues, 'the philosophy of religion is just a succession of unities, where the unity always [abides] but is continually becoming more determinate.... The main thing is the distinction of these determinations of unity. Thus the unity of God is always unity, too, though everything turns quite strictly upon the manner in which this unity is defined' (1:379–80).[6] Speculative philosophy stresses not only the fact of unity but especially the manner in which unity becomes determinate, and the latter occurs in a great diversity of ways across culture and history. Absolute knowledge is simply the knowledge of all these determinacies, and it is through these alone that it attains a knowledge of unity. But no finite human being can achieve such a knowledge; only God knows absolutely.

Thus knowledge has an aspect of mystery, a mystery that is impenetrable from the point of view of understanding (since it can recognize only contradictions). Reason may penetrate the mystery but not exhaust it. Hegel notes that the 'mystical' and the 'speculative' are similar concepts, as the Neoplatonists (Proclus in particular) recognized (1:382, 445; 3:280–2). Mystery demands a closing of eyes (*myein*, from which the words 'mystery' and 'mystical' derive) and an opening of ears and minds to self-manifesting truth (as initiates did in the Greek mystery cults). What is mirrored (*speculum*) in speculation is not simply our own thought and

of the Introduction by H. B. Nisbet (Cambridge: Cambridge University Press, 1975), 11–24.

[5] See *Elements of the Philosophy of Right*, ed. Allen W. Wood, trans. H. B. Nisbet (Cambridge: Cambridge University Press, 1991), 20. The editor's note (389–90) points out that this famous formulation is to be understood as progressive and dynamic rather than as something that is already simply achieved.

[6] Hegel makes a similar point in the *Encyclopedia*, § 573 remark (see above, Chap. 2).

speech but that of the absolute unity, which gives itself through the determinacies of history. If the mystical posture is maintained, it should help to check the excesses of reason to which speculative philosophy is prone.

## The Speculative Concept of Religion

The speculative definition of religion, Hegel writes in the 1821 manuscript (1:204–6), holds together religious consciousness and its object, which is 'the true in and for itself', God as 'the absolutely self-determining true'. Ordinarily these are known only as abstract, opposed elements, but speculation knows that religious consciousness entails a 'rising above' and 'passing over' to the absolute, and that the absolute in turn mediates itself with itself in and through the consciousness of it. 'Concrete actuality is grasped as the unity of these determinate oppositions: this is the *speculative element*' (1:205). Thus 'the infinite idea of the incarnation of God' constitutes the 'speculative midpoint' of philosophy and religion (1:245). The 'speculative intuition' grasps the 'monstrous unification of these absolute extremes'—God and humanity, love and death (3:125), and the Christian religion itself is 'wholly speculative' (3:61 n. 1).

These scattered thoughts are developed more systematically in the 1824 lectures. Religion, speculatively defined (1:314–18), is not merely our consciousness of the absolute but the self-consciousness of absolute spirit, mediated in and through finite consciousness. Religion is not merely a human but a divine process.

Absolute spirit is itself that which connects itself with what we have put on the other side to distinguish it. Thus, on a higher plane, religion is this idea, the idea of spirit that relates itself to itself, *the self-consciousness of absolute spirit*. Within this its *self-consciousness*, there falls also its *consciousness*, which was previously defined as relationship. Thus in the highest idea, religion is not the affair of the single human being; rather it is essentially the highest determination of the absolute idea itself.    (1:318)[7]

---

[7] Hotho's freely edited version of this passage reads as follows: 'Religion is *the self-consciousness of absolute spirit*—its relation to itself as the object of its knowing, which is *self*-knowing. Thus religion is the idea of spirit—it is subjective spirit or the knowing that has as its content the entire content of spirit, the truth of spirit, and knows itself to be this content. Subjective spirit is accordingly not separate from the object, and this object, or absolute spirit, is knowing itself, it is what knows the object of its knowing. Consciousness as such is finite consciousness, knowing

Religion is speculative because human knowing is a *speculum* of the divine knowing. What transpires in it is not a human projection but 'the self-knowing of divine spirit through the mediation of finite spirit' (see n. 7). Elsewhere in the 1824 lectures Hegel remarks that 'religion is a begetting of the divine spirit, not an invention of human beings but an effect of the divine at work, of the divine productive process within humanity' (1:130).

This does not mean that human knowledge is passive, a mere tool or instrument of absolute spirit. The concept of religion includes as co-constitutive moments both the object that is in religion (God) and religious consciousness itself (1:185–7). Neither can be reduced to the other, and each is necessary for the other. The two sides struggle against each other, and their initial separation and alienation must be overcome in the individual heart and through the process that constitutes the history of religion. In the lecture manuscript Hegel describes this struggle in strikingly existential terms.

In thinking, I raise myself above all that is finite to the absolute and am *infinite consciousness*, while at the same time I am *finite self-consciousness*, indeed to the full extent of my empirical condition.... These two sides seek each other and flee from each other. I am this conflict and this conciliation, which exist in myself and for myself.... I am what intuits, senses, and represents this union and conflict. I am their holding together, the effort put forth in this holding together, the labour of mind and heart to master this opposition, which likewise exists for me.  (1:212)

Also in the manuscript Hegel remarks that religion is the process of 'passing over' from consciousness to object, from finite to infinite, from the immediate to the intelligible world (1:203–4). The condition of possibility of the passing over from finite to infinite is the passing over of the infinite to the finite (the infinite idea of incarnation, the becoming human of the divine). The problem with

something that is other than the I. Religion is also consciousness, and has therefore finite consciousness within it, though sublated as finite because absolute spirit is itself the other that it knows, and it is only by knowing itself that it becomes absolute spirit. Consequently, however, it is only mediated through consciousness or finite spirit, so that it has to *finitize* itself in order by this finitization to come to know itself. However, if the divine, in order to be spirit in this way, finitizes itself so as to become human, i.e. to become a knowing, singular, immediate consciousness, [this] is not on the other hand the affair of the single human being; rather, what is singular is precisely sublated thereby, and religion is *the self-knowing of divine spirit through the mediation of finite spirit*' (1:318 n. 120). On the Hotho transcript of the 1824 lectures, see 1:16–17.

empirical approaches to religion is that they never attain to this double passing over—to the actual religious relationship as the 'unity of absolute universality and absolute singularity' (1:207).

## The Role of Phenomenology in the Speculative Concept of Religion

In the lecture manuscript Hegel arrives at the speculative concept of religion through a phenomenological approach that demonstrates the 'necessity of the religious standpoint' from the constitution of the finite world (1:221–32). 'Phenomenology' means the science of the experience of consciousness, that is, of how things appear to consciousness. The emphasis on *appearance* to consciousness, and the theme of the *odyssey* of consciousness, form the speculative element that distinguishes phenomenology from empirical description or observation. By tracing phenomenologically the immanent teleological movement of nature and finite spirit to their goal and foundation in the absolute idea, this section of the manuscript provides a summary of 'the whole sphere of the philosophical sciences'. In this way the concept of religion follows from all that precedes in philosophy, and the philosophy of religion comes last in the encyclopedia of philosophy.

A marginal reference to '*Phenomenology of Spirit*' in the manuscript (1:229 n. 119) suggests that Hegel is here summarizing the leitmotif of that work, namely the rise of finite consciousness to the absolute through a succession of increasingly adequate yet always determinate and negated shapes. A passage in the *Werke* edition of 1840 that probably derives from the lost Henning transcript of the 1821 lectures adds the following: 'To philosophical cognition, the progression is a stream *flowing in opposite directions*, leading forward to the other, but at the same time working backward, so that what appears to be the *last*, founded on what precedes, appears rather to be the *first*—the foundation' (1:227 n. 115). The image of a stream flowing in opposite directions suggests a 'speculative reversal': the rise of finite consciousness to the absolute is at the same time the return of absolute spirit to itself. What appears to be the result of the phenomenology of consciousness proves rather to be its presupposition. God is 'the absolute, all-encompassing fulfilment' in which the world's wealth immerses itself as mere appearance: everything appears *sub specie aeterni* (1:230–2).

This reading is confirmed by equivalent passages in the 1824 lectures. Stages in the phenomenology of nature and spirit are rehearsed as a way of demonstrating the necessity of the religious standpoint (1:319–24). First, 'the logical idea unlocks itself in the resolve to become nature, to pass over into nature and lose itself in this externality'. Then nature as it withdraws from externality passes over into centred consciousness or spirit, and spirit moves from its natural immediacy to its ethical and rational ground. Through this process 'absolute spirit . . . is exhibited as necessary, as the truth of all things, as the absolute truth into which, precisely through itself, all this other content returns' (1:321). This process has a one-sided and distorted character in the sense that it begins with something else (the logically abstract, nature, finite being) and arrives at the absolute as a result. 'But *absolute truth cannot be a result; it is what is purely and simply first, unique.* It is what takes up simply everything into itself—the absolute plenitude in which everything is but a moment. . . . It is in this result itself that the one-sidedness is abolished: the result casts off its position as result and develops a *counterthrust*, so to speak, against this movement' (1:322). This 'counterthrust' is the speculative reversal, the stream flowing in both directions. In the final result, '*absolute spirit, conscious of itself, is the first and alone true*' (1:322). God is alpha and omega. Two moments or movements together—God creating the world, and the world betaking itself back to God—make up the activity of God. This process first shows itself outside religion, then within religion itself. Outside religion, there is an innocence with respect to God; within religion, it is God who is strictly the first and the last (1:323–4).

All of this means that the concept of religion is really the concept of God—God as abstract being or substance, as the creator who 'unlocks' godself and releases what is not God into existence, and as the consummator who brings all things back into relationship with God. The 1827 lectures start at this point—the speculative insight into the nature of God and religion at which the 1824 lectures arrive only at the end (through a laborious but illuminating process). We shall consider the approach of the 1827 lectures when in Chapter 5 we turn to the philosophical concept of God, a concept that focuses on the abstract being of God, the knowledge of God in the religious relationship, and the consummation of this relationship in the form of worship. In this structure the Christian Trinity is prefigured.

## CHRISTIANITY AS THE CONSUMMATE, REVELATORY RELIGION

Christianity is the religion in which the concept of religion and of God are most fully realized. For the moment we are bracketing the question as to whether any finite, historical religion can simply be identified with the concept of religion. Rather we are asking what this identification means from Hegel's perspective. It means, first, that the inner structure or elements of the Christian religion correspond to moments in the life of the triune God. This is the topic of the first subsection. It means further that the Christian religion possesses distinct attributes or qualities by which it is named philosophically. These seem to divide into three sets in Hegel's treatment: Christianity is (a) the consummate or absolute religion; (b) the revelatory and revealed religion; and (c) the religion of truth, freedom, and reconciliation. These are the topics of the remaining subsections.

### The Three Elements or 'Kingdoms'

In the lecture manuscript, Hegel's treatment of the Christian religion is structured into two triads, one within the other.[8] The outer triad is an analytic framework already applied to each of the determinate religions in part 2 of the lectures. This analysis considers (A) the 'abstract concept' of God in the religion in question (including proofs of the existence of God associated with the religion); (B) its 'concrete representation' of God and of humanity's relationship to God in terms of specific symbols, images, and other thought-categories (the 'theoretical' relationship to God); (C) its 'cultus' by means of which an actual participation in or communion with God occurs (the 'practical' relationship). In the 1827 lectures, as we shall see in the next chapter, Hegel also uses this framework to structure his presentation of the concept of religion in part 1. If the concept of religion is absolute spirit in its self-mediation, then we can expect that religion as such will reflect the development or self-realization of absolute spirit in the three moments of its substantial self-unity (the abstract being of

---

[8] The following discussion draws upon the editorial introduction to vol. 3 (3:11–14). See the table that provides a comparative analysis of the structure of the Consummate Religion on 54–5.

God), its self-differentiation (the knowledge of God), and its self-reunification or return to self (the worship of God).

The inner triad of the 1821 lectures is a subset of section B of the outer triad: it sets forth the 'concrete representation' of God that is found in the Christian religion. As is clear from the outline at the beginning of this section (3:73–7), the triad is composed of: (a) the idea of God in and for itself (the immanent Trinity); (b) the idea in diremption or differentiation (creation and preservation of the natural world); (c) the appearance of the idea in finite spirit (the history of estrangement, redemption, and reconciliation). At this point a tension in Hegel's thought emerges. If what constitutes the 'concrete representation' of God in the Christian religion is the self-mediation of the triune God, then we would expect a trinitarian structure. But what is in fact offered is a philosophical triad, drawn from the three branches of philosophy: the logical idea, nature, and (finite) spirit—a triad that is recapitulated in Hegel's treatment of 'the revealed religion' in §§ 567–70 of the *Encyclopedia of Philosophical Sciences*.[9] It has the peculiar result that the 'Son' (anthropology and christology) occupies the third moment of the triad rather than the second. Or more precisely, the Son is distributed across two moments: the eternal Son or Logos by whom God

---

[9] The *Encyclopedia* anticipates the arrangement found in the lecture manuscript. The later lectures return to an arrangement hinted at in the *Phenomenology of Spirit*. Hegel experiments with both arrangements, one of which is more christological, the other more pneumatological. See my discussion of this matter in *G. W. F. Hegel: Theologian of the Spirit* (Minneapolis: Fortress Press, and Edinburgh: T&T Clark, 1997), 23–4, 144–5, 275 n. 11. The dilemma faced by Hegel arises partly from the fact that if the third moment of the philosophical triad is limited to finite spirit, there seems to be no place in the system for religion and the relationship to absolute spirit. It is noteworthy that in his earliest system outline of 1802–3 Hegel envisions a *fourfold* division: logic, philosophy of nature, philosophy of ethical life (finite spirit), and religion as 'the resumption of the whole into one' (absolute spirit). Just a year later he converted this to a triadic plan—logic, nature, spirit—with the third part understood to include both finite and infinite spirit (i.e. both ethical life and religion, to which philosophy is added as the consummation of the whole). See *Hegel: Theologian of the Spirit*, 85; and H. S. Harris's Introduction to his edition of *System of Ethical Life (1802/3) and First Philosophy of Spirit (1803/4)* (Albany: State University of New York Press, 1979), esp. 6. When the triad is applied to Christianity and the Trinity, the three moments must accommodate four themes: the idea of God in and for itself (the Father), the diremption of the idea into nature, the appearance of the idea in finite spirit (humanity, Christ), and the return of the idea to itself as absolute or Holy Spirit. The second and third themes together comprise the second trinitarian moment. In the philosophical triad, finite and infinite spirit are combined in the third moment; in the theological trinity, nature and finite spirit are combined in the second moment.

creates appears in the second moment (3:87, 99), while the incarnate, historical Son appears in the third (3:109 ff.). The third trinitarian moment, the Spirit, becomes a kind of appendage, treated under section C of the outer triad, 'community, cultus'. What is required, then, to have an adequate account of the distinctively Christian idea of God is to combine the second and third moments of the philosophical triad (nature and finite spirit) in the second moment of the trinitarian dialectic (God's self-differentiation or diremption by creating a world of both nature and finite spirit as God's own otherness *ad extra*), and to incorporate the third moment of the outer triad (community, cultus) into the third moment of the trinitarian mediation (God's return-to-self in and through the transfigured subjectivity of the community of the Spirit). The philosophical triad is grounded in the dialectic of thought itself, namely, the three logical moments of the syllogism: universality (*Allgemeinheit*), particularity (*Besonderheit*), and individuality or subjectivity (*Einzelheit*).[10] But trinitarian speculation requires a modification so that the moments become: abstract unity (universality), differentiation (particularity + finite subjectivity), return (infinite subjectivity)—or, as Hegel finally expresses it in 1831, the kingdoms of the Father, Son, and Spirit. The modification does not change the basic dialectical structure but is simply a concrete application of it to the Christian idea of God.

Hegel makes just such an adjustment in the later lectures. The first section of the manuscript's inner triad in section B (concrete representation) becomes the 'first element' in the development of the idea of God (the idea of God in and for itself, the immanent Trinity) in the 1824 and 1827 lectures, or the 'kingdom of the Father' in 1831. The second and third sections of the inner triad become the 'second element' (representation and appearance, or differentiation and reconciliation) in 1824 and 1827, or the 'kingdom of the Son' in 1831. And section C of the manuscript (community, cultus) becomes the 'third element' (community, spirit) in 1824 and 1827, or the 'kingdom of the Spirit' in 1831.[11] Thus the

---

[10] See *Science of Logic*, trans. A. V. Miller (London: George Allen & Unwin, 1969), 600 ff., 664 ff.; and *Encyclopedia*, §§ 181–93 (*The Encyclopedia Logic*, 256–71).

[11] See 3:185–8 (1824), 3:271–4 (1827), 3:362–3 (1831). There is already an anticipation of these changes in the words Hegel added to the heading of Section B in the manuscript—whether immediately or in preparation for the 1824 lectures is not certain—namely, that 'concrete representation' involves the 'determination', i.e. the 'development of the idea [of God]', and 'weaves itself by itself into the cultus'

original analytic scheme of 'abstract concept', 'concrete representation', and 'community, cultus', is broken apart, and the inner triad is converted into trinitarian moments. With respect to the second moment of the latter (namely, God's worldly appearance or the kingdom of the Son), there are still two poles, but they no longer correspond to the philosophical distinction between nature and finite spirit. Rather they are the phase of differentiation (including now not only the creation of the natural world but also the fall of humanity into estrangement and evil) and the phase of reconciliation (beginning with the appearance of the idea of divine–human unity in a single individual). The 'turning-point'—the extreme of divine self-divestment and the moment initiating the return—is no longer the creation of the first Adam (as the manuscript depicts it, 3:90–1[12]) but the incarnation and crucifixion of the second Adam (as in the 1824 lectures, 3:215).

If Christ is now the turning-point, the Spirit is the consummation of the whole process, and Hegel can be seen to be moving toward a more pneumatological Trinitarianism. Whereas in the 1821 arrangement the Son appears both in the second moment as the eternal Logos by which God creates and in the third moment as the incarnate Christ who sends or commissions the Spirit upon his departure from the world, in the later arrangement the two Sons are combined into the second moment and the Spirit constitutes the third moment as the final figure in whom the first two are sublated. The first pattern seems to entail a subordination of the Spirit to Christ. Does the second pattern suggest rather a super-

---

(see 3:73 n. 39). Section A of the manuscript, 'abstract concept', which treats the ontological proof of God, is taken over into the 1824 and 1831 lectures, where it precedes the three 'elements' or 'kingdoms'. The 1827 lectures shift all the proofs to *The Concept of Religion*.

[12] The arrangement of the manuscript might give the impression that evil is present in nature and that the 'turning' from evil to redemption occurs with the appearance of human beings. However, Hegel never regards nature as intrinsically evil in Gnostic fashion. The 'primal division' or creative scission that brings nature into being as different from God provides the condition of possibility for good and evil, but is not evil as such. In the manuscript, estrangement and evil belong to the third moment (the appearance of the idea in finite spirit), not the second, and are the product of human actions. Divinity arrives at 'its most extreme mode of being outside itself' not in nature but in human evil, which, in symbolic terms, begins with the fall of Adam and reaches its culmination with the crucifixion of Christ. This is the 'pinnacle of divestment' (3:91). Christ represents a second turning-point for the manuscript, the beginning of the history of redemption and reconciliation.

session of Christ by the Spirit? This is a question for Chapters 8 and 9.

Hegel is at pains to point out that the 'elements' or 'kingdoms' referred to are not to be construed literally in temporal and spatial terms. They are constitutive aspects of the activity and eternal life of absolute spirit, which is 'a development and a return of this development into itself'. They can be thought of more strictly as God in the three modes of thought (*Denken*), representation (*Vorstellung*), and subjectivity (*Subjektivität*); or the eternal idea of God in and for itself, God as present to sensible intuition and representation, and God as the Spirit engendering the (inter)subjectivity of the community of faith (3:185–8, 271–4). The second and third moments do have objective referents in the spatiotemporal world: the life and death of Christ and the formation and duration of the community of the Spirit. The 'representation' of God is not simply a human way of thinking about God but God's real setting-forth (*vor-stellen*) of godself in the world. And the 'subjectivity' of God arises out of the intersubjectivity of the spiritual community.

## The Consummate, Absolute Religion

The terms by which Hegel names the Christian religion in his speculative redescription of it are noteworthy. The philosophical naming of the religions means that their significance is not to be identified principally from their historical aspect. Characteristically, Hegel employs several concepts and moves dialectically among them. His is the sort of thinking that speaks/thinks across differences 'dia-lectically' and grasps and holds together in a 'concept' (*Be-griff*) disparate aspects of a whole. Rarely will a single category suffice for him.

The name given to Christianity in the heading to part 3 of the 1821 manuscript is 'the Consummate Religion' (*die vollendete Religion*), to which Hegel adds below the heading, 'or Revelatory' (*oder offenbare*) (3:61). We may assume, then, that the two preferred names are 'consummate' and 'revelatory'. Hegel reminds his hearers (3:61–2) that this religion was earlier defined (1:110–11) as the one in which the concept of religion has returned to itself or become objective to itself by becoming an object of human consciousness explicitly. Since the concept of religion *is* the relationship of finite consciousness to its absolute object, and ultimately the unity between them based on the absolute's self-mediation or self-consciousness, the religion in which this relationship is made fully manifest is the 'consummate' and the 'revelatory' religion. The concept of religion is consummated or fulfilled in Christianity because at the centre of this religion is the 'infinite idea of the incarnation of God' in which the extremes of finite and infinite, consciousness and object, are unified: this is the 'speculative midpoint' of religion; it is what makes the Christian religion 'wholly speculative' (1:245; 3:61 n. 1, 3:125).

Christianity is also 'the absolute religion' (*die absolute Religion*), and the term 'absolute' forms a set with 'consummate', but with distinctive nuances. The absoluteness of Christianity points to the fact that in it the concept of religion, the *relatedness* of divinity and humanity, is consummated, fully accomplished. 'Absolute' for Hegel is not a static but a dynamic, relational concept. Absolute spirit is utterly connected with everything: it is nothing but relationality. God is absolutely free within godself, and it is precisely in this absolute freedom that God 'absolves' or 'releases' [*entläßt*] the other to exist as a free and independent being. This other, released [*entlassen*] as something free and independent, is the world as such' (3:292).[13] The world that God releases is a genuine otherness with which God has reciprocal relations, but it is not something that resides 'beyond' the absolute by which the latter might be externally limited and rendered finite; the divine life is all-encompassing.[14] The verb *entlassen*, 'to release', is a Germanic equivalent to the Latin verb *absolvere*, 'to loosen from' or 'let go', from which the word 'absolute' derives. Hegel's association of 'release' with the concept of the absolute shows that the latter has for him just the opposite meaning from its conventional usage.

A modification of the conventional usage is found in Pseudo-Dionysius, who on the one hand speaks of the God beyond being as 'absolutely absolved from all and beyond the whole'. But on the other hand there is a double ecstasis, from humanity to divinity and from divinity to humanity. The disciple who enters into mystical contemplation is elevated by an 'absolving ecstasis' into 'the rays of the divine darkness beyond being'; and divinity not merely abides within itself but is the be-ing that lets beings be and in that

---

[13] See also *Encyclopedia*, § 244 (*The Encyclopedia Logic*, 307). See n. 2 above.
[14] Whether nondualistic otherness is intelligible is a question for the concluding chapter. It is a question that points to the contrast between Hegel and Levinas.

respect comes forth out of itself ecstatically.[15] If we apply this
suggestive language to Hegel, we can say that God is both absolved
and absolving, utterly self-contained and utterly releasing, and the
two-way movement of the 'absolving ecstasis' between divinity
and humanity is what constitutes 'religion'.

In the 1824 lectures Hegel remarks: 'Universal and singular
spirit, infinite and finite spirit, are here [in the Christian religion]
inseparable; their absolute identity is religion, and absolute religion is awareness of just this content. . . . One can say that what is at
issue here, the whole, the absolute, *is* religion'—and as religion it is
relationality. 'Absolute' does not refer to the 'majesty of God',
known only 'as an object that stands over and above us for all time'.
At first sight this is what theology seems to be about, God as an
external object of consciousness. But what is involved in the concept of the absolute religion 'is not this external object but religion
itself, i.e. the unity of this object with the subject, the way in which
it is in the subject' (3:165–6). The absolute religion has the character of both subjectivity and substance. 'This subjectivity . . . is
infinite form, the infinite elasticity of substance that enables it to
dirempt itself inwardly and make itself its own object' (3:169).

Nothing could make it clearer that for Hegel the absolute is at
the farthest remove from what is transcendent, immutable, disen-
gaged, cut off, superior, supreme, and unrelated. It is unfortunate,
therefore, that through the *Werke* edition[16] of Hegel's lectures
Christianity came to be known principally as 'the absolute religion'. The editors ignored the fact that this was not Hegel's preferred name for the Christian religion. Nonetheless, understood in
the sense intended by Hegel, it is not an inappropriate name—not
inappropriate, that is, if Christianity as a historically determinate
religion really can be identified with the consummation of the

---

[15] Pseudo-Dionysius Areopagite, *The Divine Names and Mystical Theology*,
trans. John D. Jones (Milwaukee: Marquette University Press, 1980), 3–4, 145,
211, 222. Pseudo-Dionysius is mentioned in Hegel's *Lectures on the History of
Philosophy*, ed. Robert F. Brown, vol. 3 (Berkeley and Los Angeles: University of
California Press, 1990; Oxford: Oxford University Press, forthcoming), 52, 61, but
only in reference to John Scotus Erigena, who translated his works into Latin, and
Albert the Great, who wrote on him. But Hegel was well-acquainted with Proclus,
upon whom Pseudo-Dionysius was dependent.

[16] The lectures on the philosophy of religion were first published in volumes
11–12 of the *Werke*, a complete edition of Hegel's works published by 'an association of friends'. The first edition of the philosophy of religion (1832) was edited by
Philipp Marheineke; the second (1840) by Marheineke and Bruno Bauer. Part 3 was
titled *Die absolute Religion*.

concept of religion and with the absolute relationality of God. Hegel defended this identification. But from a postmodern point of view that accepts the historical relativity of religions and affirms religious pluralism, these terms must point to an ideal that, while active in history, is never fully accomplished in it and keeps referring to new possibilities. From this point of view it seems obvious to say that the concept of religion is consummated and God becomes absolutely relational only in and through the entire history of religion, which is inexhaustibly rich and still very much an open history.

## *The Revelatory and Revealed Religion*

As we have seen, Hegel's other preferred name for the Christian religion is 'revelatory' (*offenbar*), and this is an attribute that seems more palatable to postmodern sensibilities. Indeed, when Hegel elaborates on the characteristics of Christianity at the beginning of the lecture manuscript, it is revelatoriness that is highlighted, not consummation or absoluteness.

The Christian religion is the religion of *revelation*. What God is, and the fact that he is known *as* he is, not merely in historical or some similar fashion as in the other religions, is manifest [*offenbar*] in it. Revelation [*Offenbarung*], manifestation [*Manifestation*] is itself its character and content. That is to say, revelation, manifestation [is] the being [of God] for consciousness. . . . God is *only* manifest as one who particularizes himself and becomes objective, initially in the mode of finitude, which is his own.   (3:63)

Christianity is the revelatory religion because 'revelatoriness' [*Offenbarkeit*] is an attribute, perhaps the defining attribute, of God. The later lectures make this point quite explicitly. The word 'revealing', the 1824 lectures tell us, 'refers to the primal division of infinite subjectivity or infinite form; it means determining oneself to be for an other. This revealing or self-manifesting belongs to the essence of spirit itself. *A spirit that is not revelatory is not spirit*. . . . It is the essence of God as spirit *to be for an other*, i.e. to *reveal* himself' (3:170). In similar terms, the 1827 lectures claim that God is intrinsically revelatory, self-manifesting; God is not jealous, does not withhold or conceal godself, as Plato and Aristotle contended against the mystery cults. What God reveals is not so much truths or information *about* God but rather that revelatoriness and self-communication are essentially what God is. This is what it means to say that God is 'spirit', for spirit is essentially a being *for* spirit, for another, a relating, revealing, self-opening, self-dirempting spirit (1:382–3; 3:250–1). However, Christianity is also the 'revealed' (*geoffenbart*) religion, and indeed this is the more customary way of speaking of it.[17] 'Revealed' suggests something that has been given in a historical, positive fashion through a direct epiphany, an inspired writing, or an authoritative tradition. The term does have this connotation for Hegel, but he insists that in the first instance what has been *revealed* about God is simply that God is intrinsically *revelatory, manifest* (3:170–1, 252). The past participle *geoffenbart* points to the present tense verb *offenbaren* and its adjectival and noun derivatives *offenbar, Offenbarung,* and *Offenbarkeit.* What is revealed is revelatoriness, openness. Revelation has no object or content other than itself. The coincidence of *offenbar* and *geoffenbart* means that for Hegel the whole debate in late Enlightenment thought over reason versus revelation was misplaced. What is revealed (*geoffenbart*) is precisely the process in which reason and truth make themselves open, manifest (*offenbar*).

In contrast to the somewhat dismissive attitude of the lecture manuscript toward the historical revelation of God, it is just this aspect that is emphasized in the 1827 lectures. Not only the spirituality but also the positivity of the Christian religion must be recognized (3:251–62). Christianity is a 'positive' religion, whose truth is mediated in sensible, historical fashion through external authorities. This is the case because 'everything that is *for* consciousness is *objective* to consciousness. *Everything must come to us from outside*' (3:252)—including both God and Christianity. Of course what comes to us from outside must be inwardly appropriated, and in the process it makes contact with what we know intuitively or potentially: it discloses itself also to be rational and internal. Hegel is suspicious of a purely Kantian doctrine of subjectivity or a purely Platonic doctrine of recollection. The truth

---

[17] In the *Phenomenology of Spirit*, in the heading of section C of chapter VII, Christianity is named *Die offenbare Religion*, while in the *Encyclopedia*, §§ 564 ff., it is called *Die geoffenbarte Religion*. Unfortunately in translation these terms are not consistently distinguished. While Hegel intended the use of both terms, the usage in the philosophy of religion lectures indicates a preference for the earlier (and more suggestive) designation.

may be within, but given the sensible and sinful nature of human beings it must be awakened and brought forth by an outward educational process in the form of objective truths, doctrines, laws, persons, and practices. Thus even God must come to humanity from without, giving godself for human beings in external, sensuous, historical forms. The revelatoriness of God requires a historical mediation.

Hegel also emphasizes, however, that despite the necessity of historical mediation the essentially rational truth revealed in Christianity derives from its spirituality, not its positivity, and can be verified only by the witness of the Spirit, not by historical proofs or miracles or testimonies (3:254–7). 'The spiritual as such cannot be directly verified by the unspiritual, the sensible.' Hegel finds it interesting that, in the biblical accounts, miracles are often put aside as having little or no demonstrative value. So, for example, the Egyptian magicians were able to imitate the miracles performed by Moses, and Christ himself rejected miracles ('signs and wonders') as a genuine criterion of truth. Neither verification by miracles, nor attacks on miracles, nor rationalistic explanations of them, should be of interest to us. The witness of the Spirit is the only authentic witness.

But what does this mean? The expression *Zeugniß des Geistes* contains an ambivalence or double meaning for Hegel. On the one hand, it can refer to the witness of the Holy Spirit or the Spirit of God, by which authentic faith is awakened in human subjects, or the community of faith is formed and sustained. On the other hand, it can refer to the witness of *our* spirit to spiritual truth, the witness of *my* spirit to *the* Spirit (see 1:337 n. 149). The two meanings are in fact two aspects of a single truth, since the Spirit of God witnesses only in and through our spirits: there is no divine witness apart from the activity of human spirit; however, the latter is not an autonomous, singular activity but the inner working of the one holy and universal Spirit. Thus Hegel remarks, 'In history, all that is noble, lofty, and divine speaks to us internally; to it our spirit bears witness.' This witness can range from a kind of 'general resonance' or sympathy to explicit faith, insight, and thought. Hegel thinks that the highest form of the witness of spirit is found in philosophy, but he acknowledges that human beings are at different stages of spiritual development and that many, perhaps most, need to base their trust on external authority and sensuous experience (3:254–6).

It is in this connection that Hegel mentions the Bible. While the doctrines of the Christian religion are given in the Bible in a positive fashion, they must resonate within us subjectively if we are to be touched by and appropriate them. The Bible is for Christians 'the fundamental basis, which has this effect on them, which strikes a chord within them, and gives firmness to their conviction' (3:257). The image of 'resonance' suggests a kind of spiritual attunement or interaction. On the basis of this resonance, human beings go on to *think* about the Bible and its contents, to develop a *theology* that is not simply read out of the Bible but is an *interpretation* of it. Anyone can quote the Bible (including the Devil, 3:258 n. 29), but that 'by no means makes the theologian'. Once explanation, exegesis, and interpretation are introduced in order to determine the *meaning* of the words of the Bible, we are beyond the literal text and into a process of reasoning, reflecting, thinking. The Bible itself points in this direction: 'The letter kills, but the Spirit gives life.' It is a question, then, Hegel remarks, 'as to which spirit we bring in, which spirit gives life to the positive'. Is it merely the human spirit, in which case everything in religion is reduced to human autonomy, or is it the witnessing of our spirit to the divine Spirit moving and manifesting itself in the process? (3:259–62).

In the 1827 lectures Hegel concludes the discussion of the spirituality (revelatoriness) and positivity (revealedness) of Christianity by remarking that in the present treatment 'we shall not set to work in *merely historical* fashion, which would entail starting with external matters, but rather we shall proceed *conceptually*' (3:262). The lectures on the philosophy of religion will offer not a historical description of this (or any other) religion but a conceptual redescription of it in terms appropriate to philosophical science. Such a procedure, which constitutes the true work of theology, does not at all entail a denial of the historicality of Christianity; rather it grasps what is true, actual, rational, and spiritual within this historicality. Its method is speculative rather than empirical. We shall address the matter of 'speculative redescription' in the final section of this chapter.

## The Religion of Truth, Freedom, and Reconciliation

The final set of characteristics point toward the ethical and theological *content* of Christianity in so far as this content can be distinguished from its more formal qualities (consummate, revelatory). First, Christianity is the religion of *truth*. This does not mean that it is historically accurate but rather that 'the true' (*das Wahre*) is its content. But God is the true, so God is the content; and truthful knowledge of the true is to know the true as spirit, that is, as manifest, as truth in and for itself and also for us (3:64). Thus this characteristic, as set forth in the lecture manuscript, circles back to the previous ones. The 1824 lectures take a slightly different approach but arrive at the same point. 'Truth' means that in what is objective we are not relating to something alien. In the religion of truth, it is *spirit* that is for spirit. Spirit is the 'eternal intuition of itself' as both presupposition and result, subject and object. Truth is 'the mutual adequacy to each other' of subject and object (3:171).

Likewise, therefore, Christianity is the religion of *freedom*. Abstractly defined, freedom means 'relating oneself to something objective without its being alien'. This, Hegel notes, 'is the same definition as that of truth, except that in the case of freedom the categorial moment of the negation of difference or of otherness is emphasized, and freedom therefore appears in the form of *reconciliation*' (3:171). This is because difference assumes the form of alienation, which entails not only a rupture in the relationship of divinity and humanity (which calls for *reconciliation*) but also a rupture in interhuman relations resulting in practices of slavery, oppression, injustice, etc. To address the latter what is needed is a *liberation* from such practices, and Christianity takes on the aspect of a liberatory religion, including liberation from slavery (3:172, 340). Christianity is the religion in which *all* human beings are recognized to be free, not just *one* (the ancient Oriental monarchies) or *some* (Greek and Roman societies).

In describing the relation of Christianity to the preceding religions, the 1824 lectures highlight the characteristic of freedom: the religion of freedom is the third form of religion following upon, unifying, and completing the religion of nature and the religion of finite spirit, for in it 'there is equally both the objectivity of spirit and the freedom of self-possession' (3:172–3). Self-possession or presence-to-oneself (*Beisichselbstsein*) is the essential mark of freedom. This is not principally an individualistic concept of freedom, for presence to oneself is achieved in and through presence to others; and it is free institutions, not autonomous individuals, that play the key role in the realization of freedom. For Christianity this assumes the form of the church as a community of freedom (see Chapter 9).

The highlighting of freedom as the telos of the history of religions is taken even further in the 1831 lectures, where the emergence of freedom (over against the rupture and alienation of religious consciousness) is traced back to Persian, Jewish, Egyptian, and especially Greek religion; and where, in contrast to these finite forms of freedom, Christianity is depicted as the religion of absolute freedom (2:736–60; 3:359–60). In these last lectures Hegel is especially concerned with political and social issues (an interest stimulated by recent events in France and Britain[18]) and with the actualization of freedom in both religion and the state (1:451–60).

Finally, Christianity is the religion of *reconciliation*. This means principally the reconciliation of the world with God, for the world has fallen away from God and 'fixated itself as finite consciousness, as the consciousness of idols. . . . To desist from this separation is to turn back to God' (3:65). The turning back is not an autonomous human capacity but is engendered by God's reconciliation of the world with godself, which is the central theme of religion. Indeed, we are told in 1827 that the implicit and explicit reconciliation of God and humanity is 'the foundation of all religious consciousness' (1:443–4). The 1824 lectures spell this out more fully: 'Reconciliation begins with differentiated entities standing opposed to each other—God, who confronts a world that is estranged from him, and a world that is estranged from its essence. . . . Reconciliation is the negation of this separation, this division, and means that each cognizes itself in the other, finds itself in its essence. Reconciliation, consequently, is freedom and is not something quiescent; rather it is activity, the movement that makes the estrangement disappear' (3:171–2). The unity of God and the world, or of God and humanity, is implicitly present within the divine life; but for it to become actual in the world it must be brought forth: movement and activity are required. In the first instance, this means God's movement into the world in the figure of Christ—God godself undergoes the anguish of estrangement and death—and the crucified Christ is central to the process of reconciliation for

---

[18] Specifically, the end of the Bourbon monarchy in the July Revolution of 1830, and the introduction of the Reform Bill into Parliament in 1831. Hegel's essay on 'The English Reform Bill' was his last published writing before his death (see *Hegel's Political Writings*, trans. T. M. Knox, ed. Z. A. Pelczynski (Oxford: Clarendon Press, 1964)).

Christians (see Chapter 8). But it also means that human beings must be caught up in the movement and work for the removal of estrangement: here reconciliation assumes the form of liberation.

We are led to see that all three of these movements by which Christianity is defined—truth, freedom, and reconciliation—'constitute a universal process, and thus cannot be expressed in a simple proposition, except one-sidedly' (3:172). This is characteristic, as we have noted, of Hegel's dialectical procedure: individual qualities and attributes add distinctive elements to a whole that embraces and relativizes all of them. We cannot grasp the whole all at once but only through a complex interplay of propositions.

SPECULATIVE REDESCRIPTION OF THE
CHRISTIAN METANARRATIVE

Hegel's intent is to offer not a historical description of religion but a philosophical comprehension of it. In respect to Christianity, we can say that he provides a speculative redescription of the Christian metanarrative.[19] It is this metanarrative that governs the whole of the lectures on the philosophy of religion, starting with the concept of religion and moving through the determinate religions to the consummate religion. The Christian metanarrative is fundamentally the narrative of the triune God unfolding in the three elements of unity, differentiation, and reconciliation, or the three kingdoms of the Father, Son, and Spirit. This metanarrative is read onto the whole of the history of religions, and the latter is made to subserve the Christian story.

One question raised immediately about such a procedure is whether a less distinctively Christian version of the metanarrative, yet one that retains a trinitarian or triadic structure, might be more appropriate for reading the history of religions. If the triadic structure grasps the fundamental logic of things, it would transcend every determinate articulation of it and manifest itself in a

---

[19] See Emil Fackenheim, *The Religious Dimension in Hegel's Thought* (Bloomington, Ind.: Indiana University Press, 1967), esp. chap. 6, 'The Transfiguration of Faith into Philosophy'; and Cyril O'Regan, *The Heterodox Hegel* (Albany: State University of New York Press, 1994), esp. chap. 7, 'Representation and Concept: Speculative Rewriting'. See my review of O'Regan's book in *Modern Theology* 11 (July 1995): 385–6.

diversity of forms, including the Christian Trinity but also other religious representations such as the Hindu Trimurti, Buddhist enlightenment, the Daoist way (yin–yang), the Pythagorean and Platonic triads, and various Neoplatonic and Gnostic speculations. Indeed Hegel is already pointing in this direction. Not only does he mention these diverse forms (3:80–6, 286–9); but also, as we have seen, he finds it necessary to modify the logical or philosophical triad (universality, particularity, individuality; or idea, nature, spirit) in order to generate the Christian Trinity. Perhaps the triad represents a more primordial and universal structure. These are questions to be addressed in Chapter 10.

Hegel offers not a straightforward account of the Christian metanarrative but a speculative redescription or transformation of it. The classical version of the metanarrative, with its dualistic, mythological worldview, sequential view of space/time, and representational language was seriously deficient in his view. Among other things it had the effect of locking God and the world into ontologically incommensurate realms and of requiring God to intervene supernaturally and episodically in the world. Hegel seeks to articulate an alternative that not only responds to the critiques of modernity but also introduces narrativity into the structure of the divine life. The immanent Trinity is not an Archimedean foundation but is rather an element within the revelatory dynamic as a whole—the economic or inclusive Trinity, which encompasses God and world together. The self-revealing God is *Geist,* which is not an aspect or person of the divine but the divine as such considered as an encompassing act or process, a narrative, a trinitarian unfolding.

The principal means of redescription is the translation of representational language, couched in metaphors, symbols, and stories, into speculative concepts. Narrative relations are converted into logical relations while allowing for a demythologized perdurance of narrative. Hegel's friendly demythologization of the Christian metanarrative preserves its theological referent and its deep insight while subverting the hostile demythologizations (subjectivist, materialist, atheist) that were already under way in his time.[20]

Risks are involved in this strategy. Some critics believe that the risks are too great and that Hegel in effect has thrown out the baby

---

[20] These formulations are indebted to O'Regan (see n. 19).

with the bath water.[21] Hegel himself remarks: 'The difficult thing
is to separate out from a content what pertains only to representation. In its paring away of what pertains to representation, philosophy is reproached for removing the content too. This
transformation is therefore held to be a destruction' (1:397).
Whether Hegel's transformation of Christian themes is really a
destruction or rather a deconstruction and reconstruction is the
interpretative burden of the chapters to follow. Here are some
questions with which to end the present chapter: Is a friendly
demythologization the most effective way of defending Christian
faith against hostile ones? Or is it better to ignore the latter and go
back to classical, albeit mythological, forms? Do the metaphors of
theology and religion continue to reverberate in philosophical
concepts? Or are they obliterated by the concepts? Does Hegel's
heterodox version of the Christian metanarrative come closer to
the dynamic God of biblical faith than the orthodox version? Or
does his heterodoxy simply swerve into heresy?

---

[21] This is O'Regan's view despite his brilliant and sensitive reading of Hegel. He
believes that Hegel has 'swerved' away from orthodox tradition by incorporating
elements from Gnosticism, Neoplatonism, and mysticism that subvert a properly
Christian understanding of God and the world on the model of creator and creation.
O'Regan's concerns about the Gnostic legacy are expressed more sharply in *Gnostic
Return in Modernity* (Albany: State University of New York Press, 2001) than in
*The Heterodox Hegel*. For further discussion, see below, Chap. 11, where I also
engage the criticism of William Desmond.

# 5

# The Concept, Knowledge, and Worship of God

## THE CONCEPT OF RELIGION
## AND THE CONCEPT OF GOD

We begin the first of two chapters on the concept of God: the first takes the form of a philosophical theology that reflects on the concept, knowledge, and worship of God, and it includes a consideration of the proofs of the existence of God; while the second offers a specifically Christian doctrine of the Trinity. Structural correspondences exist between these two approaches, but they represent a progression from a more generic to a more concrete treatment. The generic concept of God is at the heart of Hegel's treatment of *The Concept of Religion* in part 1 of the lectures, while the doctrine of the Trinity comprises the Christian idea of God with which the whole of part 3 is concerned either directly or indirectly. The concept of God is central to Hegel's philosophical enterprise: at the beginning of the lecture manuscript, as we have seen, he announces that God is the beginning and end of all things and is the one and only object of philosophy, the one topic in the many topics (1:84).

Hegel's treatment of *The Concept of Religion* evolved over a period of several years. In the 1821 manuscript he focuses in part 1 on the 'scientific conception of the religious standpoint' and concludes with a discussion of the relationship of religion to art and philosophy.[1] The 1824 lectures move from 'empirical observation' to the 'speculative concept of religion'. Only after he is well into the discussion does Hegel arrive at the insight that the concept of religion is absolute spirit in its self-mediation in the three

---

[1] At the heart of the 'religious standpoint' is the relationship of finite consciousness to the infinite, which speculatively understood is the return of the infinite to itself. So the concept of God is present in the concept of religion, but it is not explicitly developed in the 1821 lectures.

moments of substantial self-unity (the abstract concept of God), self-differentiation (the knowledge of God), and self-return (the worship of God). These moments produce the content of the concept of God (1:324–8). The second and third of these moments are further analysed in 1824 as comprising the 'theoretical' and the 'practical' religious relationships to God (1:328–64), while the first moment is deferred to parts 2 and 3 of the lectures where it becomes the framework for discussing the proofs of the existence of God that are associated with specific religions. This is as close as the 1824 lectures come to offering an explicit concept of God in part 1 (although many of the materials for such a concept are present).

The 1827 lectures bypass the preliminary considerations that occupy the 1821 and 1824 treatments of *The Concept of Religion* and move immediately into an exposition of the concept of God as the proper content of the concept of religion. This exposition unfolds in three steps: the abstract concept of God, religious consciousness or the knowledge of God, and the cultus or worship of God (1:366 n. 6). Much of the material from the 1821 and 1824 lectures is re-presented in clearer form. The 1831 lectures follow the 1827 structure, but with some interesting variations.[2] Our presentation in this chapter is guided by the 1827 lectures, with materials from the other lectures incorporated as needed.[3]

---

[2] 1:464–73 (see the editorial notes to this section). If Strauss's excerpts can be relied upon, it seems that the first main section in 1831 focuses on the relationship between the concept of God and the concept of religion, picking up themes from the 1824 and 1821 lectures. The 'soil of religion' is thought, which is the activity of the universal. God is not merely substance in general but self-knowing substance or subject. God is both knower and known, subject and object of divine knowing. God knows and loves godself in humanity, and humans know themselves in God. 'This is the concept of religion, that God knows himself in spirit and spirit knows itself in God.' The second main section is oriented not to the theme of the knowledge of God, as in 1827, but to the 'single forms of religion', which are feeling, representation, and faith. Rather than being viewed as the first and most immediate form, as in 1827, faith is now the highest of the religious forms of knowledge, replacing 'thought', which is treated in the first section. This intriguing valorization of faith (perhaps in response to the second edition of Schleiermacher's *Glaubenslehre*) focuses on its grounds or reasons as distinct from its basis in authority. The third main section treats the cultus in terms similar to 1827. But the 1831 lectures add a fourth section on the relationship of religion to the state, reflecting Hegel's renewed concern for this topic as a result of recent political events. Although he arrived at his mature treatment of the concept of religion in 1827, Hegel did not cease experimenting.

[3] The discussion that follows draws at several points on the editorial introduction I wrote for the one-volume edition of the *Lectures on the Philosophy of Religion: The*

## THE ABSTRACT CONCEPT OF GOD

This section appears as such only in the 1827 lectures, although analogues to it are found in the other lectures where it is used as a vehicle to present proofs of the existence of God. These proofs constitute a specific religion's 'abstract concept' or 'metaphysical concept' of God, and the proofs are discussed as they appear in the determinate religions (part 2) and the Christian religion (part 3). The 1827 lectures gather all the proofs together into a lengthy subsection ('Religious Knowledge as Elevation to God') at the end of the section on 'The Knowledge of God' in part 1; and it is in this context that we shall consider the proofs later in this chapter. As a consequence, the first section of part 1, 'The Concept of God', needed to be filled with a new content.

This content, according to the 1827 lectures, is supplied by the whole of philosophy that precedes the philosophy of religion (the science of logic and the philosophies of nature and spirit). It is the idea that 'God is the absolute truth, the truth of all things.' The highest point at which philosophy arrives is the proof that 'this universal, which is in and for itself, embracing and containing absolutely everything, is that through which alone everything is and has subsistence—that this universal is the truth. This *One* is the result of philosophy' (1:367). Hegel provides no proof of this proof, telling his hearers that at this point they have only his assurance that God is the result of philosophy (1:368). Demonstrating the proof would require retracing the whole philosophical encyclopedia. But support comes from religious consciousness, which has the conviction that God is 'the midpoint, the absolutely true, that from which everything proceeds and into which everything returns, that upon which everything is dependent and apart from which nothing other than it has absolute, true independence'. Hegel is in effect starting with the ordinary meaning and use of the word God, which is confirmed by philosophical analysis.

This definition of God as the universal truth of all things seems to be abstract. Indeed, at the beginning, we say that 'God is what is enclosed within itself [*das in sich Verschlossene*] or is in absolute

*Lectures of 1827* (Berkeley and Los Angeles: University of California Press, 1988; Oxford: Oxford University Press, 2005), 1–71. I also rely to some degree on the editorial notes, which are the same in the unabridged edition and the one-volume edition.

unity with itself.' This does not mean, however, that God is an abstract universality outside and over against which there are independent particulars, but rather that the 'development' of God does not step forth out of the universality. The universal will indeed 'show itself to be something absolutely concrete, rich, and full of content', but this development is already contained within the 'absolutely full, replete universality' that is God (1:368–9). Strictly speaking, nothing subsists 'outside' God; God is the whole, the universal, that embraces all particularity within itself. The abstract universal proves from the outset to be a very concrete universal.

Expressed in more familiar philosophical categories deriving from Spinoza,[4] we say that 'God is the absolute substance, the only true actuality'—the substance or essence upon which everything else depends for its existence (1:369). If we cling to this declaration in its abstract form, then we seem to be guilty of Spinozism or pantheism. 'But the fact that God is *substance* does not exclude *subjectivity*.' Indeed, substance is an attribute of God's absolute being-with-self and abiding-with-self that we call *spirit*, *absolute spirit*. When we speak of substance, 'the universal is not yet grasped as internally concrete'; only when it is so grasped is it spirit (1:370–1). God is not sheer, undifferentiated substance, not a 'mere soil' out of which distinctions subsequently grow, but an 'abiding unity' in which all distinctions remain enclosed: just this is the meaning of the immanent Trinity as an inexhaustible generative matrix. Thus in creating the world God does not step out of unity with godself. God remains the One, the abundant universal—'not an inert, abstract universal, but rather the absolute womb or the infinite fountainhead out of which everything emerges, into which everything returns, and in which it is eternally maintained' (1:372–4). With these sensual, sexual images drawn from a Neoplatonic-mystical trajectory, Hegel unpacks the definition of God as universal substance. At the same time he remarks that we have

---

[4] *Ethics*, part 1, esp. prop. 11 (*The Chief Works of Benedict de Spinoza*, trans. R. H. M. Elwes (New York: Dover, 1951), 2. 51–4). Spinoza's use of 'substance' derives in turn from Aristotle, for whom 'substance' (*ousia*) is the fundamental metaphysical category, designating the 'essence' of things. The absolute substance is eternal, universal, unmovable, actual, and rational: this substance is God. See *Metaphysics*, 12.7, 1072$^b$18–30 (a passage quoted by Hegel at the end of his *Encyclopedia of the Philosophical Sciences*, § 577 (*Hegel's Philosophy of Mind*, trans. William Wallace and A. V. Miller (Oxford: Clarendon Press, 1971), 315)). In Hegel's *Logic*, substance appears under the category of 'essence' (*Wesen*).

this God not primarily in the mode of feeling and sensation but in the mode of *thought*. The mystical and the rational are (typically, for Hegel) connected. 'Thought is alone the soil for this content, is the activity of the universal—the universal in its activity and efficacy.' 'Animals have feelings, but only feelings. Human beings think, and they alone have religion.' Thus religion has its 'inmost seat' in thought, though doubtless (as we shall see) it can also be felt, believed, imagined, and practised (1:372–3).

This is the abstract concept of God that emerges from speculative philosophy, and Hegel spells it out for the first time in the 1827 lectures. Some people, he adds, want to designate this idea of God as 'pantheism', and the philosophy associated with it as 'identity-philosophy' (a term used by Schelling to characterize his main writings of 1801–4). Hegel encountered the charge of pantheism directed against his own philosophy for the first time in the mid-1820s, and he took the occasion of this new section in the 1827 lectures to offer a thorough refutation (1:374–80, 432).[5] If 'pantheism' means literally that everything is God—this paper, this snuffbox, this table—then no serious philosophy has ever maintained that. Authentic pantheism (whether Spinozistic or Oriental) identifies God with the *essence*, the *substance*, the *universal power* that is in all things, not with things as such. Since this essence is what, philosophically speaking, is actual, the world in the strict sense has no 'actuality' (*Wirklichkeit*), although it is of course empirically real. The tendency of Spinoza's philosophy is toward acosmism rather than atheism (see 1:377 nn. 27, 28), since above all it is the actuality of God that is affirmed by this philosophy rather than the actuality of the world. Those who accuse Spinoza (and Hegel) of 'atheism' merely prove that they are unable to liberate themselves from finitude, since for them the 'actual' must be only what is empirical, present to sense experience.

Hegel returns to the question of pantheism in part 2 of the 1827 lectures in the context of his discussion of Buddhism (2:572–5). Here he adds a helpful clarification. The expression 'one and all' (*hen kai pan*), attributed by Jacobi to Lessing,[6] properly means, according to Hegel, 'the one All, the All that remains utterly one'.

---

[5] See 1:370 n. 11, 375 n. 20. A similar refutation is offered in the lengthy remark Hegel added to § 573 of the *Encyclopedia* when he revised this work in 1827. See *Hegel's Philosophy of Mind*, 302–13.

[6] Friedrich Heinrich Jacobi, *Briefe über Spinoza*, 22, 23, 62 (*Werke* (Leipzig, 1812–1825), 4/1. 54, 55, 89). See 1:370 n. 11, 377 n. 31.

But *pan* can also mean 'everything', in which case one understands 'pantheism' to mean that 'everything is God' (*Allesgötterei*) not that 'the All is God'. The latter is the only serious philosophical meaning of pantheism, namely that God is the All or the whole *in which* everything finite participates and has its essential being, but with which things are not identical. Such a philosophy may properly be called 'panentheism', but Hegel lacked this term. Rather he points out that 'pantheism' is a poor expression because the *pan* can be taken as a 'collective totality' (*Allesheit*), not as 'universality' (*Allgemeinheit*). This distinction is of relevance to later charges by twentieth-century critics that Hegel's philosophy is 'totalizing'. The All (*das All*) or the whole (*das Ganze*) or the universal (*das Allgemeine*) is not totalizing from Hegel's perspective because it gives to finite things their free and independent existence; it is not a homogenizing collectivity in which everything is reduced to the same.

A similar ambiguity is present in the term 'identity-philosophy'. The crucial question, which the term merely serves to obscure, is whether this identity—or, more precisely, unity—is defined as abstract substance or as concrete spirit. Philosophy is a study of how unity through its successive forms becomes continually more determinate (1:379–80). In the *Encyclopedia of the Philosophical Sciences*, Hegel remarks in a similar vein that 'the deepest and last of the determinations of unity is that of absolute spirit'.[7] Absolute spirit is not a totalizing substance but a unity that both generates and emerges from determinacy and difference.

THE KNOWLEDGE OF GOD

The abstract concept of God corresponds to the first moment of the divine life, God's primordial self-unity or the immanent Trinity of Christian theology. In the second moment, absolute universality posits its inner distinctions outwardly by means of a primal division or judgement (*Urteil*). In this way the world comes into being as the created other of God, which, according to Christian theology, is the work of the eternal Son or Logos. With the creation

---

[7] *Encyclopedia*, § 573 remark (see *G. W. F. Hegel: Theologian of the Spirit*, ed. Peter C. Hodgson (Minneapolis: Fortress Press; Edinburgh: T&T Clark, 1997), 150).

of human beings, we have for the first time two elements, God and consciousness, and God becomes an object of consciousness (1:380–1). The relationship of God and consciousness can be viewed from two perspectives. In terms of divine action, the creation of the world is precisely what it means for God to manifest or reveal godself. 'Spirit is an absolute manifesting. Its manifesting is a positing of determination and a being for an other' (1:381). God's very nature is to reveal godself, to be manifest, to be known. God is a mystery, to be sure, but not a secret. 'A mystery is something profound, and later among the Neoplatonic philosophers it is the speculative element that expresses the immediate God' (1:382 n. 44). This mystery is a rational mystery: it makes itself known, it is not jealous to the point of not communicating itself. Just as a lamp is not diminished when its light is passed on to another lamp, so 'God loses nothing when he communicates himself. Therefore this knowledge on the part of the subject is a relationship that issues from God; and, as issuing from God, it is the absolute judgement that God *is as* spirit *for* spirit' (1:382–3).

From the point of view of human beings (the second perspective), the relationship between God and consciousness yields four basic forms of the knowledge of God: immediate knowledge, feeling, representation, and thought.[8] It is these that are addressed in the second main section of the 1827 *Concept of Religion*.

## Immediate Knowledge: Certainty, Faith

Immediate knowledge is the immediate certainty that God *is*, and indeed that God is 'this universality having being in and for itself [*diese an und für sich seiende Allgemeinheit*], outside me and independent of me, not merely having being for me' (1:386). Certainty (*Gewißheit*) is the immediate relation of this content and myself. The first and most basic form of this certainty is that of *faith* (*Glaube*), which is not to be placed in opposition to knowledge (*Wissen*) but is a form of knowledge (1:386–9). Hegel does not frequently use the term 'faith', probably because of his polemic

---

[8] These forms are 'partly psychological' in character (1:385), and indeed the discussion here bears a number of resemblances to the first part of the section on 'psychology' in the *Encyclopedia* (§§ 445–68), where Hegel provides a psychology of 'theoretical mind', or what we would call 'epistemology'.

against Jacobi[9] and Schleiermacher. But he introduces it here in place of the term used in his general epistemology, 'intuition' (*Anschauung*).[10] The reason is that the certainty faith possesses of its object, God, cannot be based on any sort of immediate sensible intuition since God is not an object of sense experience. Nor does faith possess insight into the *necessity* of its content, which would be 'intellectual' intuition. In neither the Kantian (sensible) nor speculative (intellectual) senses does the word 'intuition' properly identify that form of immediate knowledge which is distinctively religious. For the latter the word 'faith' is the most appropriate.

Faith means holding something to be true (*Furwährhalten*)[11] for which we lack direct empirical evidence or intellectual intuition of its necessity. The grounds or reasons for such faith derive partly from the testimony of others whom we trust, and in this respect faith rests on external authority. But the true authority and proper testimony on which faith relies is that of the witness of the Spirit. This witness is not simply that of the Holy Spirit but 'the witness of one's own spirit … that this content conforms to the nature of my spirit and satisfies the needs of my spirit' (1:389; cf. 1:243–5). In this sense faith is an immediate knowledge and verification of an objective content, a judgement that a congruence exists between my existence and the content (e.g. the credo of the church).

Faith has two major forms or modalities: feeling (which illumines its subjective aspect) and representation (which concerns the objective mode of its content, how it is an object of consciousness for us).[12]

*Feeling*

In the 1821 lecture manuscript Hegel normally uses the term *Empfindung* (sensibility, sensation) for describing the subjectivity of faith, but in the 1824 and 1827 lectures it has been replaced by *Gefühl* (feeling). This change undoubtedly reflects the impact of

[9] In the 1824 lectures he notes that while it is correct to say that we have an immediate knowledge, it is not our *only* knowledge of God, as claimed by Jacobi, who called this immediate knowledge 'faith' (1:261).
[10] 'Intuition' is analysed in the *Encyclopedia*, §§ 446–50, and in the 1821 philosophy-of-religion lecture manuscript (1:234–7).
[11] See Hegel's Foreword to Hinrichs's *Religion*, discussed above in Chap. 2.
[12] By contrast, in the 1831 lectures faith is designated as the third and highest form of religious knowledge, into which feeling and representation issue (1:467–9). But the character of faith is described similarly in 1827 and 1831.

Friedrich Schleiermacher's *Der christliche Glaube*, first published in 1821–2, which introduced the term *Gefühl* as a major theological category and made it a topic of controversy. While *Empfindung* and *Gefühl* are closely related, there is a subtle distinction between them, as Hegel himself recognizes.[13] 'Sensibility' points to sensations, which are single and transient modifications of the self, and which are received in a mode of immediacy, as they are 'found' (*emp-finden*). 'Feeling' by contrast points to the activity of the self, which integrates the sensations into a 'reflected totality'. While feeling arises from sense, it belongs to the realm of ideality, of subjectivity. Thus it can express a relationship of immediacy to nonsensible objects such as God. When I say that 'I feel God', I mean that God is within my being: we are not two but one, yet the one remain two, for God is not a product of my feeling but exists independently of me as the ground of my being (1:268–70).

Had Hegel stressed the latter aspect, he might have come closer to Schleiermacher's understanding of religious feeling as the consciousness of being utterly or absolutely dependent on God. But instead he stresses the aspect of feeling as immediate contact, with analogies drawn from sense experience. This is an important aspect of feeling for Hegel. When I say that 'I feel something hard', the common element that links myself and the something is 'hardness': there is hardness in my feeling, and the object is also hard. In this way 'the object impinges on me, and I am filled with its determinate character' (1:270). This helps to explain why feeling is presently in vogue: when we feel something, 'we are personally and subjectively involved' in it, giving validity to ourselves as well as to the thing felt. 'Heart' is a metaphor of feeling. 'What one has in one's heart belongs to the being of one's personality, to one's inmost being.' Thus it is quite appropriate that we should be expected not only to *know* God, right, duty, and the like, but to have these things in our *feeling*; religion is a matter of the heart (and stomach) as well as of the head. We thus become physically (not just spiritually) identified with what we believe, and we act accordingly (1:390–1). It is just this role that feeling (tasting) plays in the partaking of the eucharistic elements.[14]

But there are severe limitations to feeling. As such, it is indeterminate, neither good nor evil, neither true nor false. 'Every content

---

[13] See *Encyclopedia*, §§ 402–3, and 1:268–9 n. 20.
[14] See below, Chap. 9, pp. 190–1.

is capable of being in feeling: religion, right, ethics, crime, passions.' Because of its subjective involvement, feeling has no capacity for making *judgements* with respect to the validity of its contents. Thus the feelings of the heart must be purified and cultivated, and this involves precisely *thought*. When we think, 'consciousness has made its entrance, and [with it] a parting or division that was not yet in feeling.... Consciousness is the ejection of the content out of feeling; it is a kind of liberation.' Moreover, contents such as a God, right, and duty do not belong to feeling in the sense of having been produced by it; they are determinations of the 'rational will' and hence products of thought. They may be and in fact are also in feeling, but in an 'inadequate mode'; 'thought is the soil in which this content [God] is both apprehended and engendered alike' (1:391–6, cf. 270–1, 372).

Hegel delivers the *coup de grâce* to feeling when he remarks in the 1824 lectures that 'feeling is what human beings have in common with the animals; it is the animal, sensuous form'. Feeling is the lowest form, and when a content such as right, ethical life, or God is posited in feeling, this is 'the very worst way' that it can be posited (1:273, 275). Human beings like animals feel their limit as finite creatures bounded by the world, but as spiritual beings they also *know* their limits and thus transcend them. Only human beings have religion, because only they have thought. But if, as with Schleiermacher, 'we say that religion rests on this feeling of dependence, then animals would have to have religion too, for they feel this dependence' (1:279). Here *Gefühl* seems to have devolved back into nothing but *Empfindung*, and this caricature of Schleiermacher ignores the fact that for him the feeling of *utter* or *absolute* dependence is not a sense-based experience at all but is a prereflective awareness of the whence and whither of all existence.[15] Because it is the condition of possibility for living in and knowing the world, it bears a resemblance to what Edmund Husserl calls the 'natural attitude', or *Urglaube*. It is closer to Hegel's 'immediate knowledge' or 'faith' than to the latter's depiction of feeling, except

---

[15] Schleiermacher explicitly distinguishes between feelings of relative freedom and dependence vis-à-vis the world and the feeling of utter or absolute (*schlechthinig*) dependence on God. Friedrich Schleiermacher, *Der christliche Glaube*, §§ 4–5 (*The Christian Faith*, ed. H. R. Mackintosh and J. S. Stewart (Edinburgh: T&T Clark, 1928), 12–26). However, this distinction is not as clear in the first edition of his work (1821–2), to which Hegel had access, as in the second (1830–1). See 1:279 n. 37.

that it also includes insight into the necessity of its content and thus approximates intellectual intuition. Feeling is for Schleiermacher a mode of apprehension independent of knowing and doing, yet the ground of both, whereas for Hegel it is a (limited) form of knowledge. Neither Hegel nor Schleiermacher adequately understood the position of the other, nor did they appreciate how they could make use of the same or similar terms quite differently; hence their mutual polemics were often misdirected.[16] Notably, Hegel's critique of Schleiermacher is not repeated in the 1827 lectures.

## Representation

Religion is a matter of both feeling and representation, and the question arises as to which is prior. The question can be answered in two ways. Since feeling is indeterminate and can contain any possible content, it is correct to say that it is prior. But feeling itself cannot serve as the justifying criterion for its content; it cannot determine that something is true just because it is in feeling. Hence when it comes to the matter of truth, representation is prior. Indeed, we know that religious instruction begins with representation. 'By means of doctrine and teaching the feelings become aroused and purified; they are cultivated and brought into the heart' (1:402–3).

Representation (*Vorstellung*) attends to the objective aspect, the content, of whatever it is that we are subjectively certain of, but it does not yet penetrate this content rationally or cognitively. It relies on the understanding (*Verstand*), which places images and sense impressions *under* categories (*ver-stehen*) and *before* the mind (*vor-stellen*) as objective, unmediated ideas. 'Representation is a consciousness of something that one has before oneself as something objective' (1:396). Since this is how people ordinarily think, 'religion is the consciousness of absolute truth in the way that it occurs for all human beings'. Philosophy has the same content, and its task is solely that of transforming representations into concepts. The content remains the same, although philosophy is often reproached for removing the content as it separates out from it what

---

[16] Schleiermacher certainly had Hegel in mind when he warned against the importation of speculative philosophy into Christian dogmatics. *Der christliche Glaube*, § 28.3 (*The Christian Faith*, 122).

pertains only to representation (1:396–7).[17] This operation is supposed to be not a reduction but a transformation, yet the question remains as to how and to what extent representational images continue to reverberate in concepts. Without images, concepts become dry and abstract. Hegel's own thinking is famously replete with images, metaphors, and analogies, although he is not as explicit as he might have been about the role of imagination in thought.

Representation has two basic forms, or configurations: sensible and nonsensible. The sensible forms we call 'images' (*Bilder*), for which the principal content or mode is taken from immediate, sensible intuition (1:397–400). But what the image signifies is not merely an immediate, sensible object. Rather it has a double signification, 'first the immediate and then what is meant by it, its inner meaning'. Thus the image is something symbolic, allegorical, metaphorical, mythical (Hegel does not further distinguish and define these figurative forms here). When, for example, we say that 'God has begotten a son', we know quite well that this is not meant in the literal sense but rather that it signifies 'a different relationship, which is something like this one'.

Not only what is manifestly figurative (*bildlich*) belongs to representation in its sensible aspect but also things that are to be taken as historically real. To be sure, many narratives having the appearance of history, especially religious narratives, are purely mythical, such as stories about Jupiter; but there are other narratives that are supposed to be, and in fact are, history in the proper sense, such as the story of Jesus. But this story is really 'twofold': it is both an outward history, the ordinary story of a human being, and a divine history, a divine happening, deed, action. 'This absolute divine action is the inward, the genuine, the substantial dimension of this history', and in that sense the outward history is representational of an inward action (1:399). The outward history is representational in another sense as well, as we have seen:[18] in it God sets godself forth in the world in the mode of determinacy and object-

---

[17] In the lecture manuscript Hegel remarks that nothing is further from the intention of speculative philosophy 'than to overthrow religion, i.e. to assert that the content of religion cannot for itself be the truth. On the contrary, religion is precisely the true content but in the form of representation, and philosophy is not the first to offer substantive truth. Humanity has not had to await philosophy in order to receive for the first time the consciousness or cognition of truth' (1:251).

[18] See above, Chap. 2, pp. 38–9.

ivity. Representation is a metaphysical as well as an epistemological category.

Included also under representation are nonsensible configurations (*nichtsinnliche Gestaltungen*), which do not depend on sensible images or figures, although they may originally have derived
from them (1:400–1). These have to do with spiritual (*geistige*)
contents, activities, relationships. For example, if we say, 'God
created the world', then the terms 'God' and 'world' are function-
ing as nonsensible representations, and the reference is not to an
empirical activity. God, after all, is the universal that is determined
within itself in manifold ways, but in this representational statement we have God on the one side and the world on the other.
Similarly, the world is an endlessly manifold complex, but when
we say 'world' we have it in the simple mode of representation.
Although these and other terms—indeed, the whole vocabulary of
religion and theology—proceed from thought and have their 'seat
and soil' in thought, they are representational in form, since they
exist alongside each other as independent entities, linked by conjunctions; they are not yet inwardly analysed and conceptually
mediated in such a way that their distinctions and connections
are seen to be essential.

*Thought*

The section on thought (*Denken*) in the 1827 lectures is quite long,
and we are presently discussing only the first two parts of it, which
are concerned with the relationship of thought and representation
and the question whether knowledge is immediate or mediated.
With respect to the first of these, the primary point is that representation apprehends its various contents (sensible and spiritual)
in their determinate *isolation*, whereas thought seeks for *relationships* and *universality*. 'Thought dissolves the form of the simple,
in which the content is found in representation, in such a way that
distinct determinations within this simple reality are grasped and
exhibited so that it is known as something *inwardly manifold*'
(1:404–6). Thought does this by raising representational configurations to conceptual form. A 'concept' (*Begriff*) precisely grasps-
or holds-together (*be-greifen*) those elements that remain disparate
in the simple placing-before (*vor-stellen*) the mind of various sensible or nonsensible images. Conceptual thinking for the most part
does not invent new terms or convert everything into the grammar

of logic but makes use of the materials furnished by representation. What it does is to develop arguments and hypotheses that elucidate the unity—indeed, the necessary unity—of representational features. It grasps the logical relations implicit in narrative relations. In this fashion it arrives at 'conviction' (*Überzeugung*), which is certainty in the form of thought. Thought is not a new conceptual apparatus but a way of thinking dialectically. Thus it is evident that thought continues to be fructified by the imagistic materials thrown up by representation; without representation there could be no thought, and a dialectic between representation and thought is constantly taking place—a point about which Hegel is not sufficiently clear.

As an example, Hegel offers certain of the attributes of God (1:406). Using language drawn from the Bible, we say that God is both gracious and just, or both omnipotent and wise. For representation, these qualities abide peacefully alongside each other. The task of dialectic is to show first of all that they contradict each other: benevolence contradicts justice, and the omnipotence that negates everything determinate contradicts the wisdom that wills something determinate. But then the task of dialectical thinking is to show that as applied to God these qualities are mutually and necessarily connected. The goal of thought is necessity: 'we call something "necessary" when, if one [element] exists, the other is thereby posited'.

Necessity entails mediation, and this leads Hegel into a discussion of the relationship of immediate and mediated knowledge (1:407–11). Immediacy is the principle of representation, while for thought mediation is essential. True thought or 'comprehension' (*Begreifen*) unites both of these elements. Immediate knowledge is the coherence of myself with being, while mediated knowledge concludes one thing from another by reasoning. Immediate knowledge is empirical, while mediated knowledge in its highest form is speculative. Immediacy in fact is never present to the exclusion of mediation, for there is no such thing as pure immediacy (except as an abstraction). This is because everything is connected. In place of pure immediacy we have pure relationality. Hegel offers as an example the opening moves of the logic, the dialectic that shows how being (sheer immediacy) turns into nothing (negative immediacy), and how the truth of both is becoming ('what becomes already is, although in another sense it is not but only comes to be for the first time').[19] Knowledge is always mediated because it involves both a subjective element (the act of knowing) and a content (the object that is known). The connection of immediacy and mediation is consummated when what is known corresponds fully to the act of knowing, when thought knows itself in the objects of thought. This is 'absolute knowing', but it is more a goal than an achievement, and Hegel discusses it only briefly in the concluding chapter of the *Phenomenology of Spirit*.[20] For the most part philosophy is 'on the way', not at the goal, which in religious terms could only be the beatific vision and God's self-knowing.

As far as religious knowledge is concerned (1:411–13), it is on the one hand mediated: we are educated within a religion and receive doctrinal instruction, positive religion is based on revelation, external to the individual, and so on. But on the other hand 'neither positive revelation nor education can bring about religion in such a way that religion would be effected from outside, something mechanically produced and placed within human beings'. Mediated knowledge rather brings about a 'stimulation' (*Erregung*), a 'recollection' (*Erinnerung*), of something that we originally bear within ourselves, immediately. 'Religion, right, ethics, and everything spiritual in human being is merely aroused [*erregt*]. We are implicitly spirit, for the truth lies within us and the spiritual content within us must be brought into consciousness.' Mediation is what brings it to consciousness, and without mediation it would slumber in immediacy. Something must arouse us from our slumber. That something is thought.

PROOFS OF THE EXISTENCE OF GOD

The third and final subsection of 'Thought' in the 1827 lectures, while headed 'Religious Knowledge as Elevation to God', is concerned with the proofs of the existence of God (see 1:414 n. 109). Hegel's transition to this topic is rather complex. At the beginning of the discussion of 'immediate and mediated knowledge', he says

---

[19] 1:410. See *Encyclopedia*, §§ 86–8 (*The Encyclopedia Logic*, trans. T. F. Geraets, W. A. Suchting, and H. S. Harris (Indianapolis: Hackett, 1991), 136–45).

[20] Equally brief is the concluding section on philosophy in the *Encyclopedia*, §§ 572–7, where Hegel devotes most of his attention to the relationship between philosophy and religion and then summarizes the doctrine of the triple syllogism from the logic.

that 'mediated knowledge emerges more nearly in the form of the so-called proofs for God's existence' (1:407). Knowledge of God entails a mediation between myself and an object other than myself, God. The mediation between two terms in a syllogism is provided by the third term, which has the character of a proof. Thus the knowledge of God takes the form of the proofs of God's existence. Moreover, the mediation contained in this knowledge is religion itself, for religion is an act of mediation: it is not simply a reference to an object but inwardly a movement, a passing over or an elevation to God. The passage is of a twofold sort: from finite to infinite being (or from finite being to the concept of God), and from subjective to objective infinitude (or from the concept of God to the being of God). The first of these passages corresponds to the cosmological and teleological proofs, the second to the ontological proof. The proofs, then, are the concrete forms that the knowledge of God assumes in the various religions (1:411–16).

In all the other lecture series, Hegel treats the proofs in relation to the concepts of God that appear in specific religions: the cosmological proofs in relation to the religions of nature and to Jewish and Greek religion, the teleological proof in relation to Roman religion, and the ontological proof in relation to the Christian religion. Only in the 1827 lectures does he gather all of the proofs into one section toward the end of *The Concept of Religion*. This may simply be the consequence of Hegel's continuing experimentation with the structure of the lectures. Or it may be an attempt to give the proofs a greater impact in response to the charge of atheism directed against his philosophy, or even to ward off the threat of atheism in the modern secular-bourgeois world. During his last years in Berlin, Hegel seems to have been concerned with the question of the reality-status of God; he gave separate lectures on the proofs of the existence of God in the summer of 1829 and was intending to prepare them for publication when he died in 1831.[21]

Before discussing the proofs individually, Hegel addresses two significant questions: the distortion present in most proofs, and the authentic form of the proofs. This material is new in 1827, and it

---

[21] These lectures were appended to volume 12 of the *Werke* edition of the *Lectures on the Philosophy of Religion*, and are included in the translation of the latter by E. B. Speirs and J. Burdon Sanderson (London: Kegan Paul, Trench Trubner & Co., 1895), 3. 155–327. A critical edition of this material is found in vol. 18 of Hegel's *Gesammette Werke*, ed. Walter Jaeschke (Hamburg: Felix Meiner Verlag, 1995).

seems intended to salvage the proofs from the general discredit into which they have fallen. Two sorts of distortion are present in the attempt to 'prove' God's 'existence'. The first (1:417–18) is the suggestion that God can be said to 'exist', for 'existence' (*Dasein*) refers to determinate, finite being, whereas God's being is in no way limited (see 1:415 n. 111). It would be better to say, 'God and his being, his actuality or objectivity', and the purpose of the proofs would be to show the connection or coherence (*Zusammenhang*) between God and being (*Sein, Wesen*), that is, between the concept of God and the being (or actuality, objectivity) of God. The second distortion (1:419–21) is the notion that it is possible to 'prove' or demonstrate God's being from finite being, for this would be to make God a result or a consequence, dependent upon the being of the finite, whereas God is precisely the nonderivative, is 'utterly actual being in and for itself'. But religion remains an 'elevation' to God even after this form of demonstration has been stripped away. The Kantian critique of the demonstrative form of the proofs cannot be considered to have demolished religious knowledge and activity as such. It is only that 'elevation' to God does not properly entail a 'demonstration' of the infinite from the finite on the basis of a self-projection of the finite.

This brings us to the authentic form of the proofs (1:421–5). Hegel's point, put concisely, is that the religious elevation to the infinite, which is engendered by our awareness of finitude and contingency, is not based upon an 'affirmation' of the finite, its self-extension or projection into infinitude, for that would result in the 'spurious infinite' (a merely extended finite); rather it is based on the *negation* of the finite, its self-cancelling or sublation. The finite thus becomes aware of the infinite not as one 'aspect' of a relationship but as the whole, that which overreaches both finite and infinite, includes negation within itself, and thus alone truly is. What is 'affirmative' or active is not the finite but the infinite. The religious relationship and hence the proofs are based not on an autonomous self-elevation of finite spirit, but, speculatively expressed, on the return of infinite or absolute spirit to itself in and through the self-negation of finite spirit.[22]

---

[22] In the 1824 and 1821 lectures Hegel presents the same analysis as part of developing the speculative concept of religion, which entails a 'reversal' in the relationship between finite and infinite. See our discussion of this material in Chap. 4.

*The Cosmological Proof*

Hegel's discussion of the specific proofs in the 1827 lectures simply illustrates and confirms the last two points. He starts with the cosmological proof (1:426–7), which is an attempt to argue from the contingency of the world to absolutely necessary existence. But this is not a valid argument, since something that is necessary cannot be demonstrated from something that is contingent. Hegel mentions the cosmological proof in 1827 only to dismiss it. He treats it more thoroughly in the 1821 and 1824 lectures, and in 1824 he also distinguishes between three basic forms of the cosmological proof, related to specific religions: the argument from finite to infinite (the religions of nature), the argument from the many to the one (Jewish religion), and the argument from contingency to necessity (Greek religion).[23]

In regard to the first (2:250–66), Hegel notes that at the basis of all religious proofs is the fundamental religious activity of human beings, which is that of 'rising' from finite to infinite, from singular to universal, to being-in-and-for-itself. This 'elevation' or 'transition' occurs when finitude becomes aware of its own nothingness, negation, and limit; in fact, the limit of the finite is precisely the infinite, and in this sense the finite already belongs to and 'is' its other, the infinite. However, just because what constitutes the transition is the self-*negation* of the finite, a proof cannot be based on it. To posit the infinite from the finite is to assume that the finite *is* something, but it is in fact nothing in itself. The only genuine proof of the infinite is its self-proof.

The proof based on divine unity (2:392–5) utilizes the 'quite impoverished categories of one and many. It is an ancient dictum, which we find already in Greek sources, that only the One is, and not the many.' While this may be logically correct, the question is whether the One *is* God. The concept of God is not exhausted by the category of oneness, which is an undialectical category, lacking mediation.

The proof based on the argument from contingency to necessity (2:395–404) is logically similar to that from finite to infinite, but

---

[23] In the 1821 lectures, discussion of the cosmological proof is found in relation to nature religion at 2:100–4, and in relation to Jewish and Greek religion at 2:127–34. In the 1824 lectures, the discussion is found in relation to nature religion at 2:250–66, and in relation to Jewish and Greek religion at 2:390–404. In the following we shall focus on the 1824 version.

the 'contingent' is a richer, more concrete category than the 'finite', since it contains its own negation within itself. It is precisely what is only possible, it may exist or not exist, and therefore the *truth* of contingent existence is necessity. The necessity in question must be *inner* necessity, since external necessity is itself contingent. While the proof is logically correct to conclude that an absolutely necessary cause accounts for the existence of contingent things—for otherwise we would have an infinite regress—the proof is defective in that it sets up contingent things on one side and necessity on the other, and expresses the relation between them as one of 'presupposing', 'entailing', and so forth. Thus it appears that contingent things condition absolute necessity: *their* existence is the condition for concluding that absolute necessity also exists. But absolute necessity cannot be conditioned by or dependent on anything outside itself. The authentic form of this proof would be to start with the process of mediation intrinsic to absolute necessity, and to comprehend contingent things as moments or stages in the process, posited by the absolute precisely *as contingent*, as negative, as not having being in and for themselves. But this is the ontological proof, not the cosmological proof.

*The Teleological Proof*

The teleological proof is based on the experience of purposiveness or utility (*Zweckmässigkeit*). Hegel's treatment of it is similar in all of the lectures.[24] In the form in which we usually encounter this proof (e.g. in Roman religion) it is a matter of external rather than of internal purposiveness. Given the apparent, indeed marvellous harmony between externally related things in the world, a harmony that cannot be accounted for in terms of the things themselves, we must posit a third rationally ordering principle, which arranges specific means for specific ends. This proof has God involved in quite trivial and unworthy pursuits, such as providing cork trees in order to have stoppers for bottles, or mice for cats to feed upon. This is the 'physicotheological proof', and Kant has provided the classic refutation of it in the *Critique of Pure Reason*.[25]

[24] In the 1821 lectures it is found at 2:199–206; in the 1824 lectures at 2:404–21; and in the 1827 lectures at 1:427–33. The following summary is based on 1824 and 1827.
[25] Kant, *Critique of Pure Reason*, trans. Norman Kemp Smith (London: Macmillan, 1933), B 649–58 (pp. 518–24).

Hegel does not simply accept the Kantian critique but reworks and expands it. His key point again is that we cannot argue from empirically observed worldly circumstances, which are necessarily relative and finite, to the absolute and infinite. We cannot argue from power to *omni*potence, from wisdom to *omni*science. At best, what this proof affords is a concept of *great* wisdom, power, unity, and so on. But what we want in God is *absolute* wisdom, power, unity. 'From "great" to "absolute" we make the leap.' If the aim is to stir the heart, that can be achieved by this proof—'there is nothing upon which piety cannot feed'—but to achieve cognition of God by means of it is another matter. Nor can a proof be based on the assumed predominance of good over evil in ethical matters, for the evidence is quite ambiguous.

As an alternative to external purposiveness, Kant introduced in part 2 of his *Critique of Judgement* the 'important concept' of *inner* purposiveness or organic life (*Lebendigkeit*), according to which every living thing is a telos that has its means implicit within it (1:428–31). A reciprocal causality between parts and the whole is characteristic of living things. From finite organic life the proof leads to an absolute *Lebendigkeit*, to a universally purposive life, hence to a world-soul or *Nous*—not because the latter is required to account for finite arrangements and purposes but because of the negation of the particularity of finite organic life. This version of the physicotheological proof, however, arrives only at a definition of God as 'soul' or 'power', not as 'spirit', and it cannot make judgements as to the world-soul's goodness and wisdom. In this respect it remains deficient.

Kant believed that physicotheology must be supplanted by 'ethicotheology', which he defined in the *Critique of Judgement*[26] as the attempt to infer the supreme cause and its attributes not from the ends of *nature* but from the moral end of *rational beings* in nature—an end that can be known a priori. This is the programme he carried out in the *Critique of Practical Reason*, where he argued that God, as guarantor of the kingdom of ends and thus of the reality of the highest good, is a necessary postulate of action in accord with moral ends.[27] Kant regarded this as the only valid

---

[26] Kant, *Critique of Judgement*, trans. James Creed Meredith (Oxford: Clarendon Press, 1952), 2. 100–1 (§ 85).

[27] Kant, *Critique of Practical Reason*, trans. Lewis White Beck (New York: Liberal Arts Press, 1956), 128–36. Kant actually retains the traditional metaphysical concept of God as the first, highest, most perfect, and most real being, including

The Concept, Knowledge, and Worship of God 121

proof, but Hegel does not even discuss it in his lectures. Already in the 1790s Hegel was convinced of the failure of the moral interpretations of religion; consequently, moral teleology and its accompanying doctrine of postulates were in his view completely unpersuasive.[28]

## The Ontological Proof

Valid elements are contained in both the cosmological and the teleological proofs, but they find their correction and fulfilment in the ontological proof. This proof passes over, not from (finite) being to God, but from God to being, that is, from the concept of God to the being or reality of God. The insight into this proof, the only genuine proof, was attained only in the Christian era, and indeed not until the twelfth century, by Anselm of Canterbury.[29] The problem with Anselm's argument from 'perfection'—a problem clearly exposed by Kant—is that it *presupposes* the very unity

traditional ontological attributes such as substance, unity, simplicity, immutability, and extra-worldliness. Thus Kant's God cannot move, change, suffer, or interact with the world. The categories of temporality and historicality do not apply to God. In this respect Hegel's concept of God is much more radical than Kant's. However, Kant concludes that the existence of such a God cannot be demonstrated by rational, speculative, or transcendental theology. His critique of the ontological proof is at the core of his argument. The cosmological and physicotheological proofs depend on the validity of the ontological proof, although Kant has more sympathy for the physicotheological proof because it is based on empirical rather than transcendental principles. The alternative to rational theology is moral or ethicotheology, which provides a secure basis for faith in God. This is because the existence of God is a necessary postulate of practical reason: without a God of holiness, benevolence, justice, and infinite causality, and without a future world of moral perfection, there would be no incentives to act in accordance with moral duties. Here again a very traditional understanding of God comes back into the picture, one that Hegel found distinctly unattractive. Religion, rather than being a cultic and intellectual elevation to God (Hegel's mystical-speculative perspective), becomes a utility in the advance of moral behaviour. Kant's views are clearly set forth in his *Lectures on Philosophical Theology*, trans. Allen W. Wood and Gertrude M. Clark (Ithaca, NY: Cornell University Press, 1978).

[28] See Walter Jaeschke, *Reason in Religion: The Foundations of Hegel's Philosophy of Religion*, trans. J. Michael Stewart and Peter C. Hodgson (Berkeley and Los Angeles: University of California Press, 1990), chap. 1. Hegel's silence in respect to the moral proof is both puzzling and disappointing. Obviously he is utilizing Kant for his own philosophical agenda, and he scarcely can be regarded as an unbiased interpreter. The temptation (perhaps the necessity) of each new philosophical system is to 'destroy' its predecessors. Kant as interpreted by Hegel is deconstructed, and Hegel has suffered the same fate.

[29] Anselm, *Proslogion*, chap. 2 (*Anselm of Canterbury: The Major Works*, ed. Brian Davies and G. R. Evans (Oxford: Oxford University Press, 1988), 87–8).

of concept (thought) and being (reality) that must be demonstrated. Hegel responds to the Kantian critique with a post-Kantian version of the ontological proof, one based on his own logic. His first efforts at this in the 1821 and 1824 lectures are halting despite detailed analyses; in 1827 he goes considerably further toward his own position; but the 1831 lectures present the clearest argument.[30]

Kant claimed[31] that reality cannot be 'plucked' from the concept of God (as that being than which nothing greater can be thought) because 'being' is not a predicate that adds anything to a content: the existence of a hundred thalers adds nothing to the concept of a hundred thalers (I can imagine them without having them). Hegel's rejoinder is that 'concepts' such as these are ordinary representations, not concepts properly speaking. The true concept is not a subjective idea or a fantasy of the imagination. The true concept contains objectivity within itself.[32] It is alive and active; it mediates itself with itself; it is the movement or process of self-objectifying by which its subjectivity is sublated—just as, when human beings realize their drives or purposes, what was at first only ideal becomes something real (1:434–6, 438–9). 'We may concede that being is not a predicate, but we are not ... adding anything to the concept. Rather we are removing from it the shortcoming that it is only something subjective, not the idea.' The identity of the concept with being is not a presupposition but a result—the result of its own self-determining movement. The concept 'makes itself reality and thus becomes the truth, the unity of subject and object' (3:354–6). The most perfect concept is

---

[30] The 1821 text is found in 3:65–73; the 1824 text in 3:173–84; the 1827 text in 1:433–41. The *Werke* (2nd edn. (Berlin, 1840), 12. 546–53) provides in an appendix a full text of the ontological proof in the 1831 lectures; it is translated in 3:351–8. The following summary draws on the 1827 and the 1831 versions. For a recent and detailed study of Hegel's ontological proof, see Patricia Marie Calton, *Hegel's Metaphysics of God: The Ontological Proof as the Development of a Trinitarian Divine Ontology* (Aldershot: Ashgate, 2001). As the subtitle indicates, Calton regards the ontological proof as the key to Hegel's trinitarian ontology as a whole. It is possible to read the philosophy of religion from this perspective, but in my opinion such an approach overemphasizes the rational, conceptual aspect of religion in Hegel's treatment at the expense of the cultic, representational, and ethical aspects. With the idea that philosophical thinking reconciles humanity with God and completes the extrinsic or economic Trinity (95), Calton accepts too readily the Hegelian sublation of theology in philosophy, a topic to which I return at the end of Chap. 9.

[31] Kant, *Critique of Pure Reason*, B 620–30 (pp. 500–7).

[32] *Encyclopedia*, § 213 (*The Encyclopedia Logic*, 286).

the most perfectly real, and God is the most perfect concept. This logical truth becomes fully manifest in the Christian religion, which is the religion of incarnation: God takes on finite, worldly, determinate being (*Dasein*) in and through the process of self-diremption and self-return by which God becomes absolute spirit (1:437; 3:356–7). In this sense it is not, after all, inappropriate to speak of the *Dasein Gottes*. The proof of this sort of divine existence does not involve some illicit logical trick but is provided by God's self-involvement in world-process. God, who is utterly actual being (*das Seiende*), takes on worldly, determinate, existential being (*Dasein*). The religious elevation to God presupposes this divine descent.

Of course this proof will not work for those who have no concept of God, no knowledge of God, and no religious experience of elevation to God. There is no way of 'proving' a person into being religious. What is required is involvement in the practice of a religious community, its cultic activity, its worship of God.

## THE WORSHIP OF GOD

The third moment in the *Concept of Religion* corresponds to the third moment of the trinitarian dialectic, the return to and participation in God of all creatures through the sanctification of the Spirit. It is the most concrete and richest of the moments, building upon and subsuming the first two. Yet it was not until the 1827 lectures that a discussion of the cultus (*der Kultus*) or worship found its appropriate place in the structure of presentation. Moreover, the treatment of the cultus is quite brief. This is accountable in light of the fact that cultic activities are also discussed in relation to each of the determinate religions and to the Christian religion.[33]

In the case of the knowledge of God, the theoretical religious relationship, I am immersed in my object and know nothing of

---

[33] In the 1824 lectures, the cultus is taken up under the Speculative Concept of Religion as the second of two relationships to God, theoretical and practical (1:336–64). This section is a pot-pourri of topics and lacks the systematic discussion of the 1827 lectures. It focuses first on faith as the characteristic epistemological activity of the cultus, and on the verification of faith (whether by external authority or the inner witness of the Spirit); second, it provides a defence of speculative theology against the charge of pantheism; and finally it offers a survey of the history of the cultus in the religions (tracing a movement from 'restricted cultus' to 'cultus in the element of freedom'). The first two topics are treated elsewhere in the 1827 lectures.

myself. But the true situation is the *relationship* of myself and this object; I must *know myself* as filled by it. What accomplishes this unity is *action*, the activity of the cultus, which is accordingly the practical religious relationship (1:441–3). What I know theoretically becomes existentially relevant and involving. In the practical domain I exist on my own account and am free. I assimilate the object to myself and reinstate my feeling of self. Cultus is 'the including, within my own self, of myself with God, the knowing of myself within God and of God within me' (1:443). This is accomplished through the act of 'enjoyment', 'partaking', 'communion', or 'eucharist', which is the definitive cultic act (1:443). To describe it Hegel uses the term *Genuß*, which has at its root the physical image of eating and drinking: symbolically we ingest or assimilate the crucified God, who is really present in the sacramental elements.[34] This action does not *bring about* the reconciliation of God and humanity by a substitutionary atonement, for example, or by sacrifices pleasing to God. Rather it presupposes reconciliation, participates in it as something already implicitly and explicitly accomplished by the grace of God (1:443–4).[35]

Hegel remarks that 'today this aspect of the cultus is more or less pushed to one side and no longer stands forth in all its importance'. The preoccupation today (in Protestant churches) seems to be solely with subjective faith, not with participation in God through ritual practice. Yet 'in dogmatic theology the traditional chapter *de unione mystica* deals with the cultus. As a whole the mystical [*das Mystische*] is everything speculative [*Spekulative*], or whatever is concealed from the understanding. Feeling [*Gefühl*]—the gratification [*Genuß*] that I am with God in his grace and that God's spirit is alive within me, the consciousness of my union and reconciliation with God—this is the innermost feature of the cultus' (1:444–5). The juxtaposition of the categories *Mystische, Spekulative, Gefühl,* and *Genuß* in this passage is fascinating. The mystical union of the divine and the human, which is at the heart of speculative theology, is accomplished by a sensuous ritual action: here feeling understands more than the understanding, is more attuned to God's spiritual presence than hearing. The proclamation of the

[34] This point is elaborated more fully in the discussion of the cultus in the Christian religion (see Chap. 9 below).
[35] This matter is emphasized especially in the 1831 lectures. See 1:447 n. 180.

Word of God seems to be displaced as the central liturgical act by the celebration of Communion. Hegel distinguishes three basic forms of the cultus (1:445–6). The first is devotion (*Andacht*), which is 'not the mere faith that God is, but is present when the faith becomes vivid, when the subject prays and is occupied with this content not merely in objective fashion but becomes immersed therein; the essential thing here is the fire and heat of devotion'. *Andacht* is not irrational but a passionate, engaged thinking (*Denken*). Then there are two external cultic forms, the *sacraments* (reconciliation brought into feeling, into present sensible consciousness) and *sacrifice* (the negation of the finite by offering it up to God). An advance must occur from sacrifice (a negative action) to enjoyment, to consciousness of being in unity with God by means of the ritual action (the Christian eucharist). The third and highest form is *repentance*, whereby one not only renounces external things but also offers one's heart or inmost self to God.

When purity of heart is properly 'cultivated', it issues in *ethical life*, which is 'the most genuine cultus', but only to the extent that consciousness of God remains bound up with it (1:446). Thus social and political ethics represent an extension and 'realization' of the religious cultus—a point that Hegel briefly elaborates at the end of the 1827 lectures, in his treatment of the Christian cultus (3:341–2).[36]

The discussion concludes with the observation that 'philosophy [too] is a continual cultus; it has as its object the true, and the true in its highest shape as absolute spirit, as God. To know this true not only in its simple form as God, but also to know the rational in God's works— ... that is philosophy' (1:446–7). In this fashion Hegel reprises a theme with which he begins the lectures, namely that 'philosophy *is* theology, and [one's] occupation with philosophy—or rather *in* philosophy—is of itself the service and worship of God [*Gottesdienst*]' (1:84).[37] But, we may wonder, if philosophy

---

[36] In 1831, Hegel adds a section on 'The Relationship of Religion to the State' at the end of *The Concept of Religion*, immediately following 'The Cultus'. The text is reproduced in the *Werke* and is translated at 1:451–60.
[37] Hegel provides a brief summary of the whole of *The Concept of Religion* at the end of the 1827 lectures, at least according to Lasson's text (1:448–9): 'Stated in a cursory way, religion is our relation to God. We have said that this relation is found in thinking. The primal division [or judgement] of this implicit and explicit universal, or the creation, is self-particularizing, the differentiating of the particular spirit over against the absolute spirit. The first relationship that we considered was

does the work of theology, both intellectual and practical, what happens to theology itself? Does it simply disappear as an integral discipline? Or is it relegated to the realm of representational thinking? The Hegelian embrace of theology is a bit suffocating—a matter to which I return at the end of Chapter 9.

that of knowledge, the theoretical relationship. The second is the practical relationship or the knowledge of this elevation (and the elevation is itself knowledge). The third moment is the knowing of this knowing. That is actual religion.'

# 6

# Trinity:
# God as Absolute Spirit

## ABSOLUTE SPIRIT AND TRINITY

We come now to the concept of God as it 'develops' in the Christian religion. According to Hegel, this development unfolds in three 'elements', 'moments', 'spheres', or 'kingdoms':[1] the idea of God in and for itself (the immanent trinitarian relations as symbolized by divine 'persons'), the idea of God in representation and appearance (the history of the natural and human worlds coming to focus on the figure of Christ), and the idea of God in community and as the Holy Spirit (the presence of God in the community of the Spirit, which anticipates the redemption and consummation of all things in God).[2] In the first moment God subsists in abstract universality; then the universal 'sets itself forth' or appears as finite, particular, differentiated, separated; finally the now-concretized universal returns to itself as absolute subjectivity, absolute presence-to-self, or absolute spirit. 'It is in these three forms that the divine idea explicates itself. Spirit is the divine history, the process of self-differentiation, of diremption and return into self' (3:186–7). By this trinitarian self-mediation, God goes from being absolute substance to absolute subject. Subjectivity is 'the infinite elasticity of substance that enables it to diremt itself inwardly and make itself its own object'. God as spirit is 'infinite substantial subjectivity' (3:169).

---

[1] The language of 'elements' or 'moments' is used in the 1824 and 1827 lectures, while that of 'spheres' and 'kingdoms' is found in the 1831 lectures. Hegel's treatment of the topics covered in this chapter differs little from one lecture series to the next; hence I do not identify the sources for references except when there are reasons for doing so.

[2] 3:185–8 (1824); 3:271–4 (1827). On the evolution of this structure for treating the Christian religion, see 3:185 n. 65 and Chap. 4 above.

Hegel's clearest summary of this divine history is found in the 1827 lectures:

(1) First, in and for itself, God [is] in his eternity before the creation of the world and outside the world.

(2) Second, God creates the world and posits the separation. He creates both nature and finite spirit. What is thus created is at first an other, posited outside of God. But God is essentially the reconciling to himself of what is alien, what is particular, what is posited in separation from him. He must restore to freedom and to his truth what is alien, has fallen away in the idea's self-diremption, in its falling away from itself. This is the path and the process of reconciliation.

(3) In the third place, through this process of reconciliation, spirit has reconciled with itself what it distinguished from itself in its act of diremption, of primal division, and thus it is the Holy Spirit, the Spirit [present] in its community.

These are not external distinctions, which *we* have made merely in accord with what we are; rather they are the activity, the developed vitality, of absolute spirit itself.   (3:273–4)

When fully articulated this summary produces Hegel's speculative redescription of the Christian metanarrative. He sets it forth in the third part of the lectures on the philosophy of religion, to which we direct attention in the next four chapters.

The first of these chapters (the present one) focuses on the concept of God as absolute spirit, which is intrinsically a trinitarian concept. Spirit constitutes itself as spirit through a trinitarian dialectic. This is evident from the following compact definition of God: 'God in his eternal universality is the one who distinguishes himself, determines himself, posits an other to himself, and likewise sublates the distinction, thereby remaining present to himself, and is spirit only through this process of being brought forth' (3:284–5). Spirit is a process of being brought forth, or of bringing itself forth. It brings itself forth out of nature, out of God's created otherness, which it necessarily presupposes since spirit entails consciousness or cognition, and consciousness is always embodied. The self-cognition of absolute spirit rises up out of the multiple consciousnesses of finite spirit.[3] God as absolute spirit is the *unity* of spirit and nature: spirit is on one side of the union but also 'overreaches the other side; hence it is the unity of

---

[3] We have already noted in Chap. 1 the sensuous mystical imagery that Hegel employs in the 1824 lectures: 'Spirit is an eternal process of self-cognition,

itself and an other' (1:325, 352). Nature is other than spirit but ultimately not foreign or alien to spirit. It is encompassed within the divine life.

What makes spirit absolute and infinite is that all of its relationships occur within a divinely constituted community of recognition. The other that it absolves or releases to be an other is not posited as something beyond the range of absolute spirit such that it would delimit the absolute and render it finite. What limits God is brought inside God, so to speak. It is a spatial way of thinking that locates the world 'outside' of God. Hegel makes use of spatial imagery (as in the passage quoted above), but also makes clear that it is conceptually inadequate, just as temporal imagery is inadequate for grasping the eternal divine history (3:187–8). Finite spirits, of course, have external relations: just this is the meaning of their finitude, of their existence in space and time. Absolute spirit incorporates this externality, but its own relations are properly internal, which is to say that they are moments or dimensions of an organic intersubjectivity, an inwardly differentiated whole. The terms of these relations are genuinely but not totally other; they are often recalcitrant but cannot sever their connection with God. This is a topic to which we shall return in the last chapter.

As absolute spirit God is 'the whole' (*das Ganze*): 'Universal spirit—the whole [*das Ganze*] that it is—posits itself in its three determinations, i.e. it develops itself, realizes itself; and it is complete only at the end, which is at the same time its presupposition.'[4] Hegel uses the terms *Ganze*, *Ganzheit*, and *Totalität* interchangeably, which suggests that his 'totality' is to be construed holistically rather than totalistically. In a holistic system the other is not reduced to the same, but neither are the same and the other viewed as mutually exclusive atoms. Hegel's holism seeks a middle ground between atomism and monism.

In accord with classical theology, Hegel seems to identify two Trinities: an immanent or preworldly Trinity and an economic or

---

dividing itself into the finite flashes of light of individual consciousness, and then re-collecting and gathering itself up out of this finitude—inasmuch as it is in the finite consciousness that the process of knowing spirit's essence takes place and that the divine self-consciousness thus arises. Out of the foaming ferment of finitude, spirit rises up fragrantly' (3:233 n. 191).

[4] 3:186. The English edition here translates *das Ganze* as 'totality'. See n. 66 for a discussion of the wordplay between 'posits itself' (*setzt sich*) and 'presupposition' (*Voraussetzung*).

worldly Trinity. The immanent Trinity is God in eternity, the idea of God in and for itself, prior to and apart from the creation of the world, the inward dialectic of identity, difference, and mediation symbolized by the figures of Father, Son, and Spirit. The economic Trinity is the 'diremption' (the taking apart or separation) of the divine idea in the divine *oikonomia*: the creation of the natural and human worlds and their fall into evil, the appearance of God in Christ, the history of reconciliation and redemption, the consummation of all things in God (3:77, 86–91, 273–5). These two Trinities do not subsist externally to each other such that where one stops the other begins. Rather the economic Trinity is the outward re-enactment (not simply repetition) of the inward trinitarian dialectic—a re-enactment that is necessary to the self-realization of God and that is already implicit in the trinitarian play of love with itself. God is *ideally* (logically) complete apart from the world, yet needs the world for the *real* (existential) completion of the divine life, which is not merely a play of love with itself but an engaged and serious love for others.

Hegel himself does not use the terms 'immanent' and 'economic', and the reference to two Trinities is misleading. The economic Trinity overreaches and includes the immanent Trinity as the first of its moments. Thus a more accurate designation is that of the *inclusive*[5] or *holistic* Trinity. The inclusive Trinity

---

[5] For this term I am indebted to Cyril O'Regan. See *The Heterodox Hegel* (Albany: State University of New York Press, 1994), chap. 6. See also Emil Fackenheim's discussion of the 'two Trinities' in *The Religious Dimension in Hegel's Thought* (Bloomington, Ind.: Indiana University Press, 1967), 205–6, 218–19. What I am calling the inclusive Trinity incorporates the two aspects of Hegel's thought that Fackenheim rightly regards as essential: 'We have long rejected a right-wing dissipation of the actual world into the logical realm: this would be specified by the dissipation of the worldly trinitarian incursion into a timeless trinitarian play, and we have also rejected a left-wing reduction of Idea and Spirit to worldly finitude: this would be specified by the reduction of the worldly trinitarian incursion to a divine self-realization which, bereft of a preworldly Trinity to sustain it, could never be complete. ... The preworldly trinitarian play is complete, apart from its worldly manifestation; yet this latter—no mere repetition of the play—is as real for philosophic comprehension as it is for Christian faith. The trinitarian God is wholly real apart from the world and wholly real in it, and only because of His preworldly reality can His worldly manifestation be complete' (205). In my view the converse judgement also holds: it is only because of the worldly manifestation that God's preworldly reality (or better, ideality) is complete. Completion or consummation comes only at the end; but, as Hegel notes, the end is also the beginning.

encompasses both the inner, preworldly dialectic of the divine life and the outward mediations by which the world is created and redeemed and God becomes absolute spirit. The whole Trinity comprises the three elements or spheres of the divine life, and it is confusing to speak of two Trinities along with three elements. Rather there is one Trinity of three elements with replicating patterns. In so far as the language about elements and spheres suggests temporal or spatial distinctions, it is misleading, for God is eternal and omnipresent; but temporal and spatial realities are constituted by God's creation of and movement within the world, and God participates in these realities. The 'eternal divine history' incorporates but is not reducible to temporal and spatial history. It is a rational process and as such trans-temporal and trans-spatial.

Understanding Hegel's Trinity as inclusive enables us to see that God's external relations are not something extrinsic to God. The divine life *ad intra* (the immanent Trinity) and *ad extra* (the economic Trinity) both contribute to the divine life as a whole. That which is not-God, the world, is a moment within God, and the distinction between two Trinities is an abstraction as compared with the concrete wholeness of God. The inclusive Trinity incorporates external relations, makes them internal to itself without annihilating their exteriority vis-à-vis each other and toward God. The world remains world, not-God within God.

The elements or spheres of the Trinity cannot be prioritized or ranked; they are co-essential. Classical theology accorded precedence to God's ideal self-relations, of which the world is an epiphenomenal reflection. Modern theology has prioritized the economic Trinity, God's appearance and work in the world as Son and Spirit, on the grounds that nothing can be known of God's inner life, of what God is in and for godself. Hegel will have nothing of this division, for it destroys the very heart of what God is. The elements are distinguishable but not separable. While in a discursive treatment they are unavoidably discussed in linear fashion, they are related not linearly but spirally or concentrically, with each spiral overlapping and encompassing the previous ones. The pattern is that of a trinity within a trinity, of Father within Son within Spirit. Only when we arrive at the final spiral do we fully understand what God is. We start in this chapter with the most abstract spiral.

THE CHRISTIAN DOCTRINE OF THE TRINITY

At the abstract level God is defined as 'universal spirit that particularizes itself'. This is what Christian theology calls 'the Trinity'—the doctrine that describes how God differentiates godself
but remains self-identical in the process. The Trinity constitutes
the *mystery* of God: 'its content is mystical, i.e. speculative'
(3:192). It is a *rational* mystery, intelligible to a way of thinking
that comprehends distinctions not as sense-based quantities that
can be counted but as logical elements of a living rational process.
The problem with the Christian doctrine of the Trinity is that it is
couched in representational language that introduces numbers and
persons. Hegel's task is to deconstruct such language in order to
articulate the truth that it represents: *Vorstellung* gives way to
thought.

As to *numbers*, the Trinity cannot be a matter of quantity or of
counting; it cannot be digitalized. Counting yields the unmathe-
matical conclusion, suggested by the word 'tri-une' itself, that
'three equals one'. The problem is that numbers indicate fixed
quantities rather than analogical and dialectical relations. Digital
thinking cannot grasp how unity manifests itself in diversity, difference. Thus Hegel concludes that 'reason can employ all the
*relationships* of the understanding, but only in so far as it destroys
the *forms* of the understanding' (3:192, cf. 81–2, 285). For the form
of understanding (*Verstand*), the Trinity is a suprarational paradox, something to be accepted on the authority of faith; it is not a
truth of reason itself (*Vernunft*).

As to *persons*, it can only be misleading to introduce the familial relationships expressed by 'Father' and 'Son'. 'This is a childlike
relationship, a childlike form. The understanding has no other
category, no other relationship that would be comparable with
this in respect of its appropriateness. But we must be aware that
it is merely a figurative [*bildliches*] relationship; the Spirit does not
enter into this relationship' (3:194). In truth, 'all three [persons]
are spirit'—the universal working through its process, differentiating itself, bringing forth what is already there from the beginning. 'The differentiation that the divine life goes through is not an
external [process] but must be defined solely as internal, so that the
first, the Father, is to be grasped just like the last [the Spirit]. Thus

the process is nothing but a play of self-maintenance, a play of self-confirmation' (3:195).

From the 1831 lectures it is evident that Hegel regards 'the Father' not as a specific divine person but as a symbol designating the 'kingdom' of the immanent Trinity—the movement by which God is present to godself through a differentiation that has not yet been replicated in the world (3:362). Dogmatic theology says that God as Father eternally begets his Son, that God does this in order to have a son. 'But all of this "doing" is God himself; he is only the totality, and taken abstractly as the Father, he is not the true God.' 'It is as totality that God is the Spirit' (3:363–4, 283 n. 93). Similarly, in the 1831 lectures we find this provocative statement: 'The abstractness of the Father is given up in the Son—this then is death. But the negation of this negation is the unity of Father and Son—love, or the Spirit.'[6] This does not mean that the Father and the Son simply disappear into the Spirit, but rather that the Spirit is the most concrete and encompassing of the trinitarian symbols. The death of Christ signifies the death of the transcendent father-figure and of the individual saviour-figure. But there can be no Spirit apart from the abstractness of the Father and the death of the Son—apart, that is, from the dialectic of identity and difference, universality and particularity. An advantage of this sublation (annulment *and* preservation) of the Father and the Son in the Spirit, though not one thematized by Hegel himself, is that it minimizes gender-specific language about God. Spirit is beyond gender distinctions. It is the most retrievable of the classical trinitarian figures.

Hegel notes that *predicates* are employed by the understanding in its effort to define God: justice, goodness, omnipotence, etc. These do not merely describe our relations to God, as Schleiermacher thought,[7] or God's relations to the world (as distinct from

---

[6] 3:370. This formulation is from David Friedrich Strauss's excerpts of an unidentified transcript of the 1831 lecture, but it is confirmed by the *Werke* text of the same material (3:324 n. 199). Admittedly, the latter is less dramatic: 'Just as in the first sphere the seclusion of God came to an end, and his original immediacy as abstract universality, according to which he is the essence of essences, has been sublated, so here [in the second sphere] the abstraction of humanity, the immediacy of subsisting singularity, is sublated, and this is brought about by death. But the death of Christ is the death of this death itself, the negation of negation.' Whether Strauss's source is the same one that underlies the *Werke* text is not known.

[7] Friedrich Schleiermacher, *The Christian Faith*, ed. H. R. Mackintosh and J. S. Stewart (Edinburgh: T&T Clark, 1928), § 50 (p. 194).

God's self-relations). Nor do they designate different external aspects of God—determinate, particular qualities that fall into opposition and can be endlessly multiplied. 'Predicates as particular characteristics are not appropriate to the nature of God.' The predicates work only as they relate to the *movement* by which God is God and as they proceed from the modes of divine self-differentiation (3:76, 277–8). In other words, the predicates properly refer to trinitarian relations.

Hegel does not attend to any of the technicalities of the classical trinitarian debates—the questions, for example, of the *homoousian* (the equality or identity of being) of the Son and the Spirit with the Father, or of the procession of the Spirit from the Father alone or from the Father and the Son. These debates and their categories (one substance, two processions, three persons, four relations, five characteristics, etc.) remain at the level of representational fictions from Hegel's perspective and do not adequately grasp the logic of trinitarian relations. At the same time, Hegel's speculative redescription of the doctrine accords with an orthodox version of it. Clearly the divinity of God for him is not diminished but enhanced in the second and third moments of the divine life (it is God who dies on the cross and is present to the spiritual community); and the Spirit proceeds of necessity from the second as well as the first moment, linking and completing them. In terms of its logical structure, Hegel's version of the doctrine is closer to that of Augustine (the trialectical model of subject and object mediated by a third) than to that of Thomas Aquinas (the triangular model of Father, Son, and Spirit connected by relations of begetting and spirating). As far as we know, Hegel had no direct knowledge of Augustine's theology, but he was familiar with Gnostic and Neoplatonic sources.[8]

---

[8] I discuss the Augustinian, Thomistic, and Hegelian models of the Trinity in *God in History: Shapes of Freedom* (Nashville: Abingdon Press, 1989), 55–70. Given the similarities between Augustine and Hegel, it is remarkable that no direct influence is evident; they share rather a Neoplatonic heritage. The third person is logically necessary for Augustine and Hegel, but not for Aquinas. The latter's model is 'triangular' in the sense that the Spirit is not the link between the Father and the Son or the completion of a circuit but a third person who is dependent on and subordinate to both; scripture, not reason, requires the inclusion of the Spirit in the Trinity.

## THE SPECULATIVE IDEA OF THE TRINITY

Hegel's speculative reconstruction of the Trinity[9] is already evident from his critique of the classical doctrine and from his conception of God as absolute spirit. God is to be understood not as three persons but as infinite personality or infinite subjectivity, which constitutes distinctions within itself but suspends these distinctions and remains in unity with itself. Personality is not a dead, unmoving substance but a living play of relationships, relationships formed by love and friendship. Only speculative thinking is able to grasp how distinctions are both posited and resolved, and why contradictions are present in everything living and concrete. The triune God appears to be a secret or mystery for sense perception and representational thinking, whereas speculative theology comprehends the rationality of the mystery. It does so not only in terms of the logical paradigm with which we are already familiar but also by introducing the analogy of ethical relationships and by describing the nature of personality.

Here is a suggestive passage on relationships from the 1824 lectures:

> Everything concrete, everything living, contains contradiction within itself; only the dead understanding is identical with itself. But the contradiction is also resolved in the idea, and the resolution is spiritual unity. The living thing is an example of what cannot be grasped by the understanding. 'God is love' is an expression very much to the point; ... as 'love' God is a person, and the relationship is such that the consciousness of the One is to be had only in the consciousness of the other. God is conscious of himself ... only in the other, in absolute externalization. This is spiritual unity in the form of feeling. In the relationship of friendship, of love, of the family, this identity of one with the other is also to be found.... [This is] the substantial, universal *ethical* relationship as such. (3:192–3)

Here is a similar passage from the 1827 lectures:

> When we say, 'God is love', we are saying something very great and true.... Love is a distinguishing of two, who nevertheless are absolutely not distinguished for each other. The consciousness or feeling of the identity of the two—to be outside of myself and in the other—this is

[9] It is set forth in basically similar terms in the 1821 manuscript (3:78–83), in the 1824 lectures (3:191–5), and in the 1827 lectures (3:275–86).

love. I have my self-consciousness not in myself but in the other. . . . This other, because it likewise exists outside itself, has its self-consciousness only in me, and both the other and I are only this consciousness of being-outside-ourselves and of our identity; we are only this intuition, feeling, and knowledge of our unity. This is love, and without knowing that love is both a distinguishing and the sublation of the distinction, one speaks emptily of it.  (3:276)

In these passages the logical categories of identity, difference, and mediation have been converted into the ethical relationships of love and friendship. Love is a distinguishing of two and the sublation of the distinction. Just such a process constitutes the divine life inwardly and outwardly, and thus the simplest and truest statement about God is that 'God is love'. Love requires the trinitarian dialectic.

So also does life. Life has drives and needs, and thus has distinction within itself. However, the satisfaction of the needs annuls the contradiction. 'Life is the resolving of the contradiction, the satisfying of the need, giving it peace, though in such a way that the contradiction emerges once more. The distinction, the contradiction, and its annulment alternate back and forth' (3:281–2). Expressed otherwise, life maintains itself by entering into differentiation and struggling with particularity, finding itself therein and moving on to new forms. It is a continuous process of diversification and unification (3:195). God is an eternally living, moving, dynamic process. Thus it is equally true to say that 'God is life'.

God's loving and living prove to be superabundant: that is, they overflow the inner dynamism of the godhead and pour outward in the creation of a finite world that God loves, struggles with, suffers in, and saves. The inward 'play of love with itself' (3:195, 292) becomes deadly serious. This is the topic of the next chapter. Here we should remind ourselves that the world is not in a literal sense spatially exterior to God, but encompassed within the totality of the divine life, which is enlarged by the act of creation.

As love and life, God is personal—supremely, absolutely personal. Hegel notes in the manuscript (3:82–3) that classical theology spoke of 'persons' in the godhead, but that abstract understanding cannot grasp the meaning of personality if it attributes three persons or centres of consciousness to God. Personality 'is the infinite subjectivity of self-certainty; it is reflection into self through distinction'. Personality already includes plurality within itself: God is *one* person in a trinity of personifications or gestalts. This can be understood analogously from nature. Parents who are of the same species but sexually distinct give birth to a child; thus 'a family [is] a natural unity of members who are persons, and its ethical unity [subsists] in love'. On this analogy God is a familial or corporate person. As such God incorporates sexual distinction within godself and is not gendered.[10] In the 1824 lectures (3:193–4), Hegel explains that the Trinity is comprised not of three separate gods or persons (which are posited merely as 'a transient moment or aspect') but of one person, or of personality (*Persönlichkeit*) as such. Personality is accomplished when persons maintain themselves in love and friendship, and through their love for another achieve their own subjectivity. The 1827 lectures (3:285–6) affirm that persons do not stand on their own but surrender their isolation and separateness. 'Ethical life, love, means precisely the giving up of particularity, of particular personality, and its extension to universality—so, too, with friendship. In friendship and love I give up my abstract personality and thereby win it back as concrete. The truth of personality is found precisely in winning it back through this immersion, this being immersed in the other.' God is the utterly concrete, universal personality, accomplished in and through the totality of the divine life, not in the abstraction of purely interior relations. An infinity of persons contributes to the divine personality; God's family is the whole earth, the whole realm of spirits.

## TRACES AND ANTICIPATIONS OF THE TRINITY

Hegel's speculative reconstruction of the Trinity was scandalous enough from the point of view of orthodox theology.[11] But he adds insult to injury by suggesting that the doctrine is not unique to Christianity. 'Reminiscences and traces'[12] of the Trinity, or at least of the triad, are found in earlier religions such as Hinduism—the

[10] Unlike Friedrich Schelling and Ludwig Feuerbach, Hegel did not identify masculine and feminine principles in the godhead. See Feuerbach's *The Essence of Christianity*, trans. George Eliot (New York: Harper & Brothers, 1957), chap. 7.

[11] We shall explore in the final chapter whether Hegel's 'swerves' from orthodoxy are productive or not productive for contemporary theological reflection.

[12] The language of 'traces' (*Spuren*) is certainly reminiscent of Augustine's *vestigia trinitatis* (*De Trinitate*, 8.10), although Hegel himself seems unaware of it. Augustine's trinitarian traces are found in perceptual, psychological, and

triad of Brahma, Vishnu, and Shiva, although the third element here 'is not the Spirit, not genuine reconciliation, but rather origin and passing away'. The triad also played an important role for the Pythagoreans as reported by Aristotle (everything is determined by the number three), for Plato (the three forms of the World Soul: sameness, difference, existence), for Philo and the Alexandrian Jews, for Valentian Gnosticism, and for Neoplatonists such as Proclus (3:79–81, 286–9).[13] The form of triplicity was revised in modern times by Kant, but only in a peripheral way as a schema for thought.[14] Hegel's point in citing these precedents is that the triadic structure is deeply ingrained in human consciousness, which suggests that it reflects something basic about the structure of reality itself. 'The ancients did not know what they really possessed in these forms, namely, that they contained the absolute consciousness of truth' (3:81). This consciousness was most fully developed in the Christian doctrine of the Trinity. Hegel is challenging Enlightenment theologians such as W. A. Teller and J. G. Töllner, and possibly also Friedrich Schleiermacher,[15] who neglected or downplayed the doctrine of the Trinity; and the Neopietist F. A. G. Tholuck, who regarded the Trinity as a pagan import and as mere 'decorative timbering' for Christian theology (1:157 n. 17; 3:81 nn. 61, 63).

Hegel devotes the most attention in his lectures to the Neoplatonists and to the Gnostic systems of Valentinus and the Valentinians, with which he was familiar from the work of August Neander (3:84 n. 71).[16] For both, a distinction emerges between the divine One (the first, the inconceivable, the abyss, the eternal

epistemological analogies (vision, love, knowledge, etc.), whereas Hegel has in mind precedents from the history of religions and philosophy.

[13] See Aristotle, *De caelo*, 1.1; Plato, *Timaeus*, 34c–35b; Proclus, *Platonic Theology*, 3.9–14.

[14] In the *Critique of Pure Reason*, trans. Norman Kemp Smith (London: Macmillan, 1933), в 110 (p. 116), Kant claims that, while the a priori division of concepts must be dichotomous, in each class the number of categories is always three, and that the third category in each class always arises from the combination of the first two. This is a precedent for Hegel's dialectic.

[15] Schleiermacher treats the doctrine of the Trinity in the concluding propositions of the *Glaubenslehre*, where it is described as merely an 'appended proposition' (*The Christian Faith*, 738–51).

[16] See August Neander, *Genetische Entwickelung der vornehmsten gnostischen Systeme* (Berlin, 1818). Cyril O'Regan discusses the influence of Valentinian Gnosticism on Hegel in *The Heterodox Hegel*, 19–20, 231–5. See also his later study, *Gnostic Return in Modernity* (Albany: State University of New York Press, 2001).

ground) and the self-emerging or self-manifesting of God as *nous*, *logos*, *sophia*, the only-begotten Son or *Monogenes*, who is the archetype of humanity, Adam Kadmon (3:84–5, 196–7, 288). The Only-begotten remains, however, in the bosom of God, so that the distinction is no distinction. The Spirit proceeds from the Son but lacks 'defining importance'. Thus from Hegel's perspective there is no genuine differentiation here and likewise no genuine closure. Or as he puts it, 'The defect in all these representations is that what is first is not grasped in the determination of totality, as what is last [also]' (3:197). For Gnosticism the natural world does not derive from the creative act of God but from a second material source, the Demiurge. Hegel will have nothing to do with such a dualism.

In the 1827 lectures Hegel summarizes his remarks about antecedents of the Trinity as follows: 'These are forms in which this truth, this idea, has fermented. The main point is to know that these appearances, wild as they are, are rational—to know that they have their ground in reason, and to know what sort of reason is in them. But at the same time one must know how to distinguish the form of rationality that is present and not yet adequate to the concept' (3:288–9). In this connection he mentions Jacob Boehme, who was the first to recognize the Trinity as universal. 'His way of representing and thinking is rather wild and fanciful; he has not yet risen to the pure forms of thinking. But the ruling foundation of the ferment [in his mind] . . . was the recognition of the presence of the Trinity in everything and everywhere. He said, for example, that it must be born in the hearts of human beings' (3:289).[17]

This is very close to Hegel's own agenda, namely to recognize the presence of the Trinity in everything and everywhere, but in a philosophical form adequate to the concept. When the idea of the Trinity is recognized as the essential and sole nature of God, 'it must not be regarded as something above and beyond, as it was formerly; rather it is the goal of cognition to know the truth in particular things as well. . . . [To show] that this idea is what is true as such, and that all categories of thought are this movement of determining, is the [task of] logical exposition' (3:289–90). In other

---

[17] See Jacob Boehme, *Aurora, oder Morgenröhte im Aufgang*, in *Theosophia revelata* (1715), 10.116. O'Regan discusses at length the influence of Boehme on Hegel; see the index of references in *The Heterodox Hegel* and *Gnostic Return in Modernity*.

words, the Trinity is the truth not only about God but about the whole of reality in all its determinacy and particularity. In this sense the created world images the Creator: the structure of the whole is replicated in every part.

# 7

# Creation, Humanity, and Evil

## CREATION OF THE WORLD

### From Internal Differentiation to External Diremption

In this chapter we begin a discussion of the second of the elements or spheres of the divine life, that of the creation of the world, its fall into estrangement, and its reconciliation through Christ. Expressed metaphorically, this is the 'kingdom of the Son'.

The condition of possibility for the creation of a world that is distinct from God (although still embraced within the totality of God) is the internal differentiation within the divine life that makes God a subject and not a windowless monad. God creates out of God's own internal fecundity or generative power and not out of something alien or external to God. In the act of creation the logically other within God is posited as existentially other. 'The differentiation, which in the first [moment] of the idea was only a show [*Schein*], now comes into its right' (3:365). It does so as appearance or manifestation, *Erscheinung*. 'It is no longer absolute but finite spirit that is posited; and inasmuch as what is differentiated is itself something internally differentiated into nature and finite spirit, we have the creation of the world, the form in which the Son actually becomes the other' (3:365, cf. 294 n. 128). In the movement from *Schein* to *Erscheinung*, the ideal and eternal Son (God's intrinsic self-othering) becomes a real flesh-and-blood historical Son. Historical appearance has a positive, empirical quality; but, as we shall see, everything that appears also disappears, and thus the element of *Schein* lingers in the *Erscheinung*.

On the one hand, the absolute idea, subsisting in and for itself, is complete. On the other hand, in its 'subjective' aspect it is not complete, for it is not yet concrete, it is not yet reflected into itself, is not posited as differentiated. This is the second element, that of appearance, and according to the 1824 lectures there are two sides from which it may be grasped (3:198–9). First, from the side of the divine idea, we can say that spirit in the mode of universality posits itself in the mode of particularity, but in so doing it remains the eternal idea: 'God is the entire totality [*die ganze Totalität*]', embracing both universal and particular, both internal distinction and external diremption. As we suggested in the preceding chapter, this externality is incorporated into the inclusive Trinity and thereby rendered interior to the divine life. Or we can say that the Son unites the two modalities: the Son constitutes the *reality* (as well as ideality) of difference, 'but in love, and in the Spirit', which means that the Son remains identical with the idea in the form of universality. The two modalities of universal and particular, identity and difference, are 'to be posited as distinct—but only for an instant, as it were, since they are not truly distinct'. By this Hegel means that the spatio-temporal world is only a passing instant in the divine eternity. It is representation that holds the two sides apart in time and traces the history of creation, fall, and redemption. This points to the second side from which the second element is to be grasped, that of finite spirit, which is 'intrinsically the process of elevation' from finite to infinite, from creation to creator.[1]

## Creation as Primal Division and Release of Otherness

Hegel develops a distinctive terminology for describing the act or process of creation. He refers to it on the one hand as a *positing* (*Setzen*) or as a *primal judgement or division* (*Urteil*); and on the other hand as a *release* (*Entlassen*).

*Setzen* and *Urteil* have a logical-grammatical-juridical connotation, suggesting that the divine creativity is exercised by a primordial saying or decree, a calling into being, a verbal shaping, a discriminating judgement. Creation is not so much a physical as it is an intellectual act: God creates by speaking a word. Thus we read in the 1821 manuscript (3:86) that 'it is the absolute judge-

---

[1] In the 1827 lectures, the two sides are discussed in reverse order. From the point of view of the thinking subject, the idea of divine appearance must become an objectively certain truth; while from the point of view of the idea, 'eternal being-in-and-for-itself is what discloses itself, determines itself, divides itself, posits itself as what is differentiated from itself, but the difference is at the same time constantly sublated' (3:291).

ment or primal division [*Urteil*] that grants independence to the side of other-being; it is goodness that grants the idea as a whole to [this] side in its estrangement.' The manuscript goes on to suggest (3:87–8) that *two* judgements or divisions occur: one is interior to the divine life while the other posits the world in distinction from God. While the two judgements are implicitly the same, representation rightly holds them apart as distinct acts, for the eternal Son of the Father is *not* the same as the physical and spiritual world. God in the moment of self-differentiation is not simply identical with the world. Rather the divine differentiation *ad intra* is the ground for the possibility of creating a world of nature and finite spirit whose vocation as not-God is to be God's otherness. Yet there are not two eternal activities of God, but only one. Thus 'this differentiating [of worldly entities] as something independent is only the explicitly negative moment of other-being, of being-external-to-self, which as such has not truth but is only a moment.... In God himself this is the *disappearing moment of appearance*.' What for the world is a spatially and temporally extended moment of appearance is for God an immediately disappearing moment: 'it is only a flash of lightning that immediately vanishes, the sound of a word that is perceived and vanishes in its outward existence the instant it is spoken'. These mystical images convey a sense of the qualitative difference between the eternity of God and the temporality of creation, as well as of the radical dependence of the world upon God, and of the non-objectifiability of the creative act (a flash of light, a vanishing sound). From God's point of view, the world is a disappearing instant, called into being ('posited') by a fleeting word; from the world's point of view, creation hovers on the brink of non-being and is sustained solely by the divine goodness.

These themes are developed with a different emphasis in the 1827 lectures (3:291–3). Here we are told that without creation and appearance, 'we have a relationship of God, of the idea, merely to himself. The act of differentiation is only a movement, a play of love with itself, which does not arrive at the seriousness of other-being, of separation and rupture.... The distinguished elements are posited as the same; they have not yet come to be defined so that they are distinctly determined.' Precisely this is what must happen if the other within God, the eternal Son, is to obtain 'the determinacy of other-*being*, of an actual entity'. 'Otherness is requisite in order that there may be difference; it is necessary

144        *Creation, Humanity, and Evil*

that what is distinguished should be the otherness of an entity.' The text continues with a critical statement:

> Only the absolute idea determines itself and is certain of itself as absolutely free within itself because of this self-determination. For this reason its self-determination involves letting this determinate [entity] exist as something free [*als Freies zu entlassen*], something independent, or as an independent object. It is only for the being that is free that freedom *is*; it is only for the free human being that an other has freedom too. It belongs to the absolute freedom of the idea that, in its act of determining and dividing, it releases [*entläßt*] the other to exist as a free and independent being. This other, released as something free and independent [*dies Andere, als ein Freies, Selbständiges entlassen*], is the world as such. (3:292)

Here the other key metaphor used by Hegel to describe the act of creation, 'release' or 'letting exist' (*Entlassen*), comes into play. Note the context for its usage: the absolute freedom of the absolute idea (God) is such that it is able to release the otherness that is intrinsic to its own being into actual, independent existence, which is the world vis-à-vis God. Only an utterly free being can do this; an unfree or partially free being would of necessity cling to its otherness as essential to its self-constitution. God is able to create the world without any threat to God's own radical freedom, which is complete in and for itself, and which gratuitously overflows into the world without any self-diminishment. God is an inexhaustible fount that releases its fecundity into that which is not-God.[2] In this way the non-serious play of love with itself becomes deadly serious, subject to the ruptures, conflicts, and suffering of the finite world. God is not thereby diminished but enlarged, for the world (precisely in its otherness from God) remains a moment within the divine life. God does not abandon this world but preserves and

---

[2] The language of 'release', 'overflow', 'expansion', etc. echoes the German mystical tradition. Hegel had some familiarity with Meister Eckhart (see 1:347 n. 166), and the latter's use of *lassen* and *gelassen* to describe release from worldly attachments may lie in the background: human detachment mirrors the divine release. See Robert Forman, *Meister Eckhart: The Mystic as Theologian* (Rockport, Mass.: Element, 1991), 77–80; and Oliver Davies, *Meister Eckhart: Selected Writings* (Harmondsworth: Penguin Books, 1994), pp. xxix–xxxi. Jacob Boehme is mentioned in the present context, but only in reference to his distinction between two Sons, the first of whom, Lucifer, fell and became the external world (3:293, cf. 200, 289). The influence of the Jewish Kabbalah may also be felt here, although for the Kabbalah it is not so much a release or expansion of God that allows the world to exist as free and independent as it is a withdrawal or contraction of God. Perhaps this difference between Christian and Jewish mysticism is reflected in Emmanuel Levinas's critique of Hegelian 'totality' (see Chap. 11 below).

saves it, and indeed is enriched and completed by it; but this is an existential, not a logical, completion. Both truths must be maintained: that God is complete apart from the world, and that God achieves completion through the world.

Hegel goes on in the 1827 lectures (3:293) to stress that 'the truth of the world is only its *ideality*'. The world is, to be sure, real, but it lacks 'genuine actuality [*wahrhafte Wirklichkeit*]' on its own account. The truth of its reality (*Realität*) is its ideality (*Idealität*), which means that 'it is not something eternal in itself but rather something created, whose being is only posited'.[3] Its destiny is 'to have being only for an instant, so to speak', to annul its separation and estrangement from God, to return to its origin, to enter into the relationship of love and the Spirit—which is the third element of the inclusive Trinity. 'The second element is, therefore, the process of the world in love by which it passes over from fall and separation into reconciliation.' This theme is also adumbrated in the lecture manuscript (3:88–9). Here Hegel stresses that the materiality of the world has the status of something 'posited' by God as the negative of ideality. As such, the natural world is 'relative', is 'appearance'—not only for us but also in itself. 'This is its quality, namely, to pass over, moving itself forward, so as to take itself back into the final idea.' While it endures temporally, its ontological status is that of disappearing, passing. Whatever appears also disappears: it is a disappearing appearance (*eine verschwindende Erscheinung*).

The question as to whether creation and fall are coterminous for Hegel (that is, the question whether separation or differentiation from God necessarily entails estrangement and resistance) will be considered later in this chapter. For the moment the point is that the world in its finitude, transience, and contingency is not an end in itself but finds its goal only in its return to God. This need not be viewed as a Gnostic denigration of the goodness of the material world but as the restatement of a classical Christian theme. The world, while good, is a relative good, an appearance that will ultimately disappear.[4]

---

[3] See the discussion in Chap. 1 of the connection for Hegel between ideality and reality.

[4] We might note that the fragility and passing character of the world has in our own time become a scientific and ecological as well as a religious theme.

For this very reason, the themes of creation and preservation are identical on Hegel's interpretation (3:89–90). Because self-subsistent independence is not attributable to the world, its preservation entails a continuous creation, and conversely its creation is also preservation because the moment of other-being is itself an enduring moment of the idea. If creation entails a divine release of the world, preservation entails a divine holding onto the world. Just this continuous creation/preservation is the *wisdom* of God in nature, a theme that is lacking in earlier religions, we are told, but is found especially in Judaism. Hegel believes that it is the task of philosophical cognition 'to recognize this concept [of wisdom] in nature and to grasp nature as a system, as an organization, in which the divine idea is mirrored'. This is a task Hegel himself addresses in the second part of the *Encyclopedia of the Philosophical Sciences*, the 'Philosophy of Nature'. It is sometimes regarded as the weakest part of his system, but in fact Hegel was engaged with nature from his earliest studies on, and it plays a crucial role in his thought. In the *Philosophy of Religion* lecture manuscript he provides a very brief summary of the central theme, namely that life is the highest exhibition of the idea in nature. But natural life means 'precisely the sacrifice of self—the negativity of the idea vis-à-vis this its existence—and the coming into being of spirit', that is, of human beings (3:90).

Thus the finite world divides into the realms of the natural world and finite spirit (3:293–4). On its own account, nature knows nothing of God and is not related to God except through humanity, of which it provides the 'dependent side'. It is humanity that recognizes the presence of the divine idea in nature and raises nature to its truth. This is the extent of Hegel's discussion of nature in its own right, although these brief remarks are somewhat expanded in the 1831 lectures.[5] The remainder of the 'second element' is devoted to a discussion of humanity, its fall into estrangement, and its reconciliation in Christ. Hegel's approach to

---

[5] 3:294–5 n. 128. Hegel does not discuss nature as such even here but rather the relationship of nature and spirit. 'Nature is for human beings not only the immediate, external world but rather a world in which humanity knows God; in this way nature is for humanity a revelation of God.' For the nature religions, God appears as a natural power, but such a perception is no longer adequate for the religions of spirit. Hegel quotes Job 37:5 to the effect that God is not recognized when God thunders with a thundering voice. 'In order to be recognized as spirit, God must do more than thunder.'

nature is clearly anthropocentric in the sense that nature has no relationship to God apart from humanity, and it serves human purposes. Yet the divine idea is present in nature, where it 'slumbers' in the modality of pre-selfhood. An ecologically sensitive theology of nature could conceivably be constructed on the basis of this insight, but the hierarchy of spirit over nature would have to be revised in a more dialectical direction—a direction that arguably is more faithful to Hegel's deepest intuitions. Nature and spirit each serve the other in the triple mediation of philosophy, and thus nature is an end in itself. It has the critical function of differentiation, without which there would be no process and life, only dead identity. Perhaps Hegel's suspicion of the romantic idealization of nature prevented him from articulating a nature spirituality.[6] And of course he was still unaware of the adverse impact on nature of human technology.

HUMAN NATURE

The expression 'human nature' contains an ambiguity. It can refer to what is essential (*wesentlich*) about humanity, or it can indicate that human beings belong to nature, that their existence is finite and natural, that theirs is a 'natural humanity' (*natüricher Mensch*). Regarding the latter, Hegel's central questions are whether this natural humanity is good or evil, and how humans raise themselves from a natural to a spiritual state. His treatment of these questions is nuanced slightly differently from one year to the next.

In the 1821 manuscript (3:92–5) the emphasis falls on the fact that natural humanity 'is an internally unresolved *contradiction*'. If

---

[6] Hegel does say in his lectures on the philosophy of nature that God reveals godself in two ways, as nature and as spirit, and that 'both manifestations are temples of God' that are filled by the divine presence. The goal of the philosophy of nature is to achieve nature's liberation by discovering the presence of reason and spirit in it. 'The very stones cry out and raise themselves to spirit.' Nature must be liberated from its bondage to externality, from its tendency toward singularization (or isolation, *Vereinzelung*) and chaos (spirit in nature is 'a Bacchic god unrestrained and unmindful of itself'). The outward, disintegrating pull of natural forces is countered by the inward, unifying pull of spirit. See *Encyclopedia of the Philosophical Sciences*, §§ 246–8 additions (*Hegel's Philosophy of Nature*, trans. A. V. Miller (Oxford: Clarendon Press, 1970), 13, 14–16, 18–19). These hints at a nature spirituality are found not in the text of the *Encyclopedia* but in additions from students' lecture notes. For the first time transcriptions of the *Encyclopedia* lectures on the philosophy of nature are being published (see the Bibliography).

human beings are spirit, and if spirit is essentially something that mediates itself with itself, then humans cannot remain in the state of natural immediacy. 'Natural humanity does not exist in the form that it ought to.' In the state of nature it is determined by the *singularity* of its existence. It is a *willing, desiring* being but not yet a *thinking* being. 'Thus the natural human being is not liberated[7] within itself vis-à-vis itself and external nature. It is the human being of desire, of savagery and self-seeking, of dependence and fear.' Hegel continues here with a depiction of primitive peoples drawn from travel accounts, the theme of which is that 'spirit's vocation does not lie in the direction of this naturalness and innocence, which is contrary to its concept'. The state of innocence lies prior to the distinction between good and evil, and in this state human beings are not yet actually human (3:102–3).

The 1824 lectures (3:202–5) emphasize that humanity's true 'nature' is to abandon its immediacy, to renounce its natural state. Does this mean, as is often said, that 'human beings are evil by nature'? But cannot it equally well be said that 'human beings are good by nature'? For humanity's true nature is to be rational, spiritual, to be in the image of God, and this is surely good. The problem is that in the state of nature humans are only *implicitly* rational and spiritual. Just this is the deficiency, 'for spirit ought not to be implicitly spirit—it is spirit because it is so *explicitly*'. The state of nature as such is not evil, but it can become such when humans choose to remain in that state, to exist according to nature rather than according to the spirit. Thus it is misleading to say that humans are evil 'by nature'. Children are not evil; rather they are innocent, lacking insight, will (in the sense of the capacity to make decisions), and accountability. 'It pertains to evil to be able to decide, to have a will, to possess insight into the nature of actions.' But the same pertains to the good. Thus by nature human beings are neither good nor evil; they *become* good or evil as they rise out of nature through discipline, education, laws, cultural practices, etc.

The 1827 lectures (3:295–300) take the analysis a step further. It is true to say that humans are implicitly good; but the 'implicitly' means that they have not yet become explicitly what they are in truth. Their destiny is to move beyond the implicitness of nature,

---

[7] On the possible allusion here to Friedrich Schleiermacher's definition of religion as the 'feeling of dependence', see 3:93 n. 93.

to step forth as spirit out of natural life. This stepping forth leads to a 'separation' (*Trennung*) between the concept of humanity and its immediate existence; it engenders a 'cleavage' (*Entzweiung*) within humanity. This cleavage is intrinsic to spirit, for spirit is precisely a dividing of oneself from oneself in order to become conscious of oneself. As we shall see, separation or cleavage is the condition of possibility for estrangement (*Entfremdung*) and evil, but it is not yet evil itself in the strict sense. Evil occurs in two ways: when the division into two (*Ent-zweiung*) turns into an alienating division (*Ent-fremdung*), or when humans retreat from the necessary cleavage and exist only 'according to nature' (*nur nach der Natur*) in a state of immediacy. The latter phrase is a clear allusion to the Pauline *kata sarka* ('according to the flesh') as contrasted with *kata pneuma* ('according to the spirit'). Existence according to the flesh is a lapse into a state of innocence (*Unschuld*), whereas living according to the spirit is an advance into responsibility (*Schuld*). Only with such an advance do good and evil in the strict sense become possible. 'It is false to ask whether humanity is only good by nature or only evil.... In the same way, it is superficial to say that humanity is both good and evil equally.' Humans cannot remain in the state of nature without falling into natural evil, which takes the form of selfishness and struggle for survival. But in rising out of nature through consciousness and cognition, they fall into spiritual evil by converting cleavage into alienation. They realize their goodness, their *imago Dei*, in a mode of estrangement and fragmentation. The dilemma is that we humans are both natural and spiritual, finite and infinite. In this divided state evil seems to be inescapable: it lies, as it were, both behind us (in nature) and ahead of us (in *hubris*).

Hegel does not attend at any length to the story of the creation of human beings in the first and second chapters of Genesis, though he turns to the third chapter when (as we shall see) his concern is to account for the fall into estrangement and evil. Regarding the so-called original condition in which humans were created, Hegel notes that it entails the myth of an original or paradisaical state (3:96–9). He is suspicious of philosophical arguments that depict this state as one of 'the highest spiritual perfection, of human being in unity with nature, hence as an untroubled intelligence, which does not turn away from nature and into itself by means of reflection'. He has in mind the work of Friedrich Schlegel, who was attracted to Hindu and other ancient mythologies, and of Friedrich

150 Creation, Humanity, and Evil

Schelling, who accepted as historically actual a state of original perfection and idealized the elements of feeling, intuition, and prereflective intelligence.[8] Hegel's version of the original condition of humanity is quite different, and he will have nothing to do with a romantic myth of origins. The notion that humanity is good 'by nature' is, he asserts, a 'doctrine of recent times', which he attributes erroneously to Kant rather than to Rousseau.[9] He is especially concerned with the implications for pedagogy of a view that idealizes natural principles, regards civilization as contaminating an original innocence, and fails to recognize the necessity of discipline and acquired knowledge.[10]

## THE STORY OF THE FALL

The Bible describes the transition from the state of innocence to the state of responsibility and guilt as a 'fall'. This is 'a fall from the divine idea, from the image of God' (3:101); but it is also, paradoxically, a rise into the divine idea and the image of God. By eating of the tree of knowledge of good and evil, Adam and Eve become 'like God', but they also lose their immortality and become subject to death like all other creatures. In the 1821 manuscript (3:104–7), Hegel emphasizes the 'contradictions' in the story. If the knowledge of good and evil constitutes 'spirit', why should God forbid eating precisely that which elevates humans into the divine likeness? Why should knowledge be regarded as a temptation when God confirms that knowledge is the divine in humanity? Is mortality to be viewed as punishment for sin or as the natural condition of finitude? The contradictions reflect the ambiguities that are present in consciousness and knowledge—ambiguities that only speculative thinking is able to grasp. 'The deep insight of this story is that the eternal history of humanity, to be consciousness, is

[8] 3:97 n. 99. See Friedrich Schlegel, *Ueber die Sprache und Weisheit der Indier: Ein Beitrag zur Begründung der Alterthumskunde* (Heidelberg, 1808), 295, 303; and F. W. J. Schelling, *On University Studies* (1803), trans. E. S. Morgan (Athens, Ohio: Ohio University Press, 1966), 83.
[9] 3:100 n. 106. In opposition to Rousseau's acceptance of the goodness of human nature, Kant asserted the presence of radical evil in humanity, though he believed that an original kernel of goodness could be reawakened through adherence to the moral law.
[10] 3:100 n. 107. This system of education was known as 'philanthropinism'. Hegel's criticism of it was influenced by Friedrich Immanuel Niethammer.

contained in it.' Hegel notes that the story is not mentioned again in the Hebrew Bible, and that it is Christians who have developed the connection between the first Adam and the second. The second Adam, Christ, represents the likeness of God that is to be regained, whereas this promise, 'the infinite side of knowledge', 'slumbered' in the Jewish people.[11] Hegel's preoccupation with the story is noteworthy, and it represents his most sustained piece of scriptural exegesis.

The 1824 and 1827 lectures add little to the exegesis contained in the manuscript. Hegel notes in 1824 that the punishment for disobedience is labour, having to work for a living, but such 'labouring is at the same time the stamp of humankind's higher spiritual nature' (3:208). Humanity is driven out of paradise into history, and it is through history that spirit progresses to adulthood: without discipline and punishment, the human race would have languished in infancy. The 1827 lectures add that the faulty notion of a biological transmission of sin results from viewing humanity as literally a first man (3:302). Hegel scarcely finds it necessary to mention that the story is to be read as myth, not history.

## KNOWLEDGE, ESTRANGEMENT, EVIL[12]

The story of the fall points to a tragic view of human nature: the condition for the possibility of good includes also the possibility of evil. In order to rise out of the natural state and realize his spiritual potential, the human being must undergo a cleavage or separation that produces anxiety, estrangement, and efforts at self-securing. The knowledge that makes a human being also wounds her.

Hegel works philosophically with the paradoxes contained in the story. In the lecture manuscript (3:101–3), he notes that the idea of

---

[11] Thus in 1821, 1824, and 1827 Hegel treats the story of the fall in the context of the Christian religion. In the 1831 lectures, however, it becomes part of the discussion of the Jewish religion, which is now depicted as the religion of the good (2:739–41, see n. 64).

[12] The category of 'sin' is not as frequently employed in these lectures as that of 'evil'. While 'evil' is a more philosophical category and 'sin' more theological, I can discern little distinction between the terms as Hegel uses them. Evil applies to human beings, not to nature. The immediacy, externality, and singularization of nature are not evil in themselves, but become evil when humans comport themselves accordingly.

'transition' is representational and entails the telling of a story, which suggests that 'there are two conditions related to each other, and not that nature itself in its immediacy is a transition'. The first condition is an immediate, natural state of desire. The second condition is that of consciousness, and consciousness brings with it the knowledge of the good, the universal. When consciousness is connected with desire, however, it is drawn toward evil, 'the willing of separation, the setting of one's singularity against others'. This evil is that of self-seeking: it is a free choice for which humans are responsible, and for which they know that they are responsible. 'Thus evil, the will of self-seeking, exists only through consciousness and cognition. . . . But the divine principle of turning, of return to self, is equally present in cognition; it gives the wound and heals it, [because] the principle is spirit and is true.'

The 1824 lectures probe the connection between cognition and evil more profoundly (3:205–6). Cognition (*Erkenntnis*) posits the antithesis (*Gegensatz*) in which evil is to be found.

Evil first occurs within the sphere of rupture or cleavage [*Entzweiung*]; it is the consciousness of being-for-myself in opposition to an external nature, but also in opposition to the objective [truth] that is inwardly universal in the sense of the concept or of the rational will. It is through this separation that I exist for myself for the first time, and that is where the evil lies. Abstractly, being evil means singularizing myself [*mich vereinzeln*] in a way that cuts me off from the universal (which is the rational, the laws, the determinations of spirit). But along with this separation there arises being-for-self and for the first time the universally spiritual, laws—what ought to be. So it is not the case that reflection [*Betrachtung*] has an external relationship to evil: it is itself what is evil. Inasmuch as it is spirit, humanity has to progress to this antithesis of being-for-self as such. . . . Spirit is free; freedom has the essential moment of this separation within itself. In this separation being-for-self is posited and evil has its seat; here is the source of all wrong, but also the point where reconciliation has its ultimate source. It is what produces the disease and is at the same time the source of health.[13]

---

[13] 3:206. The English edition inserts 'reality' rather than 'truth' in brackets following 'objective', and translates *Betrachtung* as '[rational] consideration'. See the variant to the last two sentences transmitted by Hotho (3:206 n. 115), where the separation is depicted as 'the poisoned chalice from which human beings drink death and decay'. A comparison is implicit with the life-giving chalice by which reconciliation comes.

In this passage the cleavage necessary to consciousness, to being-for-self, is drawn into a very close connection, if not identity, with evil. What prevents it from becoming sheer identity is language such as 'is found in', 'occurs within', 'has its seat in'. If evil has its 'seat' in separation, in consciousness, then it is at least logically if not existentially distinguishable from consciousness as such. It is when consciousness becomes consciousness of being-for-myself *in opposition to* the ultimate universal truth—it is when consciousness issues in a 'singularizing' of myself over against the universal and other living beings—that evil occurs. But such opposition and singularization always in fact accompany the progression to being-for-self. Herein lies the tragic element. The cost of freedom is the misuse of freedom. Estrangement and reconciliation have the same source: consciousness and cognition. Reconciliation will entail a reorientation of consciousness away from self-centredness and singularization to truth-centredness and community-formation.

The 1827 lectures continue these deep reflections (3:301–10). Here Hegel draws upon the etymological linkage between the 'judgement' or 'division' (*Urteil*) that is intrinsic to cognition as 'a self-distinguishing within oneself' and the 'cleavage' (*Entzweiung*) that is evil—or at least the seat of evil, for it is also the seat of good. Knowledge brings knowledge of both good and evil (3:301). What we come to know is not that we have transgressed this or that particular commandment, but that we are intrinsically evil inasmuch as we posit divisions among ourselves, between human beings and the world, and between humans and God. We exist in a state of rupture or antithesis vis-à-vis both God and the world (3:304–5).

Hegel elaborates on the latter point in a manner not found in the earlier lectures (3:305–10). Vis-à-vis God, we experience an infinite *anguish*, the anguish of separation from God, of absorption into ourselves, of the loss of goodness. This was the religious condition of Judaism in late antiquity. The possibility of infinite anguish presupposes faith in *one* God as a pure and spiritual God, whose judgements are certain and just. Vis-à-vis the world, we experience *unhappiness*, the awareness that we are not satisfied in the world, cannot find in the world an ultimate ground and purpose of life, and thus are driven back into ourselves, seeking happiness in inner harmony. This was the condition at which the Roman world arrived at the beginning of the common era, appearing in the form of Stoicism and Scepticism. Each of these conditions, anguish and unhappiness, is abstractly one-sided: on the one hand, an unbridgeable antithesis exists between infinite and finite; on the other hand, a despairing absorption into self by means of flight from the world. 'The concept of the preceding religions has refined itself into this antithesis; and that the antithesis has disclosed and presented itself as an actually existing need is expressed by the words, "When the time had fully come, God sent forth his Son."' With this remark a transition is provided into the theme of reconciliation, and a proof is given of the necessary appearance of Christ in a particular time and place.[14] But in point of fact anguish and unhappiness are enduring and universal marks of religious alienation. Hegel's rendition of them has a particular application to his own time and place. Jewish anguish reappears in the modern world in the form of Protestant piety, which knows nothing of God other than its distance from God; while Roman unhappiness appears in the form of Enlightenment rationalism, which valorizes the finite and is vulnerable to secularism and atheism.

It is sometimes said that Hegel trivializes the problem of evil by connecting it too closely with knowledge and failing to recognize its absurd and irrational aspects. From Hegel's point of view, what gives evil its extraordinary power is precisely its connection with knowledge. It is a distortion and perversion of what is highest in humanity, not of what is lowest, and thus it has a potency that far outstrips natural destruction as well as a capacity for self-deception that reason on its own cannot overcome. What is required is a redemption of reason, not its displacement. It is true, however, that Hegel does not reflect very much (at least in the philosophy of religion lectures) on the reinforcement and intensification of personal evil in institutional structures and social ideologies. And, while he is profoundly aware of the tragic and violent character of human history, he does not envision the sort of radical evil that is represented by the Holocaust and other forms of genocide. Whether the experience of evil in the past century calls for a fundamental rethinking is one of the questions posed to Hegel by postmodernity.

---

[14] Concern for this transition helps to explain why the 1827 lectures treat the themes of knowledge, estrangement, and evil *after* the summary of the story of the fall rather than before it, as in the earlier lectures. Our presentation follows the order of the 1827 lectures. See 3:300 n. 138.

# 8

# Christ and Reconciliation

## THE POSSIBILITY, NECESSITY, AND ACTUALITY OF RECONCILIATION

'When the time had fully come, God sent forth his Son' (3:310). For Hegel these words of the Apostle (Galatians 4:4) have deep philosophical significance. The 'sending forth' means that the eternal Son became incarnate as a temporal-historical Son, born of a woman for the sake of the reconciliation of humanity. The fullness of time means that this event occurred under specific religio-cultural conditions in a particular time and place. But because the heightening of anguish and unhappiness in the Roman world has a universal signification, this particular event is also of universal redemptive significance.

Hegel attempts to establish by philosophical arguments the possibility, necessity, and actuality of the reconciliation accomplished by the incarnation of God in Christ. In the process he reconstructs the concepts of 'reconciliation' and 'incarnation' as well as other christological categories.[1]

### Possibility: The Implicit Unity of Divine and Human Nature

The 1821 manuscript opens this theme with a powerful statement (3:109–10). The possibility of reconciliation consists in humanity's

---

[1] Hegel's christology has received more attention than most other parts of his theological system. See Emilio Brito, *La christologie de Hegel: Verbum Crucis* (Paris: Beauchesne, 1983); Hans Küng, *The Incarnation of God: An Introduction to Hegel's Theological Thought as a Prolegomenon to a Future Christology*, trans. J. R. Stephenson (New York: Crossroad, 1987); James Yerkes, *The Christology of Hegel*, 2nd edn. (Albany: State University of New York Press, 1983). These works were, however, all written before the critical edition of the *Lectures on the Philosophy of Religion* was published. Wolf-Dieter Marsch's valuable study, *Gegenwart Christi in der Gesellschaft: Eine Studie zu Hegels Dialektik* (Munich: Chr. Kaiser Verlag, 1965), is concerned not with the philosophy of religion but with Hegel's early theological writings and his social writings.

coming to consciousness of the universal in and for itself (i.e. God) as *its own* essence, its own infinity, from which it has been estranged by its willing of 'singular selfishness'. 'Belonging to self without seeking for self is the infinite form of consciousness.... God as spirit, who is infinite subjectivity,... is both the absolute truth and the absolute goal of the will.' When humanity makes this goal its own, it recognizes it to be the goal of 'infinite freedom'. As a consequence humans know themselves to be 'elevated above all locality, nationality, condition, life-situation, etc. Human beings are equal; slavery is intolerable.'[2]

The condition of possibility for reconciliation is that 'humanity implicitly bears within itself the divine idea', which is the idea of 'the unity of divine and human nature'. This idea, the *imago Dei*, is not something alien to humanity but is its own substantial, though presently lost or distorted, nature. The vocation of humanity is to regain its own nature—not through striving or merit but as a divine gift. In addition, however, because 'God is spirit in the process of differentiation and return,... the unity of divine and human nature has a significance not only for the definition of human nature but just as much for that of the divine.' God becomes fully God when the implicit unity of divinity and humanity becomes actual. The actualized unity of divine and human nature is Hegel's philosophical interpretation of 'incarnation'. The becoming-flesh (*in-carnatio*) or becoming-human (*Mensch-werdung*) of divinity is not something that happens only once as an extrinsic miracle; rather it is 'a moment in the process of the divine nature' (3:109–10). Yet according to Christian faith, so Hegel affirms, it does happen once in a revelatorily definitive way.

The 1824 lectures focus on the idea of 'reconciliation' (*Versöhnung*), which like 'incarnation' is a category that is philosophically reconstructed by Hegel (3:211–13).[3] Reconciliation has nothing to do with the extrinsic payment of a debt or atonement for a sin.

---

[2] This reference to slavery, though muted as a social criticism, is important for Hegel, for it signifies that Christianity as the religion of freedom undercuts all oppressive social practices. In the 1827 lectures, Hegel says in a different context that the 'freedom of the subject is its rationality.... Slavery contradicts Christianity because it is contrary to reason.' Thus 'reconciliation should also be accomplished in the worldly realm' (3:340).

[3] Hegel normally uses the term 'reconciliation' to connote redemption or salvation since what is principally involved is the overcoming of estrangement and the reunification of God and humanity. But he also employs the word 'redemption' (*Erlösung*), as at 3:128.

Rather, we are told, what seems to be incompatible—the infinite and the finite ego—proves not to be so. 'The truth . . . is the *unity* of the finite and infinite. . . . Divine and human nature enter into a unity wherein both have set aside their abstractness vis-à-vis each other. . . . "Divine and human nature" is a puzzling and difficult expression, and the kind of representation we associate with it should be forgotten. What it means is spiritual essentiality [*die geistige Wesenheit*]' (3:211–12). 'Spiritual essentiality' entails precisely the unity of God and the world, finite and infinite, divine and human, for *Geist* bridges all these dichotomies and is formed from their interplay. The awkward expression 'divine and human nature' cannot mean two ontologically incompatible natures, conjoined miraculously. The condition of possibility for reconciliation is that unity is the original and the final divine–human condition, not something having to be brought about by an extrinsic action. From these definitions we see that 'incarnation' and 'reconciliation' are closely connected if not ultimately synonymous terms.

The subject cannot produce reconciliation by its own agency, by 'positing' it. Instead of a positing we should speak rather of a 'presupposing' in the sense that what is posited is also something implicit. 'The truth must . . . appear to the subject as a presupposition, and the question is how and in what guise the truth can appear at the standpoint at which we now find ourselves, i.e. the standpoint of infinite flight and abstractness.' Thus to affirm that reconciliation is the original divine–human condition is not to deny or downplay the present human condition, which is one of 'infinite anguish', of 'flight from reality' and withdrawal into self. The question is how reconciliation can appear within and overcome the reality of estrangement.

The 1827 lectures continue along these lines (3:310–12). Implicitly, reconciliation is eternally accomplished and the antithesis between divinity and humanity is overcome in principle. The antithesis or anguish must be intensified to its greatest extreme in order that humans should become aware of the need for atonement (*Aussöhnung*), that is, the sublation or nullification of the antithesis. This nullification is not something that finite subjects can bring about on their own account; rather it is eternally accomplished in the divine idea: 'God is the one who as living spirit distinguishes himself from himself, posits an other and in this other remains identical with himself.' No 'harm' is done to the divine unity by the other-being, the finitude, the weakness, the frailty of human nature. 'For the Son is other than the Father, and this otherness is difference—otherwise it would not be spirit. But the other is [also] God and has the entire fullness of the divine nature within itself. . . . This otherness is what eternally posits and eternally sublates itself; the self-positing and sublating of otherness is love or spirit' (3:311–12). It is false to think of evil as being on one side and God on the other; rather God is on both sides: God undergoes the anguish of alienation and overcomes it, incorporates it into the divine life as a negated negative.

Reconciliation is possible simply because God is an eternal process of reconciliation—the dynamo of positing otherness and sublating estrangement that makes God to be God. The only question is how human beings become aware of this process and participate in it. With this question we arrive at questions about the necessity and actuality of reconciliation. Hegel himself does not precisely distinguish between the categories of 'possibility', 'necessity', and 'actuality', but they are discernible steps in his analysis.

### Necessity: The Unity Must Appear and Be Accomplished in History

For reasons that have already been adduced, having to do with conditions of finitude and estrangement, the knowledge of reconciliation, of divine–human unity, must *come* or *appear* to humanity as something that is empirically certain. Moreover, it must come 'in a wholly temporal, completely ordinary worldly appearance in a single human being—this one man who is known at the same time as the divine idea, not as a teacher, not merely as a higher being in general, but as the highest [idea], as the Son of God' (3:110). This assertion, as found in the lecture manuscript, combines the second and third steps in Hegel's argument, which we are naming 'necessity' and 'actuality'. The idea of divine–human unity must appear (a) as an empirically certain event in history, and (b) as a single human being who is recognized to be not merely a human teacher (important as this is in itself) but also the Son of God (who is the divine idea, the idea of divine–human unity).

Hegel's elaboration of the first point in the manuscript (3:110–12) is rather complex. The reason has to do with the necessity, for fallen and embodied beings, of 'the immediate certainty and presence of divinity'. This is the way in which 'the Is' (*das Ist*) exists for natural consciousness. The 'isness' of divinity is an essential theme. God's objectivity is 'realized in the *whole* of humanity immediately'. Hegel illustrates this claim with a quotation from the concluding stanza of Friedrich Schiller's poem 'Die Freundschaft' (1782): 'From the chalice of the entire realm of spirits foams forth to him [God] infinitude.'[4] To this he adds an obscure reference to Goethe's poem 'An Suleika', the meaning of which for him appears to be that just as Timur (Tamburlaine) destroyed myriads of human beings to gain a kingdom, so the perfume-maker consumes thousands of roses to produce a tiny flask of fragrant scent; likewise an entire world is needed to offer up a love worthy of God. By juxtaposing this poem with the line from Schiller, Hegel seems to be saying that the anguish or suffering (the 'chalice') of the *whole* of humanity is needed to give up to God God's own infinitude.[5] Thus reconciliation entails the action of humanity as a whole, not just of one human being; and God's incarnate presence is found in all the suffering of the world. The ideality of reconciliation becomes reality in the form of anguished love wherever it is found—a not insignificant thought as one reflects on the diversity of world religions.

The 1824 lectures approach the theme of 'necessity' more directly. For the sensible, divided human consciousness, the unity of divinity and humanity must *appear*: 'God appears as the concrete God, ... in sensible presence.' 'God is not an abstraction but what is utterly concrete.' Moreover, 'God, considered in terms of his eternal idea, *has* to generate the Son, has to distinguish himself from himself, in such a way that what is distinguished is wholly he himself; and their union is love and the Spirit.' Spirit emerges from the 'infinite anguish' of human suffering and is 'the absolute power to endure this anguish. . . . Thus the anguish itself verifies the appearance of God' (3:214–15). In other words, God *must* appear in the anguish of history to become a spiritual God; and humans *need* such an appearance as a concrete verification of their redemption.

The clearest formulation of the argument from necessity is found in the 1827 lectures. For the unity of divine and human nature to be known with certainty, it must obtain the form of

---

[4] 3:111 incl. n. 129. The same lines are quoted in slightly different form at the conclusion of the *Phenomenology of Spirit*. Both quotations differ slightly from Schiller's actual words.

[5] 3:111–13 incl. n. 131. The reference is to J. W. von Goethe's *West-Östlicher Divan*, Buch des Timur, Poem 2, 'An Suleika', published in 1819.

'immediate sensible intuition and external existence'; it must appear as something that has been seen and experienced in the world. 'For it is only what exists in an immediate way, in inner or outer intuition, that is certain. In order for it [divine–human unity] to become a certainty for humanity, God had to appear in the world in the flesh' (3:312–13). Whether this is the flesh of a single human being, or of a multiplicity of incarnations, or of humanity as a whole, is a matter to be determined by the actualities of history. The necessity of appearance does not determine the form of appearance.

## *Actuality: Reconciliation in and through a Single Human Being*

Hegel now moves to his strongest claims. The idea of reconciliation or of divine–human unity is realized (a) in the form of *human individuality*, indeed (b) in a *single human individual* who, according to Christian faith, is (c) the *particular person* Jesus of Nazareth. Thus the argument for actuality runs through three phases.

First, Hegel develops the necessary role of individuality (*Individualität, Einzelheit*). The universal is present as universal not in an abstract generic fashion or in material objects such as stone or metal, but in the concrete subjectivity of individual human beings. It is subjective consciousness that is open to the universal, and the universal appears in the form of subjectivity. Subjectivity is the place where the connection occurs between the infinite and the finite.

In a more controversial phase of the argument, Hegel goes on to emphasize that subjectivity or individuality is always unique: each subject exists on its own account and stands out from others. Thus there must be *only one individual* in whom the idea of divine–human unity appears in a revelatorily definitive way. 'In one, all [are encompassed]; in several, divinity becomes an abstraction. [This individual appears] utterly and exclusively other over against them all, in order that they might be reconstituted' (3:112–14). While there may be many possible incarnations—for example, divine men as venerated by the Greeks, Romans, and Hindus— there is only one Christ, in whom the infinite idea of humanity is fully realized (3:145).

These arguments, as adduced by the 1821 manuscript, are repeated in the 1824 and 1827 lectures, but with distinctive nuances. In 1824 Hegel tells his hearers that 'God appears in sensible presence' and 'has no other shape [*Gestalt*] than that of the sensible mode of spirit', which is 'the shape of the singular human being'. This is 'the appearance of God in the flesh' and is 'the monstrous reality [*das Ungeheure*] whose necessity we have seen. What it posits is that divine and human nature are not intrinsically different—God [is] in human shape' (3:214). The shape of God in human shape is a theme already enunciated in 'The Spirit of Christianity and Its Fate',[6] and it is a 'monstrous' reality because it entails the conjunction of two natures that are thought to be intrinsically different but that in fact share a common essence, that of spirit (*Geist*). The only *Gestalt* in which God can appear is that of *Geist*, and conversely there can be no *Geist* without *Gestalt*, no spirit without configuration or shape.

The 1827 lectures emphasize another aspect of the theme already announced in the manuscript, namely, that 'the unity of divine and human nature must appear in just one human being'. To be sure, the idea of humanity is universal, but in this case it is a matter not of human ideality but of concrete, sensible reality, and 'thus it is just one human being in whom this unity is envisaged'. 'Moreover, it is not just a matter of singularity in general, for singularity in general is something universal once more.' Universal singularity is an abstraction, whereas the concern here is with the 'certainty of intuiting and sensing'. The substantial unity of God and humanity is something that lies beyond immediate consciousness and ordinary knowledge. 'That is exactly why the unity in question must appear for others as a singular human being set apart; it is not present in the others, but only in one from whom all the others are excluded' (3:313–14).[7]

While conceding that humanity as a whole is an abstraction, it is not clear to a postmodern perspective why divinity should be regarded as any less concrete in several singular incarnations in different religio-cultural settings. The insistence on oneness, on 'once and for all' or 'one and only', reflects a prejudice that privileges unity over diversity and regards Christ as qualitatively superior to all other saviour figures. To be sure, the mediator of

---

[6] See above, Chap. 2. Cf. Philippians 2:6–8, where the Wisdom hymn to which Paul refers suggests that Christ, though in the form or shape (*morphē*) of God, emptied himself and took on the shape of a human being.

[7] Paralleling this passage from the 1827 lectures is a lengthy text from the 1831 lectures transmitted by the *Werke* (see 3:314 n. 173), which sounds basically the same themes but with greater emphasis on history-of-religions comparisons.

redemption is set apart from other human beings who are in need of what is being mediated, but this is not a persuasive argument for only one such mediator; there could be several who are set apart and who work in a diversity of ways. Indeed, Hegel's arguments for the possibility and necessity of reconciliation—the intrinsic unity of divinity and humanity, the universality of suffering and anguish, the need for empirical embodiments of divinity in shapes appropriate to concrete situations—could be viewed as pointing in the direction of diversity. His insistence on the role of concrete, singular individuals is well-taken, but his claim that one such individual stands above all the others does not resonate well with the recognition of a plurality of living world religions,[8] and it does not seem to be required by his own philosophical principles. At this point he is bending his argument to accommodate normative Christian doctrine.

Who is this one? This question introduces the final phase of the argument for actuality. The idea of reconciliation is realized in *this* single individual: Jesus of Nazareth, who is the Christ (3:114, 142–3). Here again Hegel reiterates that the divine–human unity becomes objective in only one 'this', not in several incarnations. To posit several is superfluous to the concept of individual subjectivity: 'once is always'. But, we may object, given the fact of cultural diversity this is not true: no single human subject can represent the whole of humanity. The argument is reinforced by a trinitarian claim: 'in the eternal idea, [there is] only one Son, one only exclusive of other finite beings'. Here Hegel is trading on metaphorical rather than conceptual categories in the sense that singularity is not necessarily implicit in the idea of divine–human unity, of which 'the Son' is a metaphorical representation. Despite the excessive character of the claim for only one redeemer figure, the focus on individuality per se is eloquently stated. 'The consummation of reality in immediate singular individuality [is] the most beautiful point of the Christian religion. For the first time the absolute transfiguration [of finitude is] intuitively exhibited [so that everyone can] give an account of it and have an awareness of it' (3:114–15).

[8] Part of the problem is that for Hegel most religions are no longer *living* religions, the exceptions being Christianity and Islam. This will be a major point of issue in Chap. 10.

What evidence can be adduced to support the claim that Jesus of Nazareth is the Christ? It is above all a claim of faith, but one that is congruent with historical fact. As we shall discuss in the next section, Hegel argues that the history of Jesus' teaching, life, death, and resurrection is 'strictly adequate to the idea [*schlechthin der Idee gemäß*]' (3:145–9). This is a revelatory as well as an ontological adequacy. Ontologically, the unity of divinity and humanity is already established as the condition of possibility of reconciliation: Jesus instantiates this unity but does not add to it. Reconciliation occurs in actuality when the unity *appears*, is recognized, and is put into practice—and this depends on the revelatory impact of Jesus' distinctive life and death. For this reason Jesus is revelatorily definitive more than he is ontologically definitive for Hegel. To be sure, his revelatory impact follows from the fullness of God's presence in him, so the revelatory and the ontological are connected.

To these remarks in the manuscript, the 1824 lectures add the following: the fact that God appears in *this* human being at *this* time and place is not verified by the inner necessity of God's sending forth his Son but only from the point of view of world history. That the time had come can only be discerned from history (3:215). But the discernment itself entails a judgement of faith based on the inner witness of the Spirit, not on miracle or historical proof.

## THE MINISTRY, TEACHING, AND PERSON OF CHRIST

In the 1827 lectures Hegel identifies two perspectives on Jesus of Nazareth or 'Christ':[9] nonreligious and religious (3:316). The nonreligious perspective (*die irreligiöse Betrachtung*) views him as a human being in accord with his external circumstances and depends on historical accounts of his ministry and teaching. Here

---

[9] Hegel uses the word 'Christ' (*Christus*) as a proper name that is synonymous with 'Jesus of Nazareth', while the title 'the Christ' (*der Christ*) designates the Messiah, the Son of God, the idea of divine–human unity. See 3:142–3 n. 211. It was common practice in the nineteenth century to use 'Christ' as a name for the historical Jesus, and I will so employ it, interchangeably with 'Jesus', in the following discussion. The key question for Hegel is whether and in what sense 'Christ' is also 'the Christ'.

he is seen in the same light as Socrates,[10] or as Muslims regard him, namely as a teacher of humanity, a messenger of God, a martyr to the truth. The religious perspective (*das Religiöse*) identifies him as the Christ, the God-man, the one in whom God is definitively present and revealed, and depends on the witness of the Spirit. While appearing to establish a sharp distinction between these perspectives, Hegel's treatment actually shows their congruence: the historical view confirms or corroborates the spiritual, but does not displace the necessary role of faith and spiritual discernment.[11]

The earlier lectures do not identify the two perspectives as such, but the distinction between them provides a convenient way of organizing the treatment of Christ in all the lecture series.

### *The Human, Historical Perspective: Christ as Teacher*

The first perspective incorporates two moments (3:316–17). The first moment views Christ as 'immediately a human being in all the external contingencies, in all the temporal exigencies and conditions, that this entails'. He is born like every other human being[12] and has common human needs, but does not share the corruption, passions, and evil inclinations of others, and is not involved in worldly pursuits. The second moment is that of his 'teaching office', and this is where Hegel's interest focuses.

---

[10] The 1831 lectures provide a more detailed comparison of Christ and Socrates (3:321 n. 196, cf. 368). From the nonreligious perspective, the story of Christ is quite similar to that of Socrates. Both were teachers who brought inwardness to consciousness in opposition to external authority, and both were martyrs to the truth. But, Hegel adds, Jesus' teaching about the kingdom of heaven and purity of heart contains 'an infinitely greater depth than the inwardness of Socrates'. In the miscellaneous papers a passage is found in which Hegel states that, while a teacher like Socrates, Christ is 'even more excellent than Socrates, since he was without sin' (3:244 n. 215; this passage also contains a reference to the Muslim view of Christ). Thus even from the point of view of history Christ is not simply equivalent to Socrates for Hegel. The comparison of Socrates and Christ was a common theme in the Enlightenment and in early nineteenth-century theology. Ferdinand Christian Baur adopted a position similar to Hegel in 'Das christliche des Platonismus oder Sokrates und Christus', *Tübinger Zeitschrift für Theologie* 10/3 (1837), 1–154. See also David Friedrich Strauss, 'Vergängliches und Bleibendes im Christenthum', *Freihafen* 1/3 (1838), 1–48.

[11] The 1831 lectures call the two perspectives the nonreligious way and the way of faith. 'One must be led from the former to the latter. If one starts from the appearance of Christ in external form, one can follow it up to the point of his death; but at this point a definite divorce occurs between faith and unbelief' (3:367). Even so, faith necessarily refers back to the story of his life prior to death (3:369).

[12] The story of the virgin birth is not discussed by Hegel and is obviously regarded by him as mythical.

The 1821 manuscript devotes considerable attention to the teaching of Jesus (3:115–22). We are told that the appearance of the divine idea in the whole of his life and destiny is integrated by his teaching, thus signifying a coherence between what he proclaims and who he is. His teaching, Hegel says, concerns only the universal, the universal soil, the element in which spirit must find its homeland: the heavenly kingdom or kingdom of God, an intelligible world in which all earthly values are cast away. The topic of the teaching is thus not God alone but the kingdom of God, the eternal as a homeland for spirit, a dwelling place for subjectivity.

Three aspects of the teaching are distinguished by the manuscript (3:117–22). First, as expressed in the Sermon on the Mount and elsewhere, there is a focus on inner blessedness or intention, a complete abstraction from what in the world is regarded as great. The central moral imperative here is that of love: love of neighbours, the love-relationship among the disciples (who are exhorted to share all possessions), and love of enemies. Second, Jesus emphasizes a breaking away from everything established, notably the ordinances of Judaism, which are brought to an end by the proclamation that God's kingdom is at hand.[13] This is the 'revolutionary' aspect of his teaching. He implores his followers not to be anxious over worldly affairs, and he prepares them to break all familial attachments. He scarcely mentions the state but envisions rather a withdrawal into a community that shuts itself off from the world (and thus has the potential to become fanatic). The third aspect of the teaching concerns the relationship of Christ himself to God, as expressed in the Johannine saying, 'I and the Father are one.' Hegel continues with an examination of Jesus' self-references as Son of God or Son of Man as found in the Synoptic Gospels. He assumes uncritically that the Gospels provide for the most part a reliable account of what Jesus actually said. Indeed, he warns against an exegesis that attempts to tone down or flatten out these expressions. Rather the words of Jesus confirm 'the truth of the idea'; they confirm that he is what he becomes for the community, namely, the Christ, the Son of God.

[13] This is the extent to which the philosophy of religion lectures set Jesus in opposition to Judaism, by comparison with the strong contrasts drawn in the early writings, notably 'The Positivity of the Christian Religion' and 'The Spirit of Christianity and Its Fate'. See *Early Theological Writings*, trans. T. M. Knox (Chicago: University of Chicago Press, 1948), 68 ff., 182 ff.

The life of this teacher is 'in conformity with' his teaching and 'strictly adequate to'[14] the idea of divine–human unity (3:122–4, 145). Jesus does not shun the hazards and the death he must expect as the result of his religious radicalism. The content of his life is simply the kingdom of God that he proclaims. By living it he brings it to life as a spiritual community. The kingdom enters into actuality through this individual, whose teaching of it constitutes his divinity. 'Since it is the divine idea that courses through this history, it occurs not as the history of a single individual alone, but rather it is implicitly the history of actual humanity as it constitutes itself as the existence of spirit.' These strong statements soften the distinction between irreligious (historical) and religious (faith) perspectives on the figure of Christ—a point to which we shall return in the 1827 lectures.

The 1824 lectures provide an abbreviated account of the teaching of Jesus (3:216–18), with no discussion of his life at all (see 3:219 n. 145). His teaching is not Christian dogmatics, not the doctrine of the church. Rather it is an explication of the nature of God oriented specifically to intuition rather than doctrine. The teaching gives 'a new world, a new religion, a new concept of God'. It produces the 'universal soil' for the concept of God in the form of the kingdom of God, which is 'the real divinity, God in his determinate existence, in his spiritual actuality'. The abstract universality of this teaching has 'the character of negation vis-à-vis everything in the present world.... It is a revolutionary doctrine that partly leaves all standing institutions aside and partly destroys and overthrows them.... What is brought before the imagination is an elevation to an infinite energy in which the universal demands to be firmly maintained on its own account.' Examples of this negative radicalism are adduced from the Gospels. Perfect independence of worldly relationships is 'the abstract, primal soil of spirituality'. On the positive side, love is made the principal commandment, meaning especially the mutual love of the community, but the particular duties of life are not specified, so that love too remains an abstraction.

The 1827 lectures restore the fuller discussion of the teaching of Jesus presented in 1821, and they draw out more explicitly the theological implications of his life and work (3:316–21). The

---

[14] The terms Hegel uses for 'adequate to' and 'in conformity with' are *gemäß* and *angemessen*.

summary of the teaching is similar to 1821 but with distinctive nuances: through his teaching a new world is constituted, a new consciousness of humanity, a new religion, an absolute reconciliation expressed as a state of affairs, the kingdom of God. God rules in the heart and has attained dominion. Such teaching is utterly opposed to external conditions and the later doctrine of the church. 'This is its polemical aspect, its revolutionary attitude' toward worldly institutions and settled attitudes. 'It poses the demand that one should remove oneself from finite things and elevate oneself to an infinite energy for which all other bonds are to become matters of indifference.' Normal ethical relationships are suspended in favour of the 'concentrated manifestation of the truth'. All this is 'expressed with the purest, most colossal boldness'.

This portrayal of the teaching leads Hegel to conclude that Jesus speaks not merely as a teacher who expounds on the basis of his subjective insight but as a prophet. The 1827 text continues with a statement that goes well beyond the 1821 and 1824 lectures (although hints are present in 1821).

He is the one who, because his demand is immediate, expresses it immediately from God, and God speaks it through him. His having this life of the Spirit in the truth, so that it is simply there without mediation, expresses itself prophetically in such a way that it is God who says it. It is a matter of the absolute, divine truth that has being in and for itself, and of its expression and intention; and the confirmation of this expression is envisaged as God's doing. It is the consciousness of the real unity of the divine will and of his harmony with it. In the form of this expression, however, the accent is laid upon the fact that the one who says this is at the same time essentially human. It is the Son of Man who speaks thus, in whom this expression, this activity of what subsists in and for itself, is essentially the work of God—not as something suprahuman that appears in the shape of an external revelation, but rather as [God's] working in a human being, so that the divine presence is essentially identical with this human being. (3:320)

The speech and activity of Jesus is that of a human being (a 'son of humanity'[15]), yet it is at the same time essentially the work of God. God speaks through human speech, not in an extrinsic, supernatural

[15] As the 'son of humanity' or 'son of man' Jesus is the representative human being. This title designates for Hegel Jesus' common humanity, not his divinity or his messianic role. See the summary above, in Chap. 2, of Hegel's discussion of the title in 'The Spirit of Christianity and Its Fate'.

way, but as God's working in a human being. This is Hegel's construal of the doctrine of the incarnation. Divinity and humanity fuse in the shape of a human teacher-prophet who plumbs the depths of divinity. God and humanity are connected in such a way that God works within humanity without cancelling but rather strengthening human subjectivity and personality. The awkward apparatus of orthodox christology—'two natures', 'one person', 'hypostatic union'—is replaced by a new philosophical intuition.[16]

It is startling to discover that Hegel regards all this as having being said from one side, the human historical side, and that it is not yet a 'religious view' of Christ (3:321). If so, then history surely serves as a confirmation or corroboration of the witness of faith. Without a congruence between faith and history, faith would be undercut: it would have as its object a mythical figure, not a real historical person.

### *The Religious Perspective: Christ as God-Man*

Despite the fact that much has already been said of religious significance from a historical perspective, the religious perspective properly comes into view only after and in light of the death and resurrection of Christ. The 1831 lectures remark (3:368–9) that with the death of Christ 'the reversal begins, and the contemplation of faith, of the Holy Spirit, enters into play—the *divine view* [*göttliche Betrachtung*], according to which it is the nature of God that is revealed in Christ.... The faith that God is in Christ is the certainty that this course of the divine life is and has been envisaged in the course of this [human] life.' Yet Hegel also acknowledges that in order for the divine life to be so envisaged, certain 'conditions' (*Bedingungen*) are necessary, such as the teaching of Christ, his self-references, and his miracles ('by which we do see divine power in this individual'). Miracles possess no independent corroborative power since they exist as such only for faith. But Christ's teaching, conduct (healing ministry), and self-understanding suggest that the human life in which the divine life is believed to flow is an appropriate vehicle of divinity. The faith that

---

[16] As in his discussion of the Trinity, Hegel does not delve into the technicalities of christological categories and doctrines. From his perspective the often arcane distinctions drawn in the trinitarian and christological debates amount to little of significance. The whole of classical theology, though expressing genuine insight, was burdened by an inadequate conceptuality and philosophical vision.

it does so flow is based on the witness of the Holy Spirit to individuals and to the community of faith. Only faith can see that *God* is present in Christ, but there are reasons for this envisagement; it does not run counter to the historical witness.[17]

What faith sees, according to 1827, is that Jesus is the 'God-man' —a 'monstrous compound', to be sure, which contradicts both representation and understanding. This compound expresses not only the unity of divine and human nature but also the recognition that 'the otherness, or, as we also say, the finitude, weakness, and frailty of human nature, does not damage this unity', indeed is necessary to it, for 'God in sensible presence can take no other shape than that of human being' (3:315–16). To be present in a single, immediate human being in all his contingency entails a 'divestment' (*Entäußerung*) of the divine (3:216). The term 'divestment' (used here in the 1824 lectures, but also in 1821) links Hegel with the tradition of kenotic christology that goes back to the second chapter of Philippians. The divine self-emptying or divestment does not involve an extrinsic miracle but is intrinsic to the process of divinity. It allows the human contingency of Jesus to stand uncompromised, but it also enables faith to affirm that God is present in his life in such a way as to change all other human lives. This affirmation comes from a post-death and post-resurrection perspective, and it entails the witness of spirit to spirit—of the Holy Spirit to human spirits. Sensory verification falls away, including miracles: the true miracle is spirit itself. Genuine verification is through power over minds (*Geister*)—a power that manifests itself in the community of faith over many centuries (3:115, 220–1).

### THE DEATH OF CHRIST

The death of Christ that begins the reversal in perspective can itself be viewed from two perspectives: historically, as the death of

---

[17] Hegel's position is in some respects similar to that of Søren Kierkegaard. Yes, a historical point of departure must be given for an eternal consciousness; but No, an eternal happiness cannot be based on historical knowledge. See the title page to Kierkegaard's *Philosophical Fragments*, ed. and trans. Howard V. and Edna H. Hong (Princeton: Princeton University Press, 1985), 1. Faith is rooted in history, but no proof of God can be given from history. Hegel would not concur with Kierkegaard's assertion that the sheer 'that' of God's incarnation (or of faith in such an incarnation) is sufficient; faith also needs the concrete 'what' of Jesus' life and ministry.

a criminal; and religiously, as the death of God. The reversal occurs in the movement from the first to the second perspective.

## Viewed Historically: The Death of a Criminal

The historical perspective is seen most clearly in the lecture manuscript. The discussion begins by noting that Christ's death is consistent with his life and teaching in the sense that it is the consequence of his religious radicalism and revolutionary attitude toward established orders. Christ 'seals his faith by his death'. Hegel immediately adds that this consistency between how one lives and how one dies is not too much to expect and is shared by him with a host of others (3:122). Christ dies as a martyr to the truth. In this respect his death is honourable but not unique.

In another respect it is neither honourable nor unique: Christ is executed as a common criminal, and in the most degrading manner conceivable, the torturous death on a cross (3:129–31). This is a shameful, dishonouring death. Hegel notes that for Christians what 'the state uses as an instrument of dishonour is here converted into what is highest'. But before extolling the religious symbolism of the cross, we should remember its political function: 'The cross corresponds to our gallows.' Crucifixion was the most outwardly visible sign of the cold brutality of Roman imperial authority, which 'degraded everything esteemed and prized by humanity'. By converting this symbol of dishonour into a badge of honour, Christians were in effect rejecting the authority of Rome and withdrawing from the life of the state and from civil affairs.[18] But this reversal of values is predicated on seeing something else in the death of Christ than the death of a criminal: it is also the death of God.

---

[18] Hegel does not comment on the irony in the fact that when Christianity itself acquired political authority the cross was converted back from a symbol of resistance and religious honour to a symbol of political power and even oppression: the cross became a sword. But he alludes to this irony in his treatment of the Crusades in the lectures on the philosophy of world history. See *The Philosophy of History*, trans. John Sibree (New York: Dover Publications, 1956), 389–98. Here he comments: 'Through the Crusades the Church reached the completion of its authority: it had achieved the perversion of religion and of the divine Spirit; it had distorted the principle of Christian freedom to a wrongful and immoral slavery of men's souls' (394).

*Viewed Religiously: The Death of God*

Hegel attends to this aspect of the death of Christ in all the lectures and in considerable detail. Starting with the 1821 manuscript (3:124–8), he argues that Christ's death is a moment of the divine idea in the sense that death is 'the highest pinnacle of finitude', and it is precisely finitude that is assumed by God in the act of incarnation. Incarnation entails a 'divestment' (*Entäußerung*) of the universal, the divine, 'but a divestment of itself such that it still *is* in this divestment'. Divinity divested remains divinity, remains infinite precisely in its assumption of finitude. If death, anguished death, is the highest pinnacle of finitude, then 'the highest divestment of the divine idea . . . is expressed as follows: "God has died, God himself is dead."'[19] [This] is a monstrous, fearful picture, which brings before the imagination the deepest abyss of cleavage' (3:125).

But at the same time this death is the highest love, for love is the consciousness of the identity of the divine and the human, and the finitization of the divine is carried to its extreme in death. Precisely in this monstrous picture we find an envisagement of the unity of the divine and the human at its absolute peak. Love entails a supreme surrender of oneself in the other, and the death of God in the death of Christ is the highest expression of divine love. Here we find '*divinity* in this universal identity with other-being, death. The monstrous unification of these absolute extremes is love itself—[this is] the speculative intuition' (3:125). Speculation grasps that the Son goes to death as the divine, and that in death a reversal occurs, for death becomes a moment in the life of spirit. Death represents 'both the extreme limit of finitude and the sublation of natural finitude, of immediate existence, the overcoming of divestment, the dissolution of limitation' (3:126). In sum: 'Death accomplishes the process whereby the divine idea has divested itself, divested itself unto the bitter anguish of death and the shame of a criminal, and thereby human finitude is transfigured into the highest—the highest love. That is the deepest anguish, this the highest love' (3:131).

---

[19] Hegel draws this expression from the passion hymn 'O Traurigkeit, O Herzeleid' by Johannes Rist (1641). Thus the context of the expression for him is religious, not atheistic. The atheistic interpretation of the death of God begins principally with Nietzsche.

On this basis it can be justly asserted that Christ was 'given for us', and his death may be represented as sacrificial, an act of absolute satisfaction. But this is not to be interpreted in the traditional way as meaning a substitutionary atonement or a transaction involving a debt that only Christ (as God-man) can pay. Rather the death of God in Christ 'is one that makes satisfaction for us because it presents the absolute history of the divine idea as a history that has taken place in itself and happens eternally'. Christ as an individual can do something only because reconciliation is eternally accomplished within the godhead. Satisfaction is made for us in the sense that 'it has occurred in and for itself'. 'It is not an extrinsic sacrifice that is performed, nor a matter of someone else [being] punished so that punishment might be rendered.' Everyone must live, die, and assume responsibility on his or her own. Christ is not a substitute for us. To make the reconciliation that has already been accomplished our own, we must take it into our own subjectivity, conform our lives to it, knowing that the ground of our redemption is the eternal history of God. 'It is not a capricious accident, or merely a particular deed and happening, but rather is true and consummating. . . . It is not the history of a single individual; rather it is God who accomplishes it' (3:126–8). Christ is the revealer, not the accomplisher.

To this very full discussion in the manuscript, the 1824 lectures add a further insight into the nature of satisfaction, namely that 'God cannot be satisfied by something else, only by himself.' Hegel explicates this insight with a potent formulation:

The satisfaction consists in the fact that the first moment, that of immediacy, is negated; only then does God come to be at peace with himself, only then is spirituality posited. God is the true God, spirit, because he is not merely Father, and hence closed up within himself, but because he is Son, because he becomes the other and sublates this other. . . . Through death God has reconciled the world and reconciles himself eternally with himself. This coming back again is his return to himself, and through it he is spirit. So this third moment is that Christ has risen. Negation is thereby overcome, and the negation of negation is thus a moment of the divine nature. (3:219–20)

Thus the idea of satisfaction, atonement, or reconciliation is intimately connected with the trinitarian mediation by which God is God. Just in case anyone has missed the point, Hegel reiterates: 'The meaning of the story is that it is the story of God. God is the absolute, self-contained movement that spirit is, and this movement is here represented in the individual [Christ].' He adds that there are a number of false ways in which this matter can be represented, relating to external relationships—such as, for example, the idea of a sacrificial death that makes God into a tyrant who demands sacrifice (3:220).

Also significant in this passage is the connection of the resurrection of Christ with the third trinitarian moment, that of the Spirit—a matter to which we shall turn shortly.

The 1827 lectures develop the latter point more fully (3:322–6), and with it the theme that the death of Christ represents not only a reversal but a transition, a transition into a new mode of existence, a transition from sensible to spiritual presence. Thus we must speak not merely of death but of death-and-resurrection. What is involved in the life, ministry, and death of Christ is not merely a moral teaching or human subjectivity but an infinite relationship to God. Satisfaction is found not through a substitutionary sacrifice but in the relationship to God, in the awareness that God is present, is love. This insight occurs with the formation of the community and the outpouring of the Holy Spirit. The death of Christ is now no longer seen merely as that of a teacher, friend, and martyr to the truth, but as 'the means of salvation, the focal point of reconciliation'. 'Christ's death assumes the character of a death that constitutes the transition to glory, but to a glorification that is only a restoration of the original glory. Death, the negative, is the mediating term through which the original majesty is posited as now achieved. The history of the resurrection and ascension of Christ to the right hand of God begins at the point where this history receives a spiritual interpretation' (3:325–6).

But, Hegel reminds his hearers in one of his most powerful formulations, 'this humanity in God...is natural death. "God himself is dead"', it says in a Lutheran hymn, expressing an awareness that the human, the finite, the fragile, the weak, the negative are themselves a moment of the divine, that they are within God himself, that finitude, negativity, otherness are not outside of God and do not, as otherness, hinder unity with God' (3:326). Death is the furthest extreme to which humanity is exposed, and 'God himself is [involved in] this.' The formulation is pushed further: in the history of Christ as comprehended spiritually, there is presented 'the process of what humanity, what spirit is—implicitly both God and dead' (3:326).

In respect to the themes of sacrifice, satisfaction, and reconciliation, the 1827 lectures repeat what is said in 1824 and 1821: the reconciliation in Christ 'makes no sense' if God is not known as the triune God who distinguishes otherness from God, yet sublates this otherness and returns to godself as love and the Spirit. '"To sacrifice" means to sublate the natural, to sublate otherness. It is said: "Christ has died for all." This is not a single act but the eternal divine history: it is a moment in the nature of God himself; it has taken place in God himself' (3:327–8).

Our sources allow a glimpse of Hegel's treatment of the death of Christ in the 1831 lectures.[20] While many themes are similar to what has been said before, especially in 1827, one in particular stands out, namely the connection between crucifixion and resurrection. 'The process does not come to a halt at this point [with the death of God]; rather, a reversal takes place: God, that is to say, maintains himself in this process, and the latter is only the death of death. God rises again to life, and thus things are reversed. The resurrection is something that belongs just as essentially to faith [as the crucifixion]' (3:323 n. 199). This process is connected with the trinitarian process in another passage: 'The abstractness of the Father is given up in the Son—this then is death. But the negation of this negation is the unity of Father and Son—love, or the Spirit' (3:370).

These statements should not be interpreted to mean that God only seems to die. Death is as real for God as it is for finite creatures; but it is not the final or most powerful reality. God overpowers death, not the reverse. Death is taken into the divine life as a negated moment. The death of God signifies the death of death, for God (not simply Christ) rises again to life. In the process God gives up the abstractness of divine immediacy (God as Father) and becomes a concrete, world-embracing, suffering, dying God (God as Son); but the power of divine love is such as to negate this negation and to reconcile the eternal and the temporal, the infinite and the finite (God as Spirit). Spirit, then, is the final and most adequate name of God. Whether God as Spirit has the power to prevail over death is a question that confronts faith in all ages—none more so than our own, the age of postmodernity in

---

[20] These consist of Strauss's excerpts (3:368–71) and a lengthy passage transmitted by the *Werke*, footnoted in relation to the 1827 text we have discussed above (3:323–5 n. 199).

which it is widely believed that death is the prevailing power. This is a question we shall have to consider in the final chapter.


## THE RESURRECTION AND ASCENSION OF CHRIST

The resurrection of Christ is as essential to Christian faith as the crucifixion, Hegel avers. But it is not a material event like the crucifixion. It is more like an interpretative perspective on the crucifixion, indeed on the whole of the life of Christ, a perspective that arises with the community of faith and is based on the spiritual experience of the community rather than on historical evidence or proofs. Thus Hegel makes no mention of the empty tomb and appearance stories, which he implicitly demythologizes along with the birth stories. No literal bodily resurrection occurs; Christ's sensible, bodily presence is left behind in the transition to spiritual presence. Under the motif of 'resurrection' (*Auferstehung*, literally 'standing forth' or 'rising up') Hegel offers images of the raising up, ascent, return, and consummation of the whole divine process. What is involved is an 'exaltation' (*Erhöhung*) of Christ; and indeed religion as such is an 'elevation' (*Erhebung*) to God. These images are all connected: resurrection as exaltation is intrinsic to the religious life.

Thus in the 1821 manuscript we are told that 'resurrection' and 'ascension' are the modes by which the consummation and return of the divine life to itself are 'envisaged' (3:131). What is involved is an envisagement or intuition (*Anschauung*), not a description or report, even though for immediate consciousness the exaltation of Christ appears in 'the mode of actuality'. With this said, Hegel can embrace the traditional language and metaphors: human nature is exalted to heaven 'where the Son of Man sits at the right hand of the Father'; 'the end is [presented] as a resolution into glory, the festive assumption of humanity in the divine idea'. But philosophically what is involved is 'the going forth of the divine idea into the uttermost cleavage, even to the opposite pole of the anguish of death, which is itself the absolute reversal, the highest love, containing the negation of the negative within itself [and being in this way] the absolute reconciliation' (3:132). 'Resurrection' is a metaphorical way of articulating what happens in the death of God and the divine process as a whole. It also designates a transition in focus from a single human being to the community of the Spirit (3:133).

Resurrection is not about the survival and prolongation of individual streams of consciousness but about the consummation of all things in the life of God.

The 1824 lectures make virtually no reference to the resurrection other than that it means God's 'coming back' to godself as spirit (3:220). The 1827 lectures offer the remark that 'the history of the resurrection and ascension of Christ to the right hand of God begins at the point where this history receives a spiritual interpretation' (3:326). 'This history' refers to the story of Christ as a whole,[21] and the point is that, when this story receives a spiritual interpretation in the community of faith, the history of the resurrection and ascension also begins. In other words, the resurrection of Christ is simply coterminous with the ongoing faith and life of the spiritual community. It is a communal, not an individual event. Thus the church rightly rejects historical investigations and proofs of the appearance of Christ after his death (3:330).[22]

Perhaps it is not surprising, given the growing suspicion of and opposition to his philosophical theology,[23] that Hegel does not push this demythologizing interpretation of resurrection too hard or in detail but turns directly to the theme of spiritual community.

---

[21] This is confirmed by a variant from one of Lasson's sources: 'Religious history is [found] where a spiritual interpretation of the history of Christ before his death prevails; for, of course, even the Gospels were written only after the outpouring of the Spirit' (3:326 n. 204).

[22] The 1831 lectures call attention to the fact that 'Christ appeared only to his friends', which is interpreted to mean that what is involved is not objective history but an occurrence only for faith (3:324 n. 199).

[23] Hegel's awareness of this opposition is reflected in his introductions to the philosophy of religion lectures. See above, Chap. 3.

# 9

# Spirit and Community

Hegel's treatment of the 'third element' of the idea of God, that of reunion and consummation, which for Christian theology takes the form of the Holy Spirit and the community of faith, is structurally similar in all of the lectures. Three topics are addressed: the *origin* of the community (the transition from the sensible to the spiritual presence of Christ and the unique intersubjectivity of the spiritual community), the *existence* or *subsistence* of the community (in the form of institutions, teachings, and sacraments), and the *realization* of the community (the process by which faith passes over into worldly actuality and the question as to whether the community itself passes away). The first two sections of this chapter discuss the matters included under 'origin', the third section the topic of 'existence', and the last two sections that of 'realization'.

## TRANSITION FROM THE SENSIBLE TO THE SPIRITUAL PRESENCE OF CHRIST

### Affirmation of Sensible Presence

In the lecture manuscript (and only there), Hegel begins his discussion by reaffirming the moment of sensible presence, against which a 'revolting arrogance' is often directed (3:134–5). The distinctive feature of Christianity as the religion of the Spirit is its affirmation of the sensible presence of divinity in a single individual. 'To shun the sensible in monkish fashion is to exhibit cowardice of thought. For spirit [is] at home with itself in the sensible.' 'The poet honours the sensible shape ... as having spirit within it', as does speculative intuition, which is not a sentimental attachment to feeling or subjectivity but an envisaging of love in death and a reverencing of God in the mode of

singularity.[1] The recognition of infinite freedom in anguished love
and the appropriation of it to oneself is 'the supreme miracle, the
highest in the realm of spirit'.

Hegel reiterates that the divine idea occurs for the Christian
religion 'as a present, immediate individual', who represents the
absolute unity of the universal and the singular, the spiritual and
the sensible. The next stage, however, 'is for this singularity, this
individuality, to be removed from the senses and raised to the right
hand of God'. Humanity is now directed inward, and worldly
grandeur disappears. This retreat to inwardness is not a Stoic
retreat, which derives from its own strength and lacks infinite
anguish. The Christian retreat 'endlessly divests itself of its particularity and self-possession and has its infinite value only in the
love that is contained in infinite anguish and comes from it'. In this
way it remains connected with the shameful death of the cross
(3:136–7).[2]

## Transition from Sensible to Spiritual Presence

This transition is called the *outpouring of the Holy Spirit*, which
can occur only after Christ has withdrawn and his sensible presence has ceased (3:230, 328).[3] This theme is developed in the 1824
and 1827 lectures.

The transition from sensible to spiritual presence involves two
sorts of passage that occur simultaneously: from the individual to
the community, and from externality and appearance to inwardness or subjectivity. Hegel remarks that since the appearance of
God in the flesh occurs in a specific time and individual, it necessarily 'passes by and becomes past history'. The sensible element is
preserved 'precisely by letting it pass away'. It cannot be held on to
as some sort of relic or holy image but must be allowed to pass
into new forms whereby it is remembered and re-enacted. Such
is the case with everything historical. Attempts can be made to

---

[1] Hegel adds a remark to the effect that envisaging such love is easy for persons of
tender and loving disposition, such as women, but 'infinitely hard for the independent concept, for the man' (3:135 incl. n. 191).

[2] The manuscript rather confusingly mixes this affirmation of sensible presence
with a discussion of the distinctive intersubjectivity of the spiritual community, to
which we attend in the next main section.

[3] On more than one occasion Hegel quotes John 16:7 to the effect that the Son
must depart in order for the Spirit to come (3:149, 222). See also the references to
John 15:26 (3:223, 369) and John 16:13 (3:115, 146, 149, 325, 383).

reconstitute the physical presence of Christ in the transubstantiated eucharistic elements or as a literal second coming, but a return that is 'essentially absolute' consists in a turning from externality to the inner realm, to a Comforter, the Spirit (3:222). Not a return but a *turning*—to the Spirit and to the community. The turn to the Spirit is a turn to inwardness and subjectivity, a turn from truth as something externally given and objective to truth as subjectivity. Truth is in the subject because the subject is 'filled with the truth' as it is filled with the Spirit. 'This is the turning to the inward path, and in this third realm we find ourselves on the soil of spirit as such—this is the community, the cultus, faith.' In the third realm, knowledge takes the distinctive form of faith, and the spiritual community arises with the rise of faith (3:223–6).

Thus the 1824 lectures; in 1827 Hegel emphasizes that the history and truth of the community are distinguished from individuals and stand over against them. On the one hand, faith is an immediate knowledge; on the other hand, 'the nature of spirit in itself is this process,... and this means that the subject itself becomes spirit, and thus a citizen of the kingdom of God, by virtue of the fact that the subject traverses this process in itself' (3:329). The process in question is the whole divine process of self-differentiation and self-return in which the individual subject is caught up as it is spiritualized. The process has an objectivity over against the individual, first in the form of the incarnate Christ, then in the form of the ongoing life of the community. The immediate knowledge of faith is mediated by the forms and practices of the community.

## *Faith and the Witness of the Spirit*

The community of faith arises, as we have seen, with the certainty that Jesus is the Christ, the incarnate Son of God. This faith derives from the witness of the Spirit, not proofs based on miracles (3:142–3). Hegel notes that Christ himself enjoins against the seeking of signs, proclaiming rather that 'the kingdom of God is within you' (3:144). This observation leads in the manuscript to an excursus on miracle in which Hegel argues that miracles themselves are effects produced by the power of spirit on the natural nexus. Spirit is a higher or absolute intervention in the natural process and the laws of nature. So also is life, as we see from such examples as the digestive process, death caused by fright, the healing power of joy and trust, and hypnosis. 'In all ages, [there is] infinite faith, infinite trust, [the influence of] spirit upon spirit; cripples are healed, the blind see, the deaf hear, right up to the present day. Unbelief in such effects is based on a superstitious belief in the so-called powers of nature and their independence vis-à-vis spirit' (3:146–8).[4]

But such a verification remains external and contingent. Genuine faith rests on the inner witness of the Spirit of truth. It has the truth of the idea as its basis, and its way of believing in Jesus means no longer having his sensible appearance before oneself, no longer depending on the testimony of a chain of witnesses. From the perspective of the Spirit of truth that is poured out upon the departure of Christ (John 16:7, 13), 'sensible history exists in essence only as accomplished—sublated[5] to the right hand of God; hence it exists essentially as a *past* history—past in the sense that [what is] sensible is past for representation' (3:148–9).

The 1824 lectures develop the latter point more thoroughly (3:226–32). Faith begins, to be sure, with sensible, empirical history. 'What it holds to be true is an outward, ordinary occurrence, and its verification is [by means of] the historical, juridical method of attesting a fact.' This is appropriate for the details relating to the external history of Christ (he lived in Palestine, was crucified by the Romans, etc.). But the faith that this man was the Son of God is something entirely different: it no longer refers to the sensible and empirical but to the spiritual and divine. Verification of the sensible occurs through sense intuition and empirical evidence. It is always subject to objections, qualifications, new data, etc., and in principle cannot achieve complete certainty. True certainty is

---

[4] Hegel leaves himself open here to the distortions of spiritualism, which was popular in the nineteenth century—the belief that mind or spirit can exercise direct power over nature such as communication with the dead. Possibly with this passage in mind, in the third edition of *The Life of Jesus* David Friedrich Strauss toys with spiritualist possibilities as a way of accepting the reports of Jesus' miracles, which he rejects as mythical in the other editions. See my editorial introduction to *The Life of Jesus Critically Examined* (London: SCM Press, 1973), pp. xlii–xliii. Hegel himself would repudiate the spiritualist distortion of his insight into the fluidity of the boundary between the natural and the spiritual. His whole point is that while such phenomena may occur they do not constitute a proof of faith.

[5] The use of *aufgehoben* here suggests that for Hegel the resurrection (*Auferstehung*) of Jesus entails an *Aufhebung*—an annulling of his sensible presence, yet a preservation of his real presence and its transfiguration into the modality of spirit. See the last section of the preceding chapter.

spiritual: the concept is its verification, although its point of departure is the sensible. Having left its sensible, historical starting-point, the faith of the spiritual community now stands on quite a different soil. Thus the church has rightly condemned attacks on miracles and the resurrection because such attacks assume that these things are what establish that Christ is the Son of God.[6] Hegel concludes this discussion with the (in)famous remark that 'only by philosophy can this simply present content [of faith] be justified, not by history. What spirit does is no history [*Historie*]. Spirit is concerned only with what is in and for itself, not something past, but simply what is present. This is the origin of the community' (3:232–3). The remark indicates that Hegel's suspicion of historicism is at its height in the 1824 lectures. He is not of course denying that in a more fundamental sense spirit *is* historical (*geschichtlich*) in its process of self-distinguishing and self-reintegrating. He speaks commonly of 'the divine history' (*die göttliche Geschichte*) or 'the eternal history, the eternal movement, which God himself is' (e.g. 3:77, 186–7, 327–8). But this ever-present historicality of God as spirit is not subject to the external, empirical mode of investigation suitable for data from the past. While God is *geschichtlich*, there is no proof of God from *Historie*.[7] The only witness to spirit is that of spirit itself, which is to say that God is self-attesting. It is from this divine self-attestation that the community of faith arises; its faith is the human mode of participating in the attestation.

THE INTERSUBJECTIVITY OF THE
COMMUNITY OF THE SPIRIT

Spirit is, as we know, an essentially communal or intersubjective reality for Hegel. Thus the transition to the third moment of the divine life is a transition from the individual to the communal,

---

[6] This is the obverse of the point made in the 1827 lectures, that the church rightly rejects historical investigations and proofs of the resurrection (3:300). Such proofs count neither for nor against the witness of faith.
[7] Hegel does not consistently maintain the terminological distinction between *Geschichte* and *Historie* that became common later in the nineteenth century. But he clearly intends a distinction between two senses of history: the intrinsically historical (*geschichtlich*) and 'simply present' process that spirit is, and the now-past historical (*historisch*) events in which this process 'appears'.

from the one in whom the idea of reconciliation is revealed to the
kingdom or realm in which this idea is actualized, the kingdom of
God (*basileia tou theou*) or, in Hegel's distinctive terminology, the
kingdom of the Spirit (*Reich des Geistes*)[8] or the community of the
Spirit (*Gemeinde des Geistes*). 'Spirit', 'kingdom', and 'community'
are categories that reciprocally define each other: God is redemp-
tively present in the form of the *basileia*; the kingdom of God *is* the
Spirit; and we comprise the community of the Spirit (3:142).

The 1821 manuscript develops this theme the most richly of any
of the lectures (3:133–42). In a section that serves as an introduction to the whole third part of *The Consummate Religion*, Hegel
argues that human subjectivity, when it is renewed, transfigured
by the indwelling of the Spirit of God, becomes a communal
subjectivity, giving up its old independence and exclusivity. The
infinite love that arises from infinite anguish creates a unique and
unsurpassable intersubjectivity, distinguished from all other forms
of human love and friendship. This section is much abbreviated in
the 1824 and 1827 lectures.

The discussion begins by describing the kingdom of the Spirit as
the sphere of infinite love in which the individual subject knows
itself to have infinite worth and absolute freedom, yet at the same
time 'surrenders this stability and maintains itself in what is utterly
other. Love equalizes all things, even absolute opposition' (3:135–6
incl. n. 193). The retreat to inwardness that characterizes the
Christian religion divests itself of particularity and self-possession,
and has 'its infinite value only in the love that is contained in
infinite anguish and comes from it'. Immediacy is replaced by an
'absolute mediation' wherein alone value is found. Although Hegel
does not use the term 'intersubjectivity', the idea is present when
he writes that the human subject 'is infinite only through this
mediation, not immediately' (3:137–8). He goes on as follows:
'Subjectivity has given up all external distinctions in this infinite

---

[8] Although Hegel uses the metaphor of 'kingdom' to describe the three spheres or
moments of the divine life only in the 1831 lectures (the kingdoms of the Father,
Son, and Spirit (3:362)), the expression 'kingdom of the Spirit' occurs already in the
1821 manuscript (3:135, 142). The 'kingdom' metaphor is also found in the *Philosophy of Right*, § 4, where Hegel speaks of 'the kingdom of actualized freedom
[*Reich der verwirklichten Freiheit*], the world of spirit produced from within itself as
a second nature' (*Elements of the Philosophy of Right* (see n. 23 below), 35). The
kingdom of the Spirit is a kingdom of freedom, and vice versa. 'Kingdom' and
'freedom' are linked in a passage from the lecture manuscript (3:152) quoted below
(see n. 14).

value, distinctions of mastery, power, position, even of sex[9] and wealth. Before God all human beings are equal.... Herein lies the possibility and the root of truly universal justice and of the actualization of freedom' (3:138).

Hegel refers to the love that arises from infinite anguish as 'speculative'; and the 'infinite mediation' through which it occurs 'has its objective shape [in] the life, suffering, death, and exaltation of Christ'. It forms a community in which the multiplicity of individuals is fused into the unity of faith. It is neither human (sexual) love nor noble friendship. Friendship is burdened by subjective particularity, whereas that wherein the disciples are one must be a third, a 'syllogistic connection', a substantial bond. It is based not on attraction or personal fulfilment but on the intuition of a speculative element, 'the infinite love that comes from infinite anguish, i.e. from the worthlessness of particularity and the mediation of love through it' (3:139). The anguish, the shared suffering, creates a new kind of human relationship in which one finds oneself only by losing oneself for the sake of the other. Hegel is struggling here to express the distinction between *erōs*, *philia*, and *agapē*; as we might expect, the first two are not simply left behind but fulfilled in the third. Love in the fullest sense is compassion, suffering with and on behalf of another. It is grounded in the divine compassion.

The unity formed by this love is not a sensible, worldly linkage but 'a unity simply in the Spirit. Love as [originating] in infinite anguish is precisely the concept of spirit itself.' This love becomes *objective* in Christ 'as the focal point of faith at an infinite distance and sublimity', but it becomes *actual* in the intersubjectivity of the individuals who comprise the community of faith, which is a community of the Spirit.

The Holy Spirit is in them; they are, they constitute, the universal Christian church, the communion of saints. Spirit is the infinite return into itself, infinite subjectivity, not represented but actual divinity, the *presence* of God, not the substantial in-itself of the Father or of the Son and of Christ, who is the truth in the shape of objectivity. The Spirit is rather what is subjectively present and actual; and it is only through this mediation [in the community] that it itself is subjectively present as the divestment into the objective intuition of love and its infinite anguish. This [is]

---

[9] Hegel refers specifically to 'the sexual freedom of women and monogamy', by which he is probably referring to the emancipation of women from a subservient role based on sex, especially the equality and reciprocity that should be part of the monogamous marriage relationship in the Christian community. See 3:138 n. 198.

the Spirit of God, or God as the present, actual Spirit, God dwelling in his community.   (3:140)

This packed statement is simplified in the 1827 lectures, where we are told that 'the community itself is the existing Spirit, the Spirit in its existence, God existing as community' (3:331). The infinite subjectivity of God as spirit is thus an infinite intersubjectivity, which is the actualization of the idea of reconciliation that is objectively revealed in Christ, a reconciliation that happens through the shared suffering of self-divesting love. Actualization requires subjective appropriation. Whereas Christ is revelatorily definitive of divine–human (and interhuman) unity, the community of the Spirit is ontologically definitive.[10]

'In this profound sense', Hegel continues, 'the Christian religion is the religion of spirit.' This is not to be taken in the trivial sense of being a 'spiritual religion'[11] that venerates abstraction and unworldliness. 'On the contrary, [the Christian religion is] the unification of the infinite antithesis [of God and the world], the one and only genuine speculative [enjoyment] of the nature of God, or of spirit. This is its content and its vision, and it is there for the ordinary, uneducated consciousness' (3:140–1). Sin against the Holy Spirit is the only unforgivable sin because it is sin against the 'consuming process' of the infinite anguish of love, and without being consumed by love we are lost and have no share in eternal life.[12]

---

[10] In the 1824 lectures Hegel says that it is possible that a religion may advance no further than 'the representation of the Son and those about him'. He thinks this is the case in Catholicism with its veneration of Mary and the saints and the transubstantiation of the eucharistic elements, which prolong the physical, sensible presence of God. The second moment has not yet been 'spiritualized' and the Spirit does not become an object in its own right (2:231). This critique takes a juridical version of Catholicism as normative and overlooks the strong emphasis stemming from Augustine on the Spirit as the 'soul' of the church. Hegel basically is not familiar with the Augustinian strand of Catholicism. He himself insists on the necessity of the second moment, that of objectivity and otherness, but adds that it must be 'sublated in love'. The third moment unifies the abstractness of the Father and the objectivity of the Son in the community of the Spirit (2:230–1). In this Hegel thinks very much like Augustine.

[11] The contrast in German is between *Religion des Geistes* and *geistige Religion*. For this reason, presumably, Hegel does not commonly refer to 'the spiritual community' (an expression employed by Paul Tillich) but rather to 'the community of the Spirit'. The community is *of the* Spirit, not 'spiritual' in an otherworldly sense.

[12] In this connection Hegel argues that innocence in regard to the Spirit is not an acceptable excuse, and he cites a medieval Latin proverb that satirizes human

INSTITUTIONAL FORMS OF THE
COMMUNITY OF THE SPIRIT

Just because the community of the Spirit is not 'spiritual' in the vapid sense but precisely unifies God and the world, it assumes institutional forms. The ideality of infinite love and transfigured intersubjectivity must become actual, and in the process they will be distorted and fragmented. Worldly forms are inadequate to the divine content, but without form or shape (*Gestalt*), spirit (*Geist*) dissipates into thin air. This is Hegel's version of the movement from the invisible to the visible church. The invisible church, the community of the Spirit, is an abstraction without the visible; the visible church without the invisible is a mere mechanism.

*The Church and Baptism*

The community of the Spirit *realizes* itself, and 'the real community is what we generally call the *church*. This is no longer the *emerging* but rather the *subsisting* community, which maintains itself.' It maintains itself as 'the institution whereby [its] subjects come to the truth, appropriate the truth to themselves, so that the Holy Spirit becomes real, actual, and present within them and has its abode in them; . . . it is the means whereby they as subjects *are* the active expression of the Spirit' (3:333). With these carefully chosen words the 1827 lectures state most clearly what is argued in all the lectures. The institutional forms of the church follow from the twofold task of *coming* to the truth (the role of baptism, faith, doctrine) and *appropriating* the truth (the role of repentance, worship, the sacraments). In ecclesial practices that serve the truth, the Holy Spirit has its abode and activity.

Among these institutional forms, Hegel makes no mention of governance, ordination, ministry, preaching, etc. Perhaps this is because these forms are not directly related to the process of coming to and appropriating the truth, or are considered as instrumental to this process. Another possibility is that Hegel's neglect of preaching reflects his low opinion of Protestant clergy and their

vanity, *nos poma natamus*, 'We apples swim.' The critical edition of the lectures (both German and English) misread the Latin as *nos prona natamus* and consequently misinterpreted the proverb (see 3:141 n. 210). Bengt Löfstedt has written a note on this citation in *Orpheus: Rivista di Umanità Classica e Cristiana* 19–20 (1998–9), 99–100. The Oxford edition has been corrected.

sermons. At the end of the lecture manuscript, he says that the gospel as preached today is like salt that has lost its savour, and he is critical of the clergy for having abandoned their teaching responsibility (3:160–1).[13]

Without eschewing institutional forms, the 1821 lectures emphasize an ethical dimension by suggesting that 'the church is the kingdom of God' in the sense of being 'the achieved presence, life, preservation, and enjoyment of the Spirit'. (Of course the church also is not the kingdom of God in so far as the latter is strictly an eschatological ideal.) Thus there is an initial, polemical tendency of renunciation toward worldly goods and values that echoes Jesus' radical vision of the kingdom. But such renunciation (e.g. giving all that one has to the poor) cannot long sustain itself in the world, and concerns inevitably arise about family, property, laws, governance, etc. The church is not directly responsible for these matters, its principal domain being that of the salvation of souls. What is needed, however, is that 'out of the womb of the church there be formed a free life, a civil and political life, stemming from eternal principles, a rational, worldly kingdom in accord with the idea of freedom and the absolute character of rights' (3:151–2).[14] Thus the church does have an essential role to play in the formation of the body politic: it is the provider of ideals, goals, frames of reference; and the relation of the community of faith to the world is, as we shall see, an abiding concern of Hegel's.

The first institutional form by which individuals 'come to the truth' is the sacrament of baptism, which signifies that the individual 'is already born within the community of the church' and simply has to be 'grafted' into an already existing social world. The community then has the responsibility of nurturing children in their spiritual growth until they reach an age when they can act on their own (3:233, 335).

### Faith and Truth

The community has *faith*: this is its mode of cognition. As we have seen from the discussion in Chapter 5, faith is a form of certainty. Hegel now emphasizes, in the manuscript (3:149–50), that the faith

[13] On Hegel's youthful attitude toward sermons, see H. S. Harris, *Hegel's Development: Toward the Sunlight, 1770–1801* (Oxford: Clarendon Press, 1972), 108–13, 117–19, 129 n. 1, 163, 165.

[14] See above, n. 8.

of the community is a certainty of absolute truth, of what God is. It rests not on external authority or past occurrences but 'solely on reason itself, on the Spirit'. This is not an autonomous human rationality but is 'brought about by God', whose Spirit testifies rationally to rational spirits who are created in the image of God. Thus the faith of the community is a form of objective truth, not of feeling. 'Spirit [is] higher than [what occurs] in the form of feeling.' It conquers and purifies feeling, and is liberated from feeling.

The 1827 lectures, as might be expected, focus especially on the *truth* whose mediation is the purpose of the institutional forms of the ecclesial community (3:331–3). 'The community begins with the fact that the truth is at hand; it is known, extant truth. And this truth is what God is: he is the triune God; he is life, this process of himself with himself, the determining of himself within himself.' This truth has appeared; it has a relation to the subject; and the subject is related to it. The latter relation is *faith*—the certainty that reconciliation has been accomplished in and for itself, and that individuals are meant to be children of God, citizens of God's kingdom. The difficulty involved in the fact that it is individuals who have faith, and that individuals are limited and commit errors, is removed by knowing that God looks into the heart and sees what is substantial and essential, so that externality does no damage to the absolute unity, and finitude is reduced to an 'inessential status'. What is essential and enduring is the community of the Spirit. Our 'essentialization'[15] begins when we surrender our individual subjectivity and are taken up into a new intersubjectivity. As this happens, the ecclesial community comes into being with its purpose of mediating God's truth, making it available here and now in concrete practices. To this end it employs various means: doctrine and teaching, repentance and penance, and the cultus and sacraments.

## Doctrine, Teaching

Hegel presents the role of doctrine and teaching—the German term *Lehre* connotes both the thing taught and the act of

---

[15] Hegel does not use this term, which is employed by Friedrich Schelling and Paul Tillich, but the idea is present. See Tillich's *Systematic Theology*, 3 (Chicago: University of Chicago Press, 1963), 149 ff., 400 ff. Along a similar line, in the 1831 lectures Hegel says that in the life of the community the 'privatism' of individuals is 'consumed' (3:344 n. 258).

teaching—in two rather different ways. In the lecture manuscript (3:151) he argues that the teaching of doctrine serves to awaken feelings, feelings that proceed from the representation of truth rather than from subjective experience, and which are thus 'genuine feelings for the first time'. To protect doctrine from arbitrariness and contingency, it is necessary that it be deposited in creedal symbols and bound to fixed expressions, which include not only the Bible but also the living tradition by which the Bible is interpreted. Tradition, too, Hegel insists, 'is something given, not [simply] created from itself. It is the Spirit of the community as a whole [that is creative]; the doctrine of the church [is] not produced by the church but is cultivated by the Spirit present within it.' Whether scripture or tradition is primary is not the issue, but rather the recognition that the community 'is the infinite power and authority' by which its own development and teaching are determined. In this and other aspects of his ecclesiology, Hegel displays a rather more Catholic than Protestant sensibility (despite his overly juridical portrayal of Catholicism).

In the 1827 lectures (3:333–5) Hegel begins by distinguishing between the emerging community, into which the Holy Spirit is poured, and the subsisting community, where the truth is now established and extant as doctrine, the doctrine of faith (*Glaubenslehre*). The content of this doctrine is reconciliation, and it is elaborated as something presupposed and settled. At first, in the emerging community, truth is present 'as intuition, faith, feeling— as the felt witness of the Spirit like a flame of fire'. Thus in the 1827 version feeling *precedes* rather than *proceeds* from doctrine. It is the fertile matrix of interiority from which doctrine develops, though 'intermixed with impurities' from which it is liberated through an ongoing process of thought. Spiritual truth is known not as an object of sense experience but only as something that is taught. The church is essentially a teaching church with a teaching office.

Individuals are born into this teaching; they partake of it at first implicitly, as children, not yet as spiritually realized subjects (as we have seen, this implicitness is symbolized by baptism). The truth is external to them, comes to them as presupposed and has *authority*. All truth initially comes in the form of authority and thus must be *taught* and *learned*. But the inner spirit is already the absolute possibility of assimilating and appropriating this knowledge: one recognizes the teaching as the truth in which one abides. The concern of *education* (*Erziehung*), *practice* (*Übung*), and *cultivation* (*Bildung*) is precisely with the process by which outwardly mediated truth is inwardly assimilated. The truth is drawn both into and out of the subject: Hegel wrestles with this dialectical process on more than one occasion.[16] He goes on to emphasize that children who are born into the church are born both in and to freedom and do not have to be converted from evil.[17] Evil has already been overcome in principle, and the task of cultivation is to 'habituate' the learner to the good and the true, and in that way to discourage evil from re-emerging (3:335–6).

## Repentance/Penance/Rebirth

'Spirit has the power to undo evil' (3:336): a simple yet momentous claim. Evil is monstrously present in the world, yet it encounters a greater power. Whether Hegel's tragicomic perspective is credible in the postmodern world is a question we shall have to address. The ground for it is his conviction that God prevails in the struggle with evil by taking it upon and into godself. Evil as such is not eliminated but it is 'undone': its doing is reversed.

This conviction sets the framework in the 1827 lectures for Hegel's discussion of *repentance* (*Reue*) or *penitence* (*Buße*), which are actions that signify a process of renouncing transgressions and rising to the truth. By acknowledging truth over evil and willing the good, it is possible to nullify evil. The undoing of what has been done cannot take place in a sensible, external manner, but only in a spiritual manner or inwardly. The evil deeds remain; they cannot be expunged from the record; but through the power of the Spirit their damage can be reduced and perhaps reversed: good can be brought out of evil. The concern of the church is to promote this process through the 'habituating and educating' of spirit ever more inwardly (3:336–7).[18] The 1831 lectures add this illuminating note: 'Acting in the belief that reconciliation has been implicitly

---

[16] See below, n. 21, and our discussion of education in relation to the knowledge of God in Chap. 5.

[17] In this as in several other respects, Hegel's theory of education bears some similarities to that of Horace Bushnell, whose *Christian Nurture* was written to counter the argument of evangelicals that children must be converted from sin by being made to feel their sinfulness and fear the wrath of God. See *Christian Nurture* (New York, 1861), chaps. 1–2.

[18] Hegel argues that because 'evil is known in the Spirit to be overcome in and for itself', there is no longer an unending struggle against evil and an unending

achieved is, on the one hand, the act of the subject, but on the other hand it is the act of the divine Spirit. Faith itself is the divine Spirit that works in the subject. But the subject is not a passive receptacle; rather the Holy Spirit is equally the subject's spirit to the extent that the subject has faith' (3:337 n. 239).

The 1824 lectures address the matter of the appropriation of truth and renunciation of evil under the motif of *rebirth* (*Wiedergeburt*) rather than repentance (3:234–5). 'Human beings must be born twice, first naturally, then spiritually, like the Brāhmans. Spirit is not immediate; it is only in so far as it engenders itself from itself.' In opposition to the notion of a perennial struggle against evil, spirit has within itself the power to be born anew, to make a fresh start. The only sin that cannot be forgiven is sin against the Holy Spirit, because to deny the Spirit is to deny the possibility of rebirth and thus to lock oneself into perpetual sin. 'It is the divine Spirit that effects rebirth; this is the free grace of God, for everything divine is free.' Rebirth is also, simultaneously, a human action, but only in so far as the subject gives up 'its singularized, private being-for-self' and joins the ecclesial community in common acts of penitence and partaking.

*Cultus/Sacraments*

'Partaking' points to the final and most important of the forms of the church, that of the cultus (*Kultus*) and the sacraments (3:152–4). Hegel attends to the cultic practices of each of the determinate religions, and as we have seen,[19] emphasizes the place of cultus as the culminating moment of the concept of religion. The Christian community of faith not only has but *is* a *cultus*—an activity of worship and liturgy by which the life, passion, and resurrection of Christ are eternally repeated in the members of the church. At the centre of this cultic activity are the *sacraments*, which attest to the inner certainty of the truth and the implicit unity of divine and human nature. The latter phrase indicates that Hegel means principally the sacrament of the eucharist or holy communion.[20] For it

---

progression toward the good, as suggested by Persian religion and Kantian philosophy, both of which posit good and evil in dualistic antithesis (3:337 incl. nn. 237, 239). This point is also made in the 1824 lectures (3:234 nn. 194, 195).

[19] See the discussion of the worship of God in Chap. 5.

[20] He mentions only in passing that confession is also a sacrament for Catholics (3:154), but he does not discuss other sacraments besides baptism. And baptism is

is by means of partaking of the body and blood of Christ that believers are received into the mystical union of the kingdom and become one with God in Christ. Partaking or communion (*Genuß*) thus symbolizes the fulfilment of the whole process of reconciliation. Hegel stresses, especially in the lecture manuscript, the 'immediately sensuous' aspect of communion, which is brought out by his use of the term *Genuß* with its root sense of physical enjoyment and satisfaction. The actual partaking of food and drink is important,

for, unlike breathing and the relation of skin to air and water, eating and drinking are just this: appropriating something consciously, and indeed on an individualized basis, to oneself as this and only this sensible, singular subject.... Here [the communion] occurs in the mode of an external, sensible object such that the divine is eaten and drunk—not merely a symbol of the divine, where the meaning is found only in the [mode of] representation, but rather sensible communion as such, immediate certainty. Hence the sensible as such must [be] validated, must be transformed or transubstantiated into the divine substance itself; the two become one. (3:154)

By eating and drinking the eucharistic elements, the reconciliation accomplished in Christ is actually assimilated into and becomes part of believers, who in the process are transformed.[21] For the sake of immediate certainty, the ritual action is essential. In this way the Christian eucharist is connected with primitive rituals of sacrifice, which entail a negation of the finite by offering it up to God.

Hegel stresses, especially in the 1824 and 1827 lectures, that the union accomplished through the partaking of the eucharist is a 'mystical union', not a physical union (3:235–6, 337). What is represented in the sacrament is that 'Christ is eternally sacrificed and rises again in the heart.... The eternal sacrifice is the process

---

not really treated as a sacrament; it is more a symbol of the church's responsibility for the nurture of children.

[21] Hegel applies the analogy of eating to education as well as to the eucharist. In the Preface to the *Phenomenology of Spirit*, he writes: 'Education, viewed from the side of individuals, consists in their laying hands on this element that is already available, making its inorganic nature organic to themselves and taking possession of it for themselves' (translation from *G. W. F. Hegel: Theologian of the Spirit*, ed. Peter C. Hodgson (Minneapolis: Fortress Press; Edinburgh: T&T Clark, 1997), 99). In both cases the ingestion of something external brings about an internal change.

through which single individuals make themselves their own [*Sichzueigenmachen*], the process by which their implicit being passes away.' This seems to mean that individuals come into a reconciled relationship with themselves and God by participating in the eternal sacrifice. Moreover, 'since they belong to grace and are reconciled, the resurrection of Christ also takes place within them'. The eucharist extends into the life of the community of faith the self-divestment of God in Christ. The pattern of sacrifice or self-giving is thus established, and the community itself (as we shall see) is destined to give itself up for the sake of the reconciliation of the world.

Hegel believes that the Christian confessions are distinct from one another principally in their view of what the sacrament is and how it works. He stresses this point in each of the lecture series (3:154–5, 236, 338–9); it is virtually his only discussion of confessional differences, which from his point of view seem destined to pass away as the Christian idea more adequately realizes itself. The *Catholics* venerate the host as such, even when it is not being partaken of. Christ is believed to be present in the host, once it is consecrated by the priest, in a sensible, bodily, unspiritual fashion. 'The divine is to be found in this externality', 'is literally eaten by the worshippers'. The transubstantiated elements are dispensed like items at a market or fair (*Messe*); hence the Catholic eucharist is called a 'mass'. The *Lutherans* regard the host to be consecrated only in the faith of each individual; it is actual in the partaking, which is a spiritual act. Otherwise it is 'only a piece of bread, not God'. Transubstantiation takes place not literally but 'only in the partaking of communion, in faith, and only in a spiritual fashion'. The *Reformed* view lacks the 'mystical element' that is preserved by the Lutherans—the belief that God is really present in the eucharistic celebration, that a spiritual presence occurs in the sensible act of partaking. Rather the communion becomes a memorial, an ordinary psychological relationship, and everything 'speculative' (mystical) has disappeared. 'Deity is not present here at all, but is only remembered as an image.' 'The Reformed Church is therefore the place where divinity and truth collapse into the prose of the Enlightenment and of mere understanding.'

On Hegel's account, Lutheranism holds the mean between (Catholic) supernaturalism and (Reformed) rationalism. Such an account is open to the suspicion of prejudice because of course Hegel himself was Lutheran. But in fact he makes very little of the supposed superiority of Lutheranism, and his own philosophical theology is really transconfessional. Confessional distinctions and doctrinal debates are of subordinate interest to him. His distinctive construal of the Christian idea reflects an eclectic appropriation of the doctrinal tradition, both orthodox and heterodox. In the 1831 lectures Hegel remarks that the Reformed view is that of 'Zwingli or Calvin', and it is indeed the case that he has folded the Calvinist doctrine of the Lord's Supper into the Zwinglian (3:373 incl. n. 29). Calvin himself, while rejecting a 'real presence' of Christ in the eucharist, accepts a mystical activity or presence of the transfigured heavenly body of Christ. Hegel's account of the Catholic doctrine is also something of a caricature, or at least lacks subtlety. Yet by placing the sacrament of communion at the centre of the Christian cult and de-emphasizing the proclamation of the Word, he exhibits an affinity to Catholicism. In any event, his account of historical details is often imprecise, and his emphasis lies rather on conceptual distinctions that appear in history in a variety of ways.

## THE COMMUNITY AND THE WORLD

Following its discussion of the origin and being of the community, the 1821 manuscript turns to a third and final section, the 'passing away' of the community. This third section is replaced in the 1824 and 1827 lectures by a discussion of the 'realization of faith' (1824) or of the 'realization of the spirituality of the community in universal actuality' (1827). The analysis turns from the category of 'passing away' (*Vergehen*) to that of 'realization' (*Realisierung*). Does this switch reflect an altered interpretation on Hegel's part or merely a difference of emphasis? We shall address this question in the final section of this chapter. In either case, however, some sort of divestment or transition of the community is entailed, which prolongs the eucharistic motif at the heart of its cultic practice. Just as God has given up abstract divinity in Christ, and Christ has given up the form of singularity in the community of faith, the community gives up its inward spirituality for the sake of the redemption of the world.

The discussion of 'realization' is structurally similar in the 1824 and 1827 lectures but with differences in content. In 1824 Hegel remarks that over against the community of faith as an inward community there stands an objective reality, of which three forms may be distinguished: the immediate world or the form of the heart, the form of reflection or abstract thought, and the form of the concept. Faith realizes itself in these three forms, and this realization constitutes the reconciliation of spirit (3:237). The 1827 lectures stress that the realization of the community entails its 'transformation' (*Umwandlung*) in the sense that its spirituality takes on diverse forms of worldly actuality, of which there are three stages: real, ideal, and ideal-real (3:339). These three are the same as the 1824 stages of immediate worldliness, abstract reflection, and the concrete concept, except that now the first (real) stage is seen to comprise three substages: heart, church, and ethical life (3:342). If all this seems confusing, keep in mind that Hegel is applying logical categories and distinctions to interpret a mass of material stretching over many centuries. Many readers will conclude that such an approach, even if it does not pretend to be history, is doomed to failure. In fact, it is not history but a form of eschatology in so far as it is concerned with the destiny of Christian faith and practice in the modern world.

*Three Real Stages of Reconciliation: Heart, Church, Ethical Life*

First, reconciliation occurs in the realm of immediacy or the *heart* (3:339–40). 'It is the pure heart that attains to this partaking of God's presence within it, and consequently reconciliation, the enjoyment of being reconciled. At the same time, however, this reconciliation is abstract and has the world as such over against it.' The tension between inner spirituality and worldly actuality is problematic because reconciliation demands to be realized in the form of freedom. The vocation of the subject that is inwardly infinite is its freedom, and this freedom is its rationality, its 'being at home with itself' (*bei sich selbst seiende*). It is in this context that Hegel makes the remark, quoted earlier,[22] that 'slavery contradicts Christianity because it is contrary to reason' (3:340). 'What is required, therefore, is that this reconciliation should also be accomplished in the worldly realm.' At first, however, the community resists this realization, renounces the worldly realm, and withdraws into itself in monkish fashion. This is the period in which monasticism prevails as the ecclesial ideal. 'But the

----

[22] See Chap. 8, n. 2.

very nature of spirit is to develop itself, to differentiate itself even unto worldliness.'

In the second phase, that of the *church*, religiosity and worldliness remain external to each other even as they enter into relation (3:238, 340–1). This is a relation in which one prevails over the other and there is no reconciliation at all: the church prevails over the unreconciled world. Yet ironically the dominating power takes worldliness into itself, and 'there emerges in the church itself a worldliness devoid of spirit'. In so far as the church becomes a worldly empire (the Holy Roman Empire), it takes the attributes of empire into itself. It rules over its subjects in the form of papal absolutism, and 'its ruling principle is that humanity is not at home with itself'. A general condition of servitude prevails, and the result is the direct opposite of genuine reconciliation: human freedom is lost, not gained.

In the third phase, this contradiction is resolved in the *ethical realm* (*Sittlichkeit*), where the principle of freedom penetrates into the world, and the world 'is freedom that has become concrete and will that is rational' (3:341–2). In his discussion of the cultus as the third form of the concept of religion in the 1827 lectures, Hegel remarks that 'ethical life is the most genuine cultus' (1:446). This means that the cultic practice of reconciliation, culminating in the eucharistic ritual wherein the divine suffering and sacrifice are re-enacted, is extended into the world in the form of ethical practices that serve God and humanity. The institutions of ethical life—law, family, civil society, state—are 'divine institutions', not in the sense that they are holy in contrast to what is worldly, but precisely as secular practices through which divine reconciliation and human freedom are accomplished (3:342). The modern Protestant secular-bourgeois world succeeds (or at least supplements) the church as the realm in which the kingdom of the Spirit actualizes itself. At least that is Hegel's hope, but as we shall see he also has severe questions about the condition of this world.

In the 1831 lectures, Hegel develops the role of the state in ethical life in an especially forceful way. He uses strong images when he says that it is in the organization of the state that 'the divine has broken through [*eingeschlagen*] into the sphere of actuality'. The foundation of the worldly realm is 'the divine will, the law of right and freedom. The true reconciliation, whereby the divine realizes itself in the domain of actuality, consists in the ethical and juridical life of the state: this is the authentic discipline

[*Subaktion*] of worldliness' (3:342 n. 250, cf. 374). Worldliness must be disciplined, made to serve divine purposes, rather than be allowed to pursue self-gratifying desires and idolatrous ends. The state properly governed accomplishes this discipline. The alternative to the state is anarchy and barbarism.

Recent political events in France and Great Britain—the end of the Bourbon monarchy in the July Revolution of 1830, and the introduction of the Reform Bill into Parliament in 1831—served to arouse once again Hegel's interest in and concern for the state (and social philosophy generally) that had been evident a decade earlier in his lectures and book on the philosophy of right.[23] Consequently he added a section on the relationship of religion to the state to his treatment of *The Concept of Religion* in the 1831 lectures. This material was preserved by the *Werke* and is included as an appendix to the first volume of the critical edition (1:451–60). Here Hegel develops three themes. First, the state is 'the genuine mode of actuality' by which the idea of reconciliation is realized in the world. Whereas religion is the *knowledge* of the highest truth, the truth that humans are free before God, the state is the *actualization* of freedom in the world. There can be only *one* concept of freedom that manifests itself in both religion and the state. Thus religion is a foundation of the state, and the state is a telos of religion.

The second theme concerns how this relationship of religion and state is represented. The claim is advanced, especially in Protestant states such as England, that laws, governmental authority, and political constitutions derive from God. But how is this claim justified, and how can abuses (e.g. child labour, low wages, restriction of the franchise) that result from the conjunction of religious and political power be avoided? Which laws constitute the divine will—the laws of the sovereign, or of the nobility, or of the people?

---

[23] Hegel's Heidelberg lectures of 1817–18 have been translated as *Lectures on Natural Right and Political Science* by J. Michael Stewart and Peter C. Hodgson (Berkeley and Los Angeles: University of California Press, 1995; Oxford: Oxford University Press, forthcoming). His Berlin lectures of 1819–20 are available in editions by Dieter Henrich (Frankfurt: Suhrkamp Verlag, 1983) and by Emil Angehrn, Martin Bondeli, and Hoo Nam Seelmann (Hamburg: Felix Meiner Verlag, 2000). Hegel's own textbook, published in 1820–1, has been translated as *Elements of the Philosophy of Right* by H. B. Nisbet, ed. Allen W. Wood (Cambridge: Cambridge University Press, 1991). Hegel's essay on 'The English Reform Bill' (1831) was his last published writing before his death (translated by T. M. Knox in *Hegel's Political Writings*, ed. Z. A. Pelczynski (Oxford: Oxford University Press, 1964)).

Finally, religion and state can be sundered and have different laws, as in Catholic states such as France. Here a realm of holiness and eternity is set up in opposition to that of right and temporality: thus celibacy is opposed to marriage, devotion to work, obedience to freedom. Here religion expresses itself only in negative fashion and recognizes no human rights, while the latter acquire a purely secular foundation. Or perhaps (as in America?) church and state should be separated to avoid theocratic abuses; but the danger in this separation is that political principles are not traced back to their ultimate ground in God. In the condition of separation, religion can gravitate toward unfreedom and illiberalism, while the state can gravitate toward atheism and secularism.

Thus the question of the right relationship between religion and state remains unresolved in the modern world, and perhaps also in Hegel's mind. It seems unlikely that he believes that the church should be superseded by the modern secular world, or that the state is the principal telos of religion. His critique of modern secularism precludes the former, and his conviction that religion cannot be made subservient to ends other than the knowledge and worship of God precludes the latter. His view seems to be that both religion and state are essential, that neither of them can be dissolved into or superseded by the other. The goal is the reconciliation of *the world*, and this goal requires a state (and other ethical institutions) as well as religion and a church. Religion alone is not enough, indeed is dangerous, while a purely secular state has no orientation other than to human ends; religion is its necessary foundation. The problem is one of finding a polity that adequately institutionalizes the religion–state relationship. Neither a theocratic nor a secularist state will do. Hegel does not seem to offer an alternative.[24]

### The Ideal Stage of Reconciliation: Enlightenment, Islam, Pietism

The realization of reconciliation in the church and in the institutions of ethical life appears to be ambiguous and incomplete. So a reaction sets in. The freedom of reason that has been acquired in

[24] This conclusion is consistent with what Hegel says about the relationship between religion and the state in the *Philosophy of Right*, § 270 remark and addition (pp. 291–304); and in the *Encyclopedia of the Philosophical Sciences*, § 552 (*Hegel's Philosophy of Mind*, trans. William Wallace and A. V. Miller (Oxford: Clarendon Press, 1971), 282–91).

religion 'now turns against merely spiritless externality and servitude, for the latter is utterly opposed to the concepts of reconciliation and liberation'. 'Thinking enters in, defying and destroying externality in whatever form it appears.' As a modern cultural movement, this is called the *Enlightenment* (3:238–42, 342–4). The 'reflective' thinking represented by the Enlightenment turn to subjectivity takes on the form of an abstract universality that is directed not merely against the external but also against the concrete in general. The particular sort of concreteness that Hegel focuses on as having been attacked by the Enlightenment is the doctrine of the Trinity—'the idea that God as triune is not a dead abstraction but rather relates himself to himself, is at home with himself, and returns to himself'. When everything concrete in God has been eradicated, then God is pushed into the beyond as a 'supreme being' about which we have no specific knowledge. Enlightenment rationalism accepts the reflective critique of traditional dogma but substitutes for it merely subjective criteria and ends with an abstract and empty self-identity over against the equally empty beyond ('unfreedom and servitude of spirit in the absolute region of freedom'). Hegel is harshly critical of this sort of rationalism because it represents in his view a significant step toward atheism. By attacking the centrepiece of the Christian doctrine of God, the Enlightenment opens the way for the abandonment of any concept of God and the substitution of the autonomous subject, which in its absolute freedom succumbs to a new servitude (perhaps he is thinking of the Robespierrean Reign of Terror).

Thus far the 1824 and 1827 lectures proceed in tandem. But they deviate dramatically when they turn to a second form of abstract identity. In 1824 this is *Islamic religion*: here subjectivity has no rights of its own and its vocation is to submerge itself in the unity of God, the pure infinite (3:242–4). In one respect this religion is the diametrical opposite of Enlightenment subjectivity, but in another the Enlightenment attack on the Christian Trinity and the divinity of Christ is shared and pushed by it to an extreme. 'The religion of Islam . . . hates and proscribes everything concrete; its God is the absolute One, in relation to whom human beings retain for themselves no purpose, no private domain, nothing peculiar to themselves. . . . Their purpose can only be to bring about the veneration of the One in all humanity. Thus the religion of Islam is essentially fanatical' (3:243).

Why does Hegel introduce a consideration and critique of Islam at this unlikely point? It is the only significant discussion of this religion in the lectures aside from a few brief references.[25] In fact, Islam lacks a place in Hegel's schema of determinate religions because, unlike the other religions, it does not represent an earlier phase of religious consciousness that has been or can be subsumed in the consummate religion. Rather it stands in antithesis to Christianity as a contemporary rival. Thus the proper place for its treatment is in the context of challenges to the Christian religion and to the realization of reconciliation in the modern world. Even so, the alignment of the Enlightenment and Islam is peculiar and seems improvised. A more natural place might have been the critique of modern culture and theologies found in the *Introduction* to the lectures. Even better, of course, would have been a fair and full assessment of Islam as one of the determinate religions; but for this Hegel lacked the necessary materials and an unprejudiced attitude.

In any event, Islam is replaced by *Pietism* as the contrasting form of abstract idealism in the 1827 lectures (3:343–4). Pietism fits here (more persuasively than Islam) because it represents an extreme form of subjectivity and freedom, 'which renounces the truth and its development and moves within itself, knowing that what it regards as valid is only its own definitions, and that it is the master of what is good and evil. This is an inward weaving of spirit within itself, which can just as readily assume the form of hypocrisy and extreme vanity as it can peaceful, noble, pious aspirations.' Pietism, Hegel continues, 'acknowledges no objective truth and opposes itself to dogmas and the content of religion'.[26] It retains a connection with Christ, but only in the realm of feeling. It results in a 'subjectivity devoid of content', and as such it has 'turned polemically against the philosophy that wants cognition'. The latter remark reflects the fact that by 1827 Hegel's philosophy was increasingly being attacked by Neopietists such as Friedrich Tholuck,[27] who targeted his Trinitarianism and accused him of pantheism.

---

[25] See 3:242 n. 210; also 2:156, 158; 3:121, 218, 316. An appreciative reference to the Muslim mystic Jalal al-Din Rumi is found in the *Encyclopedia of the Philosophical Sciences*, § 573 remark (*Hegel's Philosophy of Mind*, 308–10).

[26] The 1831 lectures attribute a 'privatism' to such piety that is properly 'consumed' in the life of the community for 'truly pious people' (3:344 n. 258).

[27] See above, Chap. 3, p. 62.

### The Ideal-Real Stage of Reconciliation: Philosophy

Once Enlightenment 'reflection' has invaded the sphere of religion, Hegel argues, thinking assumes a hostile attitude toward religion and its concrete content. Such thinking does not stop but carries through: 'it empties heart and heaven'. Under these circumstances religion, if it is to preserve its content, needs help: it 'takes refuge in the concept [*in den Begriff flüchtet*] and obtains its justification by thinking'—the thinking of speculative philosophy, which 'grasp[s] itself as concrete and free, not maintaining the distinctions as merely posited, but letting them go free and in that way recognizing the content as objective' (3:245–7, 345–7).

In this respect philosophy advances beyond both the church and the Enlightenment and mediates between them. It seems opposed to the church 'because it conceptualizes, it shares with the development of culture and with reflection the refusal to remain bound to the form of representation'. But it recognizes the necessity of representation and preserves its truth-content, so its opposition to the church is only formal. It is opposed to the Enlightenment because it does not share the latter's indifference to the content or its despair in regard to the truth. 'The goal of philosophy is the cognition of the truth—the cognition of God because he is the absolute truth.... Philosophy knows God essentially as concrete, as the spiritual, realized universality that is not jealous but communicates itself.' The Enlightenment—'that vanity of understanding'—vehemently opposes this sort of philosophy and objects to its demonstration of the truth of religion in general and Christianity in particular. Yet the task of philosophy as speculative theology 'is to show forth the rational content of religion [*die Vernunft der Religion*]' and 'to reconcile reason with religion in its manifold forms' (3:246–7).

The 1827 lectures accord very closely with the 1824 analysis, summarized in the preceding paragraph, but they add an interesting observation: speculative philosophy shares with reflective philosophy a recognition that the truth is 'produced' by subjective consciousness; but it also recognizes 'this truth as at the same time not produced, as the truth that subsists in and for itself'. In this respect it mediates the real and the ideal: it knows the objective content of religion in accord with its necessity and reason; it recognizes (with the Enlightenment) the limits to the objective, representational forms of religion, but it also finds in them their rational content. 'Sustained by philosophy, religion receives its justification from thinking consciousness.' Naive piety has no need of this sort of justification; it has the truth on the basis of authority. But thinking calls the concrete and authoritative into question and must work out a reconciliation between concrete forms and rational content (3:345–6).

This reconciliation is philosophy. Philosophy is to this extent theology. It presents the reconciliation of God with himself and with nature, showing that nature, otherness, is implicitly divine, and that the raising of itself to reconciliation is on the one hand what finite spirit implicitly is, while on the other hand it arrives at this reconciliation, or brings it forth, in world history. This reconciliation is the peace of God, which does not 'surpass all reason'[28] but is rather the peace that *through* reason is first known and thought and is recognized as what is true. (3:347)

This is all very nicely said, but it is based on a questionable assumption, namely that religion and its content must 'take refuge in' the concept. The image here is one of 'flight' (*Flucht*). Religion is on the run in the modern world, and its only refuge is in philosophy. But what will happen if this refuge itself should become marginalized in the postmodern world? In that case it would not be prudent for religion to have cast its lot with philosophy. Perhaps religion and theology should not take flight but stand and resist. Is it really the case that Christian theology does not have within itself the resources to criticize and rise above its own representational forms, and to do so without falling prey to the unproductive alternative of pietism versus rationalism (or fundamentalism versus atheism)? Such a theology would of course draw deeply upon the resources provided by a philosophical theology such as Hegel's. But it would not strictly be a philosophical theology. It would not take *refuge* in the concept but *make use* of the concept to interpret and reimagine its own primary symbols and practices. The representational, metaphorical language of religion would not be left behind but would continue to fructify conceptual thinking. Indeed, does not the continuing connection of Christian theology with concrete communities of faith and with concrete ethical practices give it an intrinsic advantage over the community of philosophy, which is in danger of becoming isolated from the affairs of the world and making hegemonic

---

[28] An allusion to Philippians 4:7; see 3:347 n. 266.

claims?[29] These thoughts are prompted in part by the conclusion
Hegel provides to his lectures in 1821.


### THE PASSING AWAY OF THE COMMUNITY?


In the 1821 manuscript (3:158–62)[30] Hegel speaks not of the 'realization' of the community of the Spirit in the world but of its
possible 'passing away' (*Vergehen*). He is prompted to do so by
the consideration that all historical phenomena come into being,
endure for a greater or shorter time, and eventually perish. So it
has been with the world's religions, all of which in his view are in
decline or no longer really alive. Is Christianity to be allowed an
exception? Is not an exception required if the kingdom of God has
been established eternally and the Holy Spirit has eternal life in its
community? Did not Christ himself say that 'the gates of hell shall
not prevail against my teaching'?[31] 'To speak of a passing away
would mean to end on a discordant note' (3:158).
     But such a discordant note is in fact being sounded in present-
day actuality. Hegel proceeds to enumerate signs of modern decadence, as compared with the age of the Roman Empire:[32] everything sacred is profaned when it falls into human hands and is
made an object of manipulation; rationality takes refuge in private
rights and goods, and the sense of a common life based on religion

---

[29] Similar concerns are expressed by Graham Ward in his appreciative assessment of the contribution of Hegel's philosophy of spirit to a theology of the church.
He cautions against the attempt to move to a purely conceptual language, for
'philosophy too trades in representations'. To regard the philosophical community
as superior to the religious is to undercut the concrete materiality of Christ and the
eucharist. He thinks that Hegel's tendency toward philosophical hegemony in this
regard may explain why his 'theological voice was, like his political theory, even
when attacked, either misunderstood, secularised or both'. See *Cities of God* (London and New York: Routledge, 2000), 137–46. Philip Merklinger, in his otherwise
admirable book, *Philosophy, Theology, and Hegel's Berlin Philosophy of Religion,
1821–1827* (Albany: State University of New York Press, 1993), does not address
the problem of philosophical hegemony.
[30] This passage is exceedingly fragmented and reflects the haste with which
Hegel completed his lecture manuscript. We follow the text as it is reconstructed
in the critical edition. The *Werke* in its second edition (1840) offers a more refined
and less radical version (see 3:158 n. 248).
[31] The text in Matt. 16:18 refers to the church, not the teaching of Christ. Hegel
accepts this passage as a saying of Jesus and uses it as a prooftext.
[32] This is a comparison Hegel offers several times in the lectures. See the
discussions of Roman religion in volume 2. The reference to 'signs of the times'
places the discussion in an apocalyptic frame of reference.

has disappeared; the quest for private welfare and enjoyment is the order of the day; the knowledge of God has been lost, replaced by a merely historical and technical sort of information; moralistic views and subjective feelings replace true faith; the clergy and the theologians have abandoned their calling, leaving ordinary people with no resources; the salt of the gospel has lost its savour if it is no longer preached to the poor and the teaching of love in infinite anguish is relinquished in favour of enjoyment. When all of this happens, we are left with 'finitude [turned] in upon itself, arrogant barrenness and lack of content, the extremity of self-satisfied disenlightenment[33]' (3:159–60).

Anyone who thinks that Hegel is naively optimistic about the modern world should ponder this passage! He certainly does not see things progressing toward a philosophical nirvana or a utopian state. But rather than envisioning the possibility of a revitalized church and theology that might come to terms with these modern challenges, he turns to that with which he is familiar, philosophy. The price of doing so, he acknowledges, is that the present day must be left to its own resources to solve its problems; and the philosophical resolution is only 'partial'. Philosophy forms 'an isolated order of priests—a sanctuary—[who are] untroubled about how it goes with the world, [who need] not mix with it, [and whose work is to preserve] this possession of truth. How things turn out [in the world] is not our affair' (3:161–2).

This is a remarkably stringent conclusion. We are reminded of the famous remark in the Preface to the *Philosophy of Right*, written at about the same time as the philosophy of religion manuscript, that philosophy, imaged as the owl of Minerva, 'begins its flight only with the onset of dusk'.[34] Philosophy comes on the scene after the action is over; it preserves and interprets the truth but does not create or struggle for the truth. If you want to be part of the struggle, philosophy is not your calling. Is there something a bit wistful here in respect to Hegel's own vocational choice? Of course he does not anticipate the tremendous impact his own philosophy has had on the struggles of the modern world. But why does he shut off the possibility of a revisioned theology and a prophetic church confronting these challenges with different and perhaps better resources than philosophy has to offer?

---

[33] The word *Ausklärung* is a play on *Aufklärung*. See 3:160–1 n. 255.
[34] *Elements of the Philosophy of Right*, 23.

Hegel is being too dogmatic when he suggests at the end of the 1824 lectures that religion, church, and faith are locked into the first, precritical 'estate' of the kingdom of the Spirit; that theology is locked into the second estate, that of the understanding (*Verstand*); and that 'the community of philosophy' alone occupies the third estate, that of reason (*Vernunft*) (3:247). Here the idea is that the community of the Spirit will survive by passing over into the community of philosophy. But such a prospect is neither realistic nor hopeful. The constraints on the community of philosophy identified in 1821 should not be forgotten. The better alternative is for religious communities themselves to acknowledge the challenges of modernity and to respond to them critically and prophetically, appropriating rationality while recognizing its limits. Yet the challenges are more daunting than even Hegel imagined, and the success of religion in responding to them remains ambiguous to say the least. Hegel's pessimism about theology is understandable. There are no panaceas, religious or philosophical—no adequate, and certainly no final, realization of reconciliation in history. The only consummation is in God.

# 10

# Christianity and World Religions

## WORLD RELIGIONS IN THE
## PHILOSOPHY OF RELIGION

Part Two of the lectures, *Determinate Religion (die bestimmte Religion)*, is by far the largest of the three parts. The text in the English edition runs to 607 pages, as compared with 265 pages for *The Concept of Religion*[1] and 287 pages for *The Consummate Religion*. Another book would be required to do justice to this complex range of materials. The present book focuses on Hegel's interpretation of Christian theology. In this context, the question becomes principally one of how Christianity is understood to be related to the other religions of the world. It is too simple to say, as of course Hegel does say, that Christianity is the 'consummation' of the concept and history of religions. If that is all that he intended to say, it could have been said much more briefly and with much less expenditure of effort.

By the time of the 1824 lectures Hegel had become engaged with the topic of the history of religions. It clearly fascinated him, and its proper interpretation is what most deeply challenged him toward the end of his career. This is evident from two facts: the extensive reading he undertook in primary sources and secondary literature for this part of the lectures, and his inability to arrive at a satisfactory arrangement of the materials. As for the sources, of the some 240 works upon which Hegel drew for his lectures on the philosophy of religion,[2] approximately two-thirds were used

---

[1] Hegel's *Introduction*, also contained in vol. 1, adds 102 pages. The counts do not include materials in the appendices or the editorial introductions.

[2] See the Bibliography of Sources in the appendix to vol. 2 (2:783–806). This count includes only a single standard edition for each of the many classical authors upon whom Hegel relied, so if individual classical works were included the number would increase substantially. These sources have been identified through the painstaking research of Walter Jaeschke.

206 Christianity and World Religions

primarily or exclusively for *Determinate Religion*. The editorial introduction to volume 2 (2:3–12) identifies these sources in relation to each of the major religious traditions discussed by Hegel: nature religion or 'magic', Chinese religion, Buddhism, Hinduism, Persian religion (Zoroastrianism), Egyptian religion, Judaism, Greek religion, Roman religion. Hegel obviously had an extensive knowledge of world religions for his time, but his sources left a great deal to be desired as far as a scientific study of religion is concerned (many were based on travel and missionary reports). He focused his attention on the original or classical expressions of the religions, for the most part not attending to their subsequent histories or contemporary living expressions, if any. He viewed the history of religions as primarily a thing of the past, with the exception of Christianity—and of Islam, which, as noted in the previous chapter, is missing from *Determinate Religion* and is briefly mentioned in Part Three as a contemporary rival to Christianity.[3] As we shall argue, this is one of the severest problems with Hegel's treatment. While religions continue to be practised throughout the world, *Geist* seems to have left most of them behind. Christianity alone truly lives, surrounded by fossilized forms, and it is not impossible (as we saw at the end of the preceding chapter) that it too will become a fossil. Yet Hegel is not sanguine about the prospect of a post-religious future.

Hegel's inability to arrive at a satisfactory arrangement of the materials is indicated by the fact that his organization of *Determinate Religion* differed widely in each of the four lecture series. Whereas the treatment of *The Consummate Religion* fell into place with the 1824 lectures, and of *The Concept of Religion* in 1827, Hegel experimented with yet another arrangement of *Determinate Religion* in 1831, which had as many problems as the previous arrangements. Yet all the arrangements and detailed discussions of specific religions are packed with insights. Hegel was seriously engaged with this material, and on a level of sophistication unmatched by other philosophers and theologians of his time (and of most other times as well). Despite brilliant exercises of conceptual

---

[3] Hegel's omission of Islam is puzzling, especially in light of his belief that it was a more populous religion than Christianity (see below, n. 32). Perhaps the following factors played a role: his knowledge of Islam was limited, although he was familiar with and appreciative of a few of its mystical writings (see Chap. 9, n. 25); it did not fit into his schematism of determinate religion; and he shared a long-standing European antipathy toward it.

imagination, he was finding that he could not produce a unified history of religions. What he did produce has more the character of a geography of religions or a pluralism of religions.

In the next section of this chapter, I will summarize the four renditions of *Determinate Religion* that appeared in the 1821, 1824, 1827, and 1831 lectures. This will lead to a reflection on Hegel's experimentation with the history of religions. Then I will focus on his treatment of four religions that are still living and that he brings into dialogue with his own philosophical theology: Daoism, Buddhism, Hinduism, and Judaism.[4] Finally, I will suggest that the logic of Hegel's philosophy of religion points beyond inclusivism (the idea that Christianity 'fulfils' or 'consummates' the religions) to a genuine religious pluralism in which Christianity takes its place as a determinate religion or as one of the religions of the 'Concrete Spirit'.

FOUR RENDITIONS OF DETERMINATE RELIGION[5]

*Moments of the Concept: The 1821 Lectures*

In a cancelled heading at the end of the 1821 manuscript's treatment of *The Concept of Religion* (1:255 n. 185), Hegel states that in Part Two of the lectures the concept of religion will be 'grasped in its determinate aspects', and that these aspects constitute the 'forms of consciousness of the absolute idea'. This formulation suggests that what follows in *Determinate Religion* is intended as a phenomenology of religion, that is, of the various forms of consciousness assumed by the absolute idea as it emerges and advances through the history of religions. Although data are drawn from history, what is offered is not a historical account but a philosophical description of stages of religious consciousness—a description that is at once phenomenological and speculative, phenomenological because it attends to the concrete stages of

---

[4] The omission from our discussion of the ancient religions—Greek, Egyptian, Persian, and Roman—is a deficit, for Hegel's treatment of them is fascinating, and Greek religion in particular he views as integral to the formation of Christianity. Hegel's depiction of nature religion also is not without merit. To have included all of these religions would have taken this chapter beyond reasonable bounds.

[5] In this section (and elsewhere in this chapter) I draw on materials I prepared for the editorial introduction to vol. 2 of the lectures.

religious consciousness, speculative because the interpretative perspective is already that of the absolute idea.

The description is carried out through the application of two sets of analytic categories—one internal to the religions, the other relating them externally. The internal set identifies three aspects of a religion: its abstract concept of divinity (which also forms a proof of the existence of God), the ways in which God is known representationally in the texts and symbols of the religion, and the practical relationship in which communion with the deity is established; or, in brief, a religion's metaphysical concept, its concrete representations, and its cultus. Initially Hegel envisioned only a twofold scheme, which did not distinguish between representation and cultus (2:94 incl. n. 5). The triple division was apparently worked out only in the course of treating the determinate religions, and it was applied as well to the consummate religion.

The external analysis arranges *Determinate Religion* into a triad corresponding to the fundamental moments of logic, namely, being, essence, and concept (2:95–7 incl. n. 6). But in the case of the religions, these categories are applied in the mode of determinateness and finitude; hence the operative triad is one of prereflective immediacy or undifferentiated substance (the Oriental religions of nature, though they are not discussed separately), differentiation in the form of particularity (Jewish religion) and necessity (Greek) (both categories of 'essence'), and external purposiveness or expediency (*Zweckmässigkeit*). The latter, Roman religion, though aligned with the 'concept', represents the apotheosis of finitude and thus prepares the transition from all the finite religions to the truly conceptual and consummate religion. Christianity is no longer a determinate religion, yet it is a product of history. Roman religion's transitional status justifies its treatment as a separate stage of religious consciousness: it is not higher than what has gone before but gathers up and makes explicit the limitations of determinate religion as such. On the one hand Roman religion is universal, related 'to the whole human race', not 'ethnic' or national like the preceding religions (in this sense it is conceptual or 'philosophical'[6]). But on the other hand it is finite, concerned with what is 'around us', not above or beneath us; lacking transcendence and depth, it is utterly prosaic, preoccupied with

---

[6] The reference to the 'ethnic' religions and the designation of Roman religion as 'philosophical' are suggested by Goethe; see 2:97 incl. nn. 12, 13.

'earthly circumstances and arrangements'. The one unvarying feature in Hegel's treatment of the determinate religions across all the
lecture series is this positioning of Roman religion. It plays a role
in the difficult transition from determinate to consummate religion. The idea seems to be that when finitude apotheosizes itself it
also negates itself and prepares the way for genuine infinitude.[7]
Hegel remarks that religion must pass through its determinate
forms 'in order to attain from them the nature of its concept'.
'These determinacies are the moments, the becoming of the concept, and their resolution and the return [to itself] are what constitute the concept itself. . . . It belongs to the nature of the concept, its
vitality and becoming, in fact its spirituality, that it does not exist
at the beginning, full-grown on its own account; [it is] not immediate. Truth is not [there] for consciousness at the beginning'
(2:94). Thus the second part of the philosophy of religion contains
'the path to the concept' and considers religions as 'stages of this
path'; but they are not the true religion (2:95). In other words, the
concept of religion is a product of history, not an a priori idea;
religion is what it is through history. Yet when the concept is fully
attained, it seems to leap out of history into ideality. We shall have
to ask: Is the concept ever fully attained? And is not such a leap a
betrayal of Hegel's insight into the connection between ideality
and reality, rationality and actuality, spirit and history?

In the 1821 *Concept of Religion*, Hegel remarks that rather than
simply compiling the history of religions in an external sense, the
higher need is to apprehend what it *means*, to grasp its *rationality*,
to know that there is *reason* in the religions. Such a recognition
enables us to be reconciled to what is 'horrifying and tasteless' in
them (the example given here is human and child sacrifice) but
without justifying such horrors (1:198–9). Hegel does not mince
words in describing brutal and oppressive religious practices: he
sees evidence in them of human activity, but he condemns them for
destroying rather than advancing human freedom, which for him is
the final criterion of religious truth. He also seems to recognize a
limit to the rational comprehension of the history of religion, for he

---

[7] Hegel devotes more attention in 1821 to Roman religion than to any other
determinate religion (some fourteen manuscript sheets, or nearly half the number
used for the whole of *The Consummate Religion*). His critique of Roman religion is in
part also an indirect critique of religious tendencies in his own time (see above,
Chap. 3), and of the idolatry present in human religiousness in general, which helps
to account for the extensive treatment.

adds that 'contingency and locality pervade all these forms' (1:199).

## Nature, Finite Spirit, Infinite Spirit: The 1824 Lectures

The three moments of *Determinate Religion* according to the introduction to the second lecture series are immediate, natural religion (God intuited in the natural unity of the spiritual and the natural), the religions of spiritual individuality (the reflection of spirit into itself out of nature, God represented as an individual subject or subjects), and the religion of finite purposiveness (Roman religion) (2:233–6). While this division is not based on the dialectic of being, essence, and concept, as in the manuscript, it is, according to Hegel, a 'necessary classification that follows objectively from the nature of spirit' (2:237)—but not so necessary as to prevent him from altering it in the process of lecturing.

What happens is that the threefold division is converted to a twofold one: (1) immediate or nature religion (much expanded to include for the first time a discussion of Asian and Middle Eastern religions), and (2) the religions of spiritual individuality or of finite spirit, into which Roman religion is incorporated as a third subphase following upon Jewish and Greek religion. Christianity now becomes the third moment in a larger dialectic of religions (see 2:381 n. 386). This innovative arrangement enables Hegel to suggest that the religions of spiritual individuality correspond to three forms of nature religion 'in reverse order', Jewish religion corresponding to Persian,[8] Greek religion to Hinduism, and Roman religion to the state religion of China (2:381–90). Thus the determinate or finite religions are seen to cycle back upon themselves in death and degeneracy—a return to the primitive at a more advanced level of culture—and the stage is set for the transition to the consummate religion. But the transition does not occur as a

---

[8] This reversal places Judaism at the pinnacle of the determinate religions, superseded only by Christianity, a position that it also occupies in 1827 due to a different structural arrangement. Jewish and Persian (Zoroastrian) religion are linked in 1831 under the category of the good. In 1824 Zoroastrianism is called the religion of the good or of light, light being the principal symbol of the good, in contrast to darkness, which represents evil. Judaism is also portrayed as a religion of light in the 1821 lectures, following similar allusions in the *Phenomenology of Spirit* (see the discussion below). Thus Persian and Jewish religion are linked in various ways for Hegel; but the fundamental distinction between them is that Zoroastrianism posits a cosmic dualism whereas Judaism is the purest form of monotheism.

progressive advance; the whole dialectical structure resists any monolithic, linear theory of progress. Christianity is virtually another genus of religion from that of the Roman cult and pantheon. At the same time, Christianity is drawn into the history of religions more directly than in Hegel's other arrangements; it becomes in effect the final phase of determinate religion, completing the movement from nature to finite spirit to infinite spirit. Perhaps for this reason Hegel returned in 1827 and 1831 to an internal threefold arrangement for *Determinate Religion* of which Christianity is not a part.

Apart from the structural experimentation, the most significant difference between the 1824 and 1821 lectures is the great enrichment of content. *Determinate Religion* as a whole is twice the length in 1824 as compared with 1821; but the fivefold expansion of the first part, immediate or nature religion, is the most dramatic. Now for the first time the religion of magic, the religion of ancient China, Buddhism, Hinduism, Persian religion, and Egyptian religion are discussed in detail and on the basis of a broad range of materials. Major changes also occur in the interpretation of Judaism.

In summary remarks on *Determinate Religion* at the end of the *Introduction* to the 1824 lectures, Hegel offers comments similar to those found in 1821. We are told that the concept resolves to determine itself and that spirit comes to itself through movement, mediation, distinctions. Spirit does not reach itself without having traversed the path of history, on which the determinate religions are necessary stages (1:142–5).

When we consider the sequence of the determinate religions under the guidance of the concept, ... the sequence of the historical religions emerges for us from it, and thus we have the history of religions before us at the same time. For what is *necessary* through the concept must have *existed*, and the religions, as they have followed one another, have not arisen in a contingent manner. Instead it is spirit that governs what is inward, that has brought it forth. It is not the work of chance, and it is absurd to see contingency here.... This is a purely philosophical treatment, but at the same time also a treatment of what *is*. Philosophy on the whole does not consider *what is not*; only *what is, is rational*. ([I mean] what *actually* is, not the merely phenomenal or the merely existing.)    (1:145–6)

Thus what Hegel is offering is a philosophical, not an empirical, history of religions; and philosophy grasps the necessity of what unfolds in actuality. But it is not as easy as this passage assumes to grasp the actual historical course of unfolding. At least Hegel offers several different constructions of the unfolding. If the claim were to grasp not the *sequence of unfolding* but the *diversity of determinate forms* in which the concept of religion appears, it would be closer to the mark. It would be a logical deduction of the necessity of religious pluralism. Just because spirit comes to itself only through movement and distinctions, there *must* be a diversity of historical religions. In fact what Hegel offers in the lectures (as we shall argue) is a typology and geography, not a history of religions. How typologically and geographically diverse religions actually arise and interact in history cannot be deduced logically but is a matter of historical contingency. Yet it can be affirmed that what is common to the religions is that spirit is coming to itself in them.

In a brief comment at the end of the introduction to *The Consummate Religion* in 1824, Hegel remarks that Christianity, the religion of freedom, is the third form of religion, following upon, unifying, and completing the religion of nature and the religion of finite spirit. The movement is one from consciousness to self-consciousness finitely determined, to self-consciousness self-contained (3:172–3). This confirms the distinctive structure of the 1824 lectures, which incorporates Christianity into the horizon of determinate religion as its 'third form'. If we could construe this third form less as a final and consummate form than as part of an ongoing dialectic of spirit, we would be closer to a genuine religious pluralism—closer than Hegel himself is prepared to go.

## Unity, Elevation, Annihilation of Spirit: The 1827 Lectures

The third lecture series reestablishes the threefold division of *Determinate Religion* found in 1821, but the categories are quite different from the logic of being, essence, and concept; rather they follow from the dialectic of nature and spirit (2:513–21).[9] The three stages of determinate religion according to 1827 are (1) religion as the unity of the spiritual and the natural, (2) the elevation of the spiritual above the natural, and (3) the religion in

---

[9] The categories are influenced by the projected threefold division at the beginning of the 1824 treatment, which, as we have seen, was converted into a twofold division in the course of lecturing, a conversion that generated problems Hegel apparently wished to avoid.

which purposiveness is not yet spiritual. The latter is Roman religion, which effectively annihilates spirit in the drive to attain expedient human ends, thus generating the religiocultural crisis into which Christianity is born. The first is nature religion, which is not devoid of spirit but worships it in natural and human shapes.[10] The strains in treating such religions as Buddhism and Hinduism under this category are becoming more apparent, and adjustments are made that anticipate the reorganization to come in 1831. Hegel recognizes that for the Asian religions divinity is no longer a natural but a spiritual substance.

The second stage of determinate religion is the one in which the spiritual is elevated above the natural in the form either of thought (Jewish religion) or of concrete individuality (Greek religion). Here again an alteration occurs in the course of lecturing, for the order in which Jewish and Greek religion are treated in 1821 and 1824 is reversed in 1827. Now Greek religion (the religion of beauty) comes first, followed by Judaism (the religion of sublimity). Indeed Hegel goes so far as to assert 'the necessity of the elevation of the religion of beauty into the religion of sublimity' (2:669). This reversal has the effect of putting Judaism at the pinnacle of the determinate religions, principally because of its insight into the unity, rationality, and spirituality of God. This is the necessary soil in which the consummate religion comes to birth: the God of Christianity is the God of Israel. But Judaism is still lacking in its grasp of the concrete mediation of divinity and humanity and in its appreciation of free ethical institutions. These deficits are partly supplied by Greek religion. The limitations of Jewish and Greek religion are overcome, not in Roman religion, which proves to be an abortive, retrograde, and expedient amalgamation of the religions, but in Christianity, which emerges in the context of Hellenistic Judaism and fills a void at the heart of Roman culture. Thus on the one hand Hegel accounts (briefly) for the historical context of Christian origins, while on the other

---

[10] In both 1824 and 1827, Hegel stresses that in nature religion it is not natural, physical objects that are taken to be God and revered as God. Rather it is the spiritual that is the object of nature religion as well, but recognized first in its immediate and natural mode, which is that of sensibly existing human beings who exercise power over nature (shamans, kings, priests, gurus, ancestors). The several stages of nature religion are distinguished on the basis of how humans represent, relate to, and objectify divinity. In magic, power over nature is exercised directly; in the more advanced nature religions, indirectly.

hand he (once again) lifts Christianity out of the framework of the determinate religions.

In the 'survey of the subject' at the end of the *Introduction* to the lectures in 1827, Hegel makes comments similar to those found in 1821 and 1824, but with distinctive nuances (1:181–3). Spirit in principle is not immediate but is living, acting, self-making. 'Anything alive is already this activity of mediation with itself.' All living things go through a cycle of immediacy, development, and recapitulation (the last being the fruit that bears the seed for a new cycle). Are we to understand from this analogy that the consummate religion too is not the end of the process but produces fruit for a new cycle? Hegel does not answer. What he does say is that 'in so far as it is determinate and has not yet traversed the circuit of its determinations, with the result that it is finite religion and exists as finite, religion is *historical* and is a *particular shape* of religion' (1:183). Christianity seems to present the paradox of being historical and concretely shaped, while at the same time it transcends determinacy and finitude, having completed the circuit. In any event, Hegel believes it is possible to identify the principal moments in the development of religion as a series of historical stages, and on this basis to furnish 'a single sequence of configurations, or a history of religion'. But it is just this 'single sequence' that he could never precisely determine.

*Immediacy, Rupture, Reconciliation: The 1831 Lectures*

Strauss's excerpts permit a glimpse of the structure of the 1831 lectures, but we have only fragments of actual lecture transcripts (those fragments preserved by the *Werke* editions and footnoted in relation to 1824 and 1827 texts). This is unfortunate because Hegel undertook a major reorganization of *Determinate Religion* in 1831 and introduced new materials and new interpretations. Instead of the interplay of nature and spirit, which characterizes the 1824 and 1827 arrangement, the 1831 lectures offer a more strictly dialectical approach—not of being, essence, and concept (as in 1821), but of immediacy, rupture, and reconciliation (2:515–17 n. 5, 721–2). These are not strictly logical categories but are descriptive of the life of the concept and of the dialectic of consciousness—a dialectic that is taken into the divine life and becomes genuinely trinitarian in the Christian religion.

The first moment, that of immediacy, is now limited to nature religion or magic, which is not yet properly religious. Religion emerges with a cleavage or rupture of consciousness such that consciousness distinguishes its sensuous nature from what is essential and knows the difference between natural power and God as absolute power. This rupture permits an elevation of the spiritual above the natural, and Hegel now locates the beginning of this process at a much earlier point than he did in 1827. It occurs already with the 'objectification of the divine object' in the more developed religions of magic, but its chief exemplification is found in 'the three Oriental religions of substance', namely Chinese religion (Daoism), Hinduism, and Buddhism/Lamaism (2:516 n. 5). Thus for the first time the Asian religions are distinguished from the category of 'nature religion' and analysed with a more appropriate concept, that of 'substance'.

The third stage entails the overcoming of the cleavage through a reconciliation of consciousness and its object at a higher, mediated level, where freedom becomes actual for the first time: this is the stage of the religions of (finite) freedom, which runs through three phases. The first phase is a transitional one in which subjectivity struggles to establish itself over against impersonal (and in some respects still quasi-natural) substance. This struggle has its historical existence in the religion of the good (Persian and Jewish), the religion of anguish (Phoenician[11]), and the religion of ferment (Egyptian[12]). In the second phase, the subject knows itself to be free in relation to the divine object. This is the religion of freedom proper, or Greek religion.[13] But since the subject has not yet passed through the infinite antithesis of good and evil, and since

[11] This is not a historical religion at all but a construct derived from classical mythology relating to the figure of Adonis and the sacred bird of the Egyptians, the phoenix. See 2:452–5 n. 2, 743 n. 71.

[12] In the 1824 and 1827 lectures, Egyptian religion is called the religion of the enigma (*Rätsel*), as represented by the sphinx and the pyramids, because its symbols denote something that always remains unexpressed and obscure (see 2:358 n. 314). Ferment (*Gärung*) suggests that spirit is struggling to rise out of the ferment of natural symbols (2:744 n. 73). Hegel's knowledge of Egyptian religion is based principally on classical sources such as Herodotus; in the 1831 lectures he alludes to recent archaeological discoveries, including the deciphering of the hieroglyphic system in 1824.

[13] Greek religion is still the religion of beauty. But now the beauty of Greek art is linked to its symbolic representations of free human spirituality, of which the gods also are an expression. Human beings are free individuals responsible for their actions, and they form political institutions that serve the goal of freedom. But they are also subject to the destiny or fate that governs everything and renders the

the gods are not yet infinite spirit, the reconciliation that occurs at this stage is not complete. Nor is the reconciliation completed by Roman religion, which issues instead in the infinite unhappiness and anguish that serve as the birth pangs of a new religion. Hence the third phase of the religion of reconciliation and freedom is one in which the relative reconciliation and freedom gained through the struggle of the preceding religions is undone, and the stage is set for the transition to the consummate religion, the religion of infinite freedom.

In some respects this reorganization is an improvement. It does much greater justice to the Oriental religions of substance. And it locates Christianity on a trajectory of the struggle for freedom that reaches back into ancient Egypt, Persia, Israel, and Greece. The history of religion is aligned with the history of the world: the progress of the consciousness of freedom.[14] In 1831 Hegel was especially concerned with the theme of freedom, as we have seen.[15] But in this new alignment Judaism comes off badly. It is on the way to freedom but has not arrived at its ethical actualization to the degree that Greek religion has; it remains bound to the service of its Lord, who, though good and wise, does not liberate from suffering by sharing human anguish. The lumping together of Persian, Jewish, Phoenician, and Egyptian religion as 'transitional' is distinctly unconvincing, as is the treatment of Persian and Jewish religion under the category of 'the good'. And Roman religion, the last of the religions in this chain, is in fact a religion of absolute servitude.

Hegel is now able to track the movement of spirit geographically from East to West: from China to India to the Middle East (Persia, Israel, Egypt) to Greece, Rome, and Europe (2:736 n. 57). He must have known that this is not the end of the journey. Whither spirit? An advance to the Americas, a turn to the South, a return to the East, a reconciliation of East and West? The movement obviously does not occur in a simple or single chronological sequence. It is rather that spirit emerges in a diversity of places and times,

---

struggle for justice tragic by bringing ethical powers into collision. In Greek religion aesthetics and ethics, beauty and freedom, are connected, but still at the level of finitude. See 2:752–8.

[14] See Hegel's *Lectures on the Philosophy of World History, Introduction: Reason in History*, trans. H. B. Nisbet (Cambridge: Cambridge University Press, 1975), 54.

[15] Hegel's treatment of the relationship of religion to the state in the 1831 lectures is discussed above, Chap. 9.

sweeping across the face of the earth in complex and changing patterns. Much work remained to be done on this geography of world religions, but Hegel's time had run out.

## CONCEPTUAL PLAY: A GEOGRAPHY OF RELIGIONS[16]

Hegel engaged in unrelenting efforts to work out an adequate philosophical conceptualization of the history of religions. If nothing else, his struggles with this material make it abundantly clear, in the words of Walter Jaeschke, that 'nothing is more alien to Hegel's procedure than the customary picture of the pontificating philosopher who sets out to reduce the colorful array of historical actuality to pallid reason through a prefabricated net of abstract categories'.[17] He does indeed make use of philosophical categories to interpret the religions, and these are connected in one way or another to his understanding of the concept of religion. But the categories are shaped and varied in accord with the concrete materials that need interpretation. His evident willingness to incorporate new data and experiment with new schemes underscores the fact that for him philosophy is a kind of conceptual play based on imaginative variation in order to arrive at new insights. Jaeschke remarks that 'his treatment of the history of religion forms an experimental field in which virtually everything is tried out'.[18] The medium of oral lectures was ideally suited for this purpose,[19] and Hegel was reluctant to commit anything to print as long as the process of thinking remained open and fluid. He was not a prisoner

[16] In this section I draw on ideas that Walter Jaeschke first formulated in an essay, 'Zur Logik der Bestimmten Religion', in *Hegels Logik der Philosophie: Religion und Philosophie in der Theorie des absoluten Geistes*, ed. Dieter Henrich and Rolf-Peter Horstmann (Stuttgart: Klett-Cotta, 1984). This material in revised form appears as a section of chap. 3 of Jaeschke's *Reason in Religion: The Foundations of Hegel's Philosophy of Religion*, trans. J. Michael Stewart and Peter C. Hodgson (Berkeley and Los Angeles: University of California Press, 1990), 263–84. Jaeschke draws upon the pioneering work of Reinhard Heede, *Die göttliche Idee und ihre Erscheinung in der Religion: Untersuchungen zum Verhältnis von Logik und Religionsphilosophie bei Hegel* (Dr.phil. dissertation, University of Münster, 1972). The only other published work on the subject, Reinhard Leuze's *Die außerchristlichen Religionen bei Hegel* (Göttingen: Vandenhoeck & Ruprecht, 1975) is limited by having to work with Lasson's edition of the lectures.
[17] From the Preface to the German edition, *Vorlesungen über die Philosophie der Religion*, Part 2, *Die bestimmte Religion* (Hamburg: Felix Meiner Verlag, 1985), p. ix.
[18] Jaeschke, *Reason in Religion*, 277.
[19] See above, Chap. 2, p. 50.

of his own system; for him it was not a closed system but a way and discipline of thinking.

What Hegel offers in *Determinate Religion*, suggests Jaeschke, is less a *history* of religion than a *typology* or *geography* of religion.[20] To be sure, religion is fundamentally historical, but its historicality follows from the historicality of human spirit. Since there is no single history of human spirit, there cannot be a single, unified history of religion. At best, what we can attain is a history of religions, or better, histories of religions—a diversity of histories that cannot be organized under a single, encompassing philosophical conceptuality. Hegel's claim to be able to do this is falsified by his actual achievement in the successive lectures, which should have made it clear that the objective of a logical construction of the history of religion cannot be attained. What Hegel gives us is a typology of shapes in which spirit appears in religious history and by which it develops, but these shapes need not, indeed cannot, be linked into a unitary history directed to a common goal. He is able to demonstrate the necessity of a diversity and plurality of religions, because spirit comes to itself only through movement and distinction, but not the necessity of a universal history of religion. The shapes appear as dispersed geographically in distinctive cultural trajectories rather than as linked in a temporal progression. 'The geography of religion that Hegel actually gives us fits the facts better than the kind of universal history of religion he aimed at.'[21] Hegel himself seems to recognize something like this when he remarks in the chapter on religion in the *Phenomenology of Spirit* that there is no single line of advance since each religiocultural trajectory at some point retrogresses, a 'knot' forms, and spirit moves to another trajectory, so that there are in fact many lines in history, which can be 'bundled' but not amalgamated.[22]

Our interest principally is in how Christianity as the 'consummate' religion relates to this geography of religions. Hegel does not establish the 'consummate' or 'absolute' character of Christianity directly from the course of the determinate religions. Rather than a

[20] *Reason in Religion*, 272, 277–84. Raimundo Panikkar employs the image of a 'geography of religions' (see below, n. 24).

[21] Jaeschke, *Reason in Religion*, 283.

[22] *Phenomenology of Spirit*, trans. A. V. Miller (Oxford: Clarendon Press, 1977), 414–15. See the translation of this passage in *G. W. F. Hegel: Theologian of the Spirit*, ed. Peter C. Hodgson (Minneapolis: Fortress Press; Edinburgh: T&T Clark, 1997), 114.

historical progression, what he pictures is that a break occurs and something new emerges out of crisis—a religion that corresponds fully to the concept of religion, and thus a religion in which God is known as God is in godself. This new religion seems to be released from the course of history. The identity between Christianity and the concept of religion is established on the basis of definition: the concept is what it is because Christianity is the fullest instantiation of it, and vice versa. But the geography of religions would seem to allow for a more pluralistic approach. There is no reason in principle why the concept of religion could not come to completion in different ways in a diversity of historical shapes. The argument for a single perfect religion is as specious as the argument for a single perfect incarnation of God. Absoluteness requires concreteness (individuality) but not singularity (once-and-for-allness). Hegel's geography allows us to say that God is never fully known as God is in godself. Rather there are approximations of such knowings in a diversity of forms. God as absolute spirit disperses godself into the world absolvingly[23] and is known in the mode of dispersal rather than of finality. Recognition of this fact will increase as religions become acquainted with each other across their differences. By extending Hegel's conceptual play, we shall explore this possibility in the next three sections.

### HEGEL'S AFFINITY WITH AND CRITIQUE OF ASIAN RELIGIONS

Hegel's definition of the concept of religion—the unity, differentiation, and reintegration of selfhood or spirit—is close to the core insight of Hinduism and Buddhism. Expressed in Hindu terms, spirit is *advaitic*, not-two, but also not simply one. Spiritual substance is one mediated by many through a spiralling process. Every union breaks down, original unity keeps evolving, the world becomes more diverse, and creativity is an ongoing struggle, a process of division and reunion at a higher level of complexity. Hinduism recognizes only one 'true self' for all reality: self and

---

[23] In Chap. 4, I discussed the sense in which absolute spirit is for Hegel an absolving, releasing spirit. Absoluteness designates God's dynamic relationality and in particular God's 'release' of otherness with which God nonetheless remains intrinsically connected.

highest reality (Brahman) mirror one another. To know myself fully is to know everything, because my true self (as distinct from my empirical self) *is* everything. However, this is no simple identity but a unity to be achieved out of an inexhaustible diversity and through countless cycles. Such a view requires pluralism, which, in the words of Raimundo Panikkar, 'means something more than sheer acknowledgment of plurality and the mere wishful thinking of unity'.[24]

Hegel shows a growing appreciation of this complex worldview in his successive treatments of the religions of China and India.

*Chinese Religion: The Religion of Measure*

The discussion of Chinese religion in the 1824 lectures (2:299–303) is very limited. The ancient religion of the Zhou dynasty is viewed as part of the religion of magic, but it represents the final stage in the 'formal objectification' of the divine object. In 1827 (2:547–62) the treatment is greatly expanded and the interpretation shifts: this is the religion of heaven or 'Tian', the highest ruling power, which is the power of nature bound together with moral characteristics. Hegel understands Daoism to be a sect of this religion,[25] which emphasizes that 'the way' of nature is also the way of reason. His attention is caught by the fact that 'the determination "three" immediately comes into play to the extent that the Dao is something rational and concrete. Reason has produced one, one has produced two, two has produced three, and three the universe.' The indeterminate One would be an impoverished and empty

---

[24] See Francis X. Clooney, SJ, *Hindu Wisdom for All God's Children* (Maryknoll, NY: Orbis Books, 1998), chaps. 1–2; and Raimundo Panikkar, 'The Jordan, the Tiber, and the Ganges: Three Kairological Moments of Christic Self-Consciousness', in John Hick and Paul F. Knitter (eds.), *The Myth of Christian Uniqueness: Toward a Pluralistic Theology of Religions* (Maryknoll, NY: Orbis Books, 1987), 89–116, esp. 109. Panikkar's use of the image of rivers points, he says, to a 'geography of religions', which 'is still an unexplored discipline' (98). These rivers do not meet on earth but in the form of clouds. 'Religions do not coalesce, certainly not as organized religions. They meet once transformed into vapor, once metamorphosized into Spirit, which then is poured down in innumerable tongues' (92).

[25] His knowledge of the historical details is imprecise; see 2:556 n. 115. His principal source is Jean Pierre Abel-Rémusat's *Mémoire sur la vie et les opinions de Lao-Tseu* (Paris, 1823). He regards the legendary Lao-zi to be a contemporary of Confucius, whose teaching he does not discuss other than to say that it is 'moralistic' and not 'speculative' (2:558). His reference in the 1831 lectures to the measures and their signs, the Gua, is derived from Antoine Gaubil's translation of the Shu-jing published in Paris in 1770 (2:552 n. 106).

abstraction without generating Two and eventually the Third, 'the totality, the consummation of determinateness'. Here we encounter 'the first efforts of humanity to think the form of triunity or trinity' (2:558–9). Hegel believes that the symbol of the Dao is on the one hand a triangle, and on the other hand three horizontal lines one above the other, with a vertical stroke through them as a sign that the three are to be grasped as one.[26] This way of thinking, he tells us, remains entirely abstract, and we do not yet have a higher religion.

In the 1831 lectures (2:729–30, cf. 550–2 n. 106), Chinese religion is defined as 'the religion of measure'. 'Measure' (*Maß*) in Hegel's logic is the third category of the doctrine of being in which quality and quantity, or substance and accident, are united; and as such it constitutes a transition to the doctrine of essence (*Wesen*). In Daoism, the measures take the form of the abstract categories of one and two, being and nonbeing, yes and no, yang and yin. From this basic dialectic derive all the other categorial distinctions (geographical, physical, musical, mathematical) by which the world is rationally structured. The moral and religious life requires gearing oneself into these measures and finding the mean between them in specific circumstances. The maintenance of the measures is the responsibility of the emperor, the son of heaven (Tian), and heaven is the power over the measures. Thus in Daoism Hegel finds an intuition of the dialectical structure of reality in terms similar to how he himself articulates it.

## Hinduism: The Religion of Fanciful Imagination and Abstract Unity[27]

In the 1824 and 1827 lectures, Hegel treats Buddhism prior to Hinduism on the assumption that it is the older of the two religions. In 1831 (2:731–5) he gets the historical sequence right, but

---

[26] Hegel seems to have confused the symbol of the Dao with the sign for *wang*, a king or prince (2:559 n. 128).

[27] 'Fanciful Imagination' (*Phantasie*) is the name by which Hegel designates Hinduism in the 1824 and 1827 lectures, while in 1831 he calls it the religion of 'abstract unity' (see 2:316, 729). In the English edition, *Phantasie* is translated as 'phantasy' in order to distinguish it from 'fantasy' in the sense of an illusion as well as from the Kantian term for 'imagination', *Einbildung*. Hegel's variation of the names by which he designates the religions philosophically is an indication of the conceptual play to which we have referred.

this may be partly for schematic reasons.[28] Hinduism now provides the conceptual advance from natural powers to unitary substance instead of Buddhism, and it receives a much more detailed
analysis in the 1831 lectures than Buddhism does. In Hinduism the
multiplicity of the Chinese measures is resumed into unity, into a
One that determines itself by means of thought (Brahman). But its
thinking remains locked into self-containment, so that the actual
elaboration of difference falls outside it in a 'wild infinity' where
fanciful imagination (*Phantasie*) is given free rein. Finally the unity
is taken back into itself, but in a 'spiritless' fashion. Thus the unity
of Brahman is 'abstract'.

These three moments—the inward self-containment, the outward multiplicity, and the spiritless resumption—correspond to
the three figures of the Hindu Trimurti (Brahmā, Vishnu, and
Shiva), and the bulk of the 1831 presentation is organized according to this triad. Hegel remarks that this 'trinity in unity is indis-
putably the most striking and greatest feature in Hindu
mythology. We cannot call [the figures] persons, for they lack
spiritual subjectivity as a fundamental determination. But to Euro-
peans it must have been in the highest degree astonishing to
encounter this lofty principle of the Christian religion here'
(2:587 n. 208). He attends in greater detail than before to the
Hindu cosmogonies, to epics contained in the Mahābhārata, and
especially to the Rāmāyana (2:597 n. 244); but despite this atten-
tiveness, and the more significant religiohistorical role accorded
Hinduism, the interpretation is no more favourable than in the
earlier lectures. The 'mismatch between content and form' accounts for the 'ugliness of the mythological figures'. There is no
fixed shape or determinacy in the Hindu's infinite world of deities,
powers, phenomena, incarnations. Imagination passes back and
forth between external existence and divinity and 'is not determined by a rational nexus of thought categories' (2:594 n. 234).

Hegel's negative assessment of Hinduism is attributable to several factors. Although he had some familiarity with primary texts
(the Upanishads, the Laws of Manu, the Mahābhārata, including
the Bhagavad-Gītā, and the Rāmāyana), his secondary sources

---

[28] In Hegel's time there was still scholarly uncertainty as to which of the two
religions was older. The 1831 arrangement is a clearer articulation of his basic
religio-geographical-historical schema, namely the advance of *Geist* from China to
India (and the India-born religions), then to the Middle East and the West (see
2:731 n. 30).

reflected the prejudice of the East India Company, which had a political interest in representing Indian culture and society as corrupt in order to justify its economic policies (see 2:6–7). Moreover, he was suspicious of the longing of German Romantics such as Friedrich Schlegel for a past golden age that was believed to have had its origins in India. By contrast with this attitude, Hegel was convinced that the cultic and ethical practices of Hinduism were destructive of human freedom and flourishing. He honed in on this problem in his discussion of the Hindu cultus in 1824 and 1827.

The 1824 lectures establish three points. The first is that the universal substance, Brahman, with whom individual selves are in some sense identical, is not in itself personal nor is it worshipped (2:335–41). By contrast with the God of Judaism, Brahman is the neuter One (*das Eine*), not the personal One (*der Eine*) (2:339 incl. n. 267).[29] Hegel says that this is a 'quite essential difference'. From his point of view Brahman is only the in-itself (*das Ansich*) and does not yet have being for itself (*das Fürsichsein*). Consequently it remains in itself abstract and needs human consciousnesses through which to achieve subjectivity. As the abstract supreme being, Brahman is unknowable, a negative beyond, similar to the God of the Enlightenment (2:340 n. 271). Second, just because of the abstractness and transcendence of Brahman, the human relationship to it requires renouncing everything that is living and concrete. This leads to 'austerities' or severe ascetic practices (yoga) that are required to achieve the state of Brahman and that Hegel regards as dehumanizing (2:341–4). Finally there are the caste distinctions that deify the Brahmin caste and regard all other humans as less worthy and some as utterly worthless (2:344–7). Hegel concludes that this religion is devoid of spirit: its isolated universal is not an object of worship, and the region of the particular has the character of irrationality and unfreedom (2:347–50). The only religious options are abstract absorption into the One or enslavement to sensuous activity. The elements of being-within-self and self-differentiation in the constitution of divinity have not yet been reconciled, and

---

[29] Brahman is impersonal substance, but spiritual, not material: Brahman = Atman (spirit, soul). It becomes incarnate in a multiplicity of personal deities, and the human self is implicitly identical with it. Thus Brahman must have within itself the potential for personification, even if, as Hegel asserts, it must go outside itself to achieve it.

Hinduism oscillates between extremes. 'Among the Hindus we find the most beautiful poetry, but always with an underlying element of utter irrationality: we are attracted by its grace and at the same time repelled by the sheer confusion and nonsense of it' (2:350).

To this unattractive picture, the 1827 lectures add further details on ascetic rigours and on the degradation of human life that is evident to Hegel from such practices as self-immolation, widow-burning, and superstition. 'Just as the superstition arising from this lack of freedom is unbounded, so it also follows that there is no ethics to be found, no determinate form of rational freedom, no right, no duty. The Hindu people are utterly sunk in the depths of an unethical life' (2:595–603).

Despite this unattractive picture, Hegel seems in some respects to be drawn to Hinduism. He recognizes it to be the earliest of the religions to affirm that divinity is the one substance or essence in which all things have their being, and he dismisses the charge of 'pantheism' that is brought against such a view, whether it be Oriental or Spinozistic. Brahman is substance but not yet subject; in this respect Jewish monotheism is preferable to Hindu. But Hinduism transcends monotheism: it is also polytheistic and tritheistic. Its Trimurti prefigures the Christian Trinity, although the third divine figure, Shiva, the creative-destructive energy of life, brings about sheer change instead of the return of the One to itself in the Spirit (thus there is no reconciliation in Hinduism, only restless diversity); and the second divine figure, Vishnu or Krishna, produces multiple and transitory incarnations instead of a single definitive one (2:589–93, 604). But potent elements are present for an understanding of divine–cosmic–human interaction. Hegel clearly is fascinated by Hinduism's 'vast poetic creations' (2:591) and the grand-scale mythologies that he delights in summarizing. He recognizes the imaginative power that is at work in the Vedas and epics and the intellectual depth that is evident from the Upanishads. As a more-or-less sober European he may have found himself attracted to the wild, colourful, sensuous dynamism of the religion of India, and to its sense of the presence of the divine in every facet of life, even as he was repulsed by what he took to be its ethical failures. He did not appreciate the philosophical subtlety, spiritual wisdom, and internal diversity of Hinduism to the degree that a more accurate knowledge would have permitted.

*Buddhism: The Religion of Being-Within-Self*[30]

The view prevalent in Hegel's day placed the life of Buddha around 1000 BCE, and this early dating probably led Hegel to assume that Buddhism is an older religion than Hinduism. Moreover, he seems to have confused the date of Siddhartha Gautama (which he places at 40–50 CE) with the introduction of Buddhism into China, which he calls the religion of Fo after the Chinese name for Buddha. He assumes, therefore, that Buddhism existed well before the life of Gautama, who was one of several Buddhas. His sources were mostly reports of English travellers to the Far East; he was not familiar with the main schools of Buddhism; and he regarded Chinese Buddhism and Tibetan Lamaism to be essentially identical.[31] Under the circumstances it is remarkable that Hegel's depiction of Buddhism has any accuracy at all. He makes the intriguing statement that this religion is 'the most widespread' in the world and that 'its worshippers are more numerous than those of Islam, which itself has more adherents than Christianity' (2:310, cf. 563–4).[32] One wonders how, with such an understanding of the numbers, Hegel could have so easily passed over Islam, or how he would account for the fact that Christianity has not triumphed over its rivals. If the consummate religion is destined to fulfil or replace other religions, it is far from its goal—although in fairness it must be acknowledged that Hegel does not present a triumphalist scenario. The consummation is conceptual, not historical; and there is a sense, as we shall see, in which historical

[30] Being-within-self (*Insichsein*) is the name for Buddhism in the 1824 and 1827 lectures. In 1831 it has become the 'religion of annihilation' (*Vernichtung*). If Strauss's excerpts can be relied upon, the discussion of Buddhism and Lamaism in the 1831 lectures is very brief (2:735–6). Hegel says that these religions are 'very much akin to Hinduism'. He then remarks, first, that in Lamaism 'the universal presence of substance already gives way to the concrete presence of the individual, who is worshipped as absolute power'; and second, that 'unlike Hinduism and Lamaism, Buddhism does not have a living being but a dead teacher, Buddha, as its object.... The acme is to be united with Buddha, and this *annihilation* is termed nirvana.'

[31] See 2:6, 36–7, 307–8 nn. 190, 192, 193. The main difference between Buddhism and Lamaism for Hegel seems to be that, whereas there can be several Buddhas at different times, there can be several Lamas at the same time. Moreover, all the incarnations of Buddha are now past, whereas Lamas continue into the present day, the best known of which is the Dalai Lama.

[32] I cannot verify the accuracy of Hegel's figures for the early nineteenth century. Today Christianity is the most populous religion, followed by Islam, Hinduism, and Buddhism. The missionary expansion of Christianity into Africa, Asia, and the Americas was just getting under way in Hegel's time.

Christianity is not identical with the ideality of consummate religion.

In the 1824 lectures (2:303–16) Buddhism is still treated under the general category of 'the religion of magic', although Hegel recognizes this designation to be inaccurate since in Buddhism we no longer encounter a formal but an actual objectification of the divine object. Religion is the unity of finite and infinite, of concept and reality. Prior to Buddhism (assuming now its precedence of Hinduism), the divine is not a content we can recognize as genuine but is only the power of the human mind over nature. The next advance is that consciousness comprehends essential being (*Wesen*) as independent, as having being within itself (*Insichsein*) and relating to itself. It is at this point that truly objective universality begins. 'Here lies the distinction between the naturally, contingently determined self-consciousness . . . and what rests and abides within itself, namely spirit; and here in this being-within-self the place of divinity in general emerges for the first time' (3:305). Here too free worship begins, for the community recognizes that the essential being is one of eternal rest and inner contemplation; it abides within itself in the mode of thought; and through union with it desire is transcended and tranquillity is achieved. What is this essence, this being-within-self? Well, it is essentially *nothing*—not in the sense of not-being but in the sense of being purely identical with itself and thus of being nothing determinate. 'It is thus completely pure, wholly simple and undifferentiated, eternally at rest; it has neither virtue nor power nor intelligence; it lacks these determinate distinctions. . . . With the attainment of this state of perfect impartiality or absence of concern, there is no longer any question of virtue and vice, reward and punishment, atonement, immortality of the soul, worship, and so on. All this has passed away, and human sanctity consists in finding union, in this silence, with God' (2:312). The Buddhists call this state of union 'nirvana' (2:314).

The 1827 lectures (2:562–79) elaborate on the depiction of nirvana, which, though couched in Western ontological and theistic categories, is surprisingly sympathetic. 'Here we find the form of substantiality in which the absolute is a being-within-self, the one substance; but it is not grasped just as a substance for thought and in thought (as it is in Spinoza); instead it has at the same time existence in sensible presence, i.e. in singular human beings' (2:564). The latter is a reference to the Buddhas and Lamas, and

Hegel thinks that the image of the Buddha in the thinking posture,
with a toe extending into the mouth,[33] expresses this withdrawal or
absorption into self. The ultimate reality is nothing or not-being,
the negated being of everything particular. All other actuality is
accidental and dependent, and humans must immerse themselves
in nirvana.

At first glance it must astonish us that humans think of God as nothing.
... More closely considered, however, this characterization means nothing
other than that God purely and simply is nothing determinate, is the
indeterminate.... When we say that God is the infinite, that means that
God is the negation of everything particular. When we adopt the forms
that are commonplace today, i.e. 'God is the infinite, the essence, the pure
and simple essence, the essence of essences and only the essence', then this
sort of talk is necessarily either totally or tolerably synonymous with
the claim that God is nothing. That does not mean, however, that God
is not, but rather that God is the empty, and that this emptiness is
God. (2:567–8)

Hegel goes on to remark that this negative theology is a necessary stage of religious representation, one that lays the foundation
for the further claim that God is also the absolute fullness or
substance that encompasses all determinacies within itself but is
not identical with any of them. This substance is similar to that
'unconsciously operative rationality' which the ancient Greeks
called *nous*. Hegel at this point seems to be conflating Buddhist
nirvana with Hindu Brahman, especially when he remarks that the
substantiality we have here is 'pantheism' in the proper sense—not
in the crude sense that everything is God but rather in the sense
that all things have their essential being *in* God, and that God as
'the All' is the negativity (not the apotheosis) of the finite. The All,
the *pan*, is to be taken not as a collective totality (*Allesheit*) but as
universality (*Allgemeinheit*) (2:571–3). As indicated earlier,[34] this is
a key passage for the claim that Hegel's holism is non-totalizing.

The substantiality of God is a necessary feature of 'our religion'
too, although we go on to affirm that God is subject and spirit. 'In
all higher religions, but particularly in the Christian religion, God
is the one and absolute substance; but at the same time God is also
subject, and that is something more. Just as the human being

[33] The image Hegel has in mind is actually of Brahmā Nārāyana (see 2:564
n. 142).
[34] See above, Chap. 5, p. 106.

has personality, there enters into God the character of subjectivity, personality, spirit, absolute spirit. That is a higher determination, although spirit remains nevertheless substance, the one substance.' At the standpoint of immediacy, however (which is where Hegel still locates the Oriental religions), there is not yet self-knowing spirituality but spirituality in the shape of a particular human being (2:573–6). An unresolved tension remains between the emptiness of nirvana and the 'shocking' notion that specific human beings with all their deficiencies simply *are* God.[35]

The discussion has drifted away from the Buddhist understanding of nirvana; and other aspects of Buddhism such as the Four Noble Truths, the Eightfold Path to Enlightenment, and the doctrine of the non-self are scarcely mentioned. But it is not without significance that one of Hegel's clearest evaluations of pantheism, and of the stance of Christian theology in relation to it, is found in the context of his conflated treatment of Buddhism/Hinduism. This is an indication of his recognition of the spiritual insight of the Asian religions and of his desire to protect them from crude misinterpretations. Hinduism, Buddhism, Judaism, and Christianity share the conviction that God is the one and absolute substance. Judaism and Christianity grasp the further truth that the absolute substance is also absolute subject; but they do so differently.


HEGEL'S EVOLVING TREATMENT OF JUDAISM[36]

Hegel's interpretation of Judaism undergoes a striking metamorphosis between the lectures of 1821 and 1827. The first lectures still share the perspective of the *Early Theological Writings*, where

[35] Hegel calls attention to the multiplicity of Buddhas and Lamas, and dwells on the story of the discovery of a Tibetan Lama in a still-nursing child after his predecessor had died of smallpox (2:576–9).

[36] In what follows I draw on materials I prepared for the editorial introduction to vol. 2 (2:19–21, 48–51, 69–71, 79–82). See also my article, 'The Metamorphosis of Judaism in Hegel's Philosophy of Religion', *The Owl of Minerva* 19/1 (1987), reprinted in Bernard Cullen (ed.), *Hegel Today* (Aldershot: Avebury, 1988), 88–101. At the beginning of this article I discuss a paper by Shlomo Avineri on Hegel's treatment of Judaism in which he points out that the nineteenth-century Jewish scholar Nachman Krochmal performed an *Aufhebung* of Hegel's views on Judaism from within the framework of a Hegelian philosophy of history: in virtue of the universality and spirituality of the idea of monotheism, the Jewish people are the true bearers of absolute spirit and thus have been able to transcend the temporality

the spirit of Judaism is represented as that of alienation (as expressed in the master–servant relationship), and of *The Phenomenology of Spirit*, where the Jewish idea of God is associated with light or 'luminous being' (*Lichtwesen*).[37] The one constant between 1821 and 1827 is the naming of Judaism as the religion of sublimity (*Erhabenheit*).

Hegel's interpretation is based almost entirely on his own reading of the Hebrew scriptures, which in the first three lectures is limited to the Pentateuch, Job (to whom he had long been attracted as the 'philosopher of Mosaic antiquity'), and the Psalms. In 1831 a few references are found to the universalism of the 'later prophets' (see 2:9). In each of these lectures Hegel struggles with the question of the relationship of Judaism to Christianity.

## The Fear of the Lord (1821)

The 'great thesis' of Jewish religion is that God is one God—the personal One (*der Eine*), not the neuter One (*das Eine*), not simply substance but also subject, the infinite reflected into itself as singular and concrete universality (2:127–9). This God is all-powerful, and the sublimity of God's power is such that it is expressed representationally (2:134–41) not by a physical force but by the pure word, which is pure light: 'God said, Let there be light, and there was light, ... light that is only a breath' (2:136). By contrast, the contingency and dependence of the world is expressed in the doctrines of creation, preservation, and passing

of history, being reborn like the legendary phoenix after every defeat, while all other nations eventually disappeared along with their particular spiritualities. Thus Krochmal accounts for the survival of Judaism in a way that Hegel himself could not, although he recognized the fact of survival and the anguish of being a people without a state. See Avineri, 'The Fossil and the Phoenix: Hegel and Krochmal on the Jewish Volksgeist', in Robert L. Perkins (ed.), *History and System: Hegel's Philosophy of History* (Albany: State University of New York Press, 1984), 47–63. In a similar vein, Emil Fackenheim, commenting on Karl Rosenkranz's remark that Judaism was for Hegel a 'dark riddle' that both attracted and repelled him through his life, observes that 'Jewish existence, supposedly rendered anachronistic by the Christian world if indeed not by classical antiquity, keeps reappearing in Hegel's thought.' See Fackenheim, 'Hegel and Judaism: A Flaw in the Hegelian Mediation', in J. J. O'Malley *et al.* (eds.), *The Legacy of Hegel: Proceedings of the Marquette Symposium* (The Hague: Martinus Nijhoff, 1973), 161–2.

[37] See *Early Theological Writings*, trans. T. M. Knox (Chicago: University of Chicago Press, 1948), 182–205; and *Phenomenology of Spirit*, 418–20. On this interpretation of Judaism in the *Phenomenology*, see Jaeschke, *Reason in Religion*, 198–204.

away. God's power in relation to the world remains undetermined: it does not acquire a determinate content, end, or purpose, other than the exercise of power as such, and the difference between the goodness and the justice of God is annulled. God is 'not yet inwardly concrete, not yet elaborated within himself' (2:153), but is merely abstract power, the being-for-self of the One.

The Jewish cultus (2:152–60) is a fundamental expression of the servile consciousness and of the master–servant relationship. When God is comprehended only under the abstract category of the One, then 'humanity's relationship to God takes the form of a heavy yoke, of onerous service. True liberation is to be found in Christianity, in the Trinity' (2:156). The condition of servitude is to have one's self-consciousness solely in the other and on behalf of the other. 'Fear of the Lord is the absolute religious duty, to regard myself as nothing, to know myself only as absolutely dependent— the consciousness of the servant vis-à-vis the master' (2:155). What God demands is that his people 'shall fear him, and have the basic feeling of their dependence' (2:158). This allusion to Schleiermacher's just-published *Glaubenslehre* (see 2:158 n. 138) is noteworthy in that Hegel regards Schleiermacher's famous description of religious consciousness as an expression of Jewish rather than of Christian piety.

If one has one's self-consciousness only in and through absolute dependence on the Lord, then there is also a sense in which one is absolutely reestablished in relationship to the Lord—a relationship that is singular, unique, and exclusive (2:155, 157–60). Hegel thinks this is the source of Jewish 'obstinacy' and 'particularity', the conviction that the Jewish people alone are God's people, and that the Lord alone is their God. While in this sense Judaism is a national or ethnic religion, it is not the case that this people can lay claim to the land they inhabit; it is rather solely the gift of God, who can take it from them and restore it to them.

### *The Beginning of Wisdom (1824)*

The fundamentally negative cast of the treatment of Judaism just three years earlier is replaced in 1824 by a more balanced and fully developed assessment. After a brief reference to the metaphysical concept of God in Judaism—the 'infinitely important' recognition that God is simply and solely the One, which is the ground of the absolute spirituality of God, 'the path to truth' (2:425–6)—Hegel

turns to the 'divine self-determination' as expressed representationally, discovering much that he had overlooked before
(2:426–40). The fundamental self-determination of God is not
yet internal (for then God would be triune) but external, the act
of creation and preservation. God is not the result of the creative
process—this is no theogony, an issuing-forth of the gods—but the
starting-point; and, as distinct from human production, this is an
absolute creation, *ex nihilo*, an inner, 'intuitive', eternal activity on
God's part (2:428). God's creation and preservation of the world
show forth God's goodness and justice, indicating that what is at
work here is infinite, purposive wisdom, not just abstract power.
Created things are prosaic, stripped of divinity, devoid of autonomy, and the externality of nature is clearly recognized. This de-
divinization of nature is a necessary step toward a valid understanding of the relationship of God and the world. In Jewish
religion this relationship is understood essentially in terms of
God's *sublimity*. Sublimity means that God is exalted above the
reality in which God appears, and that the reality itself is negated
or totally subjected to God's power. For example, God creates by
means of a word, which immediately passes away; or natural media
such as wind, lightning, and thunder are totally obedient to God's
bidding.

The representation of God's purpose is both theoretical and
practical. God's theoretical purpose is that God and God alone
should be recognized and glorified. God's practical, worldly purpose is now an ethical (no longer a natural) purpose, having its soil
in human self-consciousness and freedom. But we are still at the
stage of immediate, natural ethical life, and hence the family is
the ethical form in which the divine purpose is realized—the one
family, the Jewish people, to the exclusion of all others. Here we
encounter the striking, 'infinitely difficult' contradiction that is
present in Jewish religion: on the one hand God is universal, the
God of all humanity ('all peoples are called upon to recognize him
and glorify his name', Psalm 117:1–2), but on the other hand God's
purposes and operations are so limited as to be confined to just this
one people, defined by birth and race. For this reason, in Hegel's
view, the universal content of the story of the creation and fall of
humanity in Genesis 1–3 became disconnected from subsequent
Jewish piety. Jewish particularity, however, is not polemical, because there is no obligation to convert other peoples to the God of
Israel. While others are called upon to glorify the Lord, this is not a

goal, as in Islam, which is pursued with fanaticism. Judaism has become fanatical only when attacked, only when its existence has been threatened.

The cultus of Jewish religion (2:441–52) has two closely related moments, one negative, the other affirmative. The negative aspect is fear, fear of the Lord. But—and this is where 1824 departs decisively from 1821—this is no earthly lord that is feared. It is rather fear of the absolute, in which everything ephemeral and contingent is given up and through which one is elevated to the level of pure thought. 'This fear of the Lord, we are then told [Psalm 111:10], is the beginning of wisdom' (2:443). 'Wisdom' means not taking anything particular to be absolute and substantive; it means recognizing the relativity of all that is finite. Hence *this* fear of the Lord entails a fundamental liberation from all earthly forms of bondage, a letting everything go, an immersion in the Lord, 'having this unity as one's object and essence'. It is a far cry from what is termed a 'feeling of dependence' (2:443–4). Whereas in the manuscript Judaism is viewed as an embodiment of Schleiermacher's definition of religious piety, now it is just the reverse: Judaism is the first of the religions of freedom, and Schleiermacher's version of religion as dependence is now seen to apply to the Romans (see 2:443 n. 551).

The affirmative side of Jewish worship arises directly from what has just been said. The fear of the Lord that is the beginning of wisdom yields an absolute trust, an infinite faith, which passes over into a distinctive kind of existence. This trust 'is preserved through so many great victories, which are emphasized also in Christianity. It is this trust, this faith of Abraham's, that causes the history of this people to carry on' (2:446). Such an assessment undoubtedly represents an important shift from the portrayal of Abraham and his people in *The Spirit of Christianity and Its Fate*. But Hegel himself does not take into account the history of this people; his treatment is limited to what he regards as the oldest biblical expressions of Jewish faith. In effect the history of Israel is taken over in Hegel's scenario by the history of Christianity. The 1824 lectures significantly narrow the distance between Judaism and Christianity, and the profound aspects of Jewish piety (its worship of the one God, its theology of creation and of divine goodness and wisdom, its grounding of human freedom in divine sovereignty, its affirmation of God's covenantal promise) are absorbed into Christian faith, which extends the universalism implicit in Judaism and

introduces the process of divine self-determination into the divine
life itself in the form of Trinity and incarnation. Yet the people of
Israel, now tragically lacking their own state, continue to survive.

## The Infinite Subjectivity and Creativity of God (1827)

In the 1827 lectures, the order of treating Jewish and Greek
religion is reversed from that of 1821 and 1824, so that now
Judaism comes last (2:640–2). Both religions represent an 'elevation of the spiritual above the natural', and they share the characteristic of 'free subjectivity'. While free ethical institutions are
more fully developed in Greece than in Israel, its gods remain
tinged by finitude and the sensibly beautiful human shape. By
contrast, the God of Israel is infinite subjectivity and subsists
without shape. In this distinction lies 'the necessity of the elevation
of the religion of beauty into the religion of sublimity' (2:669).
This remark indicates that the 1827 lectures continue the trajectory of a favourable reassessment of Judaism established in 1824
and carry it further. Almost the entire section (2:669–87) is given
over to a careful analysis of the Jewish idea of God and to various
aspects of the relationship of God and the world.

The great contribution of Israel to the history of religion is its
comprehension of the 'spiritually subjective unity' of God. This
subjective unity is not mere substance, as in the Asian religions,
but is absolute power, wisdom, and purpose, for which reason it is
'holy', it merits the name 'God' for the first time. It is in fact
'infinite subjectivity', which is the highest philosophical concept;
as such, God subsists without sensible shape, only for thought:
'thinking is the essential soil for this object' (2:669–71).

But this one God does not remain in self-enclosed, abstract
identity. Rather God's wisdom contains the process of 'divine
particularization' (a description reserved to Greek religion in
1824), that is, divine self-determining, judging, creating (2:671–
82). This process is not yet posited *within* God concretely but
remains abstract and external; it is not yet an immanent Trinity.
But the act of creation is a highly important, in fact definitive,
determination of the Jewish God. God *is* the creator of the world.
This has implications both for the world and for God. First, the
world does not emanate from God, as in Hindu and Greek cosmogonies, but is created *ex nihilo*. This means that the subjectivity of
the One remains what is absolutely first and is not superseded by

what has gone forth. Second, God's relations to the world—the more specific moments of divine wisdom, which are goodness and justice—are definitive of God's own being, so that we do in fact know God in knowing God's relations. The categories of goodness and justice are now defined more fully. As good, God releases and sets free from godself the created world; only what is genuinely free can do this, can let its determinations go as free, can release them to 'go their separate ways', which is the totality of the finite world (2:675).[38] As just, God maintains the world in relation to godself, does not abandon it to radical autonomy, specifies its purpose. Third, the world is rendered profane, prosaic; nature is divested of divinity, and there is no cheap identity of finite and infinite. The manifestation of God in the world takes on the character of sublimity, which is its genuine form, or of miracle, which is specious. Finally, God's purpose is made manifest in the natural and human world. This purpose is simply that the whole earth and all peoples should proclaim the glory of God. This glorification of God is the 'inner aspect' of all human ethical activity. Without it, moral righteousness counts as nothing; with it, one may be confident of the fulfilment of one's worldly existence.

At the end of this sympathetic and perceptive account of the Jewish idea of God, Hegel mentions briefly certain 'limitations' (2:683–7). These are principally three: the self-determining wisdom of God is not yet an inward self-development (the idea of God as 'what is eternally self-developing within itself' is found only in the consummate religion); despite the implicit universalism, the God of Judaism remains a national God, the God of a limited national family rather than of the whole human family; and the divine purposes are abstract because they are simply commandments given by God as something prescribed and immutable, rather than purposes worked out in the conflict and dialectic of historical/ethical life. It is not surprising that precisely these limitations are overcome in Christianity, notably in the concept of God as triune, in the nonprovincial character of the community of the Spirit, and in the presence of God not simply in the Torah but in the crucified Christ. But clearly the soil in which Christianity

---

[38] As we have seen, this is a central theme in Hegel's account of the Christian doctrine of creation in the 1827 lectures (above, Chap. 7). The Christian doctrine is essentially identical with the Jewish doctrine.

emerged could only be that of Judaism, whose doctrines of God and creation are the foundation of the new religion.

## *The Religion of the Good (1831)*

Hegel's treatment of Judaism in the 1831 lectures is flawed by the new religiohistorical box into which it is squeezed, namely that of 'transitional forms' of the religion of freedom, where it is paired with Persian religion as the 'religion of the good' (2:738–42).[39] Much of the actual content of the discussion is similar to what is found in 1827, but with a highlighting of the themes of good and evil. God creates out of God's own being (rather than out of primordial matter) by a 'primal division' (*Urteil*). This constitutes the goodness of creation. What then is the source of evil? The answer is found neither in a cosmic dualism (the theogonic myth, exemplified for Hegel by Persian religion) nor in the flawed character of absolute substance (the tragic myth, as represented by the Greek theology of necessity or fate), but in the free fall of finite spirit (the Adamic myth).[40] This is the 'profoundly speculative' (2:740) feature of the story of the fall, which in 1831 has been transferred from the context of Christian theology, where it is treated in the earlier lectures,[41] to its rightful home in Judaism.

But in Judaism the story 'lay fallow' and 'attained its true meaning only in the Christian religion' (2:741). Making this point seems to be part of Hegel's purpose in now discussing the story in relation to Judaism. To be sure, the struggle between good and evil does constitute an essential feature of Jewish religion; this is especially striking in the Psalms of David, where 'anguish cries aloud from the innermost depths of the soul in the consciousness of its sinfulness, followed by the most anguished plea for forgiveness and reconciliation' (2:441 n. 541). But this depth of anguish is known only as pertaining to the single individual in contingent fashion rather than as an eternal moment of spirit, and it finally remains unresolved in Judaism. A similar tension is found between the

---

[39] Strauss's excerpts are supplemented by several important *Werke* passages on Judaism that are attributable to 1831: 2:438–41 n. 541, 452–5 n. 572, 672 n. 457, 683–5 n. 492. Our summary draws on these passages as well as the excerpts.

[40] I have appropriated Paul Ricoeur's categories here (*The Symbolism of Evil*, trans. Emerson Buchanan (Boston: Beacon Press, 1967), 306–46), but they fit Hegel's analysis nicely.

[41] See the discussion of the story of the fall in Chap. 7.

intrinsic universalism of the Jewish idea of God, as expressed by the later prophets, and the belief that Israel alone is the chosen people of God.

These tensions or limitations point to the fact, or perhaps are explained by the fact, that the laws of God as revealed to the Jews are not laws of freedom. They are not given by reason but prescribed by God—all of them, ranging from the most petty cultic regulations to the universal ethical foundations of human existence. 'All law is given by the Lord, and hence it is positive commandment throughout. There is in it a formal, absolute authority. The particular aspects of the political constitution are not developed out of the universal purpose at all, nor are they left to human beings to determine' (2:685 n. 492). The vocation of the Jewish people is to give themselves up wholly to the service of the Lord, which accounts for their 'admirable steadfastness', but which also means that 'there is no freedom vis-à-vis this firm bond' (ibid.). The Lord finally does not enter into the human combat with evil but punishes evil. The finite subject engages in an unresolved struggle between good and evil, resulting in contrition and anguish, from which there is no liberation. There can be a liberation only if the struggle and anguish are taken into the divine life itself.

Hegel thus returns to critical themes first adumbrated in the 1821 manuscript but muted in later lectures. The reason for this seems in part to be the hermeneutical and political context of the 1831 lectures. We know that, as a result of recent events, in 1830–1 Hegel had become deeply concerned once again, as he had been a decade earlier, with the question of the relationship between religion and state and especially with the task of creating and preserving free political institutions.[42] Only a free religion can serve as the foundation of a free state. In this respect Judaism is found wanting. It is on the way to freedom but has not arrived at its ethical actualization. In this respect too Greek religion and culture offer valuable resources.

In the 1827 lectures, while affirming the 'elevation' of Greek religion into Jewish, Hegel also refers to the 'one-sidedness' of both religions (2:688). It is only from particular perspectives that

---

[42] See Walter Jaeschke, 'Hegel's Last Year in Berlin', in Lawrence S. Stepelevich and David Lamb (eds.), *Hegel's Philosophy of Action* (Atlantic Highlands, NJ: Humanities Press, 1983), 31–48. In 1831 Hegel added a section on the relationship of religion to the state at the end of *The Concept of Religion* (1:451–60).

one appears as 'higher' than the other. From the point of view of the idea of God, monotheism, and spiritual unity and subjectivity, Judaism is higher. But from the point of view of the idea of the mediation of divinity and humanity (i.e. incarnation), as well as of free ethical institutions, Greek religion is higher. Their respective one-sidednesses are overcome in Christianity. Thus while the soil in which Christianity takes root is Jewish, the light by which it grows comes partly from Greece. It is not a simple development of Judaism but a genuinely new religion with a mixed geographical, ethnic, and cultural lineage—Hebraic and Hellenic, and later (from Hegel's limited point of view) Latin and Germanic. The contrasting emphases of the 1827 and 1831 lectures remind us of this fact. Our conclusion need not be, as Hegel's was, that as a consequence of this mix Christianity is the 'highest' religion. It too has its one-sidednesses, its cultural compromises, its doctrinal dogmatisms, its ethical failings; and these become apparent as it is compared with other living religions. A beneficial by-product of recognizing the novelty and limits of Christianity is that space is allowed for the continued existence of Judaism as an independent and equally valid religion. To these matters we turn in the final section.

## TOWARD A RELIGION OF THE CONCRETE SPIRIT

### Beyond Inclusivism to Pluralism

In the framework of religious pluralism, Christianity cannot claim to be the consummate religion. Rather it is one of the determinate religions. The third moment, that of consummation, occurs in each of the post-Axial[43] religious trajectories—Confucian/Daoist, Hindu, Buddhist, Jewish, Christian, Muslim—in distinctive ways. In so far as they share in each other's wisdom, they grow toward a richer, dialogical consummation. They meet, as Raimundo Panikkar suggests, when they are 'metamorphosized into Spirit'.[44] The unification of religions in the Spirit is strictly an eschatological

---

[43] Karl Jaspers identifies the 'axial period' in world history as starting about 800 BCE and continuing through the early centuries of the common era. The major religions originated or received their classical formations during this period. See *The Origin and Goal of History* (London: Routledge & Kegan Paul, 1953), chap. 1.

[44] See above, n. 24.

possibility, never achieved here on earth. On earth God's Spirit is always concretely manifested, and it cannot be domesticated by any determinate religion.

Along such lines Hegel's philosophy of religion may be adjusted to the situation of religious pluralism, which fits his dialectical way of thinking better than the Christian inclusivism or the model of fulfilment that he espouses.[45] I have already suggested that his geography of religions points in the direction of a pluralism that cannot be ordered into a historical development or a hierarchically graded sequence. His thinking is not progressivist but typological, and the transitions between types seem to involve breaks or ruptures in which new possibilities emerge. Given the fact that spirit comes to itself through movement and distinction, there must be a diversity of determinate forms in which it appears.

Empirically what we find are distinctive religiocultural trajectories that for most of history have gone their separate ways (either singly or in groupings) and that only now are beginning to engage each other on more than a superficial or antagonistic level. This is precisely what one would expect from Hegel's dialectical account of spirit in history. The concept of religion comes to completion in different ways in a diversity of historical shapes. God disperses godself into the world as absolving spirit and is known in the mode of dispersal rather than finality. The claim for a single perfect or final religion is as specious as the claim for a single saviour figure. Hegel's philosophy of religion really shows why in history God is revealed and encountered only in the mode of dispersal. The consummation and return of God to godself is an eschatological possibility accomplished fragmentarily in a plurality of religions, but perfectly in none of them. Consummation will occur not in the form of a monolithic universal religion but through the diremption and dispersal of God's Spirit unto the ends of the earth and in a diversity of shapes, religious and secular. In this way all things will be gathered into the divine life and redeemed. They will be preserved in their concreteness, not homogenized in a totality. God comes back to godself by going out from godself.

<hr>

[45] On various models for thinking theologically about the diversity of religions, see Paul F. Knitter, *Introducing Theologies of Religions* (Maryknoll, NY: Orbis Books, 2002). Knitter in this latest book prefers to avoid the term 'pluralism', which is embraced in different ways by his last two models, 'mutuality' and 'acceptance'. Hegel, while advocating the 'fulfilment' model, actually is moving toward the idea of 'acceptance' with his geography of religions.

*Concrete Spirit, Freedom, and the Consummation of Religion*

In his last published writing Paul Tillich suggests that the whole of systematic theology will have to be rethought in light of the history of religions, and his own rethinking points toward a 'religion of the Concrete Spirit'.[46] He sets forth several propositions: revelatory religious experiences are universally human; these experiences are always limited and distorted under the conditions in which they are received; thus a critical revelatory process is needed that will have mystical, prophetic, and secular elements; there *may* be a central event in the history of religions that gathers up the positive insights of diverse traditions; and finally, the sacred does not lie beside the secular but is its depth. Rather than a progressive-developmental theology of religions, Tillich offers a 'dynamic-typological' approach. There must be a sacramental basis to all religions (the concrete presence of the holy in figures such as Christ and Buddha and in rituals and liturgies), but there must also be a critical-mystical movement against the demonization of the sacramental, and a prophetic element that articulates a vision of justice in the name of holiness. Tillich imagines that these three elements come together to form 'the Religion of the Concrete Spirit'—concrete because of sacramental presence but spiritual in the mystical-prophetic transcendence of presence. Concrete spirit is concrescent spirit, coalescing into material, perceptible forms but always standing out from them. The inner aim of the history of religions is to become a religion of the concrete Spirit, but the latter cannot be identified with any actual religion, not even Christianity as a religion. It appears fragmentarily in many moments in the history of religions.

Its appearance in Christianity has certain distinctive character-istics: the triune God is an absolving, self-releasing, world-creating God; the Spirit of God concresces in Christ; the crucifix-ion of Christ is a negation of every idolatrous religious claim (just as the death of God deconstructs every theology); but the resur-rection of Christ and the presence of the Spirit in the community are the negation of negation, the victory of life over death, of love over anguish, of freedom over bondage. Here the sacramental, the mystical, and the prophetic are blended in a way that transcends

---

[46] Paul Tillich, 'The Significance of the History of Religions for the Systematic Theologian', in Jerald C. Brauer (ed.), *The Future of Religions* (New York: Harper & Row, 1966), 80–94.

Christianity as a religion and Christendom as a culture, and that anticipates the consummation of religion.

In the *Introduction* to the lectures of 1824, Hegel remarks that absolute spirit resolves to be in a determinate mode, and this means that spirit is present 'in the most *concrete* sense'. It is absolute spirit 'only in so far as it is *for* itself, i.e. in so far as it posits itself or brings itself forth; for it *is only as activity*'. Spirit comes to itself: 'this is a movement, an activity, a mediation of itself with itself. It involves distinctions and directions, and this succession of directed movements is the path by which spirit comes to itself, for spirit is itself the goal. The absolute goal is to recognize itself, to be for itself. . . . Spirit does not reach the goal without having traversed the path.' The 'distinct stages' traversed by spirit 'yield the determinate religions' (1:142–3). This is Hegel's version of the religion of concrete spirit. His version needs modification in one major respect: spirit does not reach its goal in history, and Christianity belongs among those determinate religions that constitute stages on the path to consummation.

Is there a common or underlying theme that marks the path? I believe that for Hegel there is such a theme: it is *freedom*. The theme is present in all the lectures, but most explicitly in the lectures of 1831, where it becomes a leitmotif: the history of religion is the progress of the consciousness of freedom.[47] The freedom in question is not simply human freedom but the freedom of God as absolute/absolving spirit in which human freedom is grounded. Spirit's coming to itself is a process of freedom, for freedom means presence to self (*Beisichselbstsein*) mediated in and through relationships with others. For subjective freedom to flourish an objective realm of freedom, a *Reich der Freiheit*, must be created. Religion's vocation is to contribute to this freedom project out of the depths of its knowledge of God and humanity, evil and redemption. Religion itself must be liberated from inadequate representational forms and rise to a critical and speculative thinking that recognizes the limits of all metaphors, symbols, and practices.[48] But we need not think that religion itself will be superseded

---

[47] See above, n. 14.

[48] Andrew Shanks offers an interesting observation along lines that support my pushing of Hegel toward religious pluralism. Adopting the phrase 'solidarity of the shaken' from the Czech philosopher Jan Patočka, he argues that Hegel's 'absolute knowing' signifies an absolute shakenness 'out of any fixed subjective sense of one's own identity' and 'out of any fixed metaphysical world-view'. 'Such shakenness is

by a philosophical priesthood that is withdrawn from the affairs of the world. One of the advantages of the theme of freedom is that it keeps us focused precisely on the affairs of the world. Freedom comes to consciousness in the major religions of the world. Let us summarize in Hegelian terms. For the Asian religions it is a matter of liberation from illusion, suffering, and desire by means of reconnection with ultimate reality in the form of the harmonized measures (Daoism), universal Brahman (Hinduism), or the emptiness of nirvana (Buddhism). For Judaism, the religion of sublimity, worship of the one true Lord liberates from bondage to earthly lords; this is the same Lord who freely creates the world by releasing it to go forth and to become the realm in which divine wisdom, goodness, and justice rule. Greek religion, the religion of beauty, begins the fashioning of free political and social institutions through which the divine purposes can be accomplished. Christianity, the religion of freedom, grasps the freedom of the triune God, proclaims the reconciliation of divinity and humanity revealed in Christ, forms a community of the Spirit in which

*itself* the true essence of the divine', of *Geist* as the 'infinite toil of dialectical questioning'. Absolute knowing is thus contrasted with the comfortable conventions of representational thinking, and 'consummate religion' is the ideal practice of the shaking power of *Geist*, which sets in process a transition from representation to thought. However, there is no reason why such a transfiguration should be limited just to the Christian religion. ' "Absolute knowing" ought to be seen as a state of wisdom potentially attainable within the framework of *any* authentically "religious" culture.... That is to say: within any post-Axial culture—insofar as it is purged of ideology. So that *every* form of religion, as such, has at least some capacity to become what Hegel calls "consummate".' We should not try to determine which religious traditions have the most truth-bearing potential. 'For the partisan of the solidarity of the shaken, there is surely an intrinsic value to their very plurality—as diverse systems of *sittlich* practice, each with their own distinctive perspective to contribute to the larger conversation-process on which such solidarity depends. "Absolute knowing" is not the prize in a competition, it is simply a commitment to the conversation-process at its best.' Andrew Shanks, *God and Modernity: A New and Better Way to Do Theology* (London and New York: Routledge, 2000), 86–9, 158. In a recent article ('Hegel and the Meaning of the Present Moment', *Bulletin of the Hegel Society of Great Britain* 45/46 (2002), 25–35), Shanks develops the same point rather differently. Despite Kierkegaard's claim that Hegel believed he had arrived at the possession of absolute truth, Hegel's 'absolute knowing' rather has the quality of seeking, of an ever-restless drive to truth that Kierkegaard himself embraced, along with Lessing. Because the context of such seeking has changed radically today from Hegel's time, Hegel would not set forth a 'grand narrative' as the basis of a university education designed to challenge a hegemonic church, but would rather embrace various social movements (green, feminist, peace, human rights, anti-racist, etc.) that are struggling for freedom against a hegemonic state. In a religiously pluralist society, these movements are 'trans-confessional agencies', drawing people together from every religious tradition.

human divisions and rankings (ethnic, sexual, religious, socioeco-nomic, political) are overcome in principle, and has the mission of extending this community into the world: here for the first time the possibility is envisioned that not only *one* is free (the Oriental monarchs), or that *some* are free (the people of Israel, the citizens of Greece and Rome), but that *all* human beings as such are free.[49]

These religious manifestations of freedom should not be ranked in a graded hierarchy along Hegelian lines. Hegel's understanding of Asian religious liberation was faulty at best, and he emphasized the failings and limitations of these religions from a Eurocentric perspective, just as he stressed the limitations of Judaism from a Christian perspective. But the ethical failings and doctrinal dog-matisms of Christianity are just as serious. Hegel himself notes that 'slavery contradicts Christianity' (3:340), but Christians prac-tised slavery well into the nineteenth century, to say nothing (at various times in Christian history) of pogroms against Jews, cru-sades against Muslims, burnings of 'witches', persecution of homosexuals, obliteration of native Americans, apartheid against peoples of colour, subordination of women, legitimation of West-ern colonialism. Hegel is not as outspoken about these matters as he might have been, but he does speak very sharply about the decadence of the modern world, and he is frustrated by the inabil-ity of Christian theology to come to terms with this decadence given its bondage to outmoded conceptualities. Thus really on Hegel's own terms Christianity cannot be the consummate reli-gion. The consummate religion is the religion of freedom. Religion will be consummated when freedom is, but the consummation of freedom is a long and arduous task. No religion can reach the goal on its own. A new philosophical religion, such as Hegel once envisioned,[50] is not the alternative, but a productive dialogue of

---

[49] *Lectures on the Philosophy of World History. Introduction: Reason in History*, 130.

[50] See the discussion above, Chap. 2, of Hegel's early system outline, 'The Resumption of the Whole into One'. One of its attractive features is its envisioning of the reconciliation of nature and spirit in a way that Hegel's later lectures, which stress rather the elevation from nature to spirit, do not. A philosophical religion of the spirit, Hegel imagines, will reconsecrate nature and form a basis for a free people and their political institutions. 'Reason gets its vitality and nature gets its spirit back.' See *Hegel: Theologian of the Spirit*, 85–91, incl. n. 18 on 268; and *System of Ethical Life (1802/3) and First Philosophy of Spirit (1803/4)*, ed. and trans. H. S. Harris and T. M. Knox (Albany: State University of New York Press, 1979), 180–6. What is needed in our own time is a reassessment of the nature religions and a recovery of resources for an ecological theology that would give nature its spirit back.

existing world religions, in the process of which each will change, would be a step toward the religion of the concrete Spirit. Western Christian definitions of freedom are not to be regarded as normative. Even the Hegelian understanding of freedom as 'being at home with difference', containing as it does the powerful insight that freedom is not autonomy but a mode of connectedness with others, is inadequate. Freedom is a work in progress, and it will be shaped by a diversity of religiocultural trajectories unimaginable in Hegel's time. In our time, I believe Hegel would be a religious pluralist and a partisan of freedom movements.[51]

[51] I am assuming that Emil Fackenheim is correct when he writes that 'were he alive today, so realistic a philosopher as Hegel would not be a Hegelian'. *The Religious Dimension in Hegel's Thought* (Bloomington, Ind.: Indiana University Press, 1967), 224. The point of this remark, I take it, is that Hegel's thought contains a power of self-criticism and self-transcendence that derives from the power of negation, from the recognition that each new synthesis (even the Hegelian one) is inadequate to the truth. At the same time I acknowledge that it is hazardous to second-guess Hegel as to where he might stand today. The more important question is where we stand in light of our reading of Hegel and others and our assessment of what the freedom project calls for in our own time.

# PART THREE

# Conclusion

# The Theological Significance
# of Hegel Today

Hegel believed that the theologians of his time had abandoned the most important theological questions—questions that he himself proposed to engage in his *Lectures on the Philosophy of Religion*. He claimed that philosophy is theology to the extent that it raises religious symbols to thought, shows forth the rational content of religion, and presents the reconciliation of God and the world. In a strange reversal, perhaps it is now the theologians who must address the questions abandoned by philosophy in its postmodern preoccupation with the deconstruction of meaning and truth and its scepticism about religious faith. Religion and theology can no longer take refuge in the concept; the concept affords no refuge. Rather theology must rethink its own fundamental themes (God, creation, humanity, evil, redemption, consummation), but in doing so it can draw fruitfully upon resources provided by Hegel's philosophy of religion, even as it challenges Hegel's tendency to absorb all the work of theology into philosophy.

My first task in this chapter is to consider those who question the assumption that Hegel provides fruitful resources for theological reflection. A strand of interpretation going back to Hegel's own time claims that his philosophical reconstruction of religion is really a destruction, that the outcome of his thought is atheism (or humanism) rather than theism, that the God of Hegel's system is a counterfeit rather than the true God of Christian faith. Such an interpretation has been powerfully articulated in a recent work by William Desmond, to which I attend in the first section.

Following this engagement with a contemporary critic of Hegel's speculative theology, and drawing upon issues raised by this engagement, I turn to six sets of distinctions or contested sites in postmodernity and their Hegelian resolution, which provide a framework for considering the theological significance of Hegel today. (1) In the tension between heterodoxy and orthodoxy (ontotheology) appears Hegel's philosophy of spirit. (2) Beyond the alternative of totality versus infinity lies the possibility of wholeness. (3) From the interplay of language and history, logic and time, emerges a trinitarian metanarrative. (4) Through tragedy comes a redemption that incorporates suffering and death into the life of God, a redemption mediated by the crucified and risen Christ. (5) In place of the autonomous self a community forms in which each individual exists for the sake of and from the gift of others. (6) Out of an inexhaustible diversity arises a religious unity such that an account of the consummate religion must entail an affirmation of religious pluralism. These themes of *spirit, wholeness, narrative, Christ, community*, and *pluralism* contribute to the project of theological reconstruction at the beginning of the twenty-first century. In making this case I shall be engaged especially with questions about Hegel raised by Emmanuel Levinas, and with interpretations provided by Cyril O'Regan and Robert Williams.

More could be offered by way of a survey of the critical literature and contested issues, but my purpose in this final chapter is not to research and summarize the contemporary discussion of Hegel's thought. The chapter recapitulates and draws together main themes from the preceding chapters, and it does so without repeating the references to Hegel texts that are cited earlier (except for direct quotations).

### HEGEL'S GOD: COUNTERFEIT OR REAL?

William Desmond, in a challenging and confrontational book,[1] argues that the God portrayed in Hegel's philosophy of religion is not the true and real God of Christian faith but an idol, a counterfeit. In this he articulates a critique of Hegel that goes

---

[1] William Desmond, *Hegel's God: A Counterfeit Double?* (Aldershot: Ashgate, 2003). Desmond's critique contrasts rather sharply with his appreciative assessment in *Art and the Absolute: A Study of Hegel's Aesthetics* (Albany: State University of New York Press, 1986), but is anticipated by his next book, *Beyond Hegel and Dialectic: Speculation, Cult, and Comedy* (Albany: State University of New York Press, 1992). Perhaps seeds of the later critique are already found in Desmond's assimilation of Hegel's aesthetic theodicy to a 'Pythagorean' model of harmony that underplays the dramatic and tragic elements of his thought (I am indebted to Hohyun Sohn for this observation).

back to Søren Kierkegaard and Ludwig Feuerbach, both of whom read Hegel as a pantheist. The difference between them is that Kierkegaard rejected the alleged pantheism in favour of an orthodox theism, whereas Feuerbach embraced it, moving it in the direction of atheism and humanism.

The charge of pantheism is implicit in Kierkegaard's critique of what he regards as the totalizing tendency of Hegel's system, which (he says) identifies thought and being (existence), abolishes the principle of contradiction, introduces becoming into logic, and excludes the possibility of the offence of reason. By contrast, Kierkegaard proclaims 'the infinite qualitative difference between God and man' and views God as an unmoved mover who radically transcends history and can appear and be known in history only in terms of paradox and the passion of faith. Kierkegaard's dialectic is one of disjunction rather than of mediation. From his point of view Hegel's system is a monistic pantheism that absorbs all of existence into the divine ideality and loses the absolute otherness of God.[2] I devote considerable attention to Desmond because he is a good contemporary representative of the Kierkegaardian critique of Hegel, a critique that must be heard and respected.

As for Feuerbach, the pantheism he embraces is materialistic, not idealistic, and it converts into an atheistic humanism for which 'God' is simply the projection of the human species-essence onto the screen of transcendence.[3] Feuerbach seems to align himself with Hegel in understanding religion to be a project of human self-consciousness. But, as Ferdinand Christian Baur already pointed out in the 1850s, 'everything that for Hegel has a double side, an objective and a subjective, has for Feuerbach only a single side, the

[2] See Søren Kierkegaard, *Philosophical Fragments*, ed. and trans. Howard V. and Edna H. Hong (Princeton: Princeton University Press, 1985), esp. chaps. 2–3; *Concluding Unscientific Postscript*, trans. David F. Swenson (Princeton: Princeton University Press, 1941), esp. 111 (where he remarks that 'every system must be pantheistic precisely on account of its finality'), and 203 (where he says that pantheism is 'the taking of oneself out of existence by way of recollection into the eternal'); and *Practice in Christianity*, ed. and trans. Howard V. and Edna H. Hong (Princeton: Princeton University Press, 1991), 140.
[3] See Ludwig Feuerbach, *The Essence of Christianity*, trans. George Eliot (New York: Harper & Brothers, 1957), and *Principles of the Philosophy of the Future*, trans. Manfred H. Vogel (Indianapolis: Bobbs-Merrill, 1966). Max Stirner regarded Feuerbach's species-essence (*Gattungswesen*) as still an idealist abstraction and argued that the only reality is the single isolated ego. See *The Ego and Its Own*, ed. David Leopold (Cambridge: Cambridge University Press, 1995).

subjective, which for him is the totality of things'. Thus in Hegel's view religious self-consciousness 'is only the subjective side of absolute spirit determining itself in terms of finite consciousness.... For Hegel the universal as such indeed has objective reality, while for Feuerbach all truth resides only in the sensual and actual, only in that which the human being is immediately.'[4] The Hegelian mediation of objective and subjective, divine and human, ideal and real, as distinct elements of an encompassing process, collapses for Feuerbach into a single, ultimately material element. He cannot, any more than Kierkegaard, tolerate a dialectical way of thinking about God and the world that preserves unity as well as difference. Either God and the world are related paradoxically and disjunctively, so that God's absolute transcendence is protected, or all of reality reduces to naturalism. The breakdown in mediation is what principally characterizes the post-Hegelian period, and the ongoing question is whether Hegelian mediation is possible without damaging the mediated elements. The alternative to mediation, however, is some form of either theological supernaturalism or secular naturalism.

Most contemporary scholars of Hegel do not attend to the philosophy of religion. Their interest focuses on other aspects of his thought: logic, philosophy of nature, anthropology and psychology, phenomenology, social and political philosophy, philosophy of history, aesthetics. They do not directly criticize the religious dimension of Hegel's thought but simply pass it by, assuming perhaps that Hegel shares with them the governing antimetaphysical, antireligious paradigms of postmodernity. The ontotheological foundation of Hegel's system is regarded as mythological or merely representational, but fragments, even large chunks, of the system that treat this-worldly realities are viewed as retrievable. In this fashion these scholars make sense of Hegel to a secularist mentality, even if they do not do justice to his own way of thinking (as Hegel makes very clear in his own critique of modern secularism). Such interpreters stand broadly in the tradition of Feuerbach

---

[4] Ferdinand Christian Baur, *Kirchengeschichte des neunzehnten Jahrhunderts*, ed. Eduard Zeller, 2nd edn. (Leipzig: Fues's Verlag, 1877), 415. That this is a correct reading of Hegel is evident from the passage we have quoted from the 1824 lectures (1:136–7) in our discussion (in Chap. 3, p. 67) of Hegel's critique of modern atheism and pantheism. In light of this critique it is ironic to say the least that Hegel should be charged with the very views that he so decisively repudiated and that he intended speculative theology to be a defence against.

and left-Hegelianism generally, which they believe rightly grasped the consequences of Hegel's philosophy.

Desmond, by contrast, belongs to the tradition of Kierkegaard since he brings the criteria of Christian orthodoxy to bear in his critique of Hegel.[5] Monotheistic religions, he says, offer an image of God as the unique and original absolute, utterly distinct from the created world. The divine transcendence and superiority are not negotiable, and philosophy must reflect on the truth or untruth of this transcendence, not invent its own truth. Philosophical rationality is unable to grasp the infinite, which can be described only in the mode of hyperbole and metaphor. The logic of hyperbole is that of sovereignty and mystery rather than of reciprocity and comprehension; the metaphor is one of rule rather than of community. Hegel, Desmond notes, is not bothered by whether or not his thought is orthodox, for he believes that truth comes from where it will. Yet he claims to base his account on the Bible and Christian doctrine: he mimics orthodoxy but does not really embrace it. 'Hegel, the confessed Christian, . . . remains too Eleatic, and is not Jewish enough.' (How much, one wonders, is too much, and how little is too little?) In advancing these charges, Desmond gives a narrow reading of orthodoxy and does not at all attend to the internal diversity of the Christian tradition through the ages. The Greek, mystical, and humanistic strands of the tradition are devalued. The infinite qualitative difference between eternity and time, God and humanity, is the controlling norm.

In place of the transcendent God of monotheism, Hegel offers, on Desmond's reading,[6] a philosophy of immanence based on human self-transcendence and a critique of the God who is 'beyond'. The only authentic transcendence in Desmond's view does in fact lie beyond nature and humanity. Hegel's mistake is to think of God's transcendence in terms of human self-transcending, and thus he posits God as an absolutely self-determining being in which a relating to an other occurs, but in that relating a fuller self-relating comes about such that no ultimate transcendence as other is found, only a self-completing immanence, or holism. It is

---

[5] Desmond, *Hegel's God*, 7–11, 59–60, 107, 122, 127.

[6] Ibid., 2–5, 10, 15, 66, 73–4, 108, 131. Hegel's discussion of these issues in § 573 of the *Encyclopedia of the Philosophical Sciences* (see above, Chap. 2) is worth pondering. There he anticipates many of Desmond's criticisms and refutes the charge of pantheism, as he does also in the philosophy of religion lectures (see above, Chaps. 3 and 5).

not clear from Desmond's exposition whether he regards Hegel's 'self-completing immanence' as something that is divine in nature or merely human. Does Hegel give us a God into whom all reality is absorbed without real distinction, or does he give us a religion of humanity for which 'God' is simply universal humanity writ large? In the final analysis, it seems to make no difference: pantheism and atheism/humanism are the same. Where Spinoza wrote, *Deus sive natura*, claims Desmond, Hegel might declare, *Deus sive humanitas*.

From my point of view, this interpretation of Hegelian holism as tantamount to a philosophy of immanence or a 'mystical monism'[7] is a gross caricature. For Hegel, as for Plato, the whole is not simply the one (a philosophy of identity), but the one *and the many*. A whole comprises parts. If the independence and the integrity of the parts are violated, if the many are reduced to one, then holism becomes identity or sameness. Without genuine difference and otherness, without transcendence as well as immanence, there is no whole, no system of relations, no spiralling into novelty, but simply an eternal repetition of the same. God *is* this whole, the whole in which everything finite comes into being and passes away, the whole in which time and history transpire and God becomes concretely self-determined. To insist, as Desmond does, that God is not the whole of wholes but a God beyond any whole, is to reduce holism to sameness and finitude. Hegel's holism offers an alternative to monism and dualism: it is (I have suggested) *advaitic*, not two and not one. This alternative disappears from Desmond's field of vision; he sees only monism and dualism, and opts for the latter. Panentheism reduces to pantheism, which reduces to atheism. Such charges were brought against Hegel in his own time; they represent a resistance to Hegelian dialectic and the logic of mediation.

Part of Desmond's problem arises from the way that he interprets Hegel's logic.[8] According to him, Hegel's logical formula is S(S–O), meaning that the subject is the relation of subject and object. In being related to an object, I am in relation to myself in relation to an object; I begin and end with myself. But this is not

---

[7] Desmond, *Hegel's God*, 2, 10, 66–7, 75, 88, 106, 110–11, 122. Desmond's critique of Hegelian 'monism' is similar in some respects to Levinas's critique of Hegelian 'totalizing', although Desmond does not mention Levinas. I return to this topic in the following two sections.

[8] Ibid., 79, 83, 92, 105, 117.

Hegel's logical formula. As we have seen in Chapter 1 (and further elaborate below), that formula is U–P–I, meaning that a universal principle is mediated with an individual subject by a particular quality. The formula has the character of a syllogism, not (as implied by Desmond) of a judgement, which can express only identity (S = O) or difference (S ≠ O). Everything rational, says Hegel, is a syllogism, which preserves identity *and* difference and involves mediation. The third term in the syllogism is emphatically not the same as the first. It is something new, emerging out of the moment of particularity or difference. The negation of the negative is not simply the return of the same, the self-recognition of the autonomous subject. Hegel's logic is not cast in the categories of subjectivity; he is not a Kantian subjective idealist. The logic rather describes an ontological process in which ideality and reality interact, and spirit emerges. The triple mediation of Hegel's logic, in which each of the three elements (universality, particularity, individuality) comes between and bridges the other two, is lost in Desmond's analysis, which is restricted to the disjunctive categories of the understanding (*Verstand*). He concludes that in counting to three, Hegel never really gets even to two but only to one, for the third is simply the self-recognition of the first in the second. And the first is the human self projecting itself into infinity.

Thus Desmond regards Hegel's Trinity as counterfeit—counterfeit in the sense that what he offers is a trinitarian monism, not a trinitarian monotheism (with monotheism understood to preclude 'the absolute unification of God and creation').[9] Hegel's economic Trinity is, according to Desmond, subordinated to the immanent Trinity in such a way that God's real relations to the world are simply epiphenomenal to God's ideal self-relations. Nothing is really outside the divine life but simply more complete expressions of its absolute immanence. The difference between the second moment of the immanent life of the Trinity and the creation as other is not of ultimate concern for Hegel. What seems like a double aspect for him (the immanent Son and the incarnate Son) is not a genuine double but merely a self-doubling of God. Again, from my point of view this is a perverse misinterpretation, a refusal

---

[9] Ibid., 11, 103–10. Desmond remarks that Hegel's Trinity is based not on orthodox doctrine but on 'philosophers and some heterodox sources' (107). Hegel offers a philosophical triad that appears in diverse religions, not a Christian Trinity composed of three divine Persons.

to accept that Hegel means what he says. I have argued that it is not the immanent Trinity that is primary for Hegel but the inclusive Trinity, the Trinity that comprises God and the world together, both God's ideal self-relations and God's real relations to what is not-God. These relations are not the same. If 'absolute unification' means 'identification', then it is clear that Hegel cannot identify God and the world. In such an identification, the world would lose its value vis-à-vis God, both its own intrinsic value and its value to God.

Desmond elaborates his critique further by arguing that the God–world relation must be understood to be asymmetrical.[10] By 'asymmetry' he means that God's relation to finite creation is not assimilable to the relation of finite creation to God; it cannot be made homogeneously symmetrical with it. Instead, God's relation to the world has the character of 'hyperbolic goodness', which means the gratuitous descent of the superior into finitude. Desmond believes that this entails a different sort of kenosis than that envisaged by Hegel, who is unable to grasp the genuinely agapeic character of the divine goodness—its gratuitous, non-necessary, superabundant self-giving. However, for Hegel the relationship between God and the world is not homogeneously symmetrical. Rather, the relationship of the absolute to the finite has an irreversible primacy. It is the infinite that overreaches the difference between finite and infinite and includes finitude within itself; finitude cannot do this. As we have seen, the finite can be properly related only negatively to itself and affirmatively to the infinite. The reverse of this, which claims an affirmative relation to self and a negative relation to transcendence, is the basis of atheism and agnosticism in Hegel's view. The religious relationship entails a negation of self as finite and an elevation of self into the divine milieu. Moreover, the basis of this elevation is not human self-projection but the divine descent into finitude. God as an 'affirmative infinitude' (1:294) is the condition of possibility for the relationship with God and for knowledge of God. God gives or manifests godself and does not withdraw into inaccessible mystery. 'Religion is a begetting of the divine spirit, not an invention of human beings but an effect of the divine at work, of the divine productive process within humanity' (1:130; cf. 3:337 n. 239). This is what Hegel's speculative theology grasps; it is not a truth

---

[10] Desmond, *Hegel's God*, 49, 54, 61–3.

that lies hyperbolically beyond logical articulation, as Desmond believes.

The asymmetry of divine–human relations is similar in certain respects to the asymmetry that is present in interhuman relations.[11] In the latter relationship, asymmetry is an essential aspect of reciprocal recognition for Hegel: asymmetry and reciprocity do not cancel each other out. The reason for this is that the mutuality of ethical relations is attained when each party renounces coercion and allows the other to be. Thus an element of self-renunciation or self-sacrifice is necessary if there is to be a two-way relationship. A one-way relationship in which one side utilizes the other to achieve its own ends (the master–slave relationship) is no relationship at all. In order to be in a relationship of mutuality with an other, I have to give the other primacy by giving up my own interests; and the other does the same. This is the asymmetry that is present in every relationship. It can also be seen to characterize the divine–human relationship. On the one hand, God is the condition of possibility for the relationship with God; the infinite begets the finite and is not a projection of the finite. On the other hand, God does not lord it over creation as a sovereign but lets it go as free and independent. God enters into and suffers our natural and human condition, affirms us precisely in our negativity and finitude so that we are, after all, able to affirm ourselves in turning to God. This is the death of God, which is the supreme vision of love sacrificing itself for its other, a sacrifice that does not end in isolation but in reconciliation and the establishment of community. Divine love that divests itself for the sake of reconciliation with its other—a reconciliation that has an element of the tragic[12] because of the necessity of sacrifice—is at the core of Hegel's theology and his account of ethical life. As we have seen, the eucharist establishes for him the pattern of 'eternal sacrifice' (3:236) that characterizes the divine life as well as social relations in the world. The divine sacrifice is primary; the human follows from and images it.

Thus what is involved is a *double* asymmetry between God and creation: one primary (the primacy of God's creativity vis-à-vis the

---

[11] I am guided at this point by ideas suggested by Robert R. Williams.

[12] Desmond does not, in his discussion of evil (143–66), consider the tragic as a necessary condition of the creation of a finite world distinct from God yet related to God. Perhaps he does not regard tragedy to be an authentically Christian category.

world), the other secondary and a reversal of the first (God's self-giving and self-emptying). This double asymmetry is similar to but also differs from the reciprocal asymmetry of interhuman relations, in which each party gives itself up for the sake of the other and neither is the creator of the other.

If this analysis is correct, then it is wrong to suggest, as Desmond does,[13] that Hegel's absolute is not agapeic but only erotic—not a freely self-giving God but a needy God who creates the world only to satisfy the divine desire. 'Despite a flicker here and there, Hegel's ecstasis of love remains asleep to the agape of God.' By contrast, I believe that for Hegel God's love is both agapeic and erotic, as indeed it must be if God *is* love and love in the fullest sense involves both *agapē* and *erōs*—and also *philia* or friendship. The divine eros for the other is the fullest divine ecstasis or self-giving. It is both desire and gift, and it makes of us friends of God. Friendship requires both kinds of love.

All the critical questions raised by Desmond come to focus on the question of God and creation. Desmond's view, in brief, is that Hegel's God is self-creating, not the creator of a genuinely other creation. God gives birth to godself: this is an erotics of creation, not an agapeics of creation. If Hegel's thought were 'more deeply rooted in an appreciation of agapeic love as a giving from surplus generosity, . . . giving for the sake of the other as other', then 'the results for thought would be entirely different.'[14] But what if Hegel's thought *is* deeply rooted in such an appreciation, as I believe it is? Then indeed the results are different. I believe we must say that for Hegel God is *both* self-creating *and* other-creating, both erotic and agapeic. After all, creativity *is* the divine nature. God is not a static entity but a spiritual process, a coming-to-be and a bringing-into-being.

Desmond attempts to diminish the significance of Hegel's claim that the divine idea 'releases' (*entläßt*) the other, the world, 'to exist as a free and independent being' (3:292). He dismisses those interpreters who 'trawl through' the works of Hegel, looking for such terms as *entlassen* and using them to make his thought 'more hospitable to robust otherness and irreducible plurality than can be read from the reiterated language of self-return that is all pervasive'. Is this a release of the idea into nature, he wonders, or merely

---

[13] Desmond, *Hegel's God*, 114–16.
[14] Ibid., 96, 121–40 (quotation from 137).

the *thought* of nature?[15] Such a dismissal is unable to take seriously the realistic mediation in Hegel's thought—a mediation that is absolutely critical to the system, which is not simply a logical idealism. Hegel's use of *entlassen* is not casual and insignificant, especially if, as I have argued, it is a Germanic equivalent to the Latin *absolvere*, 'to loosen' or 'let go', from which Hegel's concept of the 'absolute' as utterly relational derives. To be sure, the other that is released as other is not cut off, disconnected, and outside the divine *oikonomia*, totally different from the divine nature. Desmond believes that such a total otherness is required by Christian doctrine. But what has happened to the doctrine of the *imago Dei*, which excludes the possibility of total otherness? Obviously there is similarity as well as difference between creator and creation. The difference does not arise from the fact that the *nihil* from which finite things are created is something outside of God, as Desmond insists, thus embracing an ontological dualism. Rather the *nihil* is the pure possibility of being that subsists within God as the inexhaustible source out of which God releases otherness to become something free and independent, yet still connected. Thus Hegel is right, I believe, to affirm, contra Desmond, that *creatio ex nihilo* means *creatio ex Deo*. Such a view introduces tragedy into the divine life, whereas for Desmond evil remains external to God.

In the final analysis, which God is real, and which the counterfeit? It could be argued that the God who is totally other, the sovereign Lord beyond all thought and beyond all ontological connection with the creation, is the counterfeit, a projection of the human imagination into infinity—the sort of God *we* would like to be if we could. By contrast, the *real* God is the revelatory, self-giving God, knowing godself in our knowing, realizing godself in the ambiguities and tragedies of history, surrendering the status of abstract divinity for the sake of our salvation and the redemption of nature. The tables could be turned in this way. However, a more worthy response is to acknowledge that Desmond's interpretation of Christian theology is a valid option, and that there are many who share his criticisms and suspicions of Hegel. The texts are difficult and can be read in different ways. Rather than narrowing the range of acceptable readings of both Hegel and Christian theology, my plea is to open it up and affirm the broad stream that in fact has flowed from the beginning. Two fundamentally different

[15] Ibid., 121.

paradigms are at play in the dispute between Desmond (as alias of Kierkegaard) and Hegel. Both offer true insight into the reality of God and religion, and both have limitations.

I have discussed what I view as some of Hegel's limitations in the preceding chapters: his depiction of Christianity as the 'consummate' religion; his lack of clarity about the reciprocity between representation (religious symbols) and thought (philosophical concepts); his difficulty in accounting for radical, irrational evil; his argument for a single supreme incarnation of God; his selective account of the realization of reconciliation in the world culminating in speculative philosophy; his somewhat suffocating embrace of theology by philosophy; his attempt to construct a unitary history of religion. I acknowledge the inherent challenge he faced in preserving difference while emphasizing unity.[16] I believe that the resources offered to theology by Hegel outweigh these deficits, and the focus of this book is on the resources. Nonetheless my view is that theology should not be beholden to any philosophy, not even Hegel's.

Finally, and ironically, the contrasts between Hegel and Desmond may not be as great as they first appear. Desmond, who at one time was attracted to Hegel's thought, does not want to leave God stuck in the absolute beyond; rather he refers to the 'hyperbolic goodness' of God that somehow bridges the gap between infinite and finite. What for Hegel is intelligible when we grasp the concept of God is for Desmond something that thought cannot think. Yet he thinks it in his own way, not dialectically but metaxologically,[17] from the 'between' (*metaxu*) of difference rather than from the 'through' (*dia*) of mediation. But does not the 'between' require a 'through', and the 'through' a 'between'?

The critical questions raised by Desmond will be revisited in the following discussion of the aporia of postmodernity and their Hegelian resolutions. I start by noting that the broad stream of

---

[16] It certainly is possible to argue that Hegel belongs to a stream of interpretation that privileges unity over difference; but to conclude that difference is obliterated in Hegel's paradigm, and that his entire God-concept is counterfeit, is to engage in ideological and rhetorical overkill.

[17] Desmond, *Hegel's God*, 70. What hyperbole and metaxology precisely entail is not explained in this book. How does hyperbolic goodness differ from the concept of goodness? What does it mean to think hyperbolically? Is hyperbole a rhetorical category or a logical one?

interpretation includes both orthodoxy and heterodoxy. From the latter Hegel fashions his concept of *Geist*.

## HETERODOXY AND ONTOTHEOLOGY: SPIRIT

The speculative theology of the Hegelian middle has been criticized as 'heterodoxy' by the right and as 'ontotheology' by the left. These terms of derision can, I have argued, be turned to good effect because Hegel's heterodox conception of spirit (*Geist*) enables him to reconstruct ontotheological claims in such a way as to overcome the negative aspects of metaphysical orthodoxy. Hegelian *Geist* retrieves the truth of orthodoxy by drawing upon the resources of heterodoxy.

Hegel's project is orthodox in so far as it reestablishes the conditions of possibility of knowing God over against the modern doctrine that nothing can be known of God. His philosophy of religion is a response to the challenge of theological agnosticism, which in his view undercuts the central conviction of orthodoxy that God makes godself known, that the nature of God is manifest in the world, and that human cognition is capable of grasping the idea of God. Beyond agnosticism lie atheism and secularism, and Hegel foresees the consequences of living in a godless world. Religion, if still practised, is separated from the rest of life, limited to one day (or hour) of the week, and the truths that it apprehends are judged to be quite different from the truths of everyday life and empirical science. Hegel regards such a bifurcated existence to be deeply dissatisfying, and he longs for a reintegration of religion, rationality, and life, but under the conditions of modernity. To accomplish this is the goal of philosophy of religion, and he is convinced that more of dogmatics has been preserved in philosophy than in theology itself. This is because classical dogmatics, like speculative philosophy, assumes the rationality of faith and gives its doctrines intellectual formulation. Today, he says, the fundamental doctrines of Christianity—Trinity, sin and evil, incarnation—have for the most part disappeared from theology, and philosophy is pre-eminently what is orthodox; the basic truths of Christianity are preserved by it.

Thus Hegel declares his orthodoxy. The declaration is implicit in his critique of the theologies of his time. Theological rationalism has relinquished the project of knowing God, and its exegesis turns scripture into a 'wax nose' twisted to the shape of its own prejudices. Theological historicism is interested only in what was once believed and lacks assets of its own, so that philosophy now retains more of the teachings of the church than theology does. Theological agnosticism abandons dogmatics for ethics, but Hegel is unimpressed by the claim that belief in God provides incentives for acting in accord with moral duties: such a view corrupts religion. Nor is faith properly located in the subjectivity of religious feeling, which cannot get off the ground, cannot elevate itself from the finite to the infinite, cannot defend against the inversion of atheism, which regards belief in God as a projection of subjective needs and desires.

In all of this Hegel aligns himself with orthodoxy, yet he evinces little interest in the minutiae of confessional distinctions and doctrinal debates, as is evident from his discussion of the doctrines of the Trinity, Christ, and the sacraments. From his point of view, arguments over such details obscure the truth and serve no other purpose than to keep theologians busy. He is not a close historian of Christian dogma: that role was left to his disciple, Ferdinand Christian Baur. His construal of the Christian idea reflects an eclectic appropriation of the doctrinal tradition, orthodox and heterodox.

Much has been made of the influence on Hegel of a heterodox trajectory going back to Valentinian Gnosticism and including such figures as Joachim of Fiore, Meister Eckhart, and Jacob Boehme.[18] Of the latter, Hegel discusses only Boehme in any detail in the *Lectures on the Philosophy of Religion*. A reference to Valentinian Gnosticism, with which Hegel was familiar through the work of August Neander, appears in his discussion of the doctrine of the Trinity. But the main point in this context is that the apparent distinction between the divine One and the self-emerging Logos proves to be no distinction at all, for the Logos remains within the bosom of God and does not enter into the materiality and otherness of the world. Hegel will have nothing to do with the spirit–matter dualism and the concomitant rejection of the natural world that characterizes Gnosticism. Indeed, he warns against shunning the sensible 'in monkish fashion' and avows that 'spirit is at home with itself in the sensible' (3:134).

---

[18] See Cyril O'Regan, *The Heterodox Hegel* (Albany: State University of New York Press, 1994), 15–20, 251–9, 270–83.

Nonetheless, it is correct to suggest, as O'Regan does, following the lead of Baur,[19] not only that Hegel values *gnōsis* as a form of redemptive knowledge but also that the Hegelian metanarrative reflects the influence of a Gnostic-mystical as opposed to a Jewish form of apocalyptic in that the various phases of divine manifestation are constitutive of divine identity and personhood. Narrative not merely affects the *oikonomia* but reaches into the inner divine life, which 'undergoes a process of perfecting as it traverses the drama of fall, exile, and return'.[20] Here something quite new is introduced into the Christian mainstream from one of its side currents. How this novelty plays out in a theology of divine history, process, and suffering is one of the themes of this book.

Hegel does not shrink from such experimentation. We know that in his early writings he considers the possibility that Christianity will be superseded by a new folk religion or a philosophical religion of the spirit. Later he realizes that religions are not invented by philosophers and that he will have to make do with actuality as it presents itself in history. But he does not hesitate to replace the awkward categories of classical trinitarianism and christology with

[19] Baur was the first to suggest that a connection exists between ancient Gnostic systems and certain modern Protestant philosophies of religion (Boehme, Schelling, Schleiermacher, Hegel). Gnosticism with its theory of redemptive knowledge and universal historical process has in Baur's view a legitimate place in Christian theology, especially in the struggle of the first two centuries against the 'particularizing' tendencies of Judaism. See Ferdinand Christian Baur, *Die christliche Gnosis, oder die christliche Religions-Philosophie in ihrer geschichtlichen Entwiklung* (Tübingen: C. F. Osiander, 1835). But Baur's detailed description of the Gnostic worldview shows how antithetical it is to Hegel. Its speculative interpretation of religious history is predicated on a metaphysical dualism deriving from paganism (matter versus spirit, the historical versus the archetypal); and historical development is viewed as occurring through the interaction of dualistically opposed powers. Spirit returns to itself as pure spirit, and an infinite abyss remains between spirit and matter. It posits a determinism that excludes moral freedom and lacks a true doctrine of creation. Its christology is docetic since the redeemer figure must come into as little contact as possible with matter, and generally the positive content of Christianity evaporates. See *Das Christenthum und die christliche Kirche der drei ersten Jahrhunderte* (Tübingen: L. F. Fues, 1852), 159–213. Hegel's philosophical system, by contrast, is holistic, not dualistic; spirit and matter (or nature) are not antithetical but necessary to each other; spirit overreaches the difference between the ideal and the real, returning to itself as embodied, mediated spirit; God becomes incarnate as an individual, sensible, human being who suffers the degrading death of crucifixion; and the positivity and the spirituality of Christianity are equally affirmed. In a recent article John W. Burbidge argues along similar lines that Hegel cannot be read as a Gnostic. See 'The Word Became Flesh or the Orthodox Hegel', *Bulletin of the Hegel Society of Great Britain* 45/46 (2002), 16–24.

[20] O'Regan, *The Heterodox Hegel*, 300–10.

a new philosophical intuition, or to criticize the standard atonement theories, or to offer a demythologized interpretation of the
resurrection. He recognizes that both a deconstruction of representational forms and a reconstruction in conceptual language are
necessary; and he knows that this operation might seem to be
nothing but a destruction in which the content is lost along with
the form. He acknowledges the possibility that Christianity along
with other religions might become a fossil, but he is not sanguine
about a postreligious future, and he is convinced in any event that
the surest way of ensuring fossilization is to refuse the challenge of
reinterpretation. To take up the challenge, one must have the
courage, as did the heretics and the martyrs, to go into the water.
Hegel is neither a heretic nor a martyr, but he pushes past the
boundaries of orthodoxy on a number of key issues. One of these is
his distinctive construal of ontotheology.

Ontotheology is a name, invented by Immanuel Kant,[21] for
traditional metaphysical theology, which makes claims about the
ontological status of God and believes that such claims can be
proved or verified. God is a being, indeed the supreme and perfect
being, whose existence is necessary because the contingency of
finite being requires it and because perfection includes existence
or reality among its predicates. Now, as we have seen, Hegel
accepts Kant's critique of metaphysical theology, so the question
has to be raised how he can embrace ontotheology. He does not
embrace the term as such, but he certainly makes ontological
claims about God, and he affirms the ontological proof as the
only valid proof.

I have suggested that Hegel replaces traditional metaphysics
with his own postmetaphysical ontotheology that introduces a
new category, 'spirit'. The being of God (the *ontos* of *theos*) is not
the being of pure immediacy (the emptiest of all philosophical
categories, with which logic begins), or the being of abstract substance (Aristotle, Spinoza), or the being of the supreme being (the

---

[21] Kant actually returns to the ontotheology he criticizes, for his God is posited as
the totality of reality with all the traditional ontological qualities. While pure reason
cannot prove the existence of a concrete supreme being, God as this being is a
necessary transcendental regulative ideal of practical reason. See Immanuel Kant,
*Lectures on Philosophical Theology*, trans. Allen W. Wood and Gertrude M. Clark
(Ithaca, NY: Cornell University Press, 1978), esp. 44–80. Emmanuel Levinas
describes this Kantian version of ontotheology in *God, Death, and Time*, trans.
Bettina Bergo (Stanford, Calif.: Stanford University Press, 2000), 153–4.

rational theologians, Kant, Schleiermacher). Rather God's being is that of 'spirit' (*Geist*) in the sense of energy, movement, life, mind, manifestation, the process of differentiation and reconciliation. Spirit is an act or narrative of self-revealing and self-realizing that moves through dialectical spirals by which the divine inter-subjectivity is established and all that exists is brought into being.

While Boehme's theosophy may be one of the resources in the background of Hegel's conception,[22] it is notable that what Hegel offers is theology, not theosophy—not direct contemplative contact with divinity but the hard labour of disciplined thought; not *sophia* but *logos*—or better, *sophia* and *logos* together as *pneuma*, the richest of the biblical figures of divinity, a figure that embraces wisdom and word, thought and being, ideality and reality, mysticism and history. The unity of thought and being in spirit is at the heart of Hegel's version of the ontological proof. The true concept, he argues, contains objectivity within itself, is alive and active, is the movement of self-objectifying by which its subjectivity is sublated. But this is to say that the true concept is spirit: the final category of the logic (*Begriff*) corresponds to the final category of the system (*Geist*). God is absolute spirit, which means among other things that God absolves godself of supremacy or perfection and assumes the determinate existence of humanity, becomes involved in the brokenness of world process. All this represents a sharp break with the metaphysical tradition.

Emmanuel Levinas points out that Martin Heidegger regarded ontotheology as the fate of the Western metaphysical tradition as a whole: by identifying God as a supreme being and as the foundation of beings, it obscures the difference between *being* as an event, power, or letting-be, and *beings* as worldly entities. It mundanizes God and avoids the thinking of being. Levinas asks: 'Did onto-theo-logy's mistake consist in taking being for God, or rather in taking God for being.'[23] Heidegger assumed the former and thus

---

[22] O'Regan (*The Heterodox Hegel*, 18) argues to this effect, drawing upon the research of David Walsh in *The Mysticism of Innerworldly Fulfillment: A Study of Jacob Boehme* (Gainsville, Fla.: University Presses of Florida, 1983). O'Regan's entire introductory discussion of Hegelian ontotheology (1–25) is helpful. He concludes by suggesting that Hegel 'belongs to the heterodox margins of the ontotheo-logical tradition', but that his marginality does not take him 'outside the tradition into a kind of hermeneutic free fall' (25).

[23] Levinas, *God, Death, and Time*, 121–5; quotation from 124. See Martin Heidegger, 'The Onto-theo-logical Constitution of Metaphysics', in *Identity and Difference*, trans. Joan Stambaugh (New York: Harper & Row, 1969), 42–74.

sought to free being from the metaphysical God. Levinas assumes the latter and thus disconnects God from being: God signifies the other of being, and to know God philosophy must turn from ontology to ethics. To think God on the basis of ethics is to think the uncontainable, nonthematizable other, an infinite transcendence beyond any negative theology.[24]

Hegel's strategy differs from that of Heidegger and Levinas. Rather than disconnecting being and God, he rethinks being as spirit—a fluid, mobile, spiralling relationality—and he rethinks God as absolute/absolving spirit, thus breaking the logic of divine sovereignty and replacing it with the logic of divine subjectivity.[25] Hegel's God is not the wholly other but the whole of wholes, the universal that embraces all otherness and difference. As spirit God is both substance and subject, power and person, life and mind, essence and existence. The abiding unity that forms God's infinite subjectivity does not dissolve differentia into sameness but holds them in a play of productive relationships, as symbolized by the play of the trinitarian persons. It is an infinite *inter*subjectivity.

What makes God's spirit absolute and infinite is that all of its relationships occur within a divinely created community of recognition (imaged biblically as the kingdom of God, the *basileia tou theou*). The other that it absolves or releases does not become something beyond the range of absolute spirit, so to speak, such that it would delimit the absolute and render it finite. God has real, reciprocal, mutually affective relations with the world, and the real other of the economic Trinity is not the same as the logical other of the immanent Trinity. Hegel speaks of the divine 'externalization' or 'divestment' (*Entäußerung*), of the logical idea releasing itself into the externality of nature and finite spirit, and he uses spatial metaphors to designate the place of the world as 'outside' of God (3:91, 193). The other that God releases is something genuinely other than God, something finite and contingent, subject to the categories of space and time. But this otherness is at the same time not severed from the divine life: finitude becomes a moment in the development of spirit, and the result of the creative release is not a dualism that externally limits God or makes God one of two; nor is

[24] Levinas, *God, Death, and Time*, 136–9.

[25] For a discussion of this topic, see Dale M. Schlitt, *Divine Subjectivity: Understanding Hegel's Philosophy of Religion* (London and Toronto: Associated University Presses, 1990). See also Schlitt's earlier study, *Hegel's Trinitarian Claim: A Critical Reflection* (Leiden: E. J. Brill, 1984).

it a monism that collapses everything into the divine subject. Recognition preserves both identity and difference, and recognition constitutes a community (or 'kingdom') of freedom. The extraordinary thing about God as absolute spirit is that God encompasses what is not-God within God, and preserves it as not-God. God does not exclude space, time, and finitude but includes and saves them. They exist within God (God's *basileia*), not God within them. Nothing can be totally other than God, only relatively (often recalcitrantly) other. Thus God is the whole, the universal. Can this Hegelian holism escape the Levinasian charge of 'totalizing'?

## TOTALITY AND INFINITY: WHOLENESS

Levinas defines 'totality' in such a way as to make it difficult to escape the charge. A totality is not simply a blank sameness but the relativity in which beings are co-present, become signs of each other, form an intelligible structure or system. Structure is intelligibility, and subjectivity is subordinated to it.[26] Just this is what Hegel means by 'the whole' or 'the universal', although from his point of view subjectivity is not subordinated to but formed by systemic relations or by what might be called co-dependent origination, which means that it is always already intersubjectivity. For Levinas subjectivity depends not on co-dependent relations but on exteriority, disconnection, mutual transcendence. Truth is not a union of the knower and known but a form of contact without participation. One person is not defined by the recognition of an other; rather, revelation, the expression of a face, replaces recognition in a relationship of asymmetry.[27]

The contrast between the two thinkers is perhaps greatest at the point of interpreting the 'absoluteness' of the infinite God. For Levinas, any real relationship to the absolute would render it relative. Hence he writes that the absolute '"absolves" itself from the relation in which it presents itself', preserving its transcendence, its infinity. Or: 'The same and the other at the same time maintain themselves in relationship and *absolve* themselves

[26] Levinas, *God, Death, and Time*, 146–7.
[27] Emmanuel Levinas, *Totality and Infinity: An Essay on Exteriority*, trans. Alphonso Lingis (Pittsburgh: Duquesne University Press, 1969), 61–2, 65.

from this relation, remain absolutely separated. The idea of infinity requires this separation.'[28] For Hegel, divine absolution means just the reverse: the absolute releases itself into real relations with the other, becoming absolute not in separation but in communion. The difference here is between an atomistic and a social ontology. Levinas's atomism is evident from his statement that individuals 'stand out in themselves, breaking through, rending their forms, are not resolved into the relations that link them up to the totality'. This standing out and rending is symbolized by the nudity of the face. Over against the privileging of unity from Parmenides to Spinoza to Hegel, Levinas embraces the atomism of Leibniz and the exteriority of Descartes.[29]

The question is whether Hegel's social or holistic ontology removes all multiplicity from the infinite, whether Hegel's absolute excludes every other that might limit it and thus refers only to itself, whether the nothingness that Hegel includes within being is able to attain to the level of death, whether it is right to believe that God expands rather than contracts in the act of creation, whether Hegel allows for no mystery and transcendence in God and thus for no negative theology. These are questions and charges that Levinas brings against Hegel.[30] The differences here are very basic and occur at the level of fundamental intuitions as well as specific arguments.

In Hegel's defence, it can be said first of all that others have construed his system more rigidly than he himself does. Hegel, I have suggested, engages in conceptual play with the logical deep structures in light of concrete experience and data, and he does so in the context of oral lectures, which resist the totalization of a closed system. A case can be made that he recognizes the need for an apophatic element in theology, the element of mystery, of non-knowing, of limit, of non-dogmatism, which drives thinking beyond understanding (*Verstand*) to reason (*Vernunft*), and that drives reason to its ground in the infinite. Hegel's dialectic is a form of negative thinking that keeps knowledge open, fluid, restless, self-critical.

[28] Emmanuel Levinas, *Totality and Infinity: An Essay on Exteriority*, Levinas, *Totality and Infinity*, 50, 102.
[29] Ibid., 74–5, 101, 219. Cf. Robert R. Williams's discussion of this contrast in *Recognition: Fichte and Hegel on the Other* (Albany: State University of New York Press, 1992), 285–6, 297–300.
[30] *Totality and Infinity*, 103–5, 196–7; *God, Death, and Time*, 74–8, 203–6.

Following the lead of G. R. G. Mure,[31] Robert Williams argues that empirical reality stands over against thought for Hegel and is not totally sublated by it.[32] The Hegelian system comprises a correspondence, not an identity, between the science of logic and the philosophies of the real (nature, spirit). The system is closed in respect to its categorical structure but open toward the empirical realm, allowing the contingencies of the latter to reflect back into the logical. Thus two senses of otherness may be distinguished: the logical (the other as self-othering) and the empirical (the other broken free in 'utter dismemberment'). The logical other and the empirical other are not the same. God's logical self-othering (the immanent Trinity) is a condition of empirical relations, for only an inwardly complex being such as the triune God can be affected by others without being controlled or destroyed by them. For Hegel, in a reversal of the orthodox theological tradition, the economic or worldly Trinity subsumes or includes the immanent Trinity (hence is more properly spoken of as the inclusive Trinity); it is a production, the result of mediation between God and the world. History is not reduced to a side-show but is constitutive of the divine life. Hegel's project is to give difference its due, and thus abstract identity is replaced by recognition. The Hegelian totality is the very antithesis of sameness, of totalitarian hegemony. In the holistic super-triad of logic–nature–spirit, no absolute primacy exists, no founding and grounding, no reduction of the other to the same, but rather, as Williams puts it, 'a non-foundationalist threefold mutual mediation' in which each of the three elements assumes the middle position and each is mediated by the others.

The syllogism (reasoning to a conclusion from premises) is for Hegel the key to rationality. The three *elements* or *members* of every syllogism are U (the universal principle), P (the particular quality), and I (the individual subject or singular instantiation). The three *figures* of a syllogism (formed by differing logical relations among the members) are U–P–I, U–I–P, and P–U–I (the order of each of these is reversible: I–P–U, P–I–U, I–U–P). Hegel writes: 'The three figures of the syllogism declare that everything rational is manifested as a triple syllogism; that is to say, each one of the

[31] G. R. G. Mure, *A Study of Hegel's Logic* (Oxford: Oxford University Press, 1950).
[32] Williams, *Recognition*, 267–72.

members takes in turn the place of the extremes, as well as of the mean which reconciles them.'[33] In this way each of the premises in turn becomes a conclusion and is thus proved. Applied to the three branches of philosophy—with logic defined as the universal element, nature as the particular, and spirit as the individual—the triple syllogism can be formulated as follows. (1) The natural mediation: U–P–I. The logical idea is the universal principle of nature; spirit is embedded in nature as pre-self or other-than-self; therefore spirit is founded not in itself but in the logical idea, and the logical idea is the principle of spirit (this is the order of Hegel's system). (2) The spiritual mediation: U–I–P. The logical idea is the principle of spirit; nature has its telos in spirit; therefore nature is raised to its essence in the logical idea, and the logical idea is the principle of nature. (3) The logical mediation: P–U–I. Nature has its principle in the logical idea; spirit has its principle in the logical idea; therefore nature and spirit are independent (neither is the principle of the other) but connected (nature is the pre-self of spirit, and spirit is the telos of nature). Obviously people do not normally think in this abstract way, but the formulation exposes the logic implicit in connecting the elements.

Because each of the members is both the *mediator* between the other two and *mediated* by the other two, there is no single master syllogism and no single order among the members. Applied to the relation between God, the natural world, and humanity, the triple syllogism shows that God as the universal rational principle (the logical idea) is the ground of nature (particularity) and finite spirit (individuality) (U–P–I, U–I–P), but also that God mediates between nature and finite spirit, preventing their collapse into each other (P–U–I, I–U–P), and that God becomes a concrete universal (absolute spirit) through the mediation of nature and finite spirit (I–P–U, P–I–U). God is beginning, middle, and end; and God is God only in relation to what is not-God, nature and finite spirit. In this complex interaction God does not cease to be God (does not give up universality), but God *is* God only in relation to a multi-faceted totality. If the three members collapse into sameness, there is no syllogism, no rationality, no living process.

---

[33] *Encyclopedia of the Philosophical Sciences*, § 187 addition (*The Logic of Hegel*, trans. William Wallace, 2nd edn. (London: Oxford University Press, 1892), 322); cf. §§ 181–92. On Hegel's doctrine of the syllogism, see also above, Chap. 1, pp. 9–11.

Hegel uses the terms *Ganze, Ganzheit*, and *Totalität* inter-changeably, which suggests that his totality is to be construed holistically, as a *Ganzheit*, rather than totalistically. An example of totalizing in his time would have been Schelling's philosophy of identity, the 'night in which all cows are black' (as Hegel famously remarks in the Preface to the *Phenomenology of Spirit*). In such a philosophy the distinction between the universal, the particular, and the individual breaks down. God is not a point of indifference but 'the whole totality' (*die ganze Totalität*); not pitch blackness but the luminosity in which colours are discriminated. Moreover, 'it is as totality that God is the Spirit' (3:199, 284 n. 93). This is because the inclusive or holistic Trinity is not linear but a spiral of concentric relations: Father within Son within Spirit—just the reverse of the traditional trinitarian picture, which accords the Father priority. The spiral through the Son into the Spirit is a spiral away from the abstract supreme being into differentiation, concreteness, colour, and wholeness.

The 'whole totality' that is God as spirit is not simply everything that is, the empirical world as such. This would be crude panthe-ism, which Hegel emphatically rejects. Rather, borrowing a cat-egory from Spinoza, he says that God is the substance or essence upon which everything depends for its existence. But he immedi-ately adds that this substance is also internally concrete, it is substance as subject and spirit. God is not a mere soil out of which distinctions grow subsequently but an abiding unity in which distinctions are already potentially present. God is not an inert, abstract universal but an abundant, overflowing univer-sal. In another context he distinguishes between this abundant universality (*Allgemeinheit*) and the 'collective totality' (*Allesheit*) with which the *pan* of pantheism is commonly confused. This is as close as Hegel comes to a specific critique of totalization. God is not everything (*Allesgötterei*) but 'the All that remains utterly one' (2:573) and as such is the negativity, not the apotheosis, of the finite. Here Hegel is able to affirm the Buddhist conception of being as emptiness.

Just as absolute spirit is not a totalizing concept as Hegel con-ceives it, so also absolute knowledge is not.[34] Absolute knowledge

---

[34] Stephen Crites, commenting on the famous concluding chapter of the *Phe-nomenology of Spirit*, remarks that absolute knowledge 'is not definitive cosmology or metaphysics, nor does its absoluteness imply that the omniscience imputed to the

is not an empirical state of affairs attained once and for all but an unending quest through countless determinate negations; it comprises all the endless and inexhaustible details of life. Absolving knowledge releases itself into the life and death struggle of history; it stands out from identity into difference. Similarly, absolute spirit is the determinacy that encompasses all determinations. The chief interest of philosophy, Hegel tells us, is the manner in which unity becomes determinate. The deepest and last of the determinations of unity is that of absolute spirit.

The absoluteness of spirit means that its recognitive relationships are both internal and external within what might be called the divine milieu (or *basileia*). Pure inwardness would reduce spirit to self-contemplation; pure exteriority would render it finite. The true infinite according to Hegel must overreach and include the finite within itself. The infinite does not exclude that which limits or stands over against it but precisely includes it. This is the point of deepest contention between Hegel and Levinas. For Levinas, as for much of Jewish and Christian theology, the relationship between infinite and finite, creator and creature, must be conceived as one of radical exteriority: God is wholly other, not the whole that encompasses otherness. From Hegel's point of view, Levinas's infinite is just another finite, limited by its own exteriority; while from Levinas's point of view, Hegel's infinite is indistinguishable from a totality that homogenizes everything. The issue bears in part on the way that the doctrine of creation is construed.

We have seen that Hegel employs two sets of metaphors to describe the mysterious process by which the world comes to be in distinction from God. The first set suggests a linguistic-juridical act by which God speaks or posits a division in empirical reality

God of religion devolves upon human wisdom instead. Something of the sort may be what one might expect from "absolute knowledge", but Hegel's use of the term ironically inverts that expectation. It is, in the first place, that knowledge of human fallibility of which the *Phenomenology* provides an ample introduction.' Absolute knowledge is like 'philo-sophia's wistful love of wisdom'; it is *erōs*, not *stasis*. If absolute knowledge thus appears to be 'all too radically relative, indeed evanescent, the apparent contradiction arises only because of a long-standing habit of mind that identifies the absolute with the static. That is an assumption from which Hegel attempts again and again to wean us, insisting that what is absolute is always dynamic, self-transformative, never locked into any single unchanging form.' See *Dialectic and Gospel in the Development of Hegel's Thinking* (University Park, Pa.: Pennsylvania State University Press, 1998), 517–26 (quotations from 518–19). Andrew Shanks offers a similar perspective on 'absolute knowledge' (see above, Chap. 10, n. 48).

that corresponds to the inner differentiation within the divine life. Only in this way does the divine play of love with itself become 'serious' in the sense of undergoing separation and rupture. The second set offers the physical image of 'releasing' or 'letting go', of allowing the world to exist as something free and independent. Both images convey a sense of transition or break that prevents a strictly emanationist interpretation. There is no sameness of being that links God and the world, no common substance in which they both share, no simple 'going forth' of the world from God. Divine creative power, symbolized as a word, judgement, or release, generates something new out of the divine subjectivity that is genuinely different from God in its finitude, determinacy, and vulnerability to evil, but that is at the same time an expression of divine purpose and an object of divine care. Hegel is especially clear about this in his account of the Jewish theology of creation, from which the Christian doctrine derives. 'God creates absolutely, out of nothing': this is 'a mode of production in which God is the subject, is simply intuitive, infinite activity' (2:428). Human production requires a material with which to work; divine intuitive production is sheer inward vitality. The natural world is de-divinized, rendered prosaic in contrast to the divine sublimity. Yet it is good because it is created out of God's own potency rather than out of primordial matter. While Hegel refers to the doctrine of *creatio ex nihilo*, what it means for him is that God creates out of nothing other than God. This is a non-emanationist *creatio ex Deo*.[35] God is an inexhaustible creative fecundity by which potential divisions and distinctions within divinity are released, set forth, posited in and as world, and by which the divine ideality actualizes itself.

Hegel's description of creation as a divine 'release' and 'expansion' contrasts with the emphasis that Levinas derives from the Kabbalah on the divine 'contraction' or 'withdrawal' so as to leave space for a created order other than God. 'An infinity that does not close in upon itself in a circle but withdraws from the ontological extension so as to leave a place for a separated being exists divinely. Over and above the totality it inaugurates a society.'[36] Hegel's

[35] See O'Regan, *The Heterodox Hegel*, 169–87. O'Regan regards this as a 'swerve' from Christian orthodoxy influenced especially by Boehme. But it can also be interpreted as an attempt to make sense of an obscure theologoumenon.
[36] Levinas, *Totality and Infinity*, 104.

infinity does not in fact close in upon itself in a circle but rather expands and enacts itself in an open spiral. The question at stake is which philosophical view inaugurates a genuine society, a social whole in which genuine difference contributes to a diverse totality. It is ironic that Levinas should mention society here since for him society is secondary to the asymmetry of the ethical relationship, whereas for Hegel society is primary and constitutive: the totality *is* social.

It is true that Hegel stresses the contingency and passing character of the world ('the disappearing moment of appearance' (3:88)). The world is real, but its truth is its ideality; its destiny is to take itself back into the divine idea. This need not be viewed as a Gnostic denigration of the material world but as an articulation of a classical Christian theme that emphasizes the finitude, contingency, and dependence of everything created. The world in its difference contributes something essential to God, and that difference cannot be obliterated in the consummation of all things. Thus God not only releases the world but also holds on to it, preserves it; this is the work of divine wisdom.

The fundamental question is whether the Hegelian holism of spirit is still persuasive today. Hegel offers a vision of God as the encompassing, inexhaustible sphere of all that is—intellectual and material, eternal and temporal, infinite and finite. Nothing is outside of God, not even the most trivial or despicable. God encompasses what is not-God within God. All that comes about in the world, great good and terrible evil, is preserved in the divine life, even if only as negated and overcome. Spirit is the fluid that holds the matrix together and prevents it from becoming totalizing by continually generating and affirming difference. The prevailing view of postmodernity is that holism obscures the real differences, the power struggles, the conflicts and violence that drive the world as we know it.[37] The prevailing view of religious orthodoxy (as in

---

[37] This is the view of Jacques Derrida, Michel Foucault, and other postmodern philosophers. See Derrida's essays in, for example, *Margins of Philosophy*, trans. Alan Bass (Chicago: University of Chicago Press, 1982); *The Gift of Death*, trans. David Wills (Chicago: University of Chicago Press, 1995); and *Acts of Religion*, ed. Gil Anidjar (New York and London: Routledge, 2002). Foucault offers trenchant critiques of power and violence but no means of overcoming them; see *The Foucault Reader*, ed. Paul Rabinow (New York: Pantheon Books, 1984). Both thinkers reject a sociopolitical as well as a religious holism and thus find no possibility of achieving justice through a social process or redemption through a religious process. The only hope, if any, lies beyond politics and religion in an apocalyptic negation/gift.

the case of Desmond) is that holism compromises the transcendence and omnipotence of God. For the sake of God or for the sake
of the world, holism is rejected. But a holism of the spirit honours
the inexhaustible generative power of God as well as the irreducible wealth of the world. Equally important, it keeps God and the
world connected: God does not become an isolated supreme being
forever contemplating godself; and the world does not drift into its
own futility and decay. God actualizes godself in and through the
world, and the world's destiny is one of consummation rather than
destruction. The wholeness is fractured, yet it holds together.
Because it is a living process, it requires the telling of a story.

## LANGUAGE AND HISTORY: NARRATIVE

The relations expressed by language, namely grammatical and
logical, are synchronic in the sense that the meanings expressed
by the relations do not depend on a chronological unfolding. The
relations expressed by history as a sequence of events and actions
are diachronic: they run through time. Hegel struggles with the
tension between language and history, synchronicity and diachronicity, and finds a resolution in what is now commonly called
narrative. He does not employ the category of narrative in the
strict sense, but what he names *Geschichte*, narrated and interpreted history, approximates it.

In the philosophy of religion lectures the discussion of language
occurs principally as an analysis of forms of the knowledge of God:
immediate knowledge, feeling, representation, thought. We have
seen that for Hegel representation (*Vorstellung*) is not merely an
epistemological but an ontological category, pointing to a divine
action, God's setting-forth of godself in the spatiotemporal world.
God is both the subject and the object of representation. Epi-
stemologically speaking, representation has two forms, sensible
and nonsensible. Sensible representation expresses its contents in
the form of historical narratives, either mythical or factual. In
narrative, elements exist alongside each other as independent

Anselm Kyonsuk Min's discussion of Levinas, Derrida, and postmodernism
is helpful in this regard; see his *The Solidarity of Others in a Divided World:
A Postmodern Theology after Postmodernism* (New York: T&T Clark International,
2004).

entities, linked by conjunctions. Representation is not yet able to hold its disparate elements together in the form of a conceptual grasp of relations. The latter is the task of thought (*Denken*), which is the highest form of language in its ideality and synchronicity. Nonetheless, it draws upon materials furnished by representation, and if it cuts itself off from them it loses contact with life experience and takes on the character of formal logic or mathematics. Hegel might have been more explicit about this dependence of thought on representation. But it is clear that an aspect of narrative is always present in thought, especially in religious thought.

Hegel's suspicion of historicism and its preoccupation with what has happened in the past (*Historie*) does not lead him to deny that in a more fundamental sense God as absolute spirit is *geschichtlich*, an eternal process of self-distinguishing and self-reintegrating. He speaks commonly of 'the divine history' (*die göttliche Geschichte*) or 'the eternal history, the eternal movement, which God himself is' (3:187, 327). This eternal history is an eternal movement, that is, it is a process that entails motion, change, becoming. 'Becoming' (*Werden*) is the first of the synthetic categories of the logic (uniting being and nothing), and it is incorporated in the final categories, 'idea' (uniting concept and objectivity) and 'spirit' (uniting idea and nature). Becoming requires temporality, movement through time, and the question is how time gets introduced into the logic and the immanent divine life. Hegel's eternity is not antihistorical as it was for the whole of classical philosophy and theology. Rather he conceives of eternity as, to use Heidegger's expression, 'a more primordial and infinite temporality'.[38] In eternity the modes of time do not stand out from each other in an irreversible succession; rather they coinhere and complete each other without simply collapsing into sameness or identity. The eternal presence of God comprises a tensive interplay of past and future. God is eternally becoming what God already is, actualizing in reality the pure ideality of the divine life. In the process God incorporates the novelty that occurs in nature and history, where the modes of time do stand out from each other and where chronological succession occurs. In the divine history the synchronic and the diachronic fuse in a way that human experience only faintly glimpses.

---

[38] Martin Heidegger, *Being and Time*, trans. Joan Stambaugh (Albany: State University of New York Press, 1996), 416 n. 13.

A true narrative expresses ideal, logical, or spiritual relations in terms of a story, a dynamic process, a movement through time. The story aspect is not simply extrinsic but tells something about the ideal relations themselves, which are not static but moving and alive (everything rational is a syllogism). I have followed Cyril O'Regan[39] in suggesting that Hegel offers a speculative redescription of the Christian metanarrative, which is essentially the narrative of the triune God unfolding. The inclusive Trinity encompasses God and the world together, overcoming classical dualism; and it introduces narrativity into the divine life, overcoming static conceptions of eternity. But Hegel's 'speculative rewriting' occurs at a conceptual, not simply a representational level, and this means that narrative must be demythologized in the sense that sequential, spatially-temporally diffused metaphors and symbols must be thought through to a grasp of the primal logical structure that is expressing itself in them, that of universality–particularity–individuality or identity–difference–mediation—the syllogism that replicates itself throughout reality. Whether all stories exhibit a common formal depth structure is of course one of the contested issues of postmodernity. Clearly for Hegel they do: narrative space is a discursive projection of logical space, but at the same time logical space is constituted by a refiguration of narrative space. Narrative is logicized, and logic is narratized.

O'Regan identifies certain 'denarratizing operators' that enable Hegel to remove temporal sequence, contingency, and voluntarism from divine activity, and to break the narrative order of the master syllogism such that each of the elements (universal, particular, individual; or logical idea, nature, and spirit) assumes in turn the mediating role. The triple syllogism means that the metanarrative comprises a genuine interplay of God, nature, and humanity, but with priority given to God, the absolute idea, who remains the ultimate subject of becoming. Thus the ontotheological narrative perdures conceptually, and it does so in a way that transcends popular religious imagination and overcomes rationalism/atheism. Hostile demythologizations are subverted. Narrative perdures in that logico-conceptual space is a kind of contracted narrative (the

---

[39] See *The Heterodox Hegel*, esp. chap. 7. The following paragraphs summarize and reflect on O'Regan's interpretation. On Hegel and narrative, see also Paul Ricoeur, *Time and Narrative*, trans. Kathleen Blamey and David Pellauer (Chicago: University of Chicago Press, 1984–8), esp. vol. 3, chap. 9, 'Should We Renounce Hegel?'

dialectic of universal, particular, and individual tells a story), while narrative is an expanded syllogism (basic logical patterns replicate themselves in life). What underlies Hegel's view is a key assumption: that logic and life, language and history, synchronicity and diachronicity, are connected, that they share a common depth rationality. O'Regan suggests that the Indo-European linguistic embeddedness of narrative and knowledge is affirmed by Hegel over against purely formal and transcendental interpretations of knowledge. His revisionist view of knowledge has more in common with the mystical and esoteric traditions than with rationalism and empiricism from Descartes to Kant.

Postmodernity assumes the loss of any legitimate metanarrative with its accompanying theodicy, and thus for it reality has no intelligibility. Hegel reconstructs the narrative by a friendly demythologization that overcomes the uncritical dogmatism of tradition. From his point of view postmodernity would have to be seen as indulging its own hypercritical dogmatism. Hegel's reconstruction includes the terror of tragedy along with the triumph of redemption and meaning. Can tragedy and redemption be held together in a nondogmatic, narratively open fashion?

## TRAGEDY AND REDEMPTION: CHRIST

The Hegelian worldview is in part a tragic one. Robert Williams argues that Hegel prefers tragedy to the shallow optimism of the Enlightenment and to the divine comedy of classical Christianity.[40] If there is a divine comedy, it is a tragicomedy, a story of the crucified God who undergoes the suffering and conflicts that render historical existence tragic. To affirm tragic suffering in God is a deep revision of classical metaphysics. We have seen Hegel's critique of panlogism: the divine play of love with itself is insipid if the seriousness, anguish, patience, and labour of the negative are lacking in it. Negation and conflict are the condition of having a world of finite and free forces. Death haunts the cosmos, and Hegel identifies divine love not so much with reconciliation as with death. Yet through the infinite anguish of death comes the infinite love of reconciliation.

---

[40] Williams, *Recognition*, 228, cf. 231–40.

Human being is an internally unresolved contradiction caught between the pull of nature and the pull of spirit. Nature is not evil as such but becomes a seat of evil when humans choose to remain in the natural state and refuse to realize their spiritual capacities. Evil requires the ability to decide: humans *become* good or evil as they rise out of nature. Instead of an original state of innocence, Hegel finds a tragic condition: the condition for the possibility of good includes the possibility of evil. To rise out of nature and realize their spiritual potential, humans must undergo a cleavage or separation that produces anxiety, estrangement, efforts at self-securing. Knowledge both makes and wounds a human being; cognition posits the antithesis in which evil is found. Estrangement and reconciliation have the same source: consciousness, cognition, cleavage.

Not only personal history but also social and religious history are tragic. As Hegel remarks in the *Phenomenology of Spirit*, the history of religion yields the pretentious claim of the Romans that 'the self is absolute being'. The reduction of everything to subjectivity and self-satisfaction is seen in signs of modern decadence: profanization, privatization, loss of common life, loss of knowledge of God, finitude turned in upon itself. Our age is very much like that of the Romans. In this respect Hegel is looking backward, not forward. He does not anticipate the terrifying forms of dehumanization that have appeared in late modernity. The problem is not simply one of privatization and self-centeredness but of a capacity for violence and destructiveness that is not fully explained by the Hegelian anthropology. Evil assumes a dynamism that outstrips the capacity of reason; absurdity and chaos point to a dimension of the irrational and uncontrollable.

Are we still able to affirm with Hegel that 'spirit has the power to undo evil' (3:336)? Spirit is a power greater than evil, greater even than death. For an age such as ours that venerates death as the greatest power, this seems to be a wildly optimistic claim. But perhaps our tendency to totalize death simply feeds a comfortable cynicism and fails to recognize the actual complexity of things. If we look more closely, we see that evil can in fact be undone, that its effects can be reversed although the deeds themselves remain as part of an inexpungeable legacy. By remembering the evil and honouring its victims, we gain a certain transcendence over it and find resources to begin anew, to rebuild, to experience a new birth. Spirit is the power of rebirth, the inexhaustible movement by which opposing forces are reconciled and new connections established. It is inexhaustible because it is the power of God. Such conviction is at the heart of religious faith, and faith itself is the work of God's Spirit in and with the human spirit.

Reconciliation and redemption are the central themes of religion. Reconciliation overcomes a prior estrangement; redemption liberates from an attachment to idols and other forms of bondage. They are the bringing forth in actuality of the unity of God and humanity that is eternally present in the divine life. For this to be accomplished, actual practices of freedom and liberation must occur in history, and God must be involved in the practices because the power of reconciliation is God's power, not worldly power. Reconciliation in the form of freedom becomes the great work of God in history.[41]

God's involvement in history focuses on the figure of Christ for the Christian religion. Hegel's theology of spirit does not bypass christology but provides a different interpretative perspective on it. The themes of reconciliation and incarnation are interchangeable because incarnation means the actualized unity of divine and human nature. This unity, which is the ground of reconciliation, must appear, must come forth from the godhead into the anguish of history. 'Spirit is the absolute power to endure this anguish' (3:215). There is a divine necessity to appear and a human necessity for a concrete sensible presence of divinity. As we have seen, Hegel advances arguments for the appearance or incarnation of divine–human unity in (a) human individuality as

---

[41] A student of mine who is engaged in a comparative study of Hegel and Daoism suggests two contrasting ways by which freedom can be understood: (1) finding one's true identity in the divine identity/being, which embraces, preserves, transforms, and reconciles all differences or particular identities within its all-embracing intersubjective identity—with the soteriological consequence of being released/ liberated from one's attachment to or absolutizing of particular identities; or (2) being utterly claimed by the divine difference/nothing, which gives birth to and takes away particular identities (just as waves produce and wash away foam on the surface of the sea) without a divine self-return in and through them—yet with a similar soteriological consequence of being released/liberated from one's idolatrous attachments. The first is Hegel's understanding of freedom, while examples of the second would be the Buddhist idea of co-dependent origination or the perspectivalist idea of free self-creation in the play of difference that one finds in Nietzsche or the Daoist mystic Zhuangzi. Levinas is closer to the second type than the first. The value of this example is that it situates and relativizes Hegel's theology of freedom; but it is intriguing that the soteriological consequences of the two models are similar. My thanks to Hyo-Dong Lee for these thoughts.

such, (b) a single human being, (c) a particular human being, who is Jesus of Nazareth. However we assess the validity of these arguments, they attest to the power of the principle of positivity in Hegel's thought. The universal is an abstraction apart from its concrete instantiations, and its normative instantiation must be singular.

In this respect Hegel's christology is quite orthodox. But the construal of incarnation as appearance, as manifestation or revelation, is not so orthodox. Having a literal divine nature is not what makes Jesus to be the Christ but his function as revealer of divinity and mediator of reconciliation; he is the one filled by the power of the Spirit to manifest love and endure anguish. Thus Hegel's focus is on the teaching and the death of Christ. The teaching is not simply of moral maxims. Rather, in virtue of its centring on radical love and its revolutionary reversal of established orders, it is a proof of the truth of the divine idea that courses through his life. This is God's speaking, doing, working in a human being— not as an extrinsic miracle but as an inner empowerment. This teacher is God as teacher, and as such he becomes the teacher and saviour of humanity. Only faith can see that *God* is present in Christ, but the story of Christ, his sayings and deeds, confirm what faith sees.

The final deed of Christ is his death by crucifixion, which from a human perspective is the shameful death of a criminal but from a religious or faith perspective is the death of God. God is involved in this; it is more than a human tragedy: it is a divine tragedy, a divine divestment, a release of divinity into the anguish and otherness of history. But because God as spirit has the power to endure this anguish, a reversal and transition occur. God suffers death yet overcomes death, brings it into the divine life as a sublated moment. Resurrection is really a metaphor of the whole divine process of undergoing death and overcoming it, of bringing infinite love out of infinite anguish. On Hegel's interpretation it is not a physical miracle but a raising up, an exaltation, a return to God of not only individual believers but the community of faith. Resurrection is really a communal event more than it is an individual event. It extends the divine divestment, the losing of self for the sake of other, into the broad sweep of history. The shape of the cross becomes the pattern of intersubjectivity and social existence.

### SELF AND OTHER: COMMUNITY

Hegel offers a very rich description of the community of the Spirit, which embodies the infinite love that arises from infinite anguish. A new kind of human bond or intersubjectivity is created in which distinctions based on power, position, sex, and wealth are renounced, in which self-possession is given up in favour of compassion, of suffering with and on behalf of others. Possessions are shared in a relationship more radical than friendship; marriage is the closest analogy from ordinary life. The bond of union derives from no human power but from the presence of the Spirit and its absolving love: it is in the Spirit that we are both one and many. Sacramental partaking or communion symbolizes this mystical union because what the sacrament enacts, the sacrificial death of Christ, gives the pattern of communal intersubjectivity—namely, divestment of self and recognition, forgiveness, and releasement of the other.[42]

Is the Levinasian self truly released into otherness?[43] While the interiority of the self is constituted for Levinas by its response to the demand of an infinitely exterior other, what the other does is to confront and challenge the self but not enter into its self-constitution. The latter is what happens for Hegel through an ecstatic intersubjectivity: self-othering is intrinsic to subjectivity-in-process. The basis for self-denial is not an irruptive other but rather the self's discovery that by way of its participation in the infinite its own self is always more than it is; the self *is* the other as such. The way to genuine subjectivity occurs as a journey in and with the other in which interiority and intuition are redefined as an intersubjective, interlocutive self–other relation.

The difference between the two thinkers is traceable to a theological level: Levinas's God does not become incarnate, does not die on a cross, does not undergo diremption into otherness. Such an idea would compromise the utter transcendence of God. Nor for Levinas do humans find themselves by losing themselves, nor does community come into being through mutual acts of recognition and self-diremption. For him everything re-

---

[42] See Williams, *Recognition*, chaps. 7, 9.

[43] These thoughts are based on a conversation with Nathan Reede Kerr, a doctoral student at Vanderbilt University.

mains focused on the asymmetry and absolute demand of the ethical relationship, beyond which sociality has a derivative status; whereas for Hegel the creation of a new sociality (in which otherness precisely is not reduced to the same) is the matter of central interest.

The self-giving that forms the intersubjectivity of the community is extended when the community itself gives up its inward spirituality for the sake of the redemption of the world. Hegel traces a movement from heart to church to ethical life, a movement that points to freedom as the telos of world history. The freedom of the *basileia* community passes into social and political freedom. Whether the religious community passes away in the process is one of the puzzles we have considered. Hegel hardly places much confidence in the secular institutions of his time, and he is aware of a pervasive cultural decadence. While noting the incompatibility of slavery with Christianity, he does not (in these lectures) attend to other social injustices[44] and he seems more preoccupied with the fate of the community of philosophy than with that of the community of faith or with the affairs of the world. For him religion, like art, is mostly a thing of the past; and he does not glimpse the possibility of a religious renewal that might come through shared ethical struggles on the part of diverse religious traditions.

---

[44] The extent to which Hegel's philosophical theology is and is not socially transformative is discussed by Andrew Shanks in *Hegel's Political Theology* (Cambridge: Cambridge University Press, 1991); and *God and Modernity: A New and Better Way to Do Theology* (London and New York: Routledge, 2000). In a recent article Shanks attributes the hegemonic impulse in Hegel's philosophy that I have noted above (see Chap. 9, n. 29) to his attempt to create through philosophical education an 'elite community of scholars and civil servants' who would build a new social order and resist all authoritarian claims of truth. The *Lectures on the Philosophy of Religion*, and the depiction of Christianity as the 'consummate religion', he suggests, are part of that agenda, whereas Hegel's radical vision of a constant *search* for transformative truth is more evident in the *Phenomenology of Spirit*. Citing Emil Fackenheim's remark that today Hegel would not be a Hegelian (see above, Chap. 10, n. 51), and believing that the cutting edge of freedom is no longer to be found in the academic and political worlds but in various movements of contemporary dissident civil society, Shanks writes: 'If Hegel were alive today I have no doubt that he would therefore be a keen theological advocate of the underlying common ethos uniting the more thoughtful adherents of such movements: greens, feminists, human rights and anti-racist campaigners, peace movement activists and so forth.' 'Hegel and the Meaning of the Present Moment', *Bulletin of the Hegel Society of Great Britain* 45/46 (2002), 25–35 (quotation from 32). On Shanks, see also above, Chap. 10, n. 48.

## UNITY AND DIVERSITY: PLURALISM

'The language of pluralism', writes Diana Eck, 'is the language not just of difference but of engagement, involvement, and participation. It is the language of traffic, exchange, dialogue, and debate. It is the language of the symphony orchestra and the jazz ensemble.'[45] Is this kind of pluralism encountered in Hegel's *Lectures on the Philosophy of Religion*? The answer is both yes and no: the symphony version perhaps (if Hegel is indeed the Beethoven of philosophy), but not the jazz version. Discord is present, but it does not overwhelm the fundamental harmonies. Diversity is certainly engaged, debated, even celebrated, but only to a degree. In the final analysis, there is one God, one Christ, one Spirit, one consummate religion, one concept of religion. The generative possibilities of a trinitarian theology of the Spirit are hinted at but not explored.

Yet, the geography of religions that Hegel actually offers in the second part of the lectures points in the direction of pluralism. His philosophical history of religion grasps not the sequence of unfolding, as he intended, but the diversity of determinate forms in which the concept of religion appears, and thus it gives a kind of logical deduction of the necessity of religious pluralism. Just because spirit comes to itself only through movement and distinction, there must be a diversity of historical religions, which emerge independently and do not form a unitary developmental pattern. Yet it can be affirmed that what is common to the religions is that spirit is indeed coming to itself in them. While the consummation of spirit entails for Hegel a teleological process, this process need not be understood as a hierarchical one culminating in a single perfect exemplification. Hegel embraced the latter view, arguably against the intuition of his own logic; thus he gave expression to European cultural hegemony and offered a concession to Christian orthodoxy. Is the Hegelian absolute to be construed as monolithic or as pluralistic? The texts can be read in different ways. On my reading, if God interacts with the world, God must take on the diversity of the world, just as the world takes on the oneness of

---

[45] Diana L. Eck, *A New Religious America* (San Francisco: HarperSanFrancisco, 2001), 69.

God—a oneness that is not sameness but a perpetual play of many, unified in love. The Hegelian Spirit is one-in-many and many-in-one. Both oneness and manyness are to be affirmed. But where does the emphasis properly fall—for Hegel and for ourselves?

While Hegel's philosophy of religion fits the inclusivist model of interreligious dialogue, which holds that all religions find their fulfilment in the Christian religion, its depth logic is closer to pluralism. Hegel's dialectical way of thinking prevents closure on any cultural synthesis and keeps driving into the inexhaustible openness of the absolute. God disperses godself into the world as absolving spirit and is known in the mode of dispersal rather than finality. While a unification of religions in the Spirit may be an eschatological possibility, in history God's Spirit is always concrete. Hegel attends doggedly to this concreteness. A Hegelianism at the beginning of the twenty-first century readily acknowledges that the divine Spirit does not reach its goal in history, that Christianity belongs among other determinate religions on the path to consummation, and that the religion of freedom is a work in progress shaped by a diversity of cultural trajectories.

Today, I believe, Hegel would avow a theology of religious pluralism, just as he would avow a theology of community and freedom, a theology of Christ the crucified teacher of humanity, a theology of narrativity, a theology of the fractured/mended wholeness of God and world, and a theology of the being of God as absolute/absolving spirit. For a critically liberal revisioning of theology, these are excellent resources. Yet others are needed such as a theology of nature and a theology of social transformation. The Hegelian legacy contributes to the latter as well, but in works[46]

[46] See *Hegel's Philosophy of Nature*, Part Two of the *Encyclopedia of the Philosophical Sciences*, trans. A. V. Miller (Oxford: Clarendon Press, 1970); and *Elements of the Philosophy of Right*, ed. Allen W. Wood, trans. H. B. Nisbet (Cambridge: Cambridge University Press, 1991). For a recent study of the former, see Stephen Houlgate (ed.), *Hegel and the Philosophy of Nature* (Albany: State University of New York Press, 1998); and of the latter, Robert R. Williams, *Hegel's Ethics of Recognition* (Berkeley and Los Angeles: University of California Press, 1997). Several recent editions of Hegel's lectures on these topics have been published (see the Bibliography). Determining the significance of these materials for theology will require further interpretative efforts.

that are not an object of the present study. Resources such as these help to provide theology with an alternative to philosophical agnosticism and religious fundamentalism—the reigning dogmatisms of our time.[47]

[47] A reader for the Press points out that the issues discussed in this chapter concern not only a proper interpretation of Hegel's philosophy of religion but also an evaluation of its philosophical and theological implications. So, for example, the reader asks: Does Hegel's way of understanding the reconciliation of humanity and divinity tend to evolve into a postreligious humanism for which God is no longer a useful concept and philosophy is of more importance than religion? Do religious communities continue to play a significant role in Hegel's social vision or are they displaced and absorbed by the secular state? Would Hegel be able to accommodate a final, unsurpassable plurality of positions that resist sublation in a more comprehensive standpoint? Can Hegel's view of the rationality of the actual take account of radical, irrational evil? Are attempts at modifying or revising Hegel in terms of his own criteria for truth persuasive? These are questions worth pondering. I have discussed them in one form or another in the preceding pages, but I do not claim to have final answers. The tensions of modernity and postmodernity with which we continue to struggle run through Hegel's thought and are illuminated by it even as he attempts to overcome them. This is why he continues to be such an important thinker and why in respect to his philosophy of religion there will continue to be a conflict of interpretations.

# BIBLIOGRAPHY

## COLLECTED AND OTHER WORKS OF HEGEL

*Werke. Vollständige Ausgabe*, edited by an Association of Friends, 18 vols. (Berlin: Verlag von Duncker und Humblot, 1832 ff.). Some volumes issued in second editions. Reprinted with minor revisions and additions as *Jubiläumsausgabe*, edited by Hermann Glockner (Stuttgart: Fr. Frommanns Verlag, 1927–30); and as *Theorie Werkausgabe*, edited by Eva Moldenhauer and Karl Markus Michel (Frankfurt am Main: Suhrkamp Verlag, 1969). The *Vorlesungen über die Philosophie der Religion* appeared as vols. 11–12 of this edition, edited by Philipp Marheineke (1st edn., 1832; 2nd edn., revised by Bruno Bauer, 1840).

*Gesammelte Werke*, edited by the Academy of Sciences of North Rhineland-Westphalia in association with the Deutsche Forschungsgemeinschaft, 32 vols. projected (Hamburg: Felix Meiner Verlag, 1968 ff.). The historical-critical edition.

Vol. 1. *Frühe Schriften, Teil 1*, edited by Friedhelm Nicolin and Gisela Schüler (1989).

Vol. 2. *Frühe Schriften, Teil 2*, edited by Friedhelm Nicolin and Ingo Rill (forthcoming).

Vol. 3. *Frühe Exzerpte (1785–1800)*, edited by Friedhelm Nicolin and Gisela Schüler (1991).

Vol. 4. *Jenaer Kritische Schriften*, edited by Hartmut Buchner and Otto Pöggeler (1968).

Vol. 5. *Schriften und Entwürfe (1799–1808)*, edited by Kurt-Rainer Meist and Manfred Baum (1998).

Vol. 6. *Jenaer Systementwürfe I*, edited by Klaus Düsing and Heinz Kimmerle (1975).

Vol. 7. *Jenaer Systementwürfe II*, edited by Rolf Peter Horstmann and Johann Heinrich Trede (1971).

Vol. 8. *Jenaer Systementwürfe III*, edited by Rolf Peter Horstmann and Johann Heinrich Trede (1976).

Vol. 9. *Phänomenologie des Geistes*, edited by Wolfgang Bonsiepen and Reinhard Heede (1980).

Vol. 10. *Nürnberger Gymnasialkurse und Gymnasialreden (1808–1816)* (forthcoming).

Vol. 11. *Wissenschaft der Logik, Band 1: Die objektive Logik (1812/13)*, edited by Friedrich Hogemann and Walter Jaeschke (1978).

286        *Bibliography*

Vol. 12. *Wissenschaft der Logik, Band 2: Die subjektive Logik (1816)*, edited by Friedrich Hogemann and Walter Jaeschke (1981).

Vol. 13. *Enzyklopädie der philosophischen Wissenschaften im Grundrisse (1817)*, edited by Wolfgang Bonsiepen and Klaus Grotsch (2000).

Vol. 14. *Grundlinien der Philosophie des Rechts*, edited by Elisabeth Weisser-Lohmann (forthcoming).

Vol. 15. *Schriften und Entwürfe I (1817–1825)*, edited by Friedrich Hogemann and Christoph Jamme (1990).

Vol. 16. *Schriften und Entwürfe II (1826–1831)*, edited by Friedrich Hogemann and Christoph Jamme (2001).

Vol. 17. *Vorlesungsmanuskripte I (1816–1831)*, edited by Walter Jaeschke (1987).

Vol. 18. *Vorlesungsmanuskripte II (1816–1831)*, edited by Walter Jaeschke (1995).

Vol. 19. *Enzyklopädie der philosophischen Wissenschaften im Grundrisse (1827)*, edited by Wolfgang Bonsiepen and Hans-Christian Lucas (1989).

Vol. 20. *Enzyklopädie der philosophischen Wissenschaften im Grundrisse (1830)*, edited by Wolfgang Bonsiepen and Hans-Christian Lucas (1992).

Vol. 21. *Wissenschaft der Logik, Band 1: Die Lehre vom Sein (1832)*, edited by Friedrich Hogemann and Walter Jaeschke (1984).

Vol. 22. *Exzerpte (1816–1831)* (forthcoming).

The remaining volumes of the *Gesammelte Werke* (vols. 23–32) will contain the auditors' transcriptions (*Nachschriften*) of Hegel's lectures.

*Vorlesungen: Ausgewählte Nachschriften und Manuskripte*, edited by the staff of the Hegel Archives, 16 vols. to date (Hamburg: Felix Meiner Verlag, 1983 ff.). Selected lecture transcriptions and manuscripts edited in accord with the critical edition.

Vol. 1. *Vorlesungen über Naturrecht und Staatswissenschaft* (1817–18), transcribed by Peter Wannenmann, edited by the staff of the Hegel Archives with an introduction by Otto Pöggeler (1983).

Vol. 2. *Vorlesungen über die Philosophie der Kunst* (1823), transcribed by H. G. Hotho, edited by Annemarie Gethmann-Siefert (1998).

Vols. 3–5. *Vorlesungen über die Philosophie der Religion* (1821–31), lecture manuscript and various transcriptions, edited by Walter Jaeschke; part 1: *Der Begriff der Religion* (1983); part 2: *Die bestimmte Religion* (1985); part 3: *Die vollendete Religion* (1984).

Vols. 6–9. *Vorlesungen über die Geschichte der Philosophie* (1825–6), various transcriptions and manuscript fragments, edited by Pierre Garniron and Walter Jaeschke; part 1: *Einleitung in die Geschichte der Philosophie, Orientalische Philosophie* (1994); part 2: *Griechische*

*Philosophie I: Thales biz Kyniker* (1989); part 3: *Griechische Philosophie II: Plato bis Proklos* (1996); part 4: *Philosophie des Mittelalters und der neueren Zeit* (1986).

Vol. 10. *Vorlesungen über die Logik* (1831), transcribed by Karl Hegel, edited by Hans-Christian Lucas and Udo Rameil (2001).

Vol. 11. *Vorlesungen über Logik und Metaphysik* (1817), transcribed by Franz Anton Good, edited by Karen Gloy (1992).

Vol. 12. *Vorlesungen über die Philosophie der Weltgeschichte* (1822–3), transcribed by K. G. J. von Griesheim, H. G. Hotho, and F. C. H. von Kehler, edited by Karl Brehmer, Karl-Heinz Ilting, and Hoo Nam Seelmann (1996).

Vol. 13. *Vorlesungen über die Philosophie des Geistes* (1827–8), transcribed by Johann Erdmann and Ferdinand Walter, edited by Franz Hespe and Burkhard Tuschling (1994).

Vol. 14. *Vorlesungen über die Philosophie des Rechts* (1819–20), transcribed by Johann Rudolf Ringier, edited by Emil Angehrn, Martin Bondeli, and Hoo Nam Seelmann (2000).

Vol. 15. *Vorlesungen über philosophische Enzyklopädie* (1812–13), transcribed by J. F. H. Abegg and C. S. Meinel, edited by Udo Rameil (2002).

Vol. 16. *Vorlesungen über die Philosophie der Natur* (1819–20), transcribed by Johann Rudolf Ringier, edited by Martin Bondeli and Hoo Nam Seelmann (2002).

Other recently published lectures not in this series:

*Philosophie des Rechts. Die Vorlesung von 1819/20 in einer Nachschrift*, edited by Dieter Henrich (Frankfurt: Suhrkamp Verlag, 1983).

*Vorlesungen über Naturphilosophie: Berlin 1821/22*, transcribed by Boris von Uexküll, edited by Gilles Marmasse and Thomas Posch (Frankfurt and New York: Peter Lang, 2002).

*Vorlesungen über Naturphilosophie: Berlin 1823/24*, transcribed by K. G. J. von Griesheim, edited by Gilles Marmasse (Frankfurt and New York: Peter Lang, 2000).

The following is an important source for Hegel's early writings:

Nohl, Herman (ed.), *Hegels theologische Jugendschriften* (Tübingen: J. C. B. Mohr, 1907).

The first attempt at a critical edition of the *Vorlesungen über die Philosophie der Religion* was published by Georg Lasson, 4 vols. (Leipzig: Verlag von Felix Meiner, 1925–9).

Hegel's major works are individually available in the *Philosophische Bibliothek* series, published by Felix Meiner Verlag. These volumes are being revised in accord with the critical edition and are the most accessible form for the German texts.

## MAJOR WORKS BY HEGEL IN TRANSLATION

*The Difference between Fichte's and Schelling's System of Philosophy*, translated by H. S. Harris and Walter Cerf (Albany, NY: State University of New York Press, 1977).

*Early Theological Writings*, translated by T. M. Knox, with an introduction by Richard Kroner (Chicago: University of Chicago Press, 1948; reprint: Philadelphia: University of Pennsylvania Press, 1971).

*Elements of the Philosophy of Right*, edited by Allen W. Wood, translated by H. B. Nisbet (Cambridge: Cambridge University Press, 1991).

*Encyclopedia of the Philosophical Sciences*, part 1: *Hegel's Logic*; part 2: *Hegel's Philosophy of Nature*; part 3: *Hegel's Philosophy of Mind*; translated by William Wallace and A. V. Miller, 3 vols. (Oxford: Clarendon Press, 1892 (revised 1975), 1970, 1971).

*The Encyclopedia Logic*, translated by T. F. Geraets, W. A. Suchting, and H. S. Harris (Indianapolis: Hackett, 1991).

*Faith and Knowledge*, translated by Walter Cerf and H. S. Harris (Albany, NY: State University of New York Press, 1977).

*G. W. F. Hegel: Theologian of the Spirit*, edited by Peter C. Hodgson (Minneapolis: Fortress Press; Edinburgh: T&T Clark, 1997).

*The Hegel Reader*, edited by Stephen Houlgate (Oxford: Blackwell, 1998).

*Hegel's Political Writings*, translated by T. M. Knox, with an introductory essay by Z. A. Pelczynski (Oxford: Clarendon Press, 1964).

*The Jena System, 1804–5: Logic and Metaphysics*, translated by John W. Burbidge and George di Giovanni (Kingston, Ont., and Montreal: McGill-Queen's University Press, 1986).

*Lectures on Aesthetics*, translated by T. M. Knox (Oxford: Clarendon Press, 1975).

*Lectures on the History of Philosophy*, translated by E. S. Haldane and Frances H. Simson, 3 vols. (London: Kegan Paul, Trench, Trübner & Co., 1892, 1894, 1896).

*Lectures on the History of Philosophy: The Lectures of 1825–1826*, vol. 3: *Medieval and Modern Philosophy*, edited by Robert F. Brown, translated by R. F. Brown and J. M. Stewart with the assistance of H. S. Harris (Berkeley and Los Angeles: University of California Press, 1990; Oxford: Oxford University Press, forthcoming). Vols. 1 and 2 forthcoming.

*Lectures on Natural Right and Political Science: The First Philosophy of Right (Heidelberg, 1817–18)*, translated by J. Michael Stewart and Peter C. Hodgson (Berkeley and Los Angeles: University of California Press, 1995; Oxford: Oxford University Press, forthcoming).

*Lectures on the Philosophy of History*, translated by John Sibree, with an introduction by C. J. Friedrich (New York: Dover Publications, 1956).

*Lectures on the Philosophy of Religion*, edited by Peter C. Hodgson, translated by R. F. Brown, P. C. Hodgson, and J. M. Stewart with the
assistance of H. S. Harris, 3 vols. (Berkeley and Los Angeles: University
of California Press, 1984, 1985, 1987; Oxford: Oxford University Press,
2006). One-volume edition: *The Lectures of 1827* (California, 1988;
Oxford, 2005).
*Lectures on the Philosophy of World History. Introduction: Reason in His-
tory*, translated by H. B. Nisbet, with an introduction by Duncan
Forbes (Cambridge: Cambridge University Press, 1975).
*The Letters*, translated by Clark Butler and Christiane Seiler (Blooming-
ton, Ind.: Indiana University Press, 1984).
*Natural Law: The Scientific Ways of Treating Natural Law, Its Place in
Moral Philosophy, and Its Relation to the Positive Sciences of Law*,
translated by T. M. Knox, with an introduction by H. B. Acton (Phila-
delphia: University of Pennsylvania Press, 1975).
*Phenomenology of Mind*, translated by J. B. Baillie, 2nd edn. rev. (London:
George Allen & Unwin, 1949).
*Phenomenology of Spirit*, translated by A. V. Miller (Oxford: Clarendon
Press, 1977).
*Philosophy of Nature*, edited and translated by M. J. Petry, 3 vols. (Lon-
don: George Allen and Unwin, 1970). (*Encyclopedia*, Part 2.)
*Philosophy of Subjective Spirit*, edited and translated by M. J. Petry (Dor-
drecht and Boston: D. Reidel, 1978). (*Encyclopedia*, Part 3A.)
*Science of Logic*, translated by A. V. Miller (London: George Allen &
Unwin, 1969).
*System of Ethical Life (1802–3) and First Philosophy of Spirit (1803–4)*,
edited and translated by H. S. Harris and T. M. Knox (Albany, NY:
State University of New York Press, 1979).
*Three Essays, 1793–1795*, translated by Peter Fuss and John Dobbins
(Notre Dame, Ind.: University of Notre Dame Press, 1984).

## WORKS ON HEGEL'S RELIGIOUS THOUGHT

AVINERI, SHLOMO, 'The Fossil and the Phoenix: Hegel and Krochmal
on the Jewish Volksgeist', in Robert L. Perkins (ed.), *History and
System: Hegel's Philosophy of History* (Albany, NY: State University
of New York Press, 1984), 47–63.
BRITO, EMILIO, *La christologie de Hegel: Verbum Crucis* (Paris: Beau-
chesne, 1983).
BURBIDGE, JOHN W., *Hegel on Logic and Religion: The Reasonableness of
Christianity* (Albany, NY: State University of New York Press, 1992).
—— , 'The Word Became Flesh or the Orthodox Hegel', *Bulletin of the
Hegel Society of Great Britain* 45–6 (2002), 16–24.

CALTON, PATRICIA MARIE, *Hegel's Metaphysics of God: The Onto-logical Proof as the Development of a Trinitarian Divine Ontology* (Aldershot: Ashgate, 2001).

CHAPELLE, ALBERT, *Hegel et la religion*, 3 vols. (Paris: Éditions Universitaires, 1964–71).

CHRISTENSEN, DARRELL E. (ed.), *Hegel and the Philosophy of Religion* (The Hague: Martinus Nijhoff, 1970).

CRITES, STEPHEN, *In the Twilight of Christendom: Hegel vs. Kierke-gaard on Faith and History* (Chambersburg, Pa.: American Academy of Religion, 1972).

——, *Dialectic and Gospel in the Development of Hegel's Thinking* (University Park, Pa.: Pennsylvania State University Press, 1998).

DESMOND, WILLIAM, *Hegel's God: A Counterfeit Double?* (Aldershot: Ashgate, 2003).

DICKEY, LAURENCE, *Hegel: Religion, Economics, and the Politics of Spirit, 1770–1807* (Cambridge: Cambridge University Press, 1987).

FACKENHEIM, EMIL, *The Religious Dimension in Hegel's Thought* (Bloomington, Ind.: Indiana University Press, 1967).

——, 'Hegel and Judaism: A Flaw in the Hegelian Mediation', in J. J. O'Malley *et al.* (eds.), *The Legacy of Hegel: Proceedings of the Marquette Symposium* (The Hague: Martinus Nijhoff, 1973), 161–2.

GARAUDY, R., *Dieu est mort. Étude sur Hegel* (Paris: Presses Universitaires de France, 1962).

GASCOIGNE, ROBERT, *Religion, Rationality and Community: Sacred and Secular in the Thought of Hegel and His Critics* (The Hague: Martinus Nijhoff, 1985).

HEEDE, REINHARD, 'Die göttliche Idee und ihre Erscheinung in der Religion: Untersuchungen zum Verhältnis von Logik und *Religionsphilosophie* bei Hegel' (Dr.phil. dissertation, University of Münster, 1972).

HODGSON, PETER C., 'The Metamorphosis of Judaism in Hegel's Philosophy of Religion', *The Owl of Minerva* 19/1 (1987). Reprinted in Bernard Cullen (ed.), *Hegel Today* (Aldershot: Avebury, 1988), 88–101.

ILJIN, IWAN, *Die Philosophie Hegels als kontemplative Gotteslehre* (Bern: Francke, 1946).

JAESCHKE, WALTER, *Die Religionsphilosophie Hegels* (Darmstadt: Wissenschaftliche Buchgesellschaft, 1983).

——, 'Zur Logik der Bestimmten Religion', in Dieter Henrich and Rolf-Peter Horstmann (eds.), *Hegels Logik der Philosophie: Religion und Philosophie in der Theorie des absoluten Geistes* (Stuttgart: Klett-Cotta, 1984).

——, *Reason in Religion: The Foundations of Hegel's Philosophy of Religion*, translated by J. Michael Stewart and Peter C. Hodgson (Berkeley and Los Angeles: University of California Press, 1990).

JAMROS, DANIEL P., *The Human Shape of God: Religion in Hegel's Phenomenology of Spirit* (New York: Paragon House, 1994).

KOLB, DAVID (ed.), *New Perspectives on Hegel's Philosophy of Religion* (Albany, NY: State University of New York Press, 1992).

KÜNG, HANS, *The Incarnation of God: An Introduction to Hegel's Theological Thought as a Prolegomenon to a Future Christology*, translated by J. R. Stephenson (New York: Crossroad, 1987).

LAKELAND, PAUL, *The Politics of Salvation: The Hegelian Idea of the State* (Albany, NY: State University of New York Press, 1984).

LAUER, QUENTIN, *Hegel's Concept of God* (Albany, NY: State University of New York Press, 1982).

LEUZE, REINHARD, *Die außerchristlichen Religionen bei Hegel* (Göttingen: Vandenhoeck & Ruprecht, 1975).

LINK, CHRISTIAN, *Hegels Wort 'Gott ist tot'* (Zurich: Theologischer Verlag, 1974).

VON DER LUFT, ERIC (ed. and trans.), *Hegel, Hinrichs, and Schleiermacher on Feeling and Reason in Religion* (Lewiston, NY: Edwin Mellen Press, 1987).

MARSCH, WOLF-DIETER, *Gegenwart Christi in der Gesellschaft: Eine Studie zu Hegels Dialektik* (Munich: Christian Kaiser Verlag, 1965).

MERKLINGER, PHILIP M., *Philosophy, Theology, and Hegel's Berlin Philosophy of Religion* (Albany, NY: State University of New York Press, 1993).

OLSON, ALAN M., *Hegel and the Spirit: Philosophy as Pneumatology* (Princeton, NJ: Princeton University Press, 1992).

O'REGAN, CYRIL, *The Heterodox Hegel* (Albany, NY: State University of New York Press, 1994).

REARDON, BERNARD M. G., *Hegel's Philosophy of Religion* (London: Macmillan, 1977).

RINGLEBEN, JOACHIM, *Hegels Theorie der Sünde* (Berlin and New York: Walter de Gruyter, 1977).

SCHLITT, DALE M., *Hegel's Trinitarian Claim: A Critical Reflection* (Leiden: E. J. Brill, 1984).

——, *Divine Subjectivity: Understanding Hegel's Philosophy of Religion* (London and Toronto: Associated University Presses, 1990).

SCHMIDT, ERIK, *Hegels Lehre von Gott* (Gütersloh: Gütersloher Verlagshaus Gerd Mohn, 1952).

SHANKS, ANDREW, *Hegel's Political Theology* (Cambridge: Cambridge University Press, 1991).

——, 'Hegel and the Meaning of the Present Moment', *Bulletin of the Hegel Society of Great Britain* 45–6 (2002), 25–35.

SPLETT, JÖRG, *Die Trinitätslehre G. W. F. Hegels* (Munich: Alber, 1965).

## 292 Bibliography

THEUNISSEN, MICHAEL, *Hegels Lehre vom absoluten Geist als theolog-ish-politischer Traktat* (Berlin: Walter de Gruyter, 1970).

WAGNER, FALK, *Der Gedanke der Persönlichkeit Gottes bei Fichte und Hegel* (Gütersloh: Gütersloher Verlagshaus Gerd Mohn, 1971).

WALKER, JOHN (ed.), *Thought and Faith in the Philosophy of Hegel* (Dordrecht: Kluwer Academic, 1991).

WILLIAMS, ROBERT R., *Recognition: Fichte and Hegel on the Other* (Albany, NY: State University of New York Press, 1992).

WILLIAMSON, RAYMOND KEITH, *Introduction to Hegel's Philosophy of Religion* (Albany, NY: State University of New York Press, 1984).

YERKES, JAMES, *The Christology of Hegel*, 2nd edn. (Albany, NY: State University of New York Press, 1983).


OTHER WORKS CITED

ANSELM OF CANTERBURY, *The Major Works*, edited by Brian Davies and G. R. Evans (Oxford: Oxford University Press, 1988).

BAUR, FERDINAND CHRISTIAN, *Die christliche Gnosis, oder die christ-liche Religions-Philosophie in ihrer geschichtlichen Entwiklung* (Tübingen: C. F. Osiander, 1835).

——, *Das Christenthum und die christliche Kirche der drei ersten Jahrhun-derte* (Tübingen: L. F. Fues, 1852).

——, *Kirchengeschichte des neunzehnten Jahrhunderts*, edited by Eduard Zeller, 2nd edn. (Leipzig: Fues's Verlag, 1877).

CLOONEY, FRANCIS X., SJ, *Hindu Wisdom for All God's Children* (Maryknoll, NY: Orbis Books, 1998).

DAVIES, OLIVER, *Meister Eckhart: Selected Writings* (Harmondsworth: Penguin Books, 1994).

DERRIDA, JACQUES, *Margins of Philosophy*, translated by Alan Bass (Chicago: University of Chicago Press, 1982).

——, *The Gift of Death*, translated by David Wills (Chicago: University of Chicago Press, 1995).

——, *Acts of Religion*, edited with an introduction by Gil Anidjar (New York and London: Routledge, 2002).

ECK, DIANA L., *A New Religious America* (San Francisco: HarperSan-Francisco, 2001).

FEUERBACH, LUDWIG, *The Essence of Christianity*, translated by George Eliot, with an introduction by Karl Barth and a foreword by H. Richard Niebuhr (New York: Harper & Brothers, 1957).

——, *Principles of the Philosophy of the Future*, translated by Manfred Vogel (Indianapolis: Bobbs-Merrill, 1966).

FORMAN, ROBERT, *Meister Eckhart: The Mystic as Theologian* (Rock-port, Mass.: Element, 1991).

FOUCAULT, MICHEL, *The Foucault Reader*, edited by Paul Rabinow (New York: Pantheon Books, 1984).

JACOBI, FRIEDRICH HEINRICH, *Briefe über Spinoza, Werke* (Leipzig, 1812–25), vol. 4.

GADAMER, HANS-GEORG, *Truth and Method*, 2nd rev. edn., translated by Joel Weinsheimer and Donald G. Marshall (New York: Crossroad, 1989).

HABERMAS, JÜRGEN, *Knowledge and Human Interests*, translated by Jeremy Shapiro (Boston: Beacon Press, 1971).

HARRIS, H. S., *Hegel's Development*, vol. 1: *Toward the Sunlight, 1770–1801*; vol. 2: *Night Thoughts (Jena 1801–1806)* (Oxford: Clarendon Press, 1972, 1983).

HEIDEGGER, MARTIN, 'The Onto-theo-logical Constitution of Metaphysics', in *Identity and Difference*, translated by Joan Stambaugh (New York: Harper & Row, 1969), 42–74.

——, *Being and Time*, translated by Joan Stambaugh (Albany, NY: State University of New York Press, 1996).

HODGSON, PETER C., *God in History: Shapes of Freedom* (Nashville, Tenn.: Abingdon Press, 1989).

D'HONDT, JACQUES, *Hegel in His Time*, translated by John Burbidge (Peterborough, Ont.: Broadview Press, 1988).

HOULGATE, STEPHEN, *Freedom, Truth and History: An Introduction to Hegel's Philosophy* (London and New York: Routledge, 1991).

—— (ed.), *Hegel and the Philosophy of Nature* (Albany, NY: State University of New York Press, 1998).

JAESCHKE, WALTER, 'Hegel's Last Year in Berlin', in Lawrence S. Stepelevich and David Lamb (eds.), *Hegel's Philosophy of Action* (Atlantic Highlands, NJ: Humanities Press, 1983), 31–48.

JASPERS, KARL, *The Origin and Goal of History* (London: Routledge & Kegan Paul, 1953).

KANT, IMMANUEL, *Critique of Pure Reason*, translated by Norman Kemp Smith (London: Macmillan, 1929).

——, *Critique of Judgement*, translated by James Creed Meredith (Oxford: Clarendon Press, 1952).

——, *Critique of Practical Reason*, translated by Lewis White Beck (New York: Liberal Arts Press, 1956).

——, *Lectures on Philosophical Theology*, translated by Allen W. Wood and Gertrude M. Clark (Ithaca, NY: Cornell University Press, 1978).

KIERKEGAARD, SØREN, *Concluding Unscientific Postscript*, translated by David H. Swenson, with an introduction and notes by Walter Lowrie (Princeton, NJ: Princeton University Press, 1941).

——, *Philosophical Fragments*, edited and translated by Howard V. and Edna H. Hong (Princeton, NJ: Princeton University Press, 1985).

KIERKEGAARD, SØREN, *Practice in Christianity*, edited and translated by Howard V. and Edna H. Hong (Princeton, NJ: Princeton University Press, 1991).

KNITTER, PAUL F., *Introducing Theologies of Religions* (Maryknoll, NY: Orbis Books, 2002).

LEVINAS, EMMANUEL, *Totality and Infinity: An Essay on Exteriority*, translated by Alphonso Lingis (Pittsburgh: Duquesne University Press, 1969).

——, *God, Death, and Time*, translated by Bettina Bergo (Stanford, Calif.: Stanford University Press, 2000).

MIN, ANSELM KYONSUK, *The Solidarity of Others in a Divided World: A Postmodern Theology after Postmodernism* (New York: T&T Clark International, 2004).

MURE, G. R. G., *A Study of Hegel's Logic* (Oxford: Oxford University Press, 1950).

NEANDER, AUGUST, *Genetische Entwickelung der vornehmsten gnostischen Systeme* (Berlin, 1818).

O'REGAN, CYRIL, *Gnostic Return in Modernity* (Albany, NY: State University of New York Press, 2001).

PANIKKAR, RAIMUNDO, 'The Jordan, the Tiber, and the Ganges: Three Kairological Moments of Christic Self-Consciousness', in John Hick and Paul F. Knitter (eds.), *The Myth of Christian Uniqueness: Toward a Pluralistic Theology of Religions* (Maryknoll, NY: Orbis Books, 1987), 89–116.

PINKARD, TERRY, *Hegel: A Biography* (Cambridge: Cambridge University Press, 2000).

PSEUDO-DIONYSIUS AREOPAGITE, *The Divine Names and Mystical Theology*, translated by John D. Jones (Milwaukee: Marquette University Press, 1980).

RICOEUR, PAUL, *The Symbolism of Evil*, translated by Emerson Buchanan (Boston: Beacon Press, 1967).

——, *Time and Narrative*, translated by Kathleen Blamey and David Pellauer, 3 vols. (Chicago: University of Chicago Press, 1984–8).

ROSENKRANZ, KARL, *Georg Wilhelm Friedrich Hegels Leben* (Berlin, 1844; reprint, Darmstadt: Wissenschaftliche Buchgesellschaft, 1969).

SCHELLING, F. W. J., *On University Studies* (1803), translated by E. S. Morgan (Athens, Ohio: Ohio University Press, 1966).

SCHLEIERMACHER, FRIEDRICH, *Der christliche Glaube nach den Grundsätzen der evangelischen Kirche im Zusammenhange dargestellt*, 2 vols. (Berlin, 1st edn. 1821–2; 2nd edn. 1830–1). Sometimes referred to as *Glaubenslehre*.

——, *The Christian Faith*, translation of the second German edition, edited by H. R. Mackintosh and J. S. Stewart (Edinburgh: T&T Clark, 1928).

SCHLEGEL, FRIEDRICH, *Ueber die Sprache und Weisheit der Indier: Ein Beitrag zur Begründung der Alterthumskunde* (Heidelberg, 1808).

SHANKS, ANDREW, *God and Modernity: A New and Better Way to Do Theology* (London and New York: Routledge, 2000).

SMITH, STEVEN G., *The Concept of the Spiritual: An Essay in First Philosophy* (Philadelphia: Temple University Press, 1988).

SPINOZA, BENEDICT DE, *The Chief Works*, translated by R. H. M. Elwes, 2 vols. (New York: Dover, 1951).

STIRNER, MAX, *The Ego and Its Own*, edited by David Leopold (Cambridge: Cambridge University Press, 1995).

STRAUSS, DAVID FRIEDRICH, *The Life of Jesus Critically Examined*, translated by George Eliot, edited by Peter C. Hodgson (Philadelphia: Fortress Press, 1972; London: SCM Press, 1973).

TILLICH, PAUL, *Systematic Theology*, vol. 3. (Chicago: University of Chicago Press, 1963).

——, 'The Significance of the History of Religions for the Systematic Theologian', in Jerald C. Brauer (ed.), *The Future of Religions* (New York: Harper & Row, 1966), 80–94.

WARD, GRAHAM, *Cities of God* (London and New York: Routledge, 2000).

WIEDMANN, FRANZ, *Hegel: An Illustrated Biography*, translated by Joachim Neugroschel (New York: Pegasus, 1968).

WILLIAMS, ROBERT R., *Hegel's Ethics of Recognition* (Berkeley and Los Angeles: University of California Press, 1997).

# INDEX

absolute: as absolving,
releasing 90–1, 219, 238, 264–6;
concrete 219; meaning of 12,
90–1, 264; as spirit 33 (*see also*
absolute spirit); as substance and
subject 33
absolute knowledge: as absolute
shakenness 240–1 n. 48; as
absolving 35; achieved when
thought knows itself in the
objects of thought 115; as
knowledge of infinite
determinacies 35, 80, 270; as
wisdom about human
fallibility 269–70 n. 34
absolute spirit: as community of
recognition 129, 264, 270;
definition of 41, 90–1, 129, 264;
as determinate unity 106, 270; as
first and alone true 84; internal
relations of 19, 129; as process of
identity-difference-mediation
127–8; self-consciousness of
mediated through finite
consciousness 35–6, 81–4, 128;
shaking power of 240–1 n. 48;
treatment of in the
*Encyclopedia* 29, 40–5; and
Trinity 127–31; *see also* God;
spirit
acosmism 68, 105
actuality 68 n. 20, 105
agape 254, 256; *see also* love
agnosticism, theological 56–8,
62–3, 259
alienation, *see* estrangement
anguish 153–4, 159, 171, 182–4,
235

Anselm of Canterbury 54, 59, 121
appearance 141–3, 145, 158–60,
163
Aquinas, Thomas 59, 134
Aristotle 9, 69 n. 21, 92, 104 n. 4,
138
art 42
ascension 175
Asian religions 215, 219–28
asymmetry, in divine-human and
interhuman relations 254–6, 265
atheism 66–8, 105, 249–50, 252
atomism 266
atonement 157, 172; *see also*
reconciliation
Augustine 59, 134, 137 n. 12,
184 n. 10
Avineri, Schlomo 228–9 n. 36

baptism 186
Bauer, Bruno 15, 67
Baumgarten, Alexander
Gottlieb 53, 59
Baur, Ferdinand Christian 15,
164 n. 10, 249–50, 260–1
becoming 274
Beethoven, Ludwig van 3, 282
being 16–17, 35, 122, 262–4
being-within-self 225–7
Bible: interpretation of 60, 95; and
tradition 188
Boehme, Jacob 21, 139, 144 n. 2,
260, 263
Brahman 222–3
Buddhism 105, 221–2, 225–8,
278 n. 41
Burbidge, John W. 261 n. 19
Bushnell, Horace 189 n. 17

God: (*cont.*)

self-knowledge of mediated
through human knowledge
81–2; sensible presence
of 158–61, 169, 177–8, 191; as
Son 132–3; as Spirit 16–17,
262–4 (*see also* absolute spirit;
Holy Spirit; spirit); as subject
and substance 127, 269;
superabundance of 136; as
supreme being 54, 59, 61, 198,
262; as triune (*see* Trinity); and
the undoing of evil 189, 277; as
the unity of spirit and
nature 128–9; as the universal
truth of all things 103–4; as the
whole 7–8, 33, 104, 106, 129,
252, 264–5, 268–9, 272–3;
wisdom of 146, 231–4; and
world 44–5, 68, 113, 129–31,
141–7, 249–52, 254–6, 265–73;
worship of 123–6
Goethe, Johann Wolfgang
von 159, 208 n. 6
good 189–90
Good Friday, speculative 29
Göschel, Carl Friedrich 42
Great Britain 196
Greek religion 23–4, 31, 36, 213,
215–6 n. 13, 233, 236–7

Habermas, Jürgen 79 n. 4
heart 109, 194
Heede, Reinhard 217 n. 16
Hegel, Georg Wilhelm Friedrich:
his affinity with and critique of
Asian religions 219–28; and
Christian theology 75–204;
critics of 247–51; his critique of
the theology of his time 58–68;
his engagement with world
religions 205–6; his evolving
treatment of Judaism 228–37;
experimental character of his

thought 50, 217, 261–2, 266;
and Gnosticism 260–1;
heterodoxy of 260–2;
importance of oral lectures
for 50–1; life and career of 3–6;
limitations of his thought 258;
orthodoxy of 259–60; as a
partisan of freedom
movements 241 n. 48, 243,
281 n. 44; questions
about 284 n. 47; resources
provided to contemporary
theology by 247–8, 283–4; as a
theologian of the spirit 16–21;
theological significance of
today 247–84; tragicomic
perspective of 189, 276–7;
would not be a Hegelian
today 243 n. 51, 281 n. 44; his
writings on religion 22–51
Heidegger, Martin 263–4, 274
Henning, Leopold von 48
Herbert of Cherbury 61
Herder, Johann Gottfried 68 n. 19
heterodoxy 16, 100, 259–62
Hinduism 137–8, 219–24
Hinrichs, Hermann Friedrich
Wilhelm 45
historicism 61–2, 181
history: and concept 76–7, 95;
divine 127–8, 181; and faith 38,
168–9, 181; and freedom 216,
240–3; and narrative 273–6;
outward and inward 112;
passing away of everything
in 178, 202; and
philosophy 181; of religions (*see*
world religions); and
revelation 94–5
Hölderlin, Friedrich 3–4
holism: of absolute spirit 129; of
Hegel's system 7–9, 265–73; not
monistic 252; not
totalizing 106, 269; and

speculation, definition of 7–8, 69,
79–81
speculative concept of
religion 81–4
speculative intuition 171, 183
speculative philosophy/
theology 6–17, 68–72, 79–81,
112 n. 17, 200
speculative redescription of
Christian metanarrative 98–100,
261, 275
speculative reversal 7–8, 79,
83–4
Spinoza, Benedict 67–8, 104–5,
252
spiral of mediations 8–11, 131
spirit: as activity of self-
manifesting 77; as *advaitic* 219,
252; and community 177–204;
concrescent 239;
concrete 239–43; does not reach
its goal without traversing the
path 240; evolution of Hegel's
philosophy of 17–21; finite and
infinite 19–20; and history 181;
intersubjectivity of 181–4; and
love 182–3; meaning of 16–21,
262–4; and nature 128–9, 210,
212–13, 215, 242 n. 50; as one-
in-many and many-in-one 283;
philosophy of 10–11, 40–5; as
the power to do undo evil 189,
277; revelatory 92–3; and the
sensible 177–8; and shape 161;
triple mediation of 33, 68; as
unity of divinity and
humanity 157; witness of 94,
108; and world religions 207–18;
*see also* absolute spirit; Holy
Spirit
spiritualism 180 n. 4
state 195–7
Stirner, Max 67, 249 n. 3
Stoicism 154

Strauss, David Friedrich 15, 49,
60 n. 10, 133 n. 6, 164 n. 10,
180 n. 4
subject 33, 66, 160
subjectivity: as communal,
intersubjective 181–4, 280; and
exteriority 265; of God 104,
227–8; as subjectivism, devoid of
content 199, 252–3; turn to in
Protestantism and
Enlightenment 28–9, 66
substance 33, 104–5, 219, 223,
227–8
suffering 159; *see also* anguish
syllogism 9–11, 45, 116, 253,
267–8
*System of Ethical Life and First
Philosophy of Spirit* 18, 29–32,
86 n. 9

teleology 119–21
Teller, Wilhelm Abraham 61, 138
Tertullian 54
theology: agnostic 62–4; apophatic
(negative) 63–4, 227; as
cognitive knowledge of God 13,
15, 47; critical/prophetic 201,
203–4; of feeling 64–7;
historical 61–2; kataphatic
(positive) 63–4;
metaphysical 58–9;
natural 52–3; and
philosophy 12–16, 53–4, 125–6,
247; rational 59–61;
revealed 53; as science of
religion 15, 41;
speculative 13–17, 68–72
theosophy 263
thinking, thought: constructive
character of 72; courage of 72;
dialectical character of 9–10;
knowing itself 9, 69, 71–2, 115;
and knowledge of God 113–15;
and mediation 114–16; and

world religions: (*cont.*)
217–19, 220 n. 24; in Hegel's
early thought 30–2, 36;
inclusivist vs. pluralist views
of 237–8, 283; living and dead
(or fossilized) 206;
metanarrative of 98–9;
phenomenological treatment
of 207–8; philosophical history
of 211–12, 218; in the
philosophy of religion 205–7;
pluralism of 162, 207, 212,
218–20, 237–8, 242–3, 282–3;
and progress of the
consciousness of freedom 216,
240–3; rationality of the history
of 209; as stages on the path of
consciousness or spirit 208–9,
211–12, 214, 216; typology
of 212, 218, 239; universal
history of 218

world-soul (*Nous*) 120

worship 123–6, 190–3

Zwingli, Ulrich 193